Very few places are the source of most community crime. City managers and local law enforcement have greater ability than we realize to change these places, though it takes different approaches. *Cutting Crime* lays out tools local government leaders can use to reduce crime through a placed-based strategy.

–**Tom Carroll**, *City Manager, City of Lexington, Virginia (USA)*

Cutting Crime Using the Rule of the Few offers a clear blueprint to reduce crime by eliminating opportunities for crime. Essential reading for government executives, police departments, business owners, insurance underwriters, property managers, and anyone invested in making communities safer.

–**Edward L. Chávez**, *Chief Justice (retired), New Mexico Supreme Court (USA)*

Cutting Crime provides an innovative framework for practitioners to manage solutions for crime reduction and control. A "must read" for police leaders, and city executives, *Cutting Crime* serves as an evidence-based practical working manual designed to develop focused, purposeful and sustainable solutions to reduce crime.

–**Mike John**, *Assistant Police Chief (retired), City of Cincinnati (USA)*

The Rule of the Few is all around us. In this wide-ranging and accessible book, Linning, Gerard and Eck provide compelling evidence that crime too conforms to the Rule of the Few, with important implications for crime prevention theory and practice. This valuable book is a must-read for academics, practitioners and policymakers interested in understanding and preventing crime.

–**Aiden Sidebottom**, *Professor of Security and Crime Science, University College London (UK)*

Cutting Crime Using the Rule of the Few

Based on decades of research, this book reveals how the rule of the few can redirect your focus to create effective crime control policies. Many crime reduction strategies fail because they apply common crime fallacies. They assume that: solutions to crime need to be complicated, crime is widespread, residents matter the most, more arrests reduce crime, and police can solve all crime problems. At the heart of each fallacy is a failure to consider an old idea: the rule of the few. The rule of the few means a tiny fraction of inputs cause most of the outcomes. Research shows that: solving problems at smaller scales can cut crime substantially, crime is highly concentrated at a few places in any city, only a few residents can usually effect change, only a few people commit most of the crime, and a few everyday people can dismantle crime opportunities.

Cutting Crime Using the Rule of the Few shows that crime is not merely a police problem. It explains how those who own or manage property and design the products we use have far more power to suppress crime opportunities than they realize. *Cutting Crime* reveals how to use the rule of the few to identify and solve crime problems. It provides a set of tools and spells out specific strategies that the police, property owners, business owners, and government agencies can use to reduce crime. Just as it only takes a few to create a lot of crime, it only takes a few to prevent those crimes.

Shannon J. Linning, PhD, is an Assistant Professor of Criminology at Simon Fraser University. She teaches courses in crime prevention, policing, and research methods. Her research explores how the owners and managers of property can create safer areas by suppressing crime opportunities at and around their properties. Her research appears in many academic journals, and she is the co-author of books, including *Place Management and Crime: Ownership and Property Rights as a Source of Social Control.*

Daniel W. Gerard, MS, is a retired captain and 32-year veteran of the Cincinnati, Ohio Police Department. He has published articles in both academic and practitioner journals and has served as an invited consultant, speaker, trainer, and instructor for numerous police agencies, universities, and organizations throughout the United States and Canada.

John E. Eck, PhD, is an Emeritus Professor of Criminal Justice at the University of Cincinnati. His work spans five decades, working with police agencies around the world, conducting research and developing thinking tools to aid crime prevention. He is one of the key architects of widely used crime problem-solving tools such as the SARA model, the crime problem triangle, the CHEERS criteria, and the General Problem-Solving Matrix. He has worked for the Police Executive Research Forum as its Research Director, the Washington/Baltimore High Intensity Drug Trafficking Area as its Evaluation Director, and at the University of Cincinnati, where he taught courses on police effectiveness, crime prevention, and professional writing.

Routledge Series on Practical and Evidence-Based Policing

Books in the Routledge Series on Practical and Evidence-Based Policing disseminate knowledge and provide practical tools for law enforcement leaders and personnel to protect and serve the public and reduce crime. With an aim to bridge the "translation gap" between frontline policing and academic research, books in this series apply sound scientific methods as well as practical experience to make every day police work safer and smarter. These books are an invaluable resource for police practitioners, academic researchers, public policymakers, and students in law enforcement and criminology programs to guide best practices in all aspects of policing.

The Wicked Problems of Police Reform in Canada
Laura Huey, Lorna Ferguson, & Jennifer L. Schulenberg

Human Rights Policing
Reimagining Law Enforcement in the 21st Century
Peter Marina & Pedro Marina

Interviewing Vulnerable Suspects
Safeguarding the Process
Edited by Dr Jane Tudor-Owen, Dr Celine van Golde, Dr Ray Bull, & David Gee MBE

Reframing Police Education and Freedom in America
Martin Alan Greenberg & Beth Allen Easterling

Gold Medal Policing
Operational Readiness and Performance Excellence, 2nd Edition
Judy M. McDonald

Understanding Police Operational Performance
James E. McCabe, Paul E. O'Connell, Demosthenes Long, & Carol Rasor-Cordero

Cutting Crime Using the Rule of the Few
Shannon J. Linning, Daniel W. Gerard, & John E. Eck

Cutting Crime Using the Rule of the Few

Shannon J. Linning, Daniel W. Gerard and John E. Eck

Routledge
Taylor & Francis Group
NEW YORK AND LONDON

Designed cover image: Shannon Linning, Daniel Gerard, John Eck, &
Simon Cassegrain

First edition published 2026
by Routledge
605 Third Avenue, New York, NY 10158

and by Routledge
4 Park Square, Milton Park, Abingdon, Oxon, OX14 4RN

Routledge is an imprint of the Taylor & Francis Group, an informa business

ISBN: 978-1-032-55331-3 (hbk)
ISBN: 978-1-032-55052-7 (pbk)
ISBN: 978-1-003-43015-5 (ebk)

DOI: 10.4324/9781003430155

Typeset in Caslon
by SPi Technologies India Pvt Ltd (Straive)

We dedicate this book to Dr. Edward Latessa, in part for creating the School of Criminal Justice at the University of Cincinnati that brought us to one place, leading to our collaboration, but also for his sage, colorful advice as we worked on this book.

Contents

PREFACE

Why Us?

There are many criminology and criminal justice books, articles, podcasts, self-appointed experts, and more out there that provide suggestions on how to address crime problems. But many of these sources do not discuss the basic principles behind what works. Their suggestions are often convoluted, expensive, and impractical. These suggestions often impede progress. From the academic perspective, which two of us come from, we were frustrated with convoluted and impractical theories. From a policing perspective, which one of us comes from, we were irritated by resistance to change and a continual reliance on failed strategies. So, the three of us decided to write this book. It spells out simple, clear, and useful evidence-based strategies shown to reduce crime. But who are we? And why should you listen to us?

We are three people with different professional experiences who all saw the problems with conventional thinking about crime. We came together as members of the University of Cincinnati's School of Criminal Justice.

John was a professor in the School. He originally developed the idea of place management while conducting research with the San Diego, California Police Department for his PhD dissertation. As a senior researcher at the Police Executive Research Forum, he was also instrumental in developing problem-oriented policing around the world. His initial ideas about place management and problem-solving have evolved into the central themes in our book.

Dan spent his police career on the streets of Cincinnati, Ohio. He focused on violent people and gangs and commanded police resources in the areas they operated in. He simultaneously completed his Master's degree at the School, taking several courses with John. After retiring, he became the research manager of the Institute of Crime Science at the University of Cincinnati.

Shannon is an assistant professor at Simon Fraser University but was a PhD student in the University of Cincinnati's School of Criminal Justice when we all came together. John supervised her dissertation and Dan served in an advisory role for the project as well. Through her research, she brought fresh eyes and new actionable insights into the importance of place management and why offenders choose to operate in the areas they do.

Shannon has also served as the voice of reason in John and Dan's years-long debate about whether focusing on places or people was the most important piece in crime reduction. Dan frequently pointed out that an offender-based strategy was more effective than place management since never once in his long police career did a building pull out a gun and shoot someone. John countered that the police repeatedly arrested people at certain locations, yet crime continued to occur there, with either new or the same perpetrators.

Shannon understood John and Dan were both correct. A place-based strategy and an offender-based strategy can reduce your crime. However, to reduce crime, police agencies usually implement either a stand-alone place-based or offender-focused crime reduction strategy. A singular strategy may have been the right choice at the time. However, as we will demonstrate, it is time for new thinking and a better strategy.

Together, the three of us realized that the most effective solution to reduce crime is to combine a place-based and an offender-based strategy into one focused crime reduction strategy. A combined strategy would allow police and communities to concentrate their resources on the very few places and people who drive crime in an area. In this book, we bring together evidence and personal insights about strategies that work to reduce crime.

1

The Hockey Stick Epiphany

What can churches learn from bars? As it turns out, quite a lot. British crime scientist Aiden Sidebottom was advising his Master's student, Samantha Muncaster, about her study of lead thefts from churches. In the United Kingdom, the roofs and gutters of old churches often are made of lead. Lead is valuable, so thieves steal it from church roofs and gutters. But Muncaster found that most lead thefts only occurred at a tiny number of churches. Out of every 100 churches, only 17 had lead thefts. The problem is even tinier. Half of the lead thefts occurred in only five of every 100 churches.[1]

Why were the thefts concentrated at so few churches? Was something different happening at those few churches?

Sidebottom recalled a study he had done in London bars. He and a colleague, Kate Bowers, had tested a program to reduce thefts of purses, backpacks, and other bags. A local bar franchise agreed to let Sidebottom and Bowers study 26 of their locations. The researchers found that across the 26 bars, there were about 520 bag thefts: an average of 20 bag thefts per bar per year, and less than 2.5 per week for the average bar. But the average was not average.[2]

After they graphed their data, they discovered that one bar had 22% of all the bag thefts (Bar T in the figure 1.1). Even more striking, almost

DOI: 10.4324/9781003430155-1

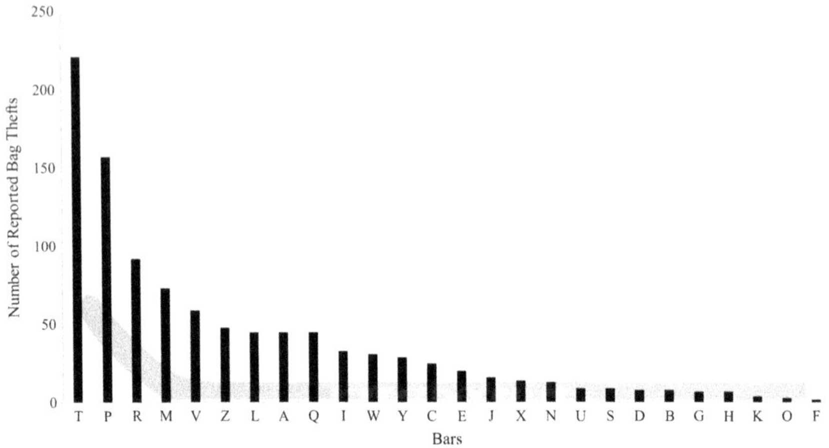

FIGURE 1.1 The Rule of the Few Looks Like a Hockey Stick

*Figure adapted from Sidebottom & Bowers (2010, p. 211)

60% of all the bag thefts clustered in only five bars (T to V). Nine bars had less than 10 bag thefts per year (bars U to F).

Sidebottom and Bowers' graph illustrates a key principle, the rule of the few: a few inputs (such as bars) produce most of the outcomes (such as crime). When you graph the rule of the few, the distributions look like hockey sticks.[3] The stick's blade covers the places on the left with lots of crime. The stick's handle covers the places on the right with little crime.

Why were so many bag thefts concentrated in a few locations, but not at most others, Sidebottom and Bowers wondered. They looked for explanations and eliminated the most obvious: it was not who owned the bars, their sizes or numbers of drinkers, or distance from public transport. So, they visited the bars and talked with local police. When they showed the police their hockey stick graph, the police quickly had an answer. Officers explained that the bars with the most crime (those in the blade) had two ways in and out. The locations with little crime (the handle) only had one way in and out. Why would this matter for crime?

Thieves look for easy opportunities, officers explained; blade locations allowed offenders to walk through one door, steal someone's bag, and leave through the other door. Bag thieves did not have to double-back and increase their risk of being caught. They could not do this at most bars. The rule of the few led to a solution: limit entrances.

Later, when studying churches, Sidebottom recalled the bars. He realized the rule of the few from the bar study may help solve the church lead theft problem. So, he and Muncaster visited the churches and consulted with local police. They showed officers the hockey stick graph and asked: why are there so many thefts at the few churches in the blade and so few thefts at the many churches in the handle? In essence, why here but not there?

The police broke it down. The roofs of churches are high. So, it is not easy for people to get onto the roofs of buildings; you usually need a ladder to access them. But thieves do not want to walk around with ladders; they are inconvenient to carry around and would make them stand out. So, thieves look for churches with easy access to roofs. Often dumpsters could give easy access. If the dumpsters have unlocked wheels, the lead thieves can push them to the right access place. The churches at the blade of the hockey stick had dumpsters with unlocked wheels. Churches whose dumpsters could not move did not provide this opportunity. Just like the bar problem, asking why a few have most of the trouble led to an easy solution: lock the wheels on church dumpsters.

Sidebottom's studies of bars and churches illustrate two important insights. First, only a few places experience most of the crime. Second, there are often simple ways to reduce crime. Sidebottom's insights illustrate a key principle: the rule of the few.

The Rule of the Few

The rule of the few states that a few inputs produce the majority of outcomes. The rule of the few explains how we can cut crime. The rule is one of those things we all have experienced but seldom put to use. This is particularly true when it comes to crime prevention. Many politicians, citizens, police, and academics are unaware of its importance and continue to demand strategies that fail to reduce crime. This is usually because they demand strategies, which we describe in later chapters, that do not apply the rule of the few. These strategies are often expensive, ineffective, and create harmful side effects. Usually, these strategies rest on at least one of these fallacies: crime is widespread, residents matter most, or that more arrests reduce crime.[4]

The facts are these. These fallacies, and several more we will introduce later, are wrong. Crime is not widespread. Just like the churches and bars, a few properties experience a lot of crime, but most properties have none.[5] Usually a tiny fraction of places experience half of the crime in any city.[6] Thus, instead of intensively policing entire neighborhoods, we need to focus on the few properties within them that have most of the crime.

Residents do not matter most because most inhabitants have no control over the areas they occupy, especially renters in high crime neighborhoods. Could local residents solve the church or bar problems? No, a few people and institutions own most of the property experiencing the crime, not residents.[7] Those who control property can control crime on their property.[8] So, instead of organizing residents, we need to persuade the owners of these high crime properties to do better.

Strategies that try to arrest as many people as possible does not reduce crime because a few offenders commit most of the crimes, but most people commit none.[9] Therefore, instead of arresting a lot of people, focus on the few prolific offenders causing the most crime. Straightforward solutions to the church and bar problems did not involve arresting people. As satisfied as some might feel to put bag and lead thieves in prison, if the opportunities for bag and lead theft are unaddressed, other offenders will replace them.

These facts we draw on come from decades of scientific research. Crime researchers have consistently found hockey stick-like graphs in their studies.[10] These patterns are not surprising. Economist Vilfredo Pareto discovered it as early as 1896 when he found that about 80% of the wealth in Italy belonged to about 20% of the people.[11;12] The rule of the few provides a different framework to understand where we have gone wrong in addressing crime. Knowing what does not work, and why, helps us understand what will be effective. The rule of the few also demands a shift in thinking about how to solve crime problems.

Shifting to the Rule of the Few

Every day, you deal with the rule of the few, often without noticing it. At home, you spend most of your time in a few areas of your house, a small area of your carpet gets the most wear, you wear a small percentage of your wardrobe most of the time.[13] In business, a small number of products make companies most of their profits, a small number of customers provide most of the sales, a small number of businesses employ most of the workers.[14] In medicine, only a few people are responsible for most of the emergency medical expenditures and a small number of people experience a large proportion of accidental injuries requiring medical attention.[15] In sports, a small number of professional teams win most championship titles. On the internet, a small number of websites get the most visits and a few people on X (formerly known as Twitter) are responsible for most of the misogynistic tweets.[16] You get the idea.

Only a small proportion of people in the community use most of the emergency care resources. Indeed, many emergency rooms see the same patients repeatedly.[17] The rule of the few is what keeps medical insurance companies in business. While millions of members pay premiums for their plans, only a few of them submit large claims. The same goes for car insurance. While all vehicle owners pay insurance premiums, a small proportion of their customers are involved in traffic crashes.[18] Often repeatedly.

Despite how often the rule of the few shows up, we design broadly. This leads to excess policies. If one person in an organization messes up, the human resources department will create a rule for everyone. If there is a spate of shootings on one block, the mayor will indict the entire neighborhood. Some governments require all vehicle owners to get their cars tested annually at emissions stations, even though only a small fraction of cars on the road emit most of the emissions, and it costs millions to construct and staff these stations.[19] Policies that incorporate the rule of the few would cost us less and reduce our aggravation: deal with the few jalopies on the road that are causing the problems.

Dan saved lives by seeing the rule of the few in fatal vehicle crashes. Fatal vehicle crashes were not spread throughout Cincinnati. While commanding the traffic section of the Cincinnati Police Department, Dan discovered there were three killer street blocks that experienced most traffic fatalities. What did these three killer blocks have that other street blocks did not? Each block was on a slope. Each block had a tight curve. Each block had fast speed limits. And on each block, when it rained, drivers skidded out of their lanes, sometimes leading to fatal head-on collisions. Dan had the roads department grind the surface, thus reducing skidding in wet conditions. These changes eliminated all fatalities on those three blocks and reduced the city's traffic fatalities by 47%.[20] If Dan had not used the rule of the few, the city would still be trying to fix 2,900

Table 1.1 Shift Your Thinking to the Rule of the Few

	Instead of Thoughts of the Many	Think Rule of the Few
Key Question	Why?	How?
Cause of Crime	Propensity	Opportunity
Explain	Offenders	Crime Events
Understand	Distant Possible Causes	Immediate Situation
Focus	Improving Processes (Means)	Solving Problems (Ends)
Undertake	Treatment of Symptoms	Treatment of Causes
Problem Solvers	Police & Residents	Place Managers
Default Intervention	Addressing Propensities	Dismantle Opportunities

lane miles, at 42 miles per year, as people continued to die on the three killer blocks.[21]

We can use the rule of the few to reduce crime. But it requires us to shift how we think about crime. It compels us to ask two questions: what is it that those few places have wrong? What is it that so many places do right? But to understand what so many people are doing well, we need to change how we think about crime (see Table 1.1).

The first change requires us to re-think offending. We are enamored with understanding why offenders commit their crimes. Hundreds of television programs and movies depict cunning offenders engaged in elaborate criminal schemes. As viewers, we are fascinated by *why*? Why did they carry out these crimes? In this book, we will show that as fascinating as this question is, it is among the least helpful questions. Simply identifying root causes does not get us very far when trying to reduce crime.

Most crimes committed are mundane.[22] Offenders commit many crimes because they are easy, safe, and useful. That is, there is a tempting opportunity for crime.[23] For example, most people do not wake up in the morning and decide to steal someone's smartphone. But if a college student goes to the library for a short study session and walks past an unoccupied cubicle with a smartphone, he may seize the opportunity. Yes, most will not. But the few that rule crime will. And of the few who will, each may have a different reason for *why* they steal the phone.

It can be inefficient to design various strategies for why they offended. Yet many of our colleagues in criminology focus on criminal propensities. They study upbringing, schooling, neighborhoods, and many other things to find the secret to criminality. They say we should offer mothers pre-natal care, we should lift people out of poverty, we should give youth better schools, offer drug treatment, and make neighborhoods healthier. Our retort is that all of these are good, and all may work. But we should aspire to do all these things even if they had no impact on crime. And if they do have an impact on crime, it can take decades for them to work.

There are enough people who have the propensity to offend.[24] If an opportunity exists, it is only a matter of time before someone comes along to exploit it. And again, each offender could have a different reason for exploiting it. So, instead of focusing on *why* a few students steal smartphones, ask *how* they steal smartphones. How will lead to a solution, such as getting students to watch their belongings, or designing study nooks to protect students' belongings. People looking to reduce crime need to ask: How did this crime opportunity emerge? How did the offender carry out his crime? How did the offender avoid detection? Asking *how* may not lead to a popular Netflix series or a political soundbite, but it often leads to a solution.[25]

Asking *how* questions leads us toward understanding and reducing crime opportunities. To do this, we look at the immediate environment that often creates crime opportunities, not at distant possible causes, such as poverty or adverse childhood experiences. There is an opportunity for a crime when a person looks at a situation and says to himself, "That offense is worth doing. It would be easy and I could get away with it." Offending decisions are often made in the moment, in a small space. This is why so few places have most of the crime. They have few enduring crime opportunities. Making crime riskier in the long run (by passing laws increasing penalties that may be imposed if one gets caught, for example) is far less effective than making crime riskier when someone is about to offend. The same is true of making crime more effort and less rewarding.[26]

To reduce crime, you need to identify the crime opportunities and who can alter the immediate environment to suppress them. Recall the story that started this chapter. Blocking secondary entrances in bars and locking the wheels on church dumpsters are prime examples of simple methods to reduce crime opportunities. These solutions became apparent when Sidebottom understood *how* thieves were committing their crimes.

We have been altering opportunities to reduce crime for years. When United States department stores first opened in the 1820s stores displayed their merchandise, including expensive silk scarves, on tables. Since these stores catered to the middle and upper middle classes, particularly women, store owners assumed their customers would be well behaved. Most were. But a few repeatedly stole the expensive merchandise. The thievery by these few middle-class women was sufficiently costly that store owners looked for a way to stop it. They started installing a design we see in most stores, a design that is so common we do not think of it as a crime prevention device: the glass display case.[27] It allows customers to see the expensive merchandise but prevents them from easily snatching it.

In the 1990s, patrons in some British pubs and nightclubs assaulted each other with glass bottles and drinking glasses. The injuries were horrific, requiring plastic surgery to restore deeply cut-up faces. One effective solution was to serve alcohol in shatter proof glasses that were either ineffective weapons or would not cut a victim when hit by it.[28]

In the early 2000s, Charlotte, North Carolina offenders routinely stole appliances from some residential developments under construction. In each case, the development was on the verge of being complete. To make the units attractive to potential buyers, developers installed appliances. In the short period between installing appliances and new owners moving in, offenders took the appliances. Despite considerable police efforts to catch the thieves, none were caught. Eventually, some developers waited to install the appliances until after the new homeowners moved in. Their theft rates plummeted.[29] Developers in Florida found similar crime reduction effects when they delayed installation of household appliances.[30]

What is common among these three examples, spanning decades and geography? All of these solutions helped drive down crime. None required us to understand *why* offenders were committing the crimes in the first place. All of the solutions relied on someone understanding *how* the crimes were committed. With the department stores, the owners had to shift their thinking from why (poverty and lower classness causes crime) to how (the expensive items are easy to snatch). With the facial glass injury problem, owners of drinking places and public health officials had to switch their thinking from why (intoxication can cause violence) to how (glass shards cut faces and intoxicated patrons have easy access to glass shards). With the appliance theft problem, developers had to switch their thinking from why (poverty compels people to steal) to how (unprotected expensive equipment is at high risk of being stolen). Once the store owners, pub and tavern keepers, and developers answered the how question, then they were able to apply effective solutions.

With this change in thinking comes a change in which steps we should take to reduce crime. The old way of thinking often touts policing strategies that try to improve processes.[31] Examples of process-focused strategies include rapid response to calls for service, investigations, increasing the number of police, or random patrolling. We cover these strategies more closely in Part 1. We show that they do not have much of an impact on crime. Having more police who can get to a shoplifted store faster after the theft does not change the fact that the store suffered a theft to begin with. Investigations may lead to an arrest but apprehending the offender does not stop someone else from stealing, as the opportunity remains. Similarly, getting the police to randomly ride past a pub with glass bottle assaults is unlikely to prevent the injuries from happening. Investigating appliance thefts did not lead to any arrests and did not solve the theft problem.

These old ways of thinking lead to strategies that are means based, as opposed to ends based.[32] Ends are the goals we want to achieve: less crime, fewer injuries, or fewer harms, to name a few. Means are the actions taken to achieve the ends, including the number of arrests, how quickly police responded, or the number of cases solved. But as we will show, these means do not necessarily lead to desired outcomes. For example, spending vast sums of money on dispatching technology may help in rare emergencies, but it is unlikely to reduce everyday crime. For example, most burglaries are discovery crimes; the crime is usually committed during the day when no one is home. The resident arrives home after work or school to discover their home has been broken into, so they call the police. This means the offense likely happened many hours before. So, the police arriving in two minutes as opposed to ten minutes will have little impact on crime. It's unlikely to improve the police's ability to solve the case. It also does not prevent the crime from happening in the first place. It merely treats the symptoms of an underlying problem.

Instead, we need to address crime opportunities and solve problems associated with them. To do this, we will also show that the key problem solvers are not who most would expect. When crime threatens the community, we default to two sets of key players to address it: police and residents. Most assume that crime is primarily the responsibility of the police to address. Some take this a step further and believe residents should partner with the police to address crime problems.

But the rule of the few suggests there is a far more powerful group in the community who can solve many crime problems: place managers. Place managers are those who own or operate property. They can organize the physical space of a location, regulate the conduct of people at the place, and control access to the place.[33] Through the legal powers granted to them due to property ownership, place managers have the authority to suppress many crime opportunities at their places.[34] And most do exactly this, hence why the rule of the few consistently shows that most properties experience no crime. But a small number of places experience a lot of crime.[35] Research suggests that the place management of these properties is different.[36] If we can partner with the managers of these places and compel them to make different decisions, we can make the biggest impact.

Recall our examples of altering the immediate environment: department store robberies, assaults in bars using glassware, construction site theft. Can the police enact the solutions we mentioned? Can the residents? No. Only the place managers can. Place managers are the ones who install locked glass display cases to reduce robberies. They are the ones who can swap easily breakable glassware for shatter-proof ones. They are the ones who decide when to install appliances in homes. If you recall the examples that started our chapter, place managers are the people who can block off entrances to their bars and lock dumpsters in place at their churches. In doing so, they are not merely disrupting potential crime opportunities. They are dismantling the opportunities entirely. This leads to sustainable crime reduction effects that will persist for much longer.

Looking Ahead

For us to understand what to do moving forward, we need to understand where we've gone wrong. We wrote this book to give people a new way to think about crime. This allows you to ask different questions and devise new ways to cut crime. We need to understand the fallacies we have about crime and why they are wrong. Part 1 addresses this. It dispels the three fallacies that most people have about crime: that crime is widespread (chapter 2); that residents matter most (chapter 3); and that more arrests reduce crime (chapter 4). We explain the research behind what works and what does not. We show how failing to apply the rule of the few explains why some seemingly useful strategies are mostly ineffective.

Part 2 re-directs us to the correct path. It demonstrates that many crimes are the product of everyday processes, products, and opportunities (chapter 5). Here, we ask you to re-think why crime opportunities exist. We urge you to break complex problems into smaller pieces so that we have hope of doing anything to fix them (chapter 6). Once we become more hyper-focused, we examine why a few places have high crime, but most do not; why a few products are stolen often, but most are not; and so on. We show how those who own or manage property and design the products we consume have far more power to suppress crime opportunities than they realize (chapter 7). Partnering with these place managers can yield great benefits.

Part 3 shows how to identify and diagnose crime problems and provides a set of tools everyday people can use to solve them. We start by defining problems (chapter 8). We then explain why many crime problems arise in the first place (chapter 9). With this knowledge, you can start problem solving yourself. We give you many tools to choose from to address problems (chapter 10). These tools can be used with or without the partnership of the police. In fact, we also show you which people or organizations can help you deal with reluctant place managers to generate results (chapter 11). We also explain why using these tools can spread crime reduction benefits as opposed to pushing them elsewhere (chapter 12).

Part 4 describes how the police can put the rule of the few into practice. It spells out specific strategies the police can use in tandem with property owners, business owners, and government agencies to cut crime (chapters 13–16). We also provide a quick reference guide to problem-solving tools in the appendix.

If you stick with us through to chapter 17, we have a present for you: a way to identify and eliminate crime reduction strategies likely to fail. We call it the SCRAP test. Using the myths we bust, the evidence we show, and the operational ideas we provide, we developed the SCRAP test to help guide you towards strategies that are likely to reduce crime.[37]

We have spent too long spinning our wheels on crime policies that are expensive, often brutal, and frequently ineffective. In hindsight, the rule of the few should have been guiding our strategies all along. We now know better. If we use the rule of the few, we can be far more effective at reducing crime. So, let's get started.

Key Points

- Many phenomena follow the rule of the few: a few inputs cause most of the outcomes.
- If events follow the rule of the few, they create a hockey stick graph.
- Comparing places on the blade of the hockey stick to the handle of the hockey stick can help us uncover ways to reduce crime.
- Ask: why here but not there?

Notes

1 Muncaster, S.J. (2012). *The theft-price relationship: Observations on the theft of lead.* Unpublished Master's thesis, Department of Security and Crime Science, University College London, United Kingdom.

2 Sidebottom, A. & Bowers, K. (2010). Bag theft in bars: An analysis of relative risk, perceived risk, and modus operandi. *Security Journal, 23*(3), 206–224. https://doi.org/10.1057/sj.2008.17

3 Gladwell, M. (2006, February 13 & 20). Million-Dollar Murray. *The New Yorker*, 96–107; Sherman, L.W. (2007). The power few: Experimental criminology and the reduction of harm: The 2006 Joan McCord Price Lecture. *Journal of Experimental Criminology, 3*(4), 299–321. https://doi.org/10.1007/s11292-007-9044-y

4 Linning, S.J., Carroll, T., Gerard, D.W., & Eck, J.E. (2024, October). Is crime widespread? *Public Management, 106*(10), 30–32. https://icma.org/articles/pm-magazine/crime-widespread; Linning, S.J., Carroll, T., Gerard, D.W., & Eck, J.E. (2024, November). Do residents matter the most in reducing crime? *Public Management, 106*(11), 30-34. https://icma.org/articles/pm-magazine/do-residents-matter-most-reducing-crime; Linning, S.J., Carroll, T., Gerard, D.W., & Eck, J.E. (2024, December). Do more arrests reduce crime? *Public Management, 106*(12), 38–41. https://icma.org/articles/pm-magazine/do-more-arrests-reduce-crime

5 Lee, Y., Eck, J.E., O, S., & Martinez, N. (2017). How concentrated is crime at places? A systematic review from 1970 to 2015. *Crime Science, 6*(1), 1–16. https://doi.org/10.1186/s40163-017-0069-x

6 Weisburd, D. (2015). The law of crime concentration and the criminology of place. *Criminology, 53*(2), 133–157. https://doi.org/10.1111/1745-9125.12070

7 Evans, R. (2019, April 17). Half of England is owned by less than 1% of the population. *The Guardian*. Retrieved July 28, 2021 from: https://www.theguardian.com/money/2019/apr/17/who-owns-england-thousand-secret-landowners-author; Lee, Y., O, S., & Eck, J.E. (2021). Why your bar has crime by not mine: Resolving the land use and crime-risky facilities conflict. *Justice Quarterly, 39*(5), 1009–1035. https://doi.org/10.1080/07418825.2021.1903068; Payne, T.C. (2010). *Does changing ownership change crime? An analysis of apartment ownership and crime in Cincinnati.* Unpublished Doctoral Dissertation, University of Cincinnati.

8 Eck, J.E., Linning, S.J., & Herold, T.D. (2023). *Place management and crime: Ownership and property rights as a source of social control.* Springer. https://doi.org/10.1007/978-3-031-27693-4; Eck, J.E. & Madensen, T.D. (2018). Place management. In G.J.N. Bruinsma & S.D. Johnson (Eds.), *The Oxford Handbook of Environmental Criminology* (pp. 629–663). Oxford University Press. https://doi.org/10.1093/oxfordhb/9780190279707.013.22

9 Martinez, N.N., Lee, Y.J., Eck, J.E., & O, S. (2017). Ravenous wolves revisited: A systematic review of offending concentration. *Crime Science, 6*(1), 1–16. https://doi.org/10.1186/s40163-017-0072-2

10 Lee, Y., Eck, J.E., O, S., & Martinez, N.N. (2017). How concentrated is crime at places? A systematic review from 1970 to 2015. *Crime Science, 6*, 1–16. https://doi.org/10.1186/s40163-017-0069-x; Weisburd, D. (2015). The law of crime concentration and the criminology of place. *Criminology, 53*(2), 133–157. https://doi.org/10.1111/1745-9125.12070; Sherman, L.W. (2007). The power few: Experimental criminology and the reduction of harm. *Journal of Experimental Criminology, 3*, 299–321. https://doi.org/10.1007/s11292-007-9044-y

11 Pareto, V. (1897). The new theories of economics. *Journal of Political Economy, 5*(4), 485–502.

12 The rule of the few has been express using different terms. Because of Pareto's wealth concentration findings, some refer to it as the Pareto principle. Statisticians refer to it as power law or fat-tailed distributions. In business circles, the rule of the few is often called the 80/20 rule (Koch, 2008, p. 4). But for the purposes of this book, we will use the rule of the few and hockey stick distributions; Koch, R. (2008). *The 80/20 Principle: The Secret to Achieving More with Less.* Currency Press, p. 4.

13 Koch, R. (2008). *The 80/20 Principle: The Secret to Achieving More with Less.* Currency Press.

14 Ijiri, Y. & Simon, H.A. (2013). Interpretations of departures from the Pareto curve firm-size distributions. *Journal of Political Economy, 82*(2), 315–331. https://doi.org/10.1086/260194; Koch, R. (2008). *The 80/20 Principle: The Secret to Achieving More with Less.* Currency Press, p. 4; Rhoades, S.A. (1993). The Herfindahl-Herschman index. *Federal Reserve Bulletin, 79*(3), 188–189.

15 Jacobi, J.V. (2012). High utilizers of ED services: Lessons for system reform. *Annals of Health Law, 21*(1), 35–44; Visser, E., Pijl, Y.J., Stolk, R.P., Neeleman, J., & Rosmalen, J.G.M. (2007). Accident proneness, does it exist? A review and meta-analysis. *Accident Analysis and Prevention, 39*(3), 556–564. https://doi.org/10.1016/j.aap.2006.09.012

16 Schmeiser, S. (2015). The size distribution of websites. *Economics Letters, 128*, 62–68. https://doi.org/10.1016/j.econlet.2015.01.019; Bartlett, J., Norrie, R., Patel, S., Rumpel, R., & Wimberley, S. (2014). *Misogyny On Twitter.* London: Demos.

17 Jacobi, J.V. (2012). High utilizers of ED services: Lessons for system reform. *Annals of Health Law, 21*(1), 35–44; Visser, E., Pijl, Y.J., Stolk, R.P., Neeleman, J., & Rosmalen, J.G.M. (2007). Accident proneness, does it exist? A review and meta-analysis. *Accident Analysis and Prevention, 39*(3), 556–564. https://doi.org/10.1016/j.aap.2006.09.012

18 Corsaro, N., Gerard, D., Engel, R., & Eck, J.E. (2012). Not by accident: An analytical approach to traffic crash harm reduction. *Journal of Criminal Justice, 40*(6), 502–514. https://doi.org/10.1016/j.jcrimjus.2012.08.003

19 Gladwell, M. (2006, February 13 & 20). Million-Dollar Murray. *The New Yorker*, 96–107.

20 Corsaro, N., Gerard, D., Engel, R., & Eck, J.E. (2012). Not by accident: An analytical approach to traffic crash harm reduction. *Journal of Criminal Justice, 40*(6), 502–514. https://doi.org/10.1016/j.jcrimjus.2012.08.003

21 In 2005 there were 36 fatal traffic crashes in Cincinnati, Ohio. In 2009, Cincinnati had 19 fatal traffic crashes. In 2022, the city had a goal of repaving 100 miles but managed to repave 42 miles of road that year. See: https://www.wcpo.com/news/local-news/hamilton-county/cincinnati/inflation-pandemic-and-insufficient-funding-cause-cincinnati-to-fall-short-on-2021-road-paving-goals

22 Felson, M. & Eckert, M. (2017). *Introductory Criminology: The Study of Risky Situations*. Routledge. https://doi.org/10.4324/9781315618739; Felson, M. & Eckert, M. (2019). *Crime and Everyday Life* (6th ed.). Sage Publications. https://doi.org/10.4135/9781506394817

23 Felson, M. & Clarke, R.V. (1998). *Opportunity makes the thief.* Police Research Series Paper 98, 1–36. Retrieved from: https://popcenter.asu.edu/sites/g/files/litvpz3631/files/opportunity_makes_the_thief.pdf

24 Andresen, M.A. (2024). *Environmental Criminology: Evolution, Theory, and Practice (3rd ed.)*. New York, NY: Routledge

25 Andresen, M.A. (2024). *Environmental Criminology: Evolution, Theory, and Practice (3rd ed.)*. New York, NY: Routledge; Brantingham, P.L. & Brantingham, P.J. (1981). Notes on the geometry of crime. In P.J. Brantingham & P.L. Brantingham (Eds.), *Environmental Criminology* (pp. 27–54). Prospect Heights, IL: Waveland Press; Eck, J.E., & Clarke, R.V. (2019). Situational crime prevention: Theory, practice, and evidence. In M.D. Krohn, N. Hendrix, G.P. Hall, & A.J. Lizotte (Eds.), *Handbook of Crime and Deviance* (2nd ed., pp. 355–376). Springer International Publishing. https://doi.org/10.1007/978-3-030-20779-3_18; Felson, M. (2017). The routine activity approach. In R. Wortley & M. Townsley (Eds.), *Environmental Criminology and Crime Analysis* (pp. 87–97). New York, NY: Routledge; Felson, M. & Eckert, M. (2015). *Crime and Everyday Life*. Sage Publications.

26 Smith, M.J. & Clarke, R. V. (2012). Situational crime prevention: Classifying techniques using "good enough" theory. In B.C. Welsh & D.P. Farrington (Eds.), *The Oxford Handbook of Crime Prevention* (pp. 291–315). Oxford, UK: Oxford University Press. https://doi.org/10.1093/oxfordhb/9780195398823.013.0015

27 Abelson, E.S. (1992). *When Ladies Go A-thieving: Middle-class Shoplifters in the Victorian Department Store*. Oxford University Press.

28 Clarke, R.V. (2020). Assaults with glasses in bars and clubs in Lancashire, England. In M.S. Scott & R.V. Clarke (Eds.), *Problem-Oriented Policing: Successful Case Studies* (pp. 128–136). New York, NY: Routledge. https://doi.org/10.4324/9780429457357-13

29 Clarke, R.V. & Goldstein, H. (2003). *Reducing theft at construction sites: Lessons from a problem-oriented project*. US Department of Justice: Office of Community Oriented Policing Services. Retrieved from: https://popcenter.asu.edu/sites/g/files/litvpz3631/files/library/CrimePrevention/Volume_13/06-Clarke.pdf

30 Boba, R. & Santos, R. (2007). Single-family home construction site theft: A crime prevention case study. *International Journal of Construction Education and Research, 3*(3), 217–236. https://doi.org/10.1080/15578770701715086
31 Goldstein, H. (1979). Improving policing: A problem-oriented approach. *Crime & Delinquency, 25*(2), 236–258. https://doi.org/10.1177/001112877902500207; Goldstein, H. (1990). *Problem-Oriented Policing*. New York, NY: McGraw-Hill Publishing Company.
32 Goldstein, H. (1979). Improving policing: A problem-oriented approach. *Crime & Delinquency, 25*(2), 236–258. https://doi.org/10.1177/001112877902500207; Goldstein, H. (1990). *Problem-Oriented Policing*. New York, NY: McGraw-Hill Publishing Company.
33 Madensen, T.D. (2007). *Bar management and crime: Towards a dynamic theory of place management and crime hotspots*. Unpublished doctoral dissertation, School of Criminal Justice, University of Cincinnati.
34 Eck, J.E., Linning, S.J., & Herold, T.D. (2023). *Place Management and Crime: Ownership and Property Rights as a Source of Social Control*. Springer. https://doi.org/10.1007/978-3-031-27693-4
35 Lee, Y., Eck, J.E., O, S., & Martinez, N.N. (2017). How concentrated is crime at places? A systematic review from 1970 to 2015. *Crime Science, 6*, 1–16. https://doi.org/10.1186/s40163-017-0069-x; Weisburd, D. (2015). The law of crime concentration and the criminology of place. *Criminology, 53*(2), 133–157. https://doi.org/10.1111/1745-9125.12070
36 Eck, J.E., Linning, S.J., & Herold, T.D. (2023). *Place Management and Crime: Ownership and Property Rights as a Source of Social Control*. Springer. https://doi.org/10.1007/978-3-031-27693-4
37 Linning, S.J., Carroll, T., Gerard, D.W., & Eck, J.E. (2025, February). How can you SCRAP crime proposals that are likely to fail? *Public Management, 107*(2), 36–40. https://icma.org/articles/pm-magazine/how-can-you-scrap-crime-proposals-are-likely-fail

PART 1

HOW MANY GET CRIME WRONG

2

Is Crime Widespread?

American crime scientist Tamara Herold has spent hundreds of hours driving around with police officers learning about the challenges they encounter. Every time she does a ride-along, she asks the officer a question, "Where would I go if I wanted to get robbed tonight?" The officer always knows immediately and says, "You want to go to this address or to this intersection." Herold would then ask, "How long has this place been that way?" Regardless of whether the officer has been on the job six months or 20 years, the answer is always the same: "forever".[1]

The information officers tell Herold is a near universal truth. But it contradicts a common fallacy people have about crime: that crime is relatively widespread, particularly in high crime neighborhoods.

Up to the 1980s, we had no reason to question this assumption. To this day, most people write off high crime neighborhoods—think Skid Row in Los Angeles, the Southside of Chicago, or the Downtown East Side in Vancouver, Canada—as widely unsafe. We call this the *crime is widespread fallacy*.[2] This fallacy is so common that it is embedded in much standard police practice and community-based crime prevention. The fallacy tells police to patrol wide areas because crime could happen anywhere at any moment with the same odds. The crime is widespread fallacy tells community crime preventers to focus on large swaths of the

DOI: 10.4324/9781003430155-3

urban landscape—neighborhoods—because crime is equally likely everywhere in the neighborhood. But in hindsight, we now know better.

Herold's story illustrates a fact that researchers have known for over 30 years: crime is highly concentrated, even within high crime areas. Lawrence Sherman and his colleagues brought this fact to light in their 1989 study of crime at addresses.[3] It was the first published study to show the concentration of crime at places.[4] Technology had improved such that researchers could map the specific addresses of where crimes occurred. Over a one-year period, Sherman's research team linked all the calls for police service in Minneapolis, MN to the precise addresses they originated from.

Their results challenged decades of past research. Of every 100 addresses, three addresses generated half the calls to the police. If we add to these three addresses, the next six highest police calling addresses, nine places total, generated almost 70% of the calls for police service. Sherman and his team found this hyper-concentration of crime even when they looked at specific types of crime. Of every 100 addresses, for example, seven places experienced all the city's assaults and 11 places experienced all of the burglaries.

They called the few addresses with a lot of crime *hotspots*. These were the places at the blade of the hockey stick. The implications of their findings were immense. If you could prevent crime at the worst 10% of a city's addresses, you would eliminate nearly 70% of the calls to the police. Even successful interventions at the worst 3% of addresses would eliminate half of the city's crime.

The other end of the distribution, the handle of the hockey stick, revealed some important insights too. Sherman's team estimated over 45,000 unique addresses in Minneapolis. Of every 100 of these addresses, 40 did not call the police and another 30 called only once in the year. So, 70 of 100 places did not show a chronic need for police response.

Researchers have found similar results in dozens of cities across multiple countries.[5] In any city, a small number of places experience most of the crime; it's a manifestation of the rule of the few. And if a place has a lot of crime, it is more likely to experience crime consistently for years.[6]

What happens when police do not account for the rule of the few? A famous 1970s police study, the Kansas City Preventive Patrol Experiment (KCPPE), provides an answer.[7] The KCPPE tested whether random preventive patrolling reduces crime. Police divided the city of Kansas City, Missouri into patrol beats: geographic areas the police make their rounds within. At the time, a typical beat would have one or two police cars assigned to it. To conduct the experiment, the police department and researchers divided the beats into three groups. In one third of these beats, police made no changes to the number of cars patrolling. These were called control beats. Another third of the beats received extra patrol cars to roam about. These were called proactive beats. And the last third of the beats had their roaming patrols removed. Police would patrol the perimeter of the beat and only enter these beats when called. These were called the reactive beats.

Researchers expected the proactive beats would experience the most benefits compared to the other beats. Adding police patrols should result in a crime reduction in the proactive beats. Adding more police roaming the streets should also increase police visibility which would reduce the public's fear of crime and increase people's overall satisfaction with the police. Reducing police patrols in the reactive beats should result in the opposite: more crime, increased public fear, and less satisfaction with the police. The researchers expected to see no changes in the control beats, where policing had not changed.

But something unexpected happened; the researchers' expectations were wrong. After running the experiment for a year, researchers found that crime was no different across the proactive, reactive, and control beats. People's fear of crime did not change. And neither did people's feelings about the police. Why did random patrolling not work?

Maybe it was the antiquated research methods of the 1970s. If re-examined, using today's methods, would the results be so pessimistic? In 2023, David Weisburd and his research team answered that question. Their re-analysis revealed that random patrolling does reduce crime, but only by a little. Random patrolling was associated with a 7% decline in crime overall. When researchers looked at violent crime only, random patrol reduced violent crime by 17%.[8] So, Weisburd and colleagues do not recommend random patrolling. They suggest a type of patrolling that was invented after the Kansas City study, based on a better understanding of crime; the rule of the few.

A key reason random patrolling did not work in the Kansas City experiment is because the police did not take the rule of the few into

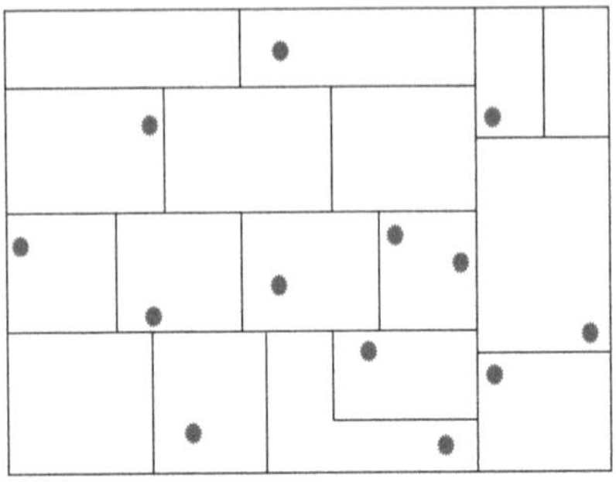

(a)

FIGURE 2.1A What Crime patterns Look Like if Crime Randomly Occurred

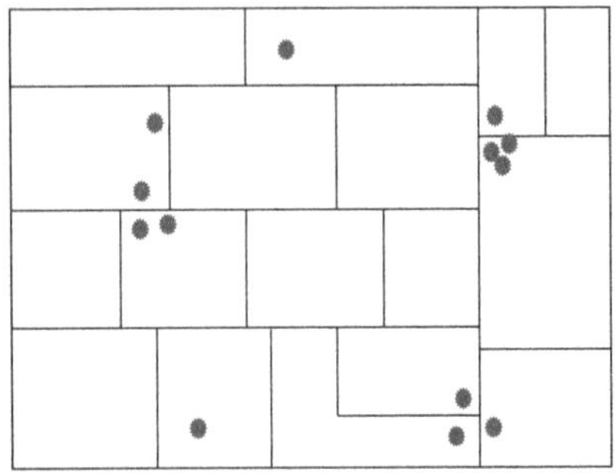

(b)

FIGURE 2.1B What Crime Patterns Look Like in Real Life

account. Random preventive patrolling assumes that crime occurs relatively uniformly across areas (Figure 2.1a). If crime occurs randomly, then random patrol makes sense. But we now know better. Because crime is concentrated in hotspots within beats then we will have beats with little or no crime (Figure 2.1b). We will also have large areas in high crime beats with no crime. In these no crime areas, increasing patrols cannot reduce crime further.

Given what we know now, if we were to run the Kansas City experiment again, we would expect it to fail. Beats with little crime simply do not need as much police attention as beats with many crime hotspots. So, if random patrol is ineffective, what can we do? The first thing the police responded with was hotspots patrols.

Cops on Dots

Considering Sherman and colleagues' findings, police started taking the rule of the few into account. They responded with hotspots patrols. These patrols, sometimes referred to as crackdowns, consist of temporary noticeable increases in police presence at known crime hotspots, giving rise to the term "cops on dots".[9] When police put cops on dots, it means they assign more officers to the dots on their city's map that have a lot of crime.

Hotspots is a term regularly used to depict places with many crimes. But there is disagreement on how to define places. Some describe neighborhoods and other large geographic areas, such as census tracts, as places. Tamara Herold (formerly Madensen) and John Eck refer to these large areas containing multiple property parcels and streets as *pooled places*.[10] Some researchers consider pooled places with a lot of crime to be hotspots.[11] Others describe street segments or street blocks as places. A segment is a length of street between two intersections (see white line between two dots in Figure 2.2) and includes all the properties on both sides of the street (parcels shaded in dark grey). Some refer to these segments as *proximal places*.[12] So, when some people are referring to hotspots, they are referring to street segments that have a lot of crime.[13]

In our own work, we have found that focusing on addresses is most useful. These places consist of land parcels with easily identifiable boundaries. Madensen and Eck classify these as *proprietary places*, which also highlights the fact that each parcel has an owner.[14] Ownership will become important later. So, moving forward, when we refer to places, we are referring to individual property parcels with a specific address. And, to us, a hotspot is a property parcel with many crimes.[15] We will show the importance of different types of proprietary places in chapter 14.

Hotspots policing provides more promising results than random patrolling (Figure 2.3). Systematic reviews of all the studies evaluating

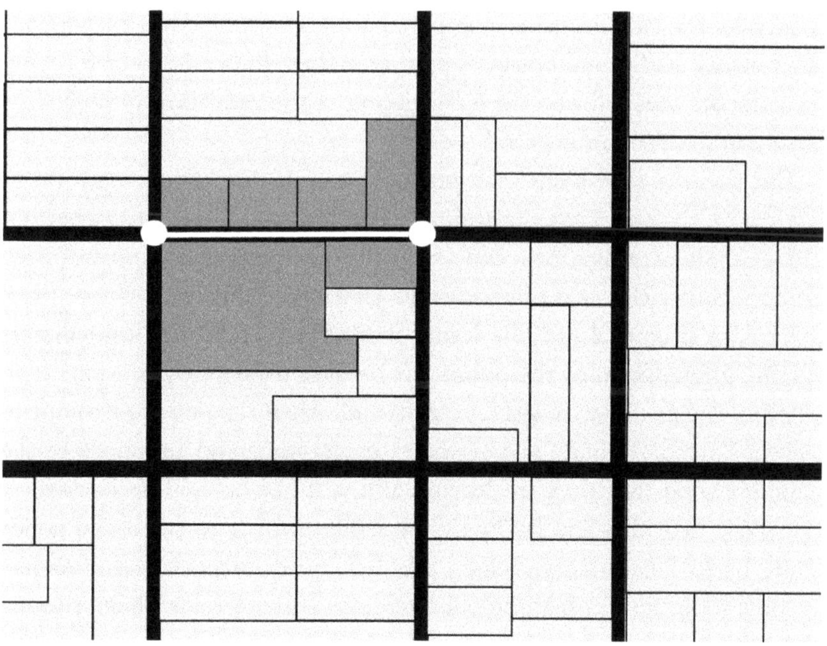

FIGURE 2.2 Types of Crime Places

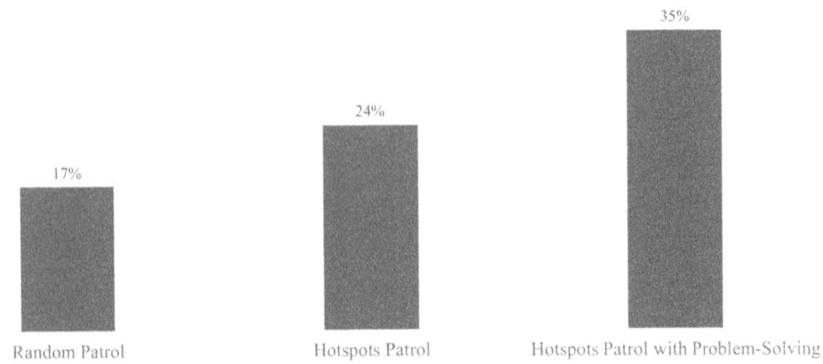

FIGURE 2.3 Violent Crime Reduction by Strategy Type

hotspots policing show that it consistently reduces crime.[16] In general, hotspots policing produces a 16% reduction in crime on average, compared to the 7% average reduction generated by random patrol.[17]

And when police incorporate problem-solving into their hotspots strategies—a topic discussed in parts 3 and 4 of this book—there is an even greater average reduction in crime.[18] For example, when reducing violent crime, using a problem-oriented hotspots approach led to a 35% reduction for violent crime compared to a 24% reduction in violence when using traditional hotspots patrols.[19] Thus, the benefits of focusing on hotspots outperforms the 17% violent crime reduction produced by having police randomly patrol the city.[20]

But there is a problem with hotspots patrols: the effects tend not to last long. Crime declines almost immediately during the intensive patrols. These declines persist for a time after the intense patrols stop, but then crime returns. This is a phenomenon Lawrence Sherman calls residual deterrence (Figure 2.4).[21] He found that offenders did not immediately resume offending once the police left because they were uncertain as to whether the crackdown was over. After all, when the police are about to leave a hotspot, they do not get out a megaphone and announce to the neighborhood that they are leaving and will not be coming back for a few days! So, offenders lay low for a while waiting to see if the police come back. Uncertainty creates this beneficial effect. Once offenders become more certain that the police are gone, they re-start their criminal

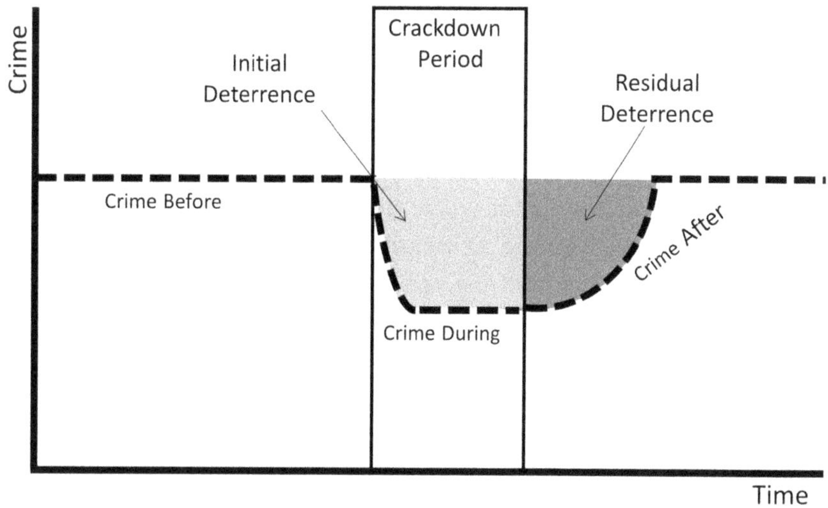

FIGURE 2.4 Residual Deterrence

activities. So, crime creeps back up. This is why officers, like the ones Tamara Herold talked with, say hotspots have been problematic forever.

To remedy this problem, Sherman suggested the police use rotating crackdowns.[22] Police would patrol a hotspot temporarily, leave to patrol another hotspot, but return once the residual effect had almost worn off. But this is a resource-intensive process leaving police playing a game of whack-a-mole by chasing crime at hotspots. Hotspots policing, therefore, is better than standard policing, but we should be able to do better, and we can. To do better, we need to answer the question: why have hotspots tended to stay hot?

From Hockey Sticks to Triangles

To understand why hotspots persist, we must understand why crime concentrates at a few places (the blade of the hockey stick) and does not concentrate elsewhere (the handle of the hockey stick). The rule of the few has the answer: because a few places have good crime opportunities, and most do not. Consider car break-ins as an example. Some areas have few cars and other areas have many cars. In areas with few cars, there are fewer opportunities for car break-ins regardless of the police patrol patterns. In the areas with many cars, such as parking lots with signs reminding people not to leave belongings in their vehicles, most people do not leave belongings in their vehicles. This too will restrict opportunities and fewer break-ins will occur. But if on a few separate blocks, there are numerous residents who routinely leave items visible in their car (this is typical around college campuses, for example), then car break-ins will concentrate on these blocks as that is where the greatest opportunities exist.

To reduce crime, we need to identify why hotspots have many crime opportunities and eliminate the opportunities. Fortunately, researchers created a tool, called the crime triangle, to help us understand why opportunities for crime exist at some places, but not others.[23] The crime triangle (Figure 2.5) depicts the elements you need for a crime to occur. Start by looking at the inner triangle coloured in black. These are the necessary conditions for a crime: you need an *offender* and a *target* to converge at a *place*. An *offender* can be anyone sufficiently motivated to commit a crime. A *target* can be a person or object that is perceived as being sufficiently attractive to an offender. The *place* is a specific property parcel. These are the three core elements needed for a crime to occur. All three elements need to converge in time and space; and when they do, this creates a crime opportunity.

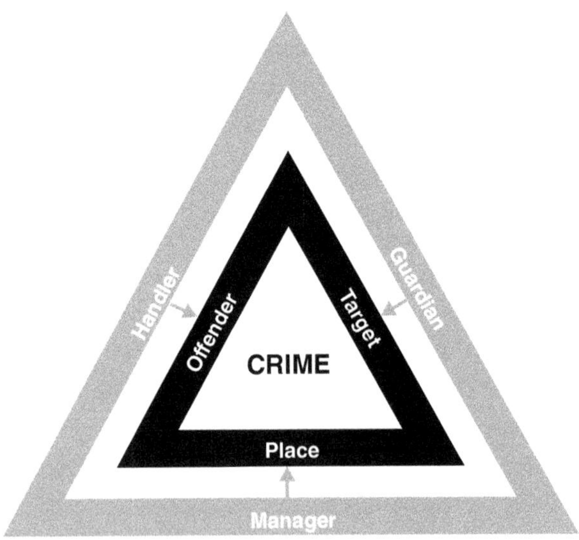

FIGURE 2.5 The Crime Triangle

The absence of any one of these three inner elements means a crime cannot occur; there is no opportunity for crime. You can have the most motivated offender in the world, but without a suitable target to tempt him, there is nothing for him to victimize. Similarly, you can have the most suitable target in the world—think of a duffle bag filled with cash sitting open in an unsupervised parking lot—but if no offender comes across it, no crime will occur.

Now direct your focus to the outer grey triangle. The three elements in the outer triangle are called controllers because they control the three inner elements. *Guardians* control targets by protecting them.[24] These could be security guards, friends, or neighbors. *Handlers* control offenders by trying to keep them out of trouble.[25] They are usually emotionally attached to the offender. Parents, for example, are handlers for juveniles. Handlers could also be teachers, coaches, friends, or spouses. *Managers* control places. They are the individuals or organizations who have legal authority over the place.[26] The most important place manager is the property owner. The owner may be a person, business, club, governmental or nongovernmental organization, religious group, college, or university.[27] Owners can delegate control to others, such as employees, to ensure the smooth functioning of the place.[28]

If a single effective controller is present and operating, then even if the three necessary conditions (depicted in the inner triangle) come together, crime is unlikely. A single crime might occur if by some odd chance the inner elements converge when all the controllers are momentarily inattentive. However, to have a recurring problem, both the convergence and inattentiveness must routinely occur. That is, when controllers routinely fail to do their jobs when the offenders are near targets, crimes repeatedly occur. This means that hotspots of crime are evidence of recurring crime opportunities. And this unveils why policing hotspots will only be temporarily effective: the patrols do nothing to address the crime opportunities.

The triangle shows that to reduce crime, we should focus on more than just offenders. There are several ways of tackling crime problems. Start with the inner triangle. Because each of these three elements are necessary conditions for a crime to occur, simply removing any one of them will prevent crime. Traditional policing strategies typically focus on offender removal through arrest. In chapter 4 we discuss why this is ineffective.

Alternative strategies using other components of the crime triangle can be more helpful. Removing targets or altering places can work well.

Consider robberies at automatic teller machines (ATMs). Keeping offenders away is difficult because we cannot predict who is and who is not an offender. Removing targets is difficult as potential victims are those who use ATMs so removing them makes ATMs useless. But removing or manipulating the place is highly feasible. In high-risk locations, we can either remove the ATM or the ATM can be situated within a protected place; instead of outside on the street, it could be put inside a store or even a police station, for example. If necessary, it can be located within a protective booth.

Though target removal is not feasible for ATM robberies, it is for some types of street robberies. Consider robberies of students or staff leaving campus late at night. Many universities offer free rides or safe walk programs across campuses or even to nearby residences off-campus. Security personnel escort students and staff to desired locations. The security personnel become added guardians making students and staff less enticing robbery targets for offenders.

Let's shift to the second triangle. It is possible to improve the effectiveness of guardians, handlers, or place managers. Some shopping malls, for example, do not allow teenagers inside on Friday or Saturday evenings without a parent present.[29] This adds handlers to a potentially troublesome situation. There are many ways to improve guardianship, in addition to adding police patrols. Encouraging young drinkers to watch out for each other is thought to reduce the incidence of sexual assault, for example. Improving place management has received considerable attention too. This usually involves getting owners to improve how they organize the physical space of the location, regulate the conduct of people at the place, and control access to the place.[30] In fact, place managers are arguably the most powerful element in the crime triangle.

When crime becomes a problem, we default to thinking the police should be summoned to solve it. This is another common fallacy about crime; we call it the *police can solve all crime problems fallacy*.[31] But many of the most effective crime reduction strategies cannot be implemented by the police. Instead, place managers are the only actors with the power to generate change. Through property ownership, many unique legal powers are bestowed upon place managers.[32] They can build on their property, they can renovate existing buildings, and they can control who they allow to use and access their property within the bounds of the law.[33] This gives place managers immense power to control crime opportunities, much of which the police do not possess. Let's re-visit some of the examples given above to illustrate the police can solve all crime problems fallacy.

The police cannot remove or relocate ATMs to different locations. This can only be done by the people who own them. Banks, for example, decide whether to locate their ATMs: on the street, inside the doors of their branches, or at other locations such as grocery stores. This is an example of place managers controlling a place.

Universities are the place managers of their campuses. They are the ones who create the safe ride and safe walk programs to transport students safely. This is an example of place managers increasing guardianship to protect targets.

In the shopping mall example, it was the place manager who created the parent-teenager policy. The mall's owner had the authority to decide who can and cannot use the shopping mall (think: no shoes, no shirt, no service); at what times of day (think: the business hours they choose to keep); and under what supervision. The policy required that teenagers have adult supervision while in the mall. This means the place manager controlled potential offenders by bringing handlers into the situation.

In the previous chapter, the place managers of the bars Aiden Sidebottom studied had the authority to block off one of the entrances of their bars to reduce bag thefts. Similarly, place managers of churches had the authority to lock the wheels on their dumpsters. Police can certainly recommend these changes. But the place managers, ultimately, are the ones who implement the changes.

Place managers can often control all other elements of the crime triangle (Figure 2.6). Just as important, no other element of the triangle can control others like place managers can. For example, mall patrons cannot change the operating hours of the mall or eliminate the parent-teenager supervision policy. Similarly, patrons or police cannot remove an ATM on the street and then move it inside the door of a building. Most people have no legal authority to do this; only place managers do. As such, place managers are the most powerful actor in the crime triangle.[34]

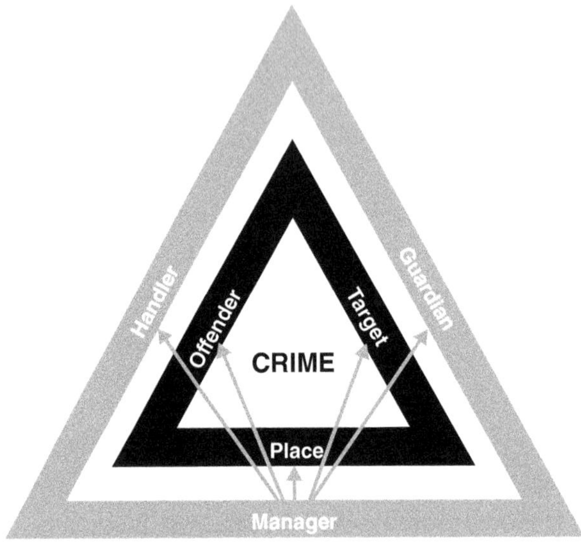

FIGURE 2.6 The Power of Place Managers

Place management provides the most comprehensive, and empirically validated, explanation for why crime concentrates at only a few places. Because place managers hold so much power in influencing all sides of the crime triangle, they are the most important in determining whether crime opportunities are present or not and to what degree. Yes, offenders matter and their motivations can play a part to a certain extent. But without opportunities, offenders cannot commit crimes no matter how motivated they are. Place management is often the key factor determining whether opportunities are present on a property or not.

All places have place managers. What distinguishes places on the blade of the hockey stick from those on the handle is the decisions place managers make about the functioning of their place. We will discuss these differences in decisions in chapters 7 and 10. But another manifestation of the rule of the few has given us insight into how we might direct place managers to make decisions on their properties.

Are All Bars Bad?

Let's return to the first hotspots study. Sherman and colleagues discovered that the 3.3% of places that contained 50.4% of the crimes in

Minneapolis were comprised of all kinds of places: bars, schools, apartment buildings, convenience stores, gas stations, banks, churches, coffee shops, restaurants, libraries, parks, transit stations, and so on.[35] The study did not assess whether certain types of places were driving this crime trend. Many people assume certain types of places are more dangerous than others; bars and liquor stores have a bad reputation, for example, when compared to coffee shops or churches. But this is a false assumption about crime.

In the 2000s, researchers examined types of places that were assumed to generate criminal activity, and they found something quite remarkable. The rule of the few applied when examining all locations of a particular type of facility. That is, if you selected a type of place—take apartments, for example—only a small number of apartments experienced most of the crime. Most apartments experienced no crime. A study of 145 high-rise apartments in Australia, for example, found that about 10% of buildings hosted half of all crime at high-rise apartments.[36]

Even places that are assumed to generate crime follow this trend. A study conducted by Tamara Madensen (now Herold) and John Eck examined all bars in Cincinnati, Ohio.[37] Of the 239 bars in the city, they were able to complete surveys at 199 of the bars and collect crime data for 184 of those bars. They found that most bars experienced no incidents of violence, while a few bars had many. Specifically, 62% had no violence, a moderate 23.4% had one incident of physical violence, and a mere 14.6% experienced two or more violent incidents. All violent incidents at bars could be traced back to 38% of bars in the city. They also found no direct link between whether high crime bars were in high crime neighborhoods. Both violent and non-violent bars were located within the same neighborhoods. This suggested to them that something else about those few problematic bars was contributing to the problem. That something was place management practices.[38] So, the type of place is not necessarily the problem. What matters is how the place is managed.

This makes intuitive sense. Consider two hypothetical bars. MacLaren's Pub might cater to young professionals looking to have a drink and dinner after work. It contains many booths and tables, but no dance floor. They have well-trained staff who regularly check patrons' identification and stop serving alcohol to noticeably intoxicated patrons. They also post rules and expected codes of conduct on the wall. They are not afraid to enforce rules and eject or ban customers who break them.

Now consider the management practices of a different bar: Puzzles. Puzzles serves no food, so patrons are more likely to become intoxicated. It contains a large dance floor, so they play loud music and run regular promotions hoping to attract college students. The owners do not regularly check patrons' identification or stop serving those who are visibly inebriated. They are also inconsistent in how they enforce rules. Rules are not posted in the premises. And bouncers are not always present to eject disruptive people.

Even though both places are bars, do you think they are equally likely to experience crime? Should patrons of MacLaren's be concerned for their safety because they are in a bar? Just as important, would motivated offenders find MacLaren's or Puzzles to be a more appealing place to spend their time?

Clearly Puzzles provides more opportunities for crime. The place management practices at MacLaren's have suppressed many crime opportunities: underage drinkers are more likely to get caught, overly intoxicated people are cut off, and rule-breakers are ejected or even banned from the place. Puzzles, on the other hand, provides a place where many offenders and targets can converge as well as the absence of sufficient controllers to prevent unwanted behavior.

Although we have used bars to illustrate how crime concentrates within a certain type of facility, it applies to all types of facilities.[39] Most apartment buildings experience no crime at all, while a few experience a lot.[40] Most motels have no crime, but a small number of them have a lot.[41] Most stores experience no shoplifting incidents, yet a few experience many.[42]

This phenomenon is so common, it has been labelled *The Iron Law of Troublesome Places*.[43] The types of facilities known to follow this law include: apartment complexes; banks; bars, pubs, and clubs; bus stop shelters; businesses; coffee shops; construction sites; convenience stores; fast food restaurants; gas stations; health care facilities; hotels and motels; parking lots; places of worship; schools; sports facilities; telephone booths; and young offender facilities.[44] To date, researchers have found no exceptions.

All of this means that the most likely cause of why the 3.3% of places experience half of all crime in Minneapolis is likely due to place management practices. Those 3.3% of places are made up of all types of facilities. But these findings suggest that the type of place is not the problem, it's how the place is managed that matters. This has important implications for crime and its prevention.

As the crime triangle indicates, the removal of offenders through arrest is a viable option to prevent crime. But as we will discuss in chapter 4, arrests are merely a tool and not the most effective tool. This is because arrests often only produce temporary fixes to problems, as the crime opportunity still remains. Uncovering the importance of place management has revealed insights into why offenders and targets are converging without any controllers to begin with. This idea will be important later in part 3 of this book. For now, we offer a few thoughts on what has been done and where we need to go.

Does a Hotspot Have to be Forever?

The police have taken the rule of the few into account since Sherman and colleagues' pivotal study on crime concentration. The police responded with hotspots patrols. Increasing police presence at hotspots is certainly a more efficient use of police resources than having them randomly patrol cities. However, the benefits of hotspots patrols tend to be short lived. Police need to repeatedly conduct the hotspots patrols for the benefits to continue. Officers simply being present at a hotspot or making arrests does not dismantle the underlying opportunities that exist at these places; they only disrupt them. Hence why crime returns.

The evidence we have presented in this chapter suggests we can rid cities of their hotspots. But to do it, we need to go a step further than putting cops on dots. We need to address the underlying crime opportunities. When fewer opportunities exist, fewer crimes will be committed. Using strategies drawn from all sides of the crime triangle can help us achieve this. At present, hotspots patrol primarily focuses on removing offenders through arrest. But to have a more long-term impact, our strategies need to focus on problem-solving that removes opportunities for crime. As we've hinted at, the best way the police can do this is with the cooperation of the community. But as we will explain in the next chapter, there is another common fallacy—one specifically about communities—that needs to be corrected using the rule of the few.

Key Points

- Crime is not widespread; crime is highly concentrated at a few places.
- Use the crime triangle; crime occurs when an offender and a target converge at a place in the absence of a controller (handler, guardian, or manager).
- The type of place does not matter for crime, what matters is how the place is managed.
- To reduce crime, you need to dismantle crime opportunities at places (instead of merely disrupting them)
- Police are not the best equipped to deal with crime opportunities, place managers are.
- Ask: who owns the problem?

Notes

1 Herold, T.D. (2019). Reducing Crime Podcast Episode 5. Retrieved from: https://www.reducingcrime.com/podcast/episodes-1-20
2 Linning, S.J., Carroll, T., Gerard, D., & Eck, J.E. (2024). Is crime widespread? *Public Management, 106*(10), 30–32. https://icma.org/articles/pm-magazine/crime-widespread
3 Sherman, L. W., Gartin, P. R., & Buerger, M. E. (1989). Hot spots of predatory crime: Routine activities and the criminology of place. *Criminology, 27*(1), 27–56. https://doi.org/10.1111/j.1745-9125.1989.tb00862.x
4 For a non-peer reviewed report with similar findings produced around the same time, see: Pierce, R.E., Spaar, S., & Briggs, L.R. (1988). *The Character of Police Work: Strategic and Tactical Implications.* Center for Applied Social Research, Northeastern University.
5 Andresen, M.A., Curman, A.S., & Linning, S.J. (2017). The trajectories of crime at places: Understanding the patterns of disaggregated crime types. *Journal of Quantitative Criminology, 33*(3), 427–449. https://doi.org/10.1007/s10940-016-9301-1; Andresen, M.A. & Linning, S.J. (2012). The (in) appropriateness of aggregating across crime types. *Applied Geography, 35*(1–2), 275–282. https://doi.org/10.1016/j.apgeog.2012.07.007; Braga, A.A., Hureau, D.M., & Papachristos, A.V. (2011). The relevance of micro places to citywide robbery trends: A longitudinal analysis of robbery incidents at street corners and block faces in Boston. *Journal of Research in Crime and Delinquency, 48*(1), 7–32. https://doi.org/10.1177/0022427810384137; Lee, Y., Eck, J.E., O, S., & Martinez, N.N. (2017). How concentrated is crime at places? A systematic review from 1970 to 2015. *Crime Science, 6*, 1–16. https://doi.org/10.1186/s40163-017-0069-x; Weisburd, D. (2015). The law of crime concentration and the criminology of place. *Criminology, 53*(2), 133–157. https://doi.org/10.1111/1745-9125.12070; Weisburd, D. & Amram, S. (2014). The law of concentrations of crime at place: the case of Tel Aviv-Jaffa. *Police Practice and Research, 15*(2), 101–114. https://doi.org/10.1080/15614263.2013.874169; Weisburd, D., Bushway, S., Lum, C., & Yang, S.M. (2004). Trajectories of crime at places: A longitudinal study of

street segments in the city of Seattle. *Criminology, 42*(2), 283–322. https://doi.org/10.4324/9781315089256-19; Weisburd, D., Zastrow, T., Kuen, K., & Andresen, M.A. (2024). Crime concentration at micro places: A review of the evidence. *Aggression and Violence Behavior, 78*, 101979. https://doi.org/10.1016/j.avb.2024.101979

6 Andresen, M.A. & Malleson, N. (2011). Testing the stability of crime patterns: Implications for theory and policy. *Journal of Research in Crime and Delinquency, 48*(1), 58–82. https://doi.org/10.1177/0022427810384136; Weisburd, D. (2015). The law of crime concentration and the criminology of place. *Criminology, 53*(2), 133–157. https://doi.org/10.1111/1745-9125.12070; Weisburd, D., Bushway, S., Lum, C., & Yang, S.M. (2004). Trajectories of crime at places: A longitudinal study of street segments in the city of Seattle. *Criminology, 42*(2), 283–322. https://doi.org/10.4324/9781315089256-19

7 Kelling, G., Pate, T., Dieckman, D., & Brown, C.E. (1974). *The Kansas City Preventive Patrol Experiment.* Washington, DC: National Policing Institute. https://www.policinginstitute.org/publication/the-kansas-city-preventive-patrol-experiment/

8 Weisburd, D., Wilson, D.B., Petersen, K., & Telep, C.W. (2023). Does police patrol in large areas prevent crime? Revisiting the Kansas City Preventive Patrol Experiment. *Criminology & Public Policy, 22*(3), 543–560. https://doi.org/10.1111/1745-9133.12623

9 Sherman, L.W. (1990). Police crackdowns: Initial and residual deterrence. *Crime and Justice, 12*, 1–48. https://doi.org/10.1086/449163

10 Madensen, T.D. & Eck, J.E. (2012). Crime places and place management. In F.T. Cullen & P. Wilcox (Eds.), *The Oxford Handbook of Criminological Theory* (pp. 1–18). Oxford University Press. https://doi.org/10.1093/oxfordhb/9780199747238.013.0029

11 For example: Farrell, G. & Sousa, W. (2001). Repeat victimization and hot spots: The overlap and its implications for crime control and problem-oriented policing. *Crime Prevention Studies, 12*, 221–240

12 Madensen, T.D. & Eck, J.E. (2012). Crime places and place management. In F.T. Cullen & P. Wilcox (Eds.), *The Oxford Handbook of Criminological Theory* (pp. 1–18). Oxford University Press. https://doi.org/10.1093/oxfordhb/9780199747238.013.0029

13 For example: Weisburd, D., Bushway, S., Lum, C., & Yang, S.M. (2004). Trajectories of crime at places: A longitudinal study of street segments in the city of Seattle. *Criminology, 42*(2), 283–322. https://doi.org/10.4324/9781315089256-19

14 Madensen, T.D. & Eck, J.E. (2012). Crime places and place management. In F.T. Cullen & P. Wilcox (Eds.), *The Oxford Handbook of Criminological Theory* (pp. 1–18). Oxford University Press. https://doi.org/10.1093/oxfordhb/9780199747238.013.0029

15 Eck, J.E., Linning, S.J., & Herold, T.D. (2023). *Place Management and Crime: Ownership and Property Rights as a Source of Social Control.* Springer. https://doi.org/10.1007/978-3-031-27693-4

16 Braga, A.A., Turchan, B.S., Papachristos, A.V., & Hureau, D.M. (2019). Hot spots policing and crime reduction: An update of an ongoing systematic review and meta-analysis. *Journal of Experimental Criminology, 15*(3), 289–311. https://doi.org/10.1007/s11292-019-09372-3; Braga, A.A. & Weisburd, D.L. (2022). Does hot spots policing have meaningful impacts on crime? Findings from an alternative approach to estimating effect sizes from place-based program evaluations. *Journal of Quantitative Criminology, 38*, 1–22. https://doi.org/10.1007/s10940-020-09481-7; Turchan, B. & Braga, A.A. (2024). The effects of hot spots policing on violence: A systematic review and meta-analysis. *Aggression and Violent Behavior, 79*, 102011. https://doi.org/10.1016/j.avb.2024.102011

17 Braga, A.A. & Weisburd, D.L. (2022). Does hot spots policing have meaningful impacts on crime? Findings from an alternative approach to estimating effect sizes from place-based program evaluations. *Journal of Quantitative Criminology, 38*, 1–22. https://doi.org/10.1007/s10940-020-09481-7; Weisburd, D., Wilson, D.B., Petersen, K., & Telep, C.W. (2023). Does police patrol in large areas prevent crime? Revisiting the Kansas City Preventive Patrol Experiment. *Criminology & Public Policy, 22*(3), 543–560. https://doi.org/10.1111/1745-9133.12623

18 Turchan, B. & Braga, A.A. (2024). The effects of hot spots policing on violence: A systematic review and meta-analysis. *Aggression and Violent Behavior, 79*, 102011. https://doi.org/10.1016/j.avb.2024.102011

19 Turchan, B. & Braga, A.A. (2024). The effects of hot spots policing on violence: A systematic review and meta-analysis. *Aggression and Violent Behavior, 79*, 102011. https://doi.org/10.1016/j.avb.2024.102011

20 Weisburd, D., Wilson, D.B., Petersen, K., & Telep, C.W. (2023). Does police patrol in large areas prevent crime? Revisiting the Kansas City Preventive Patrol Experiment. *Criminology & Public Policy, 22*(3), 543–560. https://doi.org/10.1111/1745-9133.12623

21 Sherman, L.W. (1990). Police crackdowns: Initial and residual deterrence. *Crime and Justice, 12*, 1–48. https://doi.org/10.1086/449163

22 Sherman, L.W. (1990). Police crackdowns: Initial and residual deterrence. *Crime and Justice, 12*, 1–48. https://doi.org/10.1086/449163; Sherman, L.W. & Weisburd, D. (1995). General deterrent effects of police patrol in crime "hot spots": A randomized, controlled trial. *Justice Quarterly, 12*(4), 625–648. https://doi.org/10.1080/07418829500096221

23 Eck, J.E. (2003). Police problems: The complexity of problem theory, research and evaluation. *Crime Prevention Studies, 15*, 79–114; Clarke, R.V. & Eck, J.E. (2003). *Become a Problem-Solving Crime Analyst in 55 Small Steps*. London, UK: Jill Dando Institute for Crime Science. Retrieved from: https://popcenter.asu.edu/sites/g/files/litvpz3631/files/55stepsuk_0_0.pdf; Clarke, R.V. & Eck, J.E. (2009). Crime analysis for problem solvers in 60 small steps. Washington, DC: Office of Community Oriented Policing Services. Retrieved from: https://portal.cops.usdoj.gov/resourcecenter/content.ashx/cops-w0047-pub.pdf

24 Cohen, L.E. & Felson, M. (1979). Social change and crime rate trends: A routine activity approach. *American Sociological Review, 44*(4), 588–608. https://doi.org/10.2307/2094589; Hollis, M., Felson, M., & Welsh, B. (2013). The capable guardian in routine activities theory: A theoretical and conceptual reappraisal. *Crime Prevention and Community Safety, 15*, 65–79. https://doi.org/10.1057/cpcs.2012.14; Reynald, D.M. (2009). Guardianship in action: Developing a new tool for measurement. *Crime Prevention and Community Safety, 11*, 1–20. https://doi.org/10.1057/cpcs.2008.19

25 Felson, M. (1986). Routine activities, social controls, rational decisions, and criminal outcomes. In D. Cornish & R.V. Clarke (eds.), *The Reasoning Criminal: Rational Choice Perspectives on Offending* (pp. 119–128). New York, NY: Springer-Verlag.

26 Eck, J.E. (1994). *Drug markets and drug places: A case-control study of the spatial structure of illicit drug dealing*. Doctoral dissertation, University of Maryland, College Park.

27 Eck, J.E. & Madensen, T.D. (2018). Place management. In G.J.N. Bruinsma & S.D. Johnson (Eds.), *The Oxford Handbook of Environmental Criminology* (pp. 633–667). New York, NY: Oxford University Press. https://doi.org/10.1093/oxfordhb/9780190279707.013.22

28 Eck, J.E., Linning, S.J., & Herold, T.D. (2023). *Place Management and Crime: Ownership and Property Rights as a Source of Social Control.* Springer. https://doi.org/10.1007/978-3-031-27693-4
29 Rawe, J. (2007, June 28). *Bye-Bye, Mall Rats.* Time Magazine. Retrieved from: http://content.time.com/time/subscriber/article/0,33009,1638449,00.html
30 Eck, J.E. & Madensen, T.D. (2018). Place management. In G.J.N. Bruinsma & S.D. Johnson (Eds.), *The Oxford Handbook of Environmental Criminology* (pp. 633–667). New York, NY: Oxford University Press. https://doi.org/10.1093/oxfordhb/9780190279707.013.22
31 Linning, S.J., Carroll, T., Gerard, D.W., & Eck, J.E. (2025, January). Can the police solve all public safety problems? *Public Management, 107*(1), 40–44. https://icma.org/articles/pm-magazine/can-police-solve-all-crime-problems
32 Eck, J.E., Linning, S.J., & Herold, T.D. (2023). *Place Management and Crime: Ownership and Property Rights as a Source of Social Control.* Springer. https://doi.org/10.1007/978-3-031-27693-4
33 Eck, J.E. & Madensen, T.D. (2018). Place management. In G.J.N. Bruinsma & S.D. Johnson (Eds.), *The Oxford Handbook of Environmental Criminology* (pp. 633–667). New York, NY: Oxford University Press. https://doi.org/10.1093/oxfordhb/9780190279707.013.22
34 Linning, S.J. (2026). Place management. In H. Pontell & J. Corcoran (Eds.), *Oxford Research Encyclopedia of Criminology and Criminal Justice.* Oxford University Press.
35 Sherman, L.W., Gartin, P.R., & Buerger, M.E. (1989). Hot spots of predatory crime: Routine activities and the criminology of place. *Criminology, 27*(1), 27–56. https://doi.org/10.1111/j.1745-9125.1989.tb00862.x
36 Townsley, M., Reid, S., Reynald, D., Rynne, J., & Hutchins, B. (2014). Risky Facilities: Analysis of crime concentration in high-rise buildings. *Trends & Issues in Crime and Criminal Justice, 476*, 1–7. Retrieved from: https://www.aic.gov.au/sites/default/files/2020-05/tandi476.pdf
37 Madensen, T.D. & Eck, J.E. (2008). Violence in bars: Exploring the impact of place manager decision-making. *Crime Prevention and Community Safety, 10*(2), 111–125. https://doi.org/10.1057/cpcs.2008.2
38 Lee, Y., O, S., & Eck, J.E. (2022). Why your bar has crime but not mine: resolving the land use and crime–risky facility conflict. *Justice Quarterly, 39*(5), 1009–1035. https://doi.org/10.1080/07418825.2021.1903068
39 Madensen, T.D. & Eck, J.E. (2008). Violence in bars: Exploring the impact of place manager decision-making. *Crime Prevention and Community Safety, 10*(2), 111–125. https://doi.org/10.1057/cpcs.2008.2
40 Payne, T.C. (2010). *Does changing ownership change crime? An analysis of apartment ownership and crime in Cincinnati.* Unpublished Doctoral Dissertation, University of Cincinnati.
41 Bichler, G., Schmerler, K., & Enriquez, J. (2013). Curbing nuisance motels: An evaluation of police as place regulators. *Policing: An International Journal of Police Strategies & Management, 36*(2), 437–462. https://doi.org/10.1108/13639511311329787
42 Eck, J.E., Clarke, R.V., & Guerette, R.T. (2007). Risky facilities: Crime concentration in homogeneous sets of establishments and facilities. *Crime Prevention Studies, 21*, 225–264.
43 Wilcox, P. & Eck. J. E. (2011). Criminology of the unpopular. *Criminology & Public Policy, 10*(2), 473–482. https://doi.org/10.1111/j.1745-9133.2011.00721.x
44 Wilcox, P. & Eck. J.E. (2011). Criminology of the unpopular. *Criminology & Public Policy, 10*(2), 473–482. https://doi.org/10.1111/j.1745-9133.2011.00721.x

3

Do Residents Matter Most?

For years, police officers in Kansas City, Missouri had a thorn in their side: the Creston Apartments.[1] The Creston was a single dilapidated apartment building in the Longfellow neighborhood, a middle-class area of the city. Residents and neighbors were complaining and calling the police about the Creston's illegal activities at record rates. The Creston Apartment was the #1 location for calls for service in the police's division with an average of 55 calls per month. Residents reported crime problems ranging from drug dealing, thefts, and prostitution to assaults, robberies, gunfire, and homicides. Officers spent hundreds of hours monitoring activity on the property and trying to arrest people involved in the crimes. Violence became so prominent that, to ensure officer safety, the police department dispatched four officers every time they responded to a call at the property.

Having no success with their arrest-focused approach, three officers decided to solve the problem. First, they gave nearby residents business cards with a number they could call anytime to report illegal activity. Second, the owner of a vacant apartment building across the street gave police permission to use his property to conduct surveillance of the Creston. Third, officers identified the owners of the Creston and tried to get the owner to address issues on their property. But the owners refused to co-operate.

 DOI: 10.4324/9781003430155-4

Looking further into the building, the officers discovered that there was a Housing and Urban Development (HUD) lien on the building, making HUD just as responsible for the building as the owners. So, officers began working with HUD, the fire department, and the health inspector to address the problem. Together, they deemed the building uninhabitable due to its poor condition. HUD decided to find tenants new housing. In the meantime, however, HUD also took action to improve living conditions. HUD hired 24-hour security guards and a doorman who checked everyone's identification upon entry. They also installed a metal detector at the entrance. HUD also evicted drug dealers arrested by police. These changes led to a 60% drop in calls for police service. After finding the tenants new homes, and because the building was uninhabitable, HUD demolished the Creston Apartments.

Many would classify this example as an effective use of community policing. Community policing is a strategy in which police partner with residents to address crime in the community.[2] The strategy suggests that resident involvement influences neighborhood crime levels. It is based on the idea that residents have some control over crime, so the government's role should be to facilitate the natural ability of residents to keep crime down. In theory, the police can empower residents to defend their own neighborhoods by regularly working with them. The ideas behind community policing are so appealing that police departments have been using the strategy for over 50 years.

Though the strategy sounds good in theory, does the example really illustrate community policing? While many residents were impacted by the Creston, only a few residents got involved with the police. While the few residents who were involved provided police with information, the residents did not implement the solutions at the Creston. The reason the residents could not implement the solutions is because they had no power over the place experiencing the problem. Who had this power? The place manager, HUD.

Studies show that community policing seldom reduces crime.[3] The principal reason why community policing and many other community-based strategies do not work as well as their advocates claim is because of the *residents matter most fallacy*; that residents are the most able to reduce crime in their communities.[4]

The Creston apartment example teaches us four lessons about residents' ability to influence crime and, in turn, community policing. First, we often think the people who matter most are residents. However, not every person who is part of the community is a resident. Communities also include property owners who live elsewhere, employees of businesses in the area, and people who shop and recreate there. So, we should not confuse community members with residents.

Second, residents, like any community member, can bring problems to the attention of the police. They may do this by speaking up at community or city council meetings, or by calling the police. But so can other community members who are not residents.

Third, some residents can provide useful information to police.[5] So can other community members who are not residents. In the Creston example, many residents were impacted by its problems, but few knew the source of the problem or what could be done about it. In this example, a few residents provided information that helped police build a case for HUD action. However, a community member, the property owner of the vacant building across the street who was not a resident of the building, provided police with building access so they could gather surveillance footage.

Fourth, residents are often unable to carry out solutions to crime problems.[6] Only the place manager—in this case, HUD—had the authority and ability to improve security and living conditions at the Creston, relocate residents to more livable housing, evict drug dealers, and demolish the building. Place managers are often overlooked members of the community. While they may not be residents of the places experiencing the problems, they have legal authority over the places through their ownership of the property.[7] In many of the most vulnerable areas, residents are renters. So, they seldom have the legal powers over the places they use and are unable to make changes.[8]

In this chapter we show that working with the community is highly appealing, but standard efforts to do this usually produce weak results. We've been talking as if we know what a community is, but not everyone agrees with us. In fact, there is no consensus on what the term "community" means.[9] Some people describe communities as geographic areas. Others say it's certain groups of people, usually residents of an area. There are people who insist that these residents must share some common bond – exhibit a level of cohesiveness – to be a true community rather than a collection of individuals. Still others point to specific institutions—such as churches—who facilitate the creation of community. Others claim communities are made up of people with a shared interest (e.g., stamp collecting or fans of the same football team). To add to the confusion, many call groups of people who interact online but who may have never met in-person a community (e.g., message boards, forums).

If we do not know what a community is, how can we know what a community-based strategy is? Community policing certainly has been used, but no two police agencies seem to implement the same thing, making evaluation of the overall theory difficult.

If we do not know what a community is, it is hard to create coherent crime programs that involve community. Part of the misconception of community is an implicit assumption that the more people involved the better. A community meeting of ten residents is disappointing relative to a meeting of 100, and 500 will be better. But as we show, using a widespread approach is misguided. The rule of the few is just as true of community activism as its true of everything else: in any large group of people, only a few do most of the work. So, to have the most impact, you need to identify the few people who can influence the most. We elaborate on this in chapter 7 and 16.

Another misconception common to community crime control efforts is assuming that residents are the community; they are part of the community, but in high crime areas they may not be the part of the community most important for controlling crime. So, those are our three messages: community policing has been tried and it is not very effective; only a few people in a community make most of the difference; and the most powerful crime control actors in high crime areas are often ignored in community crime control efforts. So, where did the idea of community come from and why is it a dominant idea in policing? We turn to that history next.

The Idea of Community and its Usefulness

Many of the ideas that guide community policing originated over 100 years ago. Founders of the Chicago School, sociologists Robert Park and Ernest Burgess, at the University of Chicago, were interested in city growth and how residents adapted to rapidly changing living conditions.[10] Researchers noted that cities tended to expand in a radial manner out from the city's core. People wanted to live in single family houses with white picket fences in suburban neighborhoods.

But these preferences had consequences for inner-city areas. Most investment in properties tended to go to suburban areas. This left downtown neighborhoods in a state of disarray. Researchers called it social disorganization.[11] In addition to the run-down buildings and infrastructure, they observed many social problems. There was much higher poverty and mobility, meaning people seldom resided in their homes for long. Researchers believed this disincentivized people from investing in their neighborhoods. Many residents worked long hours, 16 hours per day in some cases, for a meager wage. If their goal was to eventually move to a nicer neighborhood, they had little incentive to invest in the community.

They also found that the immigrant and rural migrant populations in the inner city created very ethnically diverse neighborhoods. However, many of these individuals were first generation immigrants who all spoke different languages and had different cultures. This hindered their ability to communicate and agree upon common norms and values they expected locals to abide by. Consequently, Park and Burgess argued that these factors—poverty, mobility, and ethnic diversity—led to social disorganization.

Several years later, in 1942, researchers Clifford Shaw and Henry McKay applied the concept of social disorganization to patterns of juvenile delinquency.[12] They consistently found that disorganized urban areas had a great deal of juvenile delinquency. They argued that three conditions—poverty, mobility, and diversity—made it difficult for residents of those areas to control deviance (Figure 3.1). Cultural differences and language barriers, for example, made it difficult for residents to agree upon rules of conduct and how to enforce them. Their harsh working

FIGURE 3.1 Crime According to Social Disorganization Theory

conditions meant they had very little time to spend at home with their own children, let alone be out in the community. All of this meant there were very few mechanisms in place to control the delinquent youths in the area. These juveniles could run wild and seldom faced consequences for poor behavior.

Some researchers say that a neighborhood's ability to control deviance hinges on the level of informal social control present. They argue that in low crime neighborhoods, residents are better able to organize themselves. They establish a common set of values or norms that they expect others in the neighborhood to adhere to and if problems arise, the residents are sufficiently organized to intervene and address the problem. In low-income neighborhoods, however, they lack this organization and are unable to exert informal social control.[13]

Robert Sampson, along with Stephen Raudenbush and Felton Earls, proposed the concept of *collective efficacy* to advance these ideas about informal social control.[14] Although they still acknowledged the importance of structural factors such as poverty and mobility, they believed collective efficacy was the crucial link between these factors and crime.

Collective efficacy is made up of two components: informal social control and social cohesion. They argued that communities are better able to exert control when there is a working trust and mutual support among residents. That is, crime is lower in neighborhoods where people believe their neighbors have a willingness to intervene for the common good. In such areas, people will keep an eye on each other to protect one another. This increases guardianship, leading to less crime. Thus, if collective efficacy is high in a neighborhood, then crime and disorder should be low. But if collective efficacy declines, there will be more crime and disorder. Where does this leave the police? Sampson and colleagues argue:

FIGURE 3.2 Crime According to Collective Efficacy Theory

> In addition to encouraging communities to mobilize against violence, through 'self-help' strategies of informal social control, perhaps reinforced by partnerships with agencies of formal social control (community policing), strategies to address the social and ecological changes that beset many inner-city communities need to be considered.[15]

This statement suggests that police can help residents build safe communities. The police role is not central to their message: it's parenthetical. It is also vague. Nevertheless, these ideas have become popular in liberal circles.

Broken windows theory is a first cousin of these ideas and has become extremely popular in conservative circles. James Q. Wilson and George Kelling originally described the theory.[16] The figure below depicts what the theory says causes crime. Broken windows theory also starts with the assertion that informal social control is the process that keeps neighborhoods safe from serious crime. This process works well as long as the occasional bit of disorder (often called "incivilities" in the theory) is addressed by community members.

Wilson and Kelling use the image of a "broken window" as a metaphor for all disorder; the theory was not about windows at all. If the broken window is immediately fixed then things continue to go well for the community. It reduces fear of crime in the neighborhood. Less fear, in turn, encourages residents to emerge into and engage with the community more readily. This enhances cooperation among community members, leading to increased informal social control that suppresses crime.

Figure 3.3 depicts the broken windows explanation of neighborhood crime. If disorder or incivilities go unaddressed for too long, this leads to more disorder. Consistent with other research in the early 1980s, disorder

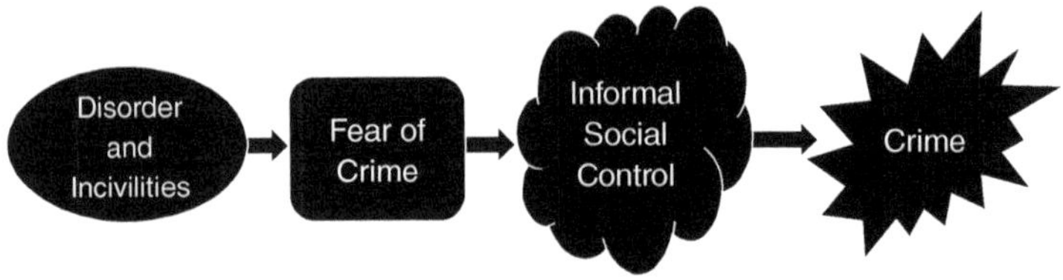

FIGURE 3.3 Crime According to Broken Windows Theory

was assumed to be a sign of crime, whether or not it is actually factually linked to crime. That is, as people experience disorder, they become anxious and increasingly fear the possibility of crime in their neighborhood. So as visible disorder leads to more disorder, it also increases fear of crime. Residents then retreat in two ways. First, local residents restrict their activities in the neighborhood. They reduce the amount of time they walk in the area and use nearby parks, restaurants, stores, and other facilities. This reduces the number of people who can act as informal guardians by watching street behavior. Second, residents pull back from participation in other civic activities in the neighborhood, such as community associations. This reduces trust among residents and their willingness to intervene to prevent disorder. As informal social controls weaken, this reinforces fear of crime. Again, note how central residents are in this theory. There is also no indication of how the police fit into this theory. We will return to the police role in the next section.

Social disorganization, collective efficacy, and broken windows theory all emphasize informal social control among residents. But in these theories, it's difficult to decipher what role the police should play in addressing crime. Exactly what the police can do to inject collective efficacy or informal social control into a neighborhood is not clear. But the idea of partnerships with communities is a common theme throughout policing strategies labelled as "community policing". We explore these in more detail in the next section.

What Role Should the Police Have?

Police and allied researchers have come up with a diverse set of tactics that are bundled into the idea of community policing. The unifying thread connecting these tactics is that police and community members are brought closer together, physically. Decentralizing police bureaucracies brings decision-making into the neighborhood so district and precinct commanders can adapt policing to the needs of their specific communities.[17] This usually involves numerous meetings with the public in formal regular settings and informal unplanned discussions. Though there are countless strategies one could place under the community policing label, we describe four common ones: citizen oversight committees, neighborhood watch and citizen patrols, foot patrols, and broken windows policing.

Example #1: Citizen Oversight Committees

Problem solving is considered an integral part of community policing. The idea is that police, with members of the community, discover, define, and analyze discrete problems and come up with tailor-made solutions, often not involving the use of criminal justice processes or sanctions. Some people advocate for a form of community policing that changes who governs the police. Citizen oversight panels, advisory groups, and other committees that give direction to the police make the police more responsive to the public and their needs.[18]

Example #2: Neighborhood Watch and Citizen Patrols

Another set of tactics does almost the opposite. Instead of putting the police under the direction of citizens, police organize citizens to work under the guidance of police. They host police citizen academies to help the public understand the nature and difficulties of policing. Citizens attend the policing academy and go through a modified training course. Sometimes, police agencies then organize graduates into citizen patrols for neighborhoods. The police coordinate these patrols, whose basic purpose is to extend the visibility of policing. Patrols are not to interfere in crimes or make arrests. Rather, their presence is supposed to deter crime. If a suspicious situation is encountered, the patrol calls the police and a fully trained officer handles it.[19]

The point of all this activity is to enhance police-community relations. This, in turn, should improve cooperation with the police by community members. If the public reports more crime, provides more information about crime and suspicious people and situations, does not interfere with police activities, and helps on joint projects, then this will help the police reduce crime.

Example #3: Foot Patrols

Foot patrols allow officers to meet people in their areas, develop useful working relationships, respect, and a shared sense of purpose. This helps police identify community priorities at the grass roots level and it helps police understand the details of neighborhood crime and disorder problems. Community policing tactics, such as foot patrols, might also reduce residents' fears of crime. As residents become less fearful, they may be more willing to work with the police. Cooperation might help stimulate more informal social control. So, the residents are more likely to intervene on minor situations without the police and thereby keep situations from escalating. Perhaps community policing tactics (some if not all) might increase collective efficacy if police-sponsored meetings bring people together who would not ordinarily meet. This could enhance trust and promote a collective sense of when and how to act.[20]

Example #4: Broken Windows Policing

Recall in our earlier explanation of broken windows theory how central residents are in the theory. They were the primary actors thought to reduce crime through informal social control. This first part of the theory says nothing about policing. In fact, it is difficult to determine what, if anything, the police can do to fight this death spiral that evolves from unaddressed disorder. Wilson and Kelling asserted that the police can do a great deal. If residents can no longer address disorder and engage in informal social control, because the social fabric has been so disrupted and disorder is too rampant, then the police need to step in.[21]

Figure 3.4 depicts Wilson and Kelling's explanation of how the police can intervene to reduce crime. They argue that deft police action to fight disorder can revitalize community cooperation. To do this, the police must engage in order maintenance tactics. That is, they must act on behalf of the community to address the disorder that plagues the neighborhood. Wilson and Kelling saw this order maintenance role of policing as carried out by foot patrol officers, who would be closer to community members and who could better learn their priorities and concerns. The police would address the forms of disorder that community members would have addressed, if fear of crime had not eroded their ability to exercise

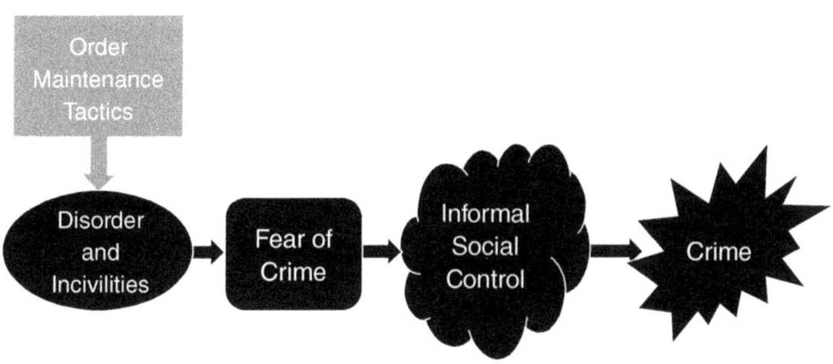

FIGURE 3.4 How to Prevent Crime According to Broken Windows Theory

informal social control. If the police do this well, disorder will decline. Then fear of crime will go down. These two things will empower communities and increase informal social control. This will further reduce disorder and it will enhance community cooperation. All of this will signal offenders that the neighborhood is not a good place for committing crimes, so crime will decline. As crime declines, people will become even less fearful, which further increases informal social control.[22] Instead of a death spiral, the police will have created a spiral of increasing virtuousness. Presumably, the neighborhood will get to the point where residents can maintain order themselves with limited police involvement.

Does Community Policing Reduce Crime?

While many of the ideas that guide community policing have been around for 100 years, few help us reduce crime. In a 2014 systematic review of 25 community policing evaluations, American researcher Charlotte Gill and her colleagues found that some community policing efforts were effective while others were not.[23] Overall, they found that community policing did not significantly reduce crime or fear of crime. However, the strategy did significantly increase citizens' satisfaction with the police.

Justin Crowl examined the evidence for community policing in 27 studies. He found that community policing did not significantly reduce crime in the majority (81.4%) of studies. Instead, community policing was much more likely to increase citizen's satisfaction with the police and officers' job satisfaction.[24]

In 2007, Trevor Bennett and colleagues conducted a systematic review of 18 evaluations of neighborhood watch programs with modest results. The review included studies from the United States and United Kingdom beginning in 1977. They found that neighborhood watch programs saw reductions in crime between 16 to 26%.[25] Other research has raised concerns about resident participation; while people are generally in favor of having a neighborhood watch program in their own neighborhood, fewer people are willing to devote time to participating in such programs.[26]

The evidence for broken windows policing is also unpromising. A single randomized controlled trial, conducted by David Weisburd and his team in 2011, found that broken windows policing had no impact on residents' fear of crime, confidence in police, or collective efficacy. Four years later, Weisburd and his colleagues published a systematic review of six broken windows policing studies.[27] The researchers assessed whether the strategies reduced fear of crime, informal social control, or crime. Not every study examined all three, though all examined fear. In only one of the five did broken windows policing reduce fear. One of the six evaluations looked at the impact of informal social control and found that broken windows had no effect. Finally, five of the six studies looked at the impact of broken windows policing on crime. In only one of the five evaluations was there reasonable evidence that it had an effect.

Similarly, Anthony Braga and colleagues conducted a systematic review of 56 police efforts to reduce disorder and their effects on crime.[28] When they looked at "aggressive" policing tactics to reduce disorder, often associated with broken windows policing, they had a nonsignificant impact on crime. Instead, they found that problem-focused strategies generated a significant 33.1% crime reduction.

In summary, the evidence that community policing reduces crime is weak at best. About 80% of the time, it does not work. To be fair, working with residents is better than ignoring them, for many reasons. It helps inform the public about government actions in their areas; it allows residents to have a voice in what is going on and it can tap people's insights into what is driving crime. But merely involving residents is not going to have a substantial impact on crime. While specific strategies, such as neighborhood watch programs, may have promise, the strategy more generally has little impact on crime. Instead, community policing can be used to achieve other outcomes, such as improving citizen-police relations. But if one's goal is to reduce crime, community policing is not the way forward. In the next section we explore the reasons why community efforts to address crime fall short.

Problems with Community Policing

We have shown that community policing does little to reduce crime. Why is that? Some have claimed that community policing fails because it is not tough on crime. This assertion is absurd and the evidence shows it. "Get tough" policies, favored under a broken windows approach are not that effective either.[29] So, the answer is not rooted in the political ideology behind the strategy. Whether approached from the left or the right, community-based programs are of limited use.

Let's look at three possible, and politically neutral, reasons for the failure. First, maybe the theory behind community-oriented strategies is correct, but police have not been implementing strategies properly. Broken windows policing, for example, suffered from this problem. Several police departments started implementing zero tolerance policing strategies in the 1990s using Wilson and Kelling's ideas as justification. Zero tolerance policing involved police pursuing lawbreakers no matter how small the infraction they committed.[30] They justified their actions, saying that smaller quality of life type of infractions, thought of as disorder or incivilities, could lead to more serious crime. There were many reports of police harassment towards citizens for minor crimes, particularly involving minority persons.[31] But this policing approach contradicts the very ideas broken windows argued for. The theory proposes a much more subtle process for policing where officers are engaged in foot patrol, get to know community members, and use discretion to deal with people involved in crime or disorder. In this case, some police agencies claimed they were using broken windows policing when in reality, they were not.

The second reason community policing may not reduce crime is because the theory is vague, ambiguous, and even muddled. As mentioned before, the term "community" is ambiguous[32] and few police departments engage in the same activities when they claim to be using community policing.

This muddle extends to the key components of community-orientation, such as *social disorganization*,[33] *neighborhood*,[34] and, in particular, *informal social control*. In theory, communities are supposed to curb crime by informally keeping youth and others from misbehaving; that is, without police becoming involved. But it is unclear what the term even means. As criminologists Francis Cullen and Teresa Kulig argue, "…nobody clearly defines what informal social control is or how precisely it works to limit crime events".[35]

Two of us recently conducted a review of criminology studies between 2010 and 2020 to see if Cullen and Kulig's claims were true. We examined criminology studies using the term informal social control to see how researchers defined it. Of the 597 studies we reviewed, 41 (6.8%) of the studies provided a definition. Analyzing the authors' definitions, we concluded that the definition of informal social control is: residents intervening on youth/children to reduce crime. Overall, this is rather vague, though it does again emphasize the centrality of residents in the theory.[36]

Informal social control is but one idea that is a muddle. Another muddled term is the concept of *disorder*.[37] Academics and policy makers have pondered concepts like disorder for over a century, using a variety of terms. In the early to middle of the 20th century, they used the word *blight*. But no one could agree on its definition.[38] So, academics and policy makers shifted to the terms *incivilities* and *disorder*.[39] But they cannot agree on the meaning of these terms either.[40] Changing the label on a concept that no one can define does not make the idea clearer.

When all the key components of the theory are unclear—community, informal social control, disorder—it's no wonder the community crime control studies find the approach is not effective at reducing crime! It might be effective if people could define these components precisely and develop a coherent strategy. But the muddle about the meaning of these terms has persisted for so long that it is doubtful someone will straighten it out anytime soon.

The third reason why community policing may not reduce crime is because the theory and strategies built around it rely on a fallacy: *residents matter most*.[41] All community-oriented strategies hinge on police and residents getting involved in jointly addressing crime problems. Recall, broken windows theory assumes that if the police can reduce residents' fear of crime, it will empower residents to start engaging in informal social control to take back control of their neighborhoods.

Here is the problem with the *residents matter most* fallacy. In areas where crime is most pervasive, residents usually have the least capability to address crime.[42] It's not merely that the residents are poor, have to move often, or come from diverse backgrounds—the causes criminologists have endorsed for decades—but that they do not control their turf. Residents who do not own their homes lack power within their turf. They rent. It is landlords and owners of businesses in the area, who usually live elsewhere, that control turf. They own. Community crime control advocates write about the need for residents to shoo miscreants from street corners as if this were control of turf. Turf control requires other powers most community crime control advocates ignore.[43]

The reality of many residents in low-income, high crime neighborhoods is that they are so busy just trying to survive that they do not have time to partner with police. Many are also aware that they do not have the power to affect change. This reality can also be quite discouraging to new police officers. In the police academy, recruits are bombarded with the importance of community policing. But once they are out patrolling, they quickly realize the disconnect between the theory of community policing and the realities of the streets; often, neither residents, nor police have the power to solve crime problems.

So, who does have this power? Place managers; the people who own or operate property: homeowners, landlords, business owners. Broken windows theory ascribes so strongly to the Chicago School ideas of residents controlling their communities that it never stops to ask "who owns that building with the broken window and why don't they fix it?"[44] Renting residents do not have the power to fix a real or metaphorical broken window on their landlord's property. Just as important, the police do not have the authority to fix broken windows. Renters and the police can try to persuade the landlord to fix the window, but at the end of the day only the owner can.[45] This is a fundamental flaw of the theory and all other theories with a community-oriented focus.

Collective efficacy theory focuses on residents and whether they can count on their neighbors to intervene if someone is engaging in unwanted behavior.[46] In fact, the collective efficacy research is largely based on surveys of residents, with the occasional nod to neighborhood businesses. There is seldom a mention, in the writings of collective efficacy proponents, of the role of landlords in neighborhoods. Like broken windows advocates, collective efficacy pushers seem blind to place management. The policies stemming from the theory focus almost exclusively on residents and their inability to organize themselves.

Yet, a small number of owners control most of the places in many neighborhoods (a point to which we will return in chapter 7). These owners are seldom residents of the high crime neighborhoods containing their properties; they own property in these neighborhoods but live elsewhere.[47] Thus, when we design strategies based solely on residents, we omit a small but extremely powerful group of people; people who can reduce crime.

All places have place managers. This is obvious for commercial sites such as bars, restaurants, and retail stores. It is also obvious for rental properties. The place managers are the owners, commercial lease holders, and employees. But place managers are important for other places. Consider vacant buildings; the manager has chosen to ignore the building but is still its legal owner with the legal owner's rights and responsibilities. Consider parks, public squares, and schools; their place managers are local governments and public institutions (city departments, park authorities, or school boards). Consider single family homes and condominiums; their place managers are the homeowners, condominium owners, and condominium associations. Like restaurant owners, these place managers' powers stem from their property rights. Property rights dictate who has the ability to control who can and cannot use their place, and what place users can and cannot do.[48]

Place managers' primary interest is on the smooth functioning of the place.[49] They typically do not think about crime unless it poses an immediate threat to the functioning of their place. If they are running a business and experience no crime, there is little need to invest time and money to implement crime prevention measures. If crime becomes a problem, however, place managers have incentives to spend the time and money to drive crime down. Crime is both a direct and indirect threat. Directly, crime takes something of value from place managers (for example, thefts of goods or vandalism to buildings). Indirectly, crime tarnishes a place's reputation. Bad reputations decrease the willingness of place users to come to the place (for example, renters or shoppers), and a bad reputation makes it harder to recruit and retain competent employees. As crime threatens place managers, it's not surprising that most places have little crime.[50]

As we have discussed, a few places have much of the crime. So, to enhance crime prevention strategies, we need to focus on the small number of places that experience much of the crime. What does "focusing" mean? It means understanding how these places are managed and how management practices can make crime possible. Some place managers may not be aware of their crime problem: for example, the absentee landlord who does not know about the vandalism, vehicle break-ins, and drug dealing on her property. Other place managers may not have enough money to address the problem. Other place managers may not know how to address the problem: for example, the landlord who bought the building as an investment but has never operated an apartment building. A few place managers may profit from the crime: for example, the corner grocery store that serves as a front for processing stolen goods.[51]

As we highlighted in the previous chapter, crime occurs when opportunities for crime arise. If there is no opportunity to exploit, even a well motivated offender has to walk the straight and narrow. But if a place manager's actions create a crime opportunity—whether unintentionally or intentionally—even a weakly motivated person can be tempted to exploit the crime opportunity.

What does this mean for community-based crime strategies? It means we have to consider place managers as parts of communities, even when the place managers live outside the neighborhood, are international corporations, or are agencies of government. They are not residents. But they shape and control property and products within neighborhoods,[52] and most have a vested interest in the vitality of the neighborhood.[53]

Crime preventers should partner with those who have control over crime opportunities. But they should do this with the rule of the few in mind. General partnerships with place managers will not solve crime problems; partnering with the owner of a clothing store who has no control over the places with crime is unlikely to be productive. Crime preventers need to identify specific place managers who can exercise control over troublesome places. If an apartment building, like the Creston apartment, is generating many calls for service, the crime preventers need to work with that specific building's owner. If thieves are stealing copper piping from homes and construction sites, the crime preventers need to work with the few metal recyclers to whom thieves sell. If a particular bar is experiencing multiple assaults, this might mean partnering with the bar's owner to develop more effective security measures. In each of these examples, the most useful community partner is the place manager where the problem resides. Partnering with all landlords, all metal recyclers, or all bar owners will have very limited utility, like all general community efforts.

Place managers shape neighborhoods; they are the ones who control the physical environment.[54] It is their rules that govern how people behave. Neighborhoods with little crime have place managers who routinely thwart crime, though even in very safe neighborhoods there will be a very few place managers who facilitate much of the limited crime that occurs. In high crime neighborhoods, most place managers work to keep crime down. But compared to low crime neighborhoods, they have more poorly managed places that make crime possible.

What then is a community? It might be best if we abandoned the term, but if we keep it, then it's all the people who reside in an area and all the people and institutions who own and operate property in the area. Just draw a line around an area on a map; everyone in it makes up the community.

What is informal social control? It may be wise to abandon this term, too. At best, it is shorthand for everything that controls crime but does not involve the police. That is a lot of different things, including the actions of parents and the actions we take to keep ourselves under control; also known as self-control. It also includes place management control. At worst, it is attempting to legislate or mandate common courtesy and common sense, which is impossible. So rather than use a vague term no one, including informal social control experts, can define, let's be specific.[55] If we are being specific, then place management is a form of control that is too important to ignore any longer.[56]

We will have more to say about places and place management in the chapters to come. That is because those who own and operate property have the powers to change how people behave. Those who do not own and operate property have far less power. This includes not only residents, but police. Police can encourage, nudge, and in special circumstances compel property owners to do the right thing. Still police powers are limited. One of their powers is that of arrest. But can more arrests reduce crime? We turn to this question in the next chapter.

Key Points

- Community-oriented policing appeals to people, yet the research shows it's not very effective at reducing crime
- A few residents may be able to influence crime, but most community members have little ability to reduce crime opportunities
- A small number of people in communities—places managers—can reduce crime
- Ask: who owns the building with the broken window and why don't they fix it?

Notes

1 Kansas City Police Department (1994). The Creston Apartments. Submission to the Herman Goldstein Awards for Excellence in Problem-Oriented Policing. Retrieved from: https://popcenter.asu.edu/sites/g/files/litvpz3631/files/library/awards/goldstein/1994/94-10(W).pdf

2 Skogan, W. (2019). Advocate: Community policing. In D. Weisburd & A. Braga (Eds.), *Police Innovation: Contrasting Perspectives* (2nd ed, pp. 27–44). Cambridge University Press. https://doi.org/10.1017/9781108278423.002

3 Gill, C., Weisburd, D., Telep, C.W., Vitter, Z., & Bennett, T. (2014). Community-oriented policing to reduce crime, disorder and fear and increase satisfaction and legitimacy among citizens: A systematic review. *Journal of Experimental Criminology, 10*(4), 399–428. https://doi.org/10.1007/s11292-014-9210-y

4 Linning, S.J., Carroll, T., Gerard, D., & Eck, J.E. (2024). Do residents matter most in reducing crime? *Public Management, 106*(11), 30-34. https://icma.org/articles/pm-magazine/do-residents-matter-most-reducing-crime

5 Salami, M. (2025). *"Residents became our eyes and ears": The role of residents in police problem-solving*. Unpublished Honours thesis, Simon Fraser University, School of Criminology.

6 Salami, M. (2025). *"Residents became our eyes and ears": The role of residents in police problem-solving*. Unpublished Honours thesis, Simon Fraser University, School of Criminology.

7 Eck, J.E., Linning, S.J., & Herold, T.D. (2023). *Place Management and Crime: Ownership and Property Rights as a Source of Social Control.* Springer Publishers. https://doi.org/10.1007/978-3-031-27693-4

8 Linning, S.J., Olaghere, A., & Eck, J.E. (2022). Say NOPE to social disorganization criminology: The importance of creators in neighborhood social control. *Crime Science, 11*(1), 1–11. https://doi.org/10.21428/cb6ab371.87801605

9 Wilcox, P., Cullen, F.T., & Feldmeyer, B. (2018). *Communities and Crime: An Enduring American Challenge*. Philadelphia, PA: Temple University Press; Leighton, B. (1988). The community concept in criminology: Toward a social network approach. *Journal of Research in Crime and Delinquency, 25*(4), 351–374. https://doi.org/10.1177/0022427888025004003

10 Park, R.E. & Burgess, E.W. (1925). *The City*. University of Chicago Press.

11 Wilcox, P., Cullen, F.T., & Feldmeyer, B. (2018). *Communities and Crime: An Enduring American Challenge*. Philadelphia, PA: Temple University Press.

12 Shaw, C.R. & McKay, H.D. (1969/1942). *Juvenile Delinquency and Urban Areas: A Study of Rates of Delinquency in Relation to Differential Characteristics of Local* Communities *in American Cities*. Revised ed. Chicago, IL: University of Chicago Press.

13 Kornhauser, R.R. (1978). *Social Sources of Delinquency: An Appraisal of Analytic Methods*. University of Chicago Press; Bursik Jr., R.J. (1988). Social disorganization and theories of crime and delinquency: Problems and prospects. *Criminology, 26*(4), 519–552. https://doi.org/10.1111/j.1745-9125.1988.tb00854.x ; Felson, M. & Eckert, M. (2017). *Introductory Criminology: The Study of Risky Situations*. Routledge. https://doi.org/10.4324/9781315618739

14 Sampson, R.J., Raudenbush, S.W., & Earls, F. (1997). Neighborhoods and violent crime: A multilevel study of collective efficacy. *Science, 277*(5328), 918–924. https://doi.org/10.1126/science.277.5328.918

15 Page 993 of: Sampson, R.J., Raudenbush, S.W., & Earls, F. (1997). Neighborhoods and violent crime: A multilevel study of collective efficacy. *Science, 277*(5328), 918–924. https://doi.org/10.1126/science.277.5328.918

16 Wilson, J.Q., & Kelling, G.L. (1982). Broken windows: The police and neighborhood safety. *Atlantic Monthly, 249*(3), 29–38.
17 Skogan, W. (2019). Advocate: Community policing. In D. Weisburd & A. Braga (Eds.), *Police Innovation: Contrasting Perspectives* (2nd ed, pp. 27–44). Cambridge University Press. https://doi.org/10.1017/9781108278423.002
18 Ferdik, F.V., Rojek, J., & Alpert, G.P. (2013). Citizen oversight in the United States and Canada: An overview. *Police Practice and Research, 14*(2), 104–116. https://doi.org/10.1080/15614263.2013.767089
19 Bennett, T., Holloway, K., & Farrington, D. (2008). The effectiveness of neighborhood watch. *Campbell Systematic Reviews, 4*(1), 1–46. https://onlinelibrary.wiley.com/doi/pdf/10.4073/csr.2008.18
20 Ratcliffe, J.H., & Sorg, E.T. (2017). *Foot Patrol: Rethinking the Cornerstone of Policing*. Springer. https://doi.org/10.1007/978-3-319-65247-4
21 Wilson, J.Q. & Kelling, G.L. (1982). Broken windows: The police and neighborhood safety. *Atlantic Monthly, 249*(3), 29–38.
22 Wilson, J.Q. & Kelling, G.L. (1982). Broken windows: The police and neighborhood safety. *Atlantic Monthly, 249*(3), 29–38.
23 Gill, C., Weisburd, D., Telep, C.W., Vitter, Z., & Bennett, T. (2014). Community-oriented policing to reduce crime, disorder and fear and increase satisfaction and legitimacy among citizens: A systematic review. *Journal of Experimental Criminology, 10*(4), 399–428. https://doi.org/10.1007/s11292-014-9210-y
24 Crowl, J.N. (2017). The effect of community policing on fear and crime reduction, police legitimacy and job satisfaction: an empirical review of the evidence. *Police Practice and Research, 18*(5), 449–462. https://doi.org/10.1080/15614263.2017.1303771
25 Bennett, T., Holloway, K., & Farrington, D.P. (2007). Does neighborhood watch reduce crime? A systematic review and meta-analysis. *Journal of Experimental Criminology, 2*(4), 437–458. https://doi.org/10.1007/s11292-006-9018-5
26 Rosenbaum, D.P. (1987). The theory and research behind neighborhood watch: Is it a sound fear and crime reduction strategy? *Crime & Delinquency, 33*(1), 103–134. https://doi.org/10.1177/0011128787033001007
27 Weisburd, D., Hinkle, J.C., Braga, A.A., & Wooditch, A. (2015). Understanding the mechanisms underlying broken windows policing: The need for evaluation evidence. *Journal of Research in Crime and Delinquency, 52*(4), 589–608. https://doi.org/10.1177/0022427815577837
28 Braga, A.A., Schnell, C., & Welsh, B.C. (2024). Disorder policing to reduce crime: An updated systematic review and meta-analysis. *Criminology & Public Policy, 23*, 745–775. https://doi.org/10.1111/1745-9133.12667
29 Braga, A.A., Schnell, C., & Welsh, B.C. (2024). Disorder policing to reduce crime: An updated systematic review and meta-analysis. *Criminology & Public Policy, 23*, 745–775. https://doi.org/10.1111/1745-9133.12667
30 Grabosky, P.N. (1999). *Zero Tolerance Policing*. Sidney, Australia: Australian Institute of Criminology. Retrieved from: https://www.aic.gov.au/sites/default/files/2020-05/tandi102.pdf
31 Greene, J.A. (1999). Zero tolerance: A case study of police policies and practices in New York City. *Crime & Delinquency, 45*(2), 171–187. https://doi.org/10.1177/0011128799045002001
32 Wilcox, P., Cullen, F.T., & Feldmeyer, B. (2018). *Communities and Crime: An Enduring American Challenge*. Philadelphia, PA: Temple University Press.
33 Braga, A.A. & Clarke, R.V. (2014). Explaining high-risk concentrations of crime in the city: Social disorganization, crime opportunities, and important next steps. *Journal of Research in Crime and Delinquency, 51(*4), 480–498. https://doi.org/10.1177/0022427814521217

34 Linning, S.J., Mierzwa, T., Cheung, J., & Eck, J.E. (2025). What is a neighborhood? A concept consensus review of recent criminological literature. *Journal of Criminal Justice, 97*, 102370. https://doi.org/10.1016/j.jcrimjus.2025.102370

35 Page 169 of: Cullen, F.T. & Kulig, T. (2018). Evaluating theories of environmental criminology: Strengths and weaknesses. In G.J.N. Bruinsma & S.D. Johnson (Eds.), *Oxford Handbook of Environmental Criminology* (pp. 160–174). Oxford University Press. https://doi.org/10.1093/oxfordhb/9780190279707.013.7

36 Linning, S.J., Eck, J.E., Olaghere, A., & Steinman, H. (2024). What is informal social control? A concept consensus review of recent criminological research. *Canadian Journal of Criminology and Criminal Justice, 66*(1), 63–86. https://doi.org/10.3138/cjccj-2023-0024

37 Kubrin, C.E. (2008). Making order of disorder: A call for conceptual clarity. *Criminology & Public Policy, 7*(2), 203–214. https://doi.org/10.1111/j.1745-9133.2008.00502.x

38 Gordon, C. (2004). Blighting the way: Urban renewal, economic development, and the elusive definition of blight. *Fordham Urban Law Journal, 31*(2), 305–337. https://ir.lawnet.fordham.edu/ulj/vol31/iss2/2

39 Wilson, J.Q. & Kelling, G.L. (1982). Broken windows: The police and neighborhood safety. *Atlantic Monthly, 249*(3), 29–38.

40 Kubrin, C.E. (2008). Making order of disorder: A call for conceptual clarity. *Criminology & Public Policy, 7*(2), 203–214. https://doi.org/10.1111/j.1745-9133.2008.00502.x; Skogan, W. (2015). Disorder and decline: The state of research. *Journal of Research in Crime and Delinquency, 52*(4), 464–485. https://doi.org/10.1177/0022427815577836; Taylor, R. (2001). *Breaking Away from Broken Windows: Baltimore Neighborhoods and the Nationwide Fight Against Crime, Grime, Fear, and Decline*. New York, NY: Routledge.

41 Linning, S.J., Carroll, T., Gerard, D., & Eck, J.E. (2024). Do residents matter most in reducing crime? *Public Management, 106*(11), 30–34. https://icma.org/articles/pm-magazine/do-residents-matter-most-reducing-crime

42 Linning, S.J., Olaghere, A., & Eck, J.E. (2022). Say NOPE to social disorganization criminology: The importance of creators in neighborhood social control. *Crime Science, 11*(1), 1–11. https://doi.org/10.21428/cb6ab371.87801605

43 Linning, S.J. & Eck, J.E. (2024). Clarifying control in criminology: A proposal for six interacting controls of crime. *Canadian Journal of Criminology and Criminal Justice, 66*(3–4), 119–141. https://doi.org/10.3138/cjccj-2024-0053; Linning, S.J. & Eck, J.E. (2025). Race-based real estate practices and spuriousness in community criminology: Was the Chicago School part of a self-fulfilling prophecy? *Criminal Justice Review, 50*(2), 117–142. https://doi.org/10.1177/07340168231175444; Linning, S.J., Olaghere, A., & Eck, J.E. (2022). Say NOPE to social disorganization criminology: The importance of creators in neighborhood social control. *Crime Science, 11*(1), 1–11. https://doi.org/10.21428/cb6ab371.87801605; Felson, M. & Eckert, M. (2017). *Introductory Criminology: The Study of Risky Situations*. Routledge. https://doi.org/10.4324/9781315618739

44 Linning, S.J. & Eck, J.E. (2021). *Whose 'Eyes on the Street' Control Crime? Expanding Place Management into Neighborhoods*. Cambridge University Press. https://doi.org/10.1017/9781108954143

45 Eck, J.E., Linning, S.J., & Herold, T.D. (2023). *Place Management and Crime: Ownership and Property Rights as a Source of Social Control*. Springer Publishers. https://doi.org/10.1007/978-3-031-27693-4

46 Sampson, R.J., Raudenbush, S.W., & Earls, F. (1997). Neighborhoods and violent crime: A multilevel study of collective efficacy. *Science, 277*(5328), 918–924. https://doi.org/10.1126/science.277.5328.918
47 Linning, S.J. & Eck, J.E. (2021). *Whose 'Eyes on the Street' Control Crime? Expanding Place Management into Neighborhoods.* Cambridge University Press. https://doi.org/10.1017/9781108954143
48 Eck, J.E., Linning, S.J., & Herold, T.D. (2023). *Place Management and Crime: Ownership and Property Rights as a Source of Social Control.* Springer Publishers. https://doi.org/10.1007/978-3-031-27693-4
49 Eck, J.E. & Madensen, T.D. (2018). Place management. In G.J.N. Bruinsma & S.D. Johnson (Eds.), *The Oxford Handbook of Environmental Criminology* (pp. 633–667). New York, NY: Oxford University Press. https://doi.org/10.1093/oxfordhb/9780190279707.013.22
50 Eck, J.E., Linning, S.J., & Herold, T.D. (2023). *Place Management and Crime: Ownership and Property Rights as a Source of Social Control.* Springer Publishers. https://doi.org/10.1007/978-3-031-27693-4
51 Eck, J. E. & Madensen-Herold, T. D. (2018). Place management, guardianship, and the establishment of order. In D.S. Nagin, F.T. Cullen, and C.L. Jonson (Eds.), *Deterrence, Choice, and Crime: Contemporary Perspectives* (pp. 269–308). New York, NY: Routledge. https://doi.org/10.4324/9781351112710
52 Linning, S.J. & Eck, J.E. (2021). *Whose 'Eyes on the Street' Control Crime? Expanding Place Management into Neighborhoods.* Cambridge University Press. https://doi.org/10.1017/9781108954143; Linning, S.J., Olaghere, A., & Eck, J.E. (2022). Say NOPE to social disorganization criminology: The importance of creators in neighborhood social control. *Crime Science, 11*(1), 1–11. https://doi.org/10.21428/cb6ab371.87801605
53 Eck, J.E., Linning, S.J., & Herold, T.D. (2023). *Place Management and Crime: Ownership and Property Rights as a Source of Social Control.* Springer Publishers. https://doi.org/10.1007/978-3-031-27693-4
54 Linning, S.J., Olaghere, A., & Eck, J.E. (2022). Say NOPE to social disorganization criminology: The importance of creators in neighborhood social control. *Crime Science, 11*(1), 1–11. https://doi.org/10.21428/cb6ab371.87801605
55 Linning, S.J. & Eck, J.E. (2024). Clarifying control in criminology: A proposal for six interacting controls of crime. *Canadian Journal of Criminology and Criminal Justice, 66*(3–4), 119–141. https://doi.org/10.3138/cjccj-2024-0053; Felson, M., & Eckert, M. (2017). *Introductory Criminology: The Study of Risky Situations.* Routledge. https://doi.org/10.4324/9781315618739
56 Eck, J.E., Linning, S.J., & Herold, T.D. (2023). *Place Management and Crime: Ownership and Property Rights as a Source of Social Control.* Springer Publishers. https://doi.org/10.1007/978-3-031-27693-4

4
Do Arrests Reduce Crime?

Imagine the following, based on true events. An intoxicated driver kills a mother and her infant daughter in a car crash. Word of the incident spreads quickly and community members request a meeting with the local police. During the meeting, attendees demand police action to address impaired driving. The police agree to ramp up publicized sobriety checkpoints, particularly at high volume times such as Friday and Saturday nights. They also pledge to assign a community liaison officer to visit all establishments with liquor licenses to assess employee training on safe serving and selling practices.

Several months later the police department holds another community meeting. They report that since their last meeting, crashes involving impaired drivers have declined, as have crashes resulting in hospitalizations, and there has been a reduction in arrests for impaired driving. Members of the audience demand to know to why the police have been arresting fewer people for impaired driving after the police agreed to take impaired driving more seriously. The police insist that they took impaired driving seriously and that is why there are fewer crashes and injuries from impaired driving. But the attendees do not accept this answer; they want more impaired drivers arrested.

Examples like this occur often. Many in the public expect the police to arrest wrongdoers for their misbehavior. They may disagree about which

DOI: 10.4324/9781003430155-5

wrongs should result in an arrest, but most people want to have someone arrested for something. People claim that more arrests reduce whatever crime they are most concerned with. And fewer arrests only encourage whatever crime is of most concern.

Arrests can serve many purposes. They temporarily remove suspected offenders from the public to keep them from committing additional crimes. Arrests may deter further offending by scaring the arrestee. And arrests may signal to the rest of us that misbehaving is a bad idea. So, the assumption is that if arrests decline, more bad things will happen. But is this true?

Consider the impaired driving example. If the police's efforts to curb impaired driving (e.g., working with alcohol retailers) worked, then fewer people are driving while impaired. And if there are fewer impaired drivers on the road, then there are fewer impaired drivers to arrest. The reduction in impaired driving crashes and injuries suggests there were fewer impaired drivers on the road. If that is the case, the police achieved the public's goal of reducing the impaired driving. Yet this arrest-focused mentality persists. We call this the *more arrests reduce crime fallacy*.[1] Although arrests can certainly contribute to reductions in harm and crime, they are merely a tool used to achieve a goal; they are a means to an end.

In this chapter we explore the more arrests reduce crime fallacy. Many crime prevention and policing strategies are based on this fallacy. So, you may not be surprised to learn that strategies which apply this fallacy have not been overly effective at reducing crime. These strategies tend to fail because the focus is on the wrong part of the crime prevention process: outputs. To be successful, you need to focus on achieving desired outcomes.

Focus on Outcomes

In our intoxicated driver example, one of the problems the community members had is that they lost sight of the outcome (or goal) that they wanted to achieve. To understand why this mistake occurred, we need to clarify the process needed to generate outcomes and what comes along with it. Let's step back from the police example for a moment and use a common illustration. Say a woman is getting married and it has been her lifelong dream to wear her mother's wedding dress in the ceremony.

But at present she cannot fit into the dress. So, she sets a goal to be able to wear that dress on her wedding day. This is her outcome: to fit into her mother's wedding dress. Now, there are several things that must take place for her to achieve this outcome: inputs, processes, and outputs.[2]

Inputs are the things you use to produce outcomes. In the example, an important input is food. So, the prospective bride starts buying more fresh vegetables and leaner meats. She also purchases some kitchen gadgets to help her make healthier meals. Her other inputs include buying workout clothes and shoes, a gym membership, and hiring a personal trainer. These inputs, she hopes, will help her achieve her goal. But the prospective bride knows that lots of inputs alone will not get her into that dress. This is where the process comes in.

A process is a sequence of activities generated by a program. In this example, it can include planning regular trips to the grocery store with pre-planned shopping lists. It can involve creating specific strength training schedules to follow throughout the week. It includes putting on the new exercise gear and shoes and doing the exercises, regularly. And it can involve excluding bad procedures; she stops going out eating and drinking with her girlfriends many nights per week. She no longer stops at the coffee shop for her daily double mocha frappuyoka latte.

These processes produce immediate outputs. The bride-to-be may make friends at the gym in her workout groups. Her overall health, such as lowered cholesterol levels and increased bone density, improves. And with all the strength training she does, she builds muscle and loses fat. In fact, if she builds enough muscle, she may lose no weight or even gain some weight. So, another output is that she becomes anxious when she sees no change (or an increase) on the scale, despite her efforts. Has she frustrated her plans? Do the outputs tell her she has failed? No. Outputs may hint at possible outcomes, but they are not the outcome.

On her goal day, she put on the wedding dress. It fit. Because her muscle weighed more than fat, but takes up less space than fat, her body shape changed. Thus, she achieved her desired outcome: to fit into her mother's wedding dress.

Many of us mistakenly focus on outputs as opposed to outcomes. Some refer to this as goal displacement.[3] Sometimes this displaced focus can derail us from achieving desired outcomes. To use an absurd example to illustrate: the bride-to-be could have amputated her leg. This would have led to weight loss (an output), but it would not have helped her fit into her mother's wedding dress (the outcome). Doesn't seem like the best option, does it? So, we need to keep our focus on outcomes, not outputs.

Now let's apply this to policing. Outcomes for police are usually some socially desirable impact on a problem that the police have to address. In the example we started with, it was the reduction of impaired driving. The inputs required to achieve this can include personnel time, equipment, fuel for police cars, and police stations that act as a home base for all operations. Processes are the methods and practices the police use to convert these inputs to results and outcomes. Some common policing processes include patrolling, investigating, meeting with community members, coordinating with other government agencies, conducting raids on locations where offenders are hiding illegal goods, and analyzing data to find patterns of illicit activities. In our impaired driving example, it also includes rolling out sobriety checkpoints throughout the city and meeting with the owners and employees of alcohol-serving establishments to discuss serving practices.

Outputs of these processes include arrests, checkpoints administered, community meetings attended, vehicles damaged in chases, successful prosecutions of offenders, cars and pedestrians stopped, and so on. These outputs are not indicators of success. They merely indicate how the process is working. Some outputs produce costs—vehicle stops interrupt peoples' lives, thereby producing a cost; arrests create even greater disruptions of lives and impose costs when the suspect is transported, booked, jailed, prosecuted, convicted, and sentenced. Vehicle checkpoints produce a cost; perhaps the police department was short-staffed and needed officers to do overtime shifts to carry them out. Community meetings may produce benefits in terms of increased trust in the police, but they also expend the time of participants that could have been used in other ways.

The outcome—reducing impaired driving—can be difficult to measure. But the reduction in crashes involving intoxicated drivers and the reduction of hospitalizations linked to collisions could be a good indicator that the police are achieving the outcome. The number of arrests is not a good measure because it is an output, not an outcome. Again, the declining number of arrests for impaired driving could simply be the

Table 4.1 Distinguishing Inputs, Processes, Outputs, and Outcomes

	Definition	Bride Example	Intoxicated Driving Example
Inputs	Resources, raw materials, clients, and staff that go into a program.	• Healthy food • Kitchen appliances • Workout clothes • Gym membership • Personal trainer	• Personnel time • Equipment • Fuel for police cars • Police stations
Processes	The sequence of activities generated by a program.	• Trips to grocery store • Workouts at the gym • Appointments with personal trainer	• Patrolling • Conducting sobriety checkpoints • Meeting with community members • Analyzing crime data
Outputs	The immediate result of the processes.	• Making new friends • Building muscle • Weight gain	• # vehicles stopped • # arrests • # community meetings attended
Outcomes	The impact that the process had on the problem.	• Fit into wedding dress	• Fewer people harmed by intoxicated drivers

result of fewer people driving while impaired. Thus, sometimes making fewer arrests can be a good sign.

But arrests continue to be a focus of the public as they are easy to count and keep track of. The police and politicians often fall into this trap too. Arrests are often mistaken for outcomes as they are easy to count and provide proof that "something" was done about the problem. Where does this obsession with arrest come from? Why do so many people falsely believe that arrest-focused strategies will reduce crime? And why don't arrest-focused strategies work? You will see that a common reason for their ineffectiveness is that the strategies often fail to consider the rule of the few.

Why Are So Many Policing Strategies Arrest-Dependent?

Some of the most common policing strategies rely heavily on arrests. They assume arrests act as the most effective deterrent to offending. Examples of these strategies include: police force size, rapid response, Compstat, and zero tolerance sweeps. In this section we review each of these strategies, the theory behind them, and why they are not overly effective long-term.

In the following section, we show that main reason these strategies are ineffective is because they do not apply the rule of the few.

Police force size is one of the most common strategies to reduce crime. When a series of crimes occur and the public demand swift action, politicians are quick to pledge hiring more police officers. This often satisfies the public. But why would adding more police reduce crime? Using the same logic, would reducing the number of police increase crime? To get answers we must first establish the underlying explanation for why these two things are connected. We are searching for a logical and plausible reason that could connect the number of police to crime.

From a theoretical standpoint, there are at least five processes that might convert more police into less crime. The first is *deterrence*. More police on the street increases police visibility, so offenders are more aware of police, and believe their risk of getting arrested increases. Thus, offenders will either refrain from committing more crimes, or they will be more careful. Either way, crime declines.

The second process is *incapacitation*. More police officers results in more arrests of offenders. Arresting more offenders, prosecuting them, and imprisoning them reduces the number of offenders in communities. While incarcerated in prison, offenders cannot commit crimes in communities.

The third process is *visibility*. More police officers on the street increases citizens' perceptions of safety. This is thought to lead to more citizens being out and about who may encounter crime and be willing to intervene or call the police about it. Offenders also see officers out more readily, so they refrain from committing as much trouble.

The fourth process is *speed*. More police officers means that there are more patrol units available to respond when trouble occurs. These additional officers can increase the speed with which the police respond to calls for service. This has a cascade effect linked to the previous three reasons. It produces greater chances of arresting offenders and then incapacitating them. Offenders, being aware of this, reduce their offending. And the public, being aware of this, feel safer and become more active.

The last process is *detection*. More police officers means there are more resources available to investigate crimes. This produces more identifications of offenders, more arrests, and more successful prosecutions. Although there may certainly be other processes, these are the five driving rationales for hiring more police officers. As you may have noticed, nearly all of them involve increasing the number of arrests.

Increased arrests are a similar belief in rapid police response. The theory of response time is both simple and plausible. Offenders, who believe they can get away with a crime, commit more crimes than offenders who believe that they face a high risk of getting caught. One way to increase the risks to offenders is for the police to race to the crime scenes when called. The faster the police get there, the less chance the offender has to escape. Thus, fast response times should have a deterrent effect. Also, arresting offenders at the crime scene "red handed" increases their chances of conviction and prison. So, there might also be an incapacitation effect. Once again, this strategy relies on an output (arrests) to produce an outcome (crime reduction).

Increased arrests also tend to appear when police adopt Compstat* models. Compstat does not provide a theory of crime or disorder. Instead, it is a theory of bureaucracy. Routinely, commanders of operational units of a police department meet with the highest officials to report on what they are doing to address crime in the areas they are responsible for. Ideally, commanders would come prepared to these meetings with statistics about the most common crimes in their patrol districts. They then describe what their officers have been doing to address problems in their districts and show statistics for before and after the actions taken. The routine meetings are believed to hold commanders accountable to what goes on in their districts.[4]

While it is good to hold commanders accountable, this pressure can sometimes lead people astray. For example, commanders will often deploy officers to problem areas, encouraging them to make arrests for minor offenses. These minor arrests result in easily quantifiable numbers. Then when they must answer to high-ranking officials in a Compstat meeting, the commanders can say they sent a certain number of officers to an area who made a certain number of arrests. In essence, the commanders demonstrate that they "did something". While this may satisfy high-ranking

* There is debate about what Compstat stands for. Some say it's "computer statistics", others say it's "compare statistics" or even "complaint statistics". Regardless of what it stands for, the theory of how to apply Compstat is the same.

officials for the meeting, it does not mean the commander solved the underlying problem. Far too often, the chosen outcome for a Compstat problem is to get the location off the problem list by the next meeting, not solve the actual problem.

Finally, zero-tolerance policing involves the police clamping down on all violations of law, no matter how minor, as well as antisocial behavior and disorder.[5] This strategy uses numbers of arrests to promote general deterrence. Generally, someone following a zero-tolerance policy does not allow any exceptions to rule breaking. So, if a school has a policy of not allowing weapons, and students found with weapons are expelled, a student found with a firearm is treated the same as one found with a small folding pocketknife. A zero-tolerance policy against drugs will treat someone with a marijuana seed in his pocket the same as someone with several ounces of cocaine. In policing, a zero-tolerance policy toward disorder means that minor and not particularly harmful behaviors will result in arrest, just like very harmful law breaking.

All of the policing strategies we have just described rely heavily on arrests.** They assume that arrests are an effective means to reduce crime. But arrests are expensive. And the evidence indicates that these strategies either do not work or have limited long-term effectiveness because of their emphasis on arrests. And a unifying reason for why reliance on arrest is ineffective is the rule of the few. In the next section we break each strategy down to show why it is ineffective or has limited long-term effectiveness.

Are Arrest-Dependent Strategies Effective?

Just because something sounds plausible in theory does not mean that it leads to desired outcomes in practice. So, we must also ask, does the evidence show whether this is effective or not? Research has consistently demonstrated that the rule of the few applies to the three most important elements of crime: offenders, victims, and places.[6] Only a few offenders commit most of the offenses,[7] a few people experience most of the

** Note: Another police strategy that relies on arrests is focused deterrence. However, this is a newer strategy that applies the rule of the few to arrests. We cover it extensively in chapters 12 and 13.

victimizations,[8] and a small percentage of places have most of the crime.[9] This has important implications for crime prevention that has yet to be fully realized.

Arrests focus mostly on incapacitating offenders, so we will focus the rest of this discussion on the concentration of offenders. Natalie Martinez and colleagues completed the most recent systematic review of studies examining this phenomenon in 2017. They found 73 studies examining the prevalence and frequency of offending. When examining both offenders and non-offenders, their research showed that "10% of the most criminally-active people account for around 66% of crime".[10] However, because most people commit no crimes, the presence of zeros can inflate concentration. So, they repeated their analysis using only individuals who had committed at least one crime. Even with this adjustment, "the most active 10% of offenders account for around 41% of crime".[11] Their review showed that most people do not commit crime. A moderate number of individuals commit crime here and there. But a tiny fraction of offenders commit dozens, if not hundreds, of crimes. These results suggest that focusing police resources on a small number of prolific offenders will reap the most benefits.

Our point is that arrests are useful, but only if they are used among the most criminally prolific people will arrests reduce crime. Arresting many people may make little difference in crime but arresting a few high rollers can. But most of the policing strategies we outlined above are almost solely focused on increasing the volume of arrests. They merely focus on the quantity of arrests and not on quality arrests.

Most people assume that the more people the police can arrest, the more crime will decline. The arrests would both incapacitate many offenders and deter others from offending. There are several problems with this:

1. Deterrence has little effect on the prolific few we need it to work on.
2. The incapacitation effects of arrest are often only temporary.
3. Arrest-focused strategies often penalize people who are not engaging in criminal behavior.

Below we break down each of these three problems and apply them to the corresponding strategies we reviewed earlier.

First, much research shows that deterrence—particularly through incarceration—has little impact on reducing criminal behavior of prolific offenders.[12] The threat of arrest certainly works on many people. If you recall before, the systematic review of offending found that most people do not commit any crimes. Deterrence could be one reason for this. But crime is driven by a very small number of prolific offenders.[13] Thus, devising strategies that focus primarily on increasing the prevalence or speed that police can make arrests is not likely to reap the most crime reduction benefits. The number of police officers and rapid response strategies are examples of such strategies.

Police force size matters, but not in the way that most people think.[14] If we had no police, crime would likely be high. Offenders would see great likelihood in their ability to get away with crime. If you were to create a police department where one did not exist before, the first few officers would have a big impact on crime, though there would still be plenty of misbehavior. A few more officers would decrease crime even more (though not as much as the decrease after you hired the first batch). With each new batch of officers you put on the street, crime would go down, but never as much as it went down from your initial hires. Eventually, adding more police would lead to no discernible impact on crime. In other words, the benefits of hiring decline as you hire more.

Declining benefits is common, so common it has a name: decreasing marginal effectiveness. You've probably heard of it as the "too many cooks in the kitchen" problem. If there are no cooks in the kitchen, no food gets made and you go hungry. One cook means you'll get a meal, eventually. Two might mean you get that meal more effectively, perhaps the second cook brings new skills that enhance the quality of the dish. Three cooks could also increase the speed with which the meal is made. But after a certain point, adding more cooks just leads to people getting into each other's way. This can even backfire and lead to increased time to complete the meal!

This means once a city has its Goldilocks number of officers, adding more is unlikely to reduce crime further. As police staffing reaches this number, it is far more important to change the policing strategy to reduce crime.[15] Beyond some base number, it's not how many officers you have, it's what you do with them that matters most. We cannot provide what the Goldilocks number of police is, and it probably varies from city to city. But we do know that police staffing is very stable over time and that adding or subtracting a few police here and there has no discernable impact on crime.[16] So, it's likely that the typical city is operating in the Goldilocks zone. In part 4 of this book, we will come back to this point and explain some strategies you can use with your officers.

Rapid response suffers from a similar plight; it is too focused on arrests and the likelihood the police will be able to make them. However, the main problem with rapid response is it only focuses on the speed of the police; it ignores something far more important. People are slow. The largest delays in police arriving come from the public's delay in reporting crimes.[17] Most crimes come to the attention of the police through citizen reporting. Studies have found that even though the police can respond quickly after being dispatched (e.g., within 60 seconds), nearly half of the calls involved citizens reporting the crimes over five minutes after seeing them. Thus, if thousands of dollars are spent to reduce a police response time from 60 seconds to 30 seconds, but the average citizen takes ten minutes to report the crime, does the 30 second reduction really make that much of a difference? It's unlikely.

Response times do matter, but not for reducing crime. They matter when there are true emergencies, where time is of the essence: a fire from which people need rescue, a traffic crash with serious injuries, an in-progress burglary, or an active shooter. The rapid intervention of well-trained police can and often does make a difference for the people involved. But the importance of rapid response when rescuers are needed does not prevent crisis events from occurring. Emergency medicine can save people from dying in car crashes, and from heart attacks, and shootings, but medical care does not prevent car crashes, heart attacks, or shootings. In short, emergency rescue and prevention are two vital functions of police but doing one successfully does not imply the other function is carried out as well.

One reason is that emergency rescue does not account for the rule of the few. Police force size and rapid response also fail to consider the concentration of crime among offenders and places. But even the strategies that have better embraced the rule of the few fall short.

This is where the second flaw, the temporary effects, comes in. The incapacitation effects of arrests seldom produce long-term crime reduction effects. Arrests seldom lead to conviction and incarceration.[18] In the case of prolific offenders, this only removes them from the street temporarily. Upon release, they return to the same places and keep offending; it's a revolving door effect.

With hotspots patrol, discussed in chapter 2, we direct police attention to places that experience disproportionately more crime. As the saying goes, the best predictor of future behavior is past behavior. Research indicates that there are almost always systematic reasons for why crime hotspots exist and that hot places usually remain hot unless the opportunities at these places are dismantled.[19] Thus, increasing police presence at these places can be useful. However, hotspots patrols tend not to go much beyond this. The police may invoke crackdowns and attempt to arrest active offenders. This usually takes the form of patrolling these places (i.e., showing up) more often. But these actions only temporarily disrupt the opportunities, they do not dismantle the underlying opportunities that exist at these places. And because arrests seldom lead to convictions, offenders are often released and simply return to business as usual at these places. Or in the rare instances where conviction occurs, it's usually only a matter of time before another motivated offender discovers and starts exploiting the opportunities at the place. Consequently, we might see declines in crime at these places temporarily.[20] But these effects are rarely sustained for the long-term.

The final flaw with arrest-focused strategies is that they often penalize people who are not engaging in criminal behavior. Again, if a small proportion of people are responsible for most of the crime committed, then we should not have to arrest scores of people to reduce crime. Strategies such as zero tolerance advocate for the police to crackdown on all transgressions no matter how minor they are. This can include forms of social and physical disorder, such as public intoxication and loitering, even if such behaviors are not inherently criminal.

Theories such as broken windows emphasize that the police use order maintenance tactics to reduce neighborhood disorder. This in turn is supposed to reduce fear of crime and lead to increased informal social control exerted by residents to suppress crime. However, many of these behaviors are minor quality of life offenses and, while annoying, are not inherently criminal. So, it should not be surprising that such strategies are less likely to reduce crime or disorder.[21]

As we have seen in recent decades, this has led to increased arrests of visible minorities, persons with mental illness, and unhoused persons. For example, policy changes that have led to de-investment in mental health services have further led to the criminalization of behaviors that are not inherently criminal. We will provide some examples of this in part 2 of this book. Arrests are not a solution to these problems. In fact, we question whether they should be police problems to address to begin with. The problems began in other sectors of society, but because the public perceives certain behaviors as a nuisance, they call the only agency who they know will pick up the phone and respond: the police.

Police response to such inquiries causes the second flaw we mentioned above: a temporary fix to the problem. Arresting an unruly person may make him go away for the time being, but it does not stop him from returning and repeating similar behaviors over again upon being released. The individuals engaged in such behaviors are usually in need of assistance that the police cannot provide. This might include help from mental health professionals or social workers. But the temporary nature of arrest provides little long-term benefit to anyone involved.

Conclusions

Arrests certainly serve an important purpose in our society. They can temporarily incapacitate those who may pose a threat to society. However, they are a means to an end. In many cases, they serve as the criminal justice equivalent of a band aid for crime problems. They can lead to temporary decreases in crime and show that "something was done". However, arrests tend not to address the true causes of problems. Arrests are an output. So, while they may be helpful in showing that a crime reduction process is underway, they should not be used as a benchmark to determine whether the process is working. Arrests tend to only be a temporary fix for an underlying problem and arrest-focused strategies run the risk of disrupting the lives of law-abiding citizens.

If you want to reduce crime, you need to focus on outcomes. In policing, outcomes can include a reduction in unwanted events, such as crime or disorder, or a reduction in harms caused by these events, such as a reduction in injuries sustained from a crime. Thus, instead of focusing on how many officers a department has or the number of arrests they are making, you should ask: what outcome do I want to achieve?

Improving outcomes requires that you adopt strategies capable of reducing crime-related harms. Often, the most effective strategies apply the rule of the few. We discuss several strategies that achieve this in chapters 12 through 16.

But before we get to those strategies, we need to explain key shifts in mindset over how to reduce crime using the rule of the few. In the next part of this book (chapters 5–7), we provide some examples of how working with specific place managers, manufacturers, and influential neighborhood outsiders can lead to effective, long-term crime solutions. Many of them illustrate that crime is often the by-product of everyday processes and conventional activities. A small number of elites, relative to the number of residents, have the most control over these processes. Invoking action from these powerful few can lead to substantial, long-term crime reductions.

Key Points

- Outcomes are the goals you want to achieve whereas outputs are the services delivered or new products produced by the process.
- Arrests are an output, not an outcome.
- A few offenders commit most of the crime, most people commit no crime.
- Ask: what is the outcome you are trying to achieve?

Notes

1 Linning, S.J., Carroll, T., Gerard, D., & Eck, J.E. (2024). Do more arrests reduce crime? *Public Management, 106*(12), 38–41. https://icma.org/articles/pm-magazine/do-more-arrests-reduce-crime

2 Brown, M. (1996). *Keeping Score: Using The Right Metrics to Drive World Class Performance*. CRC Press.

3 Bohte, J. & Meier, K.J. (2000). Goal displacement: Assessing the motivation for organizational cheating. *Public Administration Review, 60*(2), 173–182. https://doi.org/10.1111/0033-3352.00075

4 Shane, J.M. (2004). Compstat design. *FBI Law Enforcement Bulletin, 73*, 12–19.; Weisburd, D., Mastrofski, S.D., McNally, A.M., Greenspan, R., & Willis, J.J. (2003). Reforming to preserve: Compstat and strategic problem solving in American policing. *Criminology & Public Policy, 2*(3), 421–456. https://doi.org/10.1111/j.1745-9133.2003.tb00006.x; Willis, J.J., Mastrofski, S.D., & Weisburd, D. (2007). Making sense of COMPSTAT: A theory-based analysis of organizational change in three police departments. *Law & Society Review, 41*(1), 147–188. https://doi.org/10.1111/j.1540-5893.2007.00294.x

5 Grabosky, P.N. (1999, January). Zero tolerance policing. Australian Institute of Criminology; Trends & Issues in Crime And Criminal Justice, 102, 1–4.

6 Eck, J.E., Lee, Y., O, S, & Martinez, N. (2017). Compared to what? Estimating the relative concentration of crime at places using systematic and other reviews. *Crime Science, 6*(1), 1–17. https://doi.org/10.1186/s40163-017-0070-4

7 Martinez, N.N., Lee, Y., Eck, J.E., & O, S. (2017). Ravenous wolves revisited: A systematic review of offending concentration. *Crime Science, 6*(1), 1–16. https://doi.org/10.1186/s40163-017-0072-2

8 O, S., Martinez, N.N., Lee, Y., & Eck, J.E. (2017). How concentrated is crime among victims? A systematic review from 1977 to 2014. *Crime Science, 6*(1), 1–16. https://doi.org/10.1186/s40163-017-0071-3

9 Lee, Y., Eck, J.E., O, S., & Martinez, N.N. (2017). How concentrated is crime at places? A systematic review from 1970 to 2015. *Crime Science, 6*, 1–16. https://doi.org/10.1186/s40163-017-0069-x; Weisburd, D., Zastrow, T., Kuen, K., & Andresen, M.A. (2024). Crime concentration at micro places: A review of the evidence. *Aggression and Violence Behavior, 78*, 101979. https://doi.org/10.1016/j.avb.2024.101979

10 Page 7 of: Martinez, N.N., Lee, Y., Eck, J.E., & O, S. (2017). Ravenous wolves revisited: A systematic review of offending concentration. *Crime Science, 6*(1), 1–16. https://doi.org/10.1186/s40163-017-0072-2

11 Page 7 of: Martinez, N.N., Lee, Y., Eck, J.E., & O, S. (2017). Ravenous wolves revisited: A systematic review of offending concentration. *Crime Science, 6*(1), 1–16. https://doi.org/10.1186/s40163-017-0072-2

12 Nagin, D. S. (2013). Deterrence in the twenty-first century. *Crime and Justice, 42*(1), 199–263. https://doi.org/10.1086/670398

13 Martinez, N.N., Lee, Y., Eck, J.E., & O, S. (2017). Ravenous wolves revisited: A systematic review of offending concentration. *Crime Science, 6*(1), 1–16. https://doi.org/10.1186/s40163-017-0072-2

14 Lee, Y., Eck, J.E., & Corsaro, N. (2016). Conclusions from the history of research into the effects of police force size on crime—1968 through 2013: A historical systematic review. *Journal of Experimental Criminology, 12*(3), 431–451. https://doi.org/10.1007/s11292-016-9269-8

15 Lee, Y., Eck, J.E., & Corsaro, N. (2016). Conclusions from the history of research into the effects of police force size on crime—1968 through 2013: A historical systematic review. *Journal of Experimental Criminology, 12*(3), 431–451. https://doi.org/10.1007/s11292-016-9269-8

16 Eck, J.E., Lee, Y., Corsaro, N. (2017, Spring). Adding more police is unlikely to reduce crime: A meta-analysis of police agency size and crime research. *Translational Criminology*, 14–16; Lee, Y., Eck, J.E., & Corsaro, N. (2016). Conclusions from the history of research into the effects of police force size on crime—1968 through 2013: A historical systematic review. *Journal of Experimental Criminology, 12*(3), 431–451. https://doi.org/10.1007/s11292-016-9269-8

17 Spelman, W. & Brown, D.K. (1981). *Calling the police: A replication of the citizen reporting component of the Kansas City response time analysis.* In Washington, DC: Police Executive Research Forum.
18 Nagin, D.S. (2013). Deterrence in the twenty-first century. *Crime and Justice, 42*(1), 199–263. https://doi.org/10.1086/670398
19 Eck, J.E., Linning, S.J., & Herold, T.D. (2023). *Place Management and Crime: Ownership and Property Rights as a Source of Social Control.* Springer Publishers. https://doi.org/10.1007/978-3-031-27693-4
20 Sherman, L. W. (1990). Police crackdowns: Initial and residual deterrence. *Crime and Justice, 12,* 1–48. https://doi.org/10.1086/449163
21 Braga, A.A., Schnell, C., & Welsh, B.C. (2024). Disorder policing to reduce crime: An updated systematic review and meta-analysis. *Criminology & Public Policy, 23*, 745–775. https://doi.org/10.1111/1745-9133.12667

PART 2
RE-THINKING CRIME

In Part 1 we covered some common crime fallacies. We showed you that crime is not widespread, it's highly concentrated at places and among offenders and victims. We also showed you that residents are not usually the most important people for solving crime problems. Instead, place managers are better equipped to address crime problems on their properties because they control their places. We also showed you that arrest-focused strategies are not usually the most effective at reducing crime. Arrests are merely an output. Instead, we should be focusing on achieving outcomes such as reducing crime or reducing harm.

Now that you have learned about these fallacies, we want to redirect you on a new path. Part 2 of this book shows that crime is often the by-product of everyday life (chapter 5). When new products come on the market or some major shift in society changes people's daily activities, this can create crime opportunities that offenders exploit. So, to address crime, we need to dismantle crime opportunities. And as we will show, sometimes the best way to cut crime is to think small (chapter 6) and to get place managers involved (chapter 7).

DOI: 10.4324/9781003430155-6

5
Crime Is a By-Product of Everyday Life

On a rainy April evening in 2012, aspiring New York chef Hwangbum Yang was robbed, shot, and killed two blocks from his Bronx apartment. But when police and paramedics arrived, they found Yang with his wallet untouched. While this was an extreme murder case, by the early 2010s non-violent robberies had spiked in many Western nations. Many people were being robbed, but not for their wallets. When the police investigated what offenders were targeting, once again, the rule of the few showed itself. One item was driving most of the thefts and robberies, and you probably have one in your pocket: a smartphone. Yang's killer, seeing him walking home with AirPods in his ears, robbed him for his iPhone.[1]

The crime trend began in 2007, the same year Apple released their first iPhone. By 2013, thieves in New York City stole over 8,000 Apple devices annually, making up more than 18% of grand larcenies.[2] By comparison, in 2002, there were 25 thefts of Apple products in New York City. In 2011, the New York Police Department reported that in 70% of thefts on public transportation, thieves stole iPhones from transit users.[3] Thieves coveted iPhones (and later iPads) so much that police started referring to their thefts as: Apple picking.[4]

DOI: 10.4324/9781003430155-7

While Apple devices are the most popular among thieves, they are not the only devices stolen. Shortly after the iPhone's release, other companies—such as Samsung, LG, and Google—released their own smartphones. By 2011, smartphone and cellphone thefts made up 30% to 50% of all robberies in many major US cities. For example, over 40% of robberies in New York City and 38% of robberies in Washington DC involved phones.[5]

Smartphones are what crime scientist Ronald Clarke calls a hot product.[6] They are another manifestation of the rule of the few. While hotspots are addresses that experience a lot of crime, hot products are items that are most likely to be targeted by offenders. Although there are a seemingly infinite number of consumer goods that thieves could target, a small number of products are stolen far more than others. For example, in American supermarkets, offenders shoplift tobacco and liquor more than any other product. Similarly, residential burglars usually look for jewellery and electronics whenever they break into a home. They seldom take lightbulbs, spatulas, coasters, or food processors. Even cat burglars are uninterested in stealing litter boxes, scratching posts, or cat nip. Instead, there are a few products that offenders want.

So why are some products hot and others are not? Clarke devised a useful acronym to explain this: CRAVED.[7] An item is more likely to be stolen if it is:

Concealable
Removable
Available
Valuable
Enjoyable
Disposable

Offenders want items that are *concealable*, particularly on the person. This makes sense intuitively. Put yourself in an offender's shoes; if you are going to steal something for quick cash, would you be more inclined to take a Rolex watch or a stainless-steel refrigerator? Items that can be easily hidden, such as on your wrist or in your pocket, make for easier getaways. Second, offenders are more likely to seek out *removable* products. Things that are locked down are less likely to be taken than items that can be taken with little resistance. Third, offenders will steal items that are readily *available*. In the simplest terms, an item needs to exist and be present for it to be stolen. After all, there was no car theft before cars were invented.[8] Fourth, offenders are more likely to seek out *valuable* items, particularly if their goal is to sell them. As Clarke explains, for example, cars that are about five years old are more enticing "because the value of their parts is greater than that of the whole stolen vehicle".[9] Fifth, offenders will generally opt to steal *enjoyable* items. They often have more street re-sale value and are simply desired by offenders themselves should they decide to keep them. This is why electronics are more likely to be stolen than microwaves during residential burglaries, and alcohol, tobacco, or condoms are more likely to be shoplifted than bottled water or paper plates. Finally, offenders often look for items that are *disposable*. Because they often steal to make some cash, offenders want items that will be easy to sell.

Using the CRAVED criteria, it makes sense why smartphones were driving a substantial number of robberies and thefts in the 2010s. Consider each criterion. Smartphones are very *concealable*. They fit in our pockets and thus can often be taken without notice.[10] They are highly *removable*. The whole point of a smartphone is to have a portable computer to take with you, so they are seldom bolted down to anything. During the time we are discussing, they were becoming highly *available*. Thefts of smartphones started happening because a new product became available to the masses quickly; the New York City Police Department said the theft of Apple products had risen roughly 2% per year since 2007.[11]

Just as important, smartphones are *valuable*. They entice offenders because they have high street value. When smartphones first came onto the market, they could be sold for upwards of $400 online.[12] Smartphones are also *enjoyable*. While some offenders may steal the phones for cash, others want them to use for themselves. They are fun devices. Last, smartphones are *disposable*. Because of the demand for these products, offenders could easily find buyers willing to pay good money for the stolen phones. Given the CRAVED criteria, it makes sense why offenders disproportionately targeted smartphones. They are more desirable than microwaves, refrigerators, bicycles, or even formerly popular hot products like Walkmans.

The surge in smartphone theft and robbery surprised everyone, including the police. So, it's not surprising that police applied their default strategies: respond to victims' reports of theft and robbery. Of course, taking reports from victims did little other than help victims file insurance claims: this did not result in many arrests and did not deter offenders, who knew a good thing when they saw it.

Several years into the crime surge, the police across North America used the crime triangle to find a solution. The targets, smartphones, were driving much of this trend because they were such CRAVED items. Instead of trying to catch offenders, they investigated whether the attractiveness of the target could be changed. Smartphones were attractive to thieves and robbers because so many people had them, they could be easily taken, and quickly illegally re-sold. But authorities realized that if thieves or their buyers could not use the stolen phones, they would be less attractive to offenders. They would have little market value. So, police and district attorneys lobbied mobile-phone manufacturers like Apple and Samsung to develop anti-theft features for their products. One feature is called a *kill switch*. If stolen, the phone's owner could deactivate or lock the phone.[13] This made phones worthless, unless an offender had the technological wherewithal to override the phone's antitheft technology. Many thieves did not possess these skills.

Apple was the first to introduce a kill switch allowing owners to disable their stolen phones. They implemented the new technology in the fall of 2013. By the summer of 2014, officials were already seeing declines in thefts and robberies. Statistics from the New York Attorney General said that:

> In New York City, robberies and grand larcenies from a person involving Apple products dropped 19% and 29%, respectively, in the first five months of this year, compared with a year earlier. In San Francisco, iPhone robberies declined 38%. In London, Apple thefts declined 24%.[14]

During the same time, however, thefts of Samsung devices increased in the same cities.[15] This suggested to officials that offenders were adapting to the change and learned to target devices without kill switches. Smartphone manufacturers, including Samsung, Google, and Microsoft, followed suit soon after and implemented similar anti-theft technologies into their products.[16] Thefts of these devices declined thereafter as well.[17]

In October 2014, the Canadian Wireless Telecommunications Association launched a cellphone blacklist. So, in addition to having manufacturers implement kill switch technology into smartphones, devices that have been reported lost or stolen were added to the cellphone blacklist. Once added, the device "will not be able to be activated by a carrier for use—rendering it useless for web browsing, phone calls or texting".[18] The Vancouver (Canada) Police Department reported that smartphone robberies involving violence had declined by 30%.[19]

Both the smartphone kill switch technology and cellphone blacklist were effective in reducing thefts and robberies. However, these strategies did not require police intervention. Instead, they involved action by smartphone manufacturers; those who had the ability to influence the level of opportunity that these products created. Actions of the product manufacturers manipulated target attractiveness. This also produced a more long-term approach to reducing crime. Once the technology was implemented, their effects persisted. Only the most technologically skilled offenders could circumvent these changes; many did not have the skills to overcome them. Thus, crime declined overall.

The smartphone theft phenomenon teaches two important lessons. First, crime problems often arise as by-products of everyday life. They are created through legitimate processes that we never question. The engineers who designed the iPhone were focused on creating a device that revolutionized how we live. They had good intentions; they wanted to make our lives easier by putting our computer, music player, GPS device, wallet, and more in our pocket. But a by-product of this innovation is that eventually everyone would have a hot product in their pocket making them a target for thieves. This phenomenon is not new. Vehicle theft did not exist before cars were invented.[20] In fact, prior to the invention of automobiles, horse theft was a common problem.[21] Cybercrimes, such as phishing or malware attacks, did not exist until the internet was invented. And crime trends evolve with society and technological advancements. For example, offenders used to pirate movies by sneaking camcorders into cinemas, filming the movies, and selling VHS copies on the street.[22] Once the internet and digital copies of films emerged, offenders could more easily distribute advance copies and recordings of the films over the internet.[23]

The second lesson is that the police are often not best equipped to solve crime problems. We call this the *police can solve all crime problems* fallacy.[24] Instead, the people, organizations, owners, and manufacturers whose places and products created crime as a byproduct are in a better position to curb the crime opportunities they unintentionally created.[25]

In this chapter we provide some examples illustrating these two lessons. Our examples illustrate specific crime problems that the police have been called upon to solve. We show that because crime is often a by-product of other processes,[26] traditional arrest-focused strategies failed to reduce crime. Instead, crime was solved via non-police means. This has important implications. It means that addressing some crime problems should not solely be the concern of the police; others in society can take part and be far more effective. Everyone needs to understand how crime opportunities are created. Once we understand this, it is usually clearer who has the power to suppress the crime opportunities. Place managers and product manufacturers are often the ones who can solve the problem.

Crime Enterprise at a Convenience Store

While a Police Captain, Dan once dealt with a problematic convenience store that we will call the Barksdale Market. It was located in a low-income, high-crime neighborhood. Despite the mostly vacant and dilapidated buildings that surrounded it, the Barksdale was a popular place. From the outside it looked like a run-of-the-mill convenience store that sold junk food, lottery tickets, and cigarettes. But few of its customers ever bought these products. Instead, the Barksdale was popular for the unconventional items and services it had to offer. The store was the hub of a retail drug market, the center of a shoplifting enterprise, a money laundering front, and the nucleus for street robberies on the surrounding blocks.[27]

The Barksdale was located close to a central intersection that transit routes passed through. This created ample automobile and foot traffic. Interspersed between the nearby vacant buildings there were a few legitimate businesses that did attract some customers to the area, a grocery store and pharmacy, for example. Drug dealers could sell their products at the nearby bus stops, in the parking lots for the stores across the street, and in the alley behind the Barksdale.

The owner of the Barksdale had an arrangement with local drug dealers and users. He laundered money from the dealer's transactions in exchange for a cut. He also stored drugs and weapons for the dealers in the store. Drug users also benefitted from the Barksdale's illicit operations. The owner would offer users money for drugs in exchange for certain retail items, such as laundry detergent. So, the users would shoplift items from nearby businesses—like the pharmacy and grocery store across the street—to get their fix. Thus, the Barksdale did not only generate crime on its property, it also radiated crime to other places.[28]

The illicit operations at the Barksdale continued for years. The police used traditional tactics at the Barksdale and similar problematic places but saw little results. They carried out raids arresting offenders involved in crime at places like the Barksdale. But they found that at best this only produced short-term success. Crime seemed to always return to the same few places. This could have gone on for more years.

Dan became the new Captain for the district containing the Barksdale. He noticed an important pattern that occurred at these few problematic places. The police would arrest wrongdoers, sometimes even high-ranking members of the criminal enterprise. While the offenders were incarcerated, those still at large would take control of the property. They would slap a new name on the door and re-open it for business. Dan realized that this crime cycle could only continue if someone in the offender network had control of the building. He learned in John's course that the source of control is ownership; the key to solving these problems was to tackle property ownership among problem owners.[29]

Dan started researching the problem properties. He learned that properties often had more than just crime problems. The Barksdale, for example, had many. It had unpaid tax liens to the city, several building code violations, and fell short of several health violations. But many of these problems had yet to be addressed by the relevant city agencies. Because these agencies rarely collaborated with each other, they did not realize the property was of interest to multiple agencies. These problems, coupled with the crimes occurring at the Barksdale, motivated the city to shutter the business. So, Dan worked in conjunction with the local police, redevelopment foundation, city, building inspector, health inspector, and a prosecutor to address the problem. After a raid, the city seized the property for outstanding liens and code violations. The city then sold the property to the non-profit redevelopment foundation to be redeveloped into a new business.

This dramatically reduced crime at and around the Barksdale. Drug dealers no longer had their headquarters to store illicit goods and weapons. Drug users no longer had a cash outlet for their shoplifted goods. So not only did crime on the property decline, but crime at nearby properties declined as well.[30] Moreover, because the city took ownership of the property, no one in the criminal network could re-open the business to resume illegal activities. Dan's people had not merely *disrupted* the operations of the criminal network on the property, as so many previous police actions had done. They had *dismantled* the crime opportunities of the property. Thus, the crime reduction effects have persisted for over a decade.

Assaults in Bars & Pubs Involving Glassware

In 2004 on Christmas Eve, Blake Golding was working as a doorman of a nightclub in Milton Keynes, UK. When a fight broke out, he stepped in to break things up. One of the assailants proceeded to smash their pint glass and slash him in the face and throat several times with the shards of glass. Despite losing four pints of blood, he narrowly survived the attack and was left physically and mentally scarred.[31]

Unfortunately, this was not an isolated event. In the past two decades there has been a strong push by policymakers in the United Kingdom (UK) to address assaults in bars involving glassware. According to a 2010 report by the Design Council, a Royal Charter charity and the government's advisor on design, there are nearly one million violent incidents each year in the UK involving persons under the influence of alcohol.[32] The UK's National Health Service (NHS) spent an estimated £2.7 billion at the time to address alcohol-related harms, including assault injuries.[33] Police have used resources beyond that figure to respond to these incidents as well.

The Design Council report specified that over 87,000 incidents per year involved glass and "around 5,500 glassings are reported annually".[34] Glassings are "barroom assaults where glass vessels are used as weapons".[35] During altercations, bar patrons often smash pint glasses and use the remains to harm whoever they are fighting. Studies in the UK estimate that glasses and bottles are used in about 4 to 9% of all assaults that result in emergency hospitalization.[36] Facial injuries from these assaults often ensued, resulting in immense health care costs to stabilize victims and costs to carry out reconstructive plastic surgery to repair the damage.[37]

The standard police response to this problem would be to regularly patrol problem bars and await calls for service from the public. When fights break out, bar employees or bystanders call the police to stop the fight and arrest those involved. However, this is a reactive response. While this might hold involved parties criminally responsible for their bad behavior, the victims still sustain injuries. Millions of tax dollars still needed to be spent to provide medical care to those involved.[38] Was this really the best we could do?

In response to the traumatic event Golding experienced, his mother, Marjorie Golding, formed the Pop-campaign: "plastic bottles or plastic surgery". The Pop-campaign started with a petition to get glass banned from night clubs and bars in downtown areas. As Marjorie Golding states, "we are still serving a mind-altering substance in a potential weapon".[39] They proposed that these businesses use alternatives, such as polycarbonate glass, that cannot shatter.

In 2006, the Glasgow city council passed a by-law implementing a phased elimination of glassware in downtown businesses that served alcohol past midnight. They required businesses to use plastic drinkware instead.[40] Prior to the policy, there was an average of six glassings per month in the city center area. Six months after the city passed the bylaw, only five glass attacks had occurred.[41]

In England, they tested out polycarbonate glassware in bars across multiple cities, including Northampton and Lancashire. In Northampton, nine of the largest alcohol-serving businesses participated in the project and switched over to the alternative glassware. They tried both polycarbonate glasses and polyethylene terephthalate (PET) plastic bottles. The Design Council report stated:

> Within Northampton town centre the number of glassings and bottlings has significantly declined year on year from 51 in 2006 to 45 in 2007 and 31 in 2008. Since 2004 there has been a cumulative decrease of 40% in glassing incidents.[42]

Researchers in Lancashire, UK reported similar successes. They selected venues in three areas in Lancashire, Burnley, Chorley, and Preston, and had some of the businesses switch over to polycarbonate glassware (PCG) while the others kept their same drinking vessels. Over the three-month study period:

> ...there were significant decreases in the number of glass breakings in PCG venues, from an average of 17 per week (per venue) pre-trial to zero per week during the trial. Whilst the number of customer and staff injuries recorded by PCG venues was low both pre- and post-trial, there were reductions in both staff and customer injuries after the introduction of PCG. In non-PCG venues staff injuries also decreased during the trial period, but customer injuries increased.[43]

Overall, the policies show promise for the benefits of switching the type of glassware used in premises where assaults may be more likely to occur. And while this change certainly does not disrupt the likelihood of assaults occurring, they can drastically reduce the amount of injury and harm that results from these events.[44] Other policies, such as staff training on safe serving practices to cut off visibly intoxicated patrons, are required to reduce the likelihood of fights breaking out in the first place. But it is an undeniable example of how non-police persons or organizations can make changes to reduce crime problems.

Gasoline Drive-Offs

One night in 2005, a 17-year-old British Columbia (Canada) driver tried to drive off with $12 of unpaid gas. Following his employer's training, the gas station attendant, Grant De Patie, tried to record the vehicle's license plate number. But he could not see the car's license plate from inside the station, so he exited the building. The driver ran De Patie down with his vehicle. In the process, De Patie got stuck under the vehicle as the driver tried to flee. De Patie was dragged beneath the car several kilometres, leading to his death.[45] Even though the police were able to arrest and convict the driver, they could not bring De Patie back. Research suggested that very few arrests, let alone convictions, were made for gasoline theft.[46] We needed to do better.

The inclusion of this example may puzzle you. In many countries, it's impossible for people to drive off with unpaid gasoline. But in 2005, it was quite common. Gasoline drive-offs are the automotive equivalent of a dine-and-dash. Gas stations used to have payment structures like sit-down restaurants where you received your food first and paid after. Gas stations worked the same way; you drove into a station, pumped gasoline into your vehicle, and then walked into the station to pay for the amount you pumped.

This system created an opportunity for crime, most commonly gasoline theft.[47] People could pump gas into their vehicles and then drive off without paying. Using this payment model, oil companies collectively lost profits when motorists drove away with gas they did not pay for. These lost profits have cost us a great deal in terms of insurance costs and increased gas prices to law-abiding consumers.[48] It also created a lot of problems for the police. For example, in the 1990s, an analysis of calls for police service from "38 convenience stores in Austin, TX reveals that gasoline drive-offs account for 48% of all convenience store calls".[49] Some incidents also involve serious crimes, like the De Patie example.

Clearly, the standard response to this problem was ineffective. It involved having gas station attendants record the license plate numbers of the vehicles whose drivers gas-and-dashed. Companies would then report this to the police and make claims to their insurance companies with hopes of recouping their losses. This strategy was reactive and police-dependent. It also did not guarantee the police could identify offenders nor hold them accountable.[50] Even if this method could result in an arrest, it cannot undo some of the more serious consequences that ensued from these events, like in De Patie's case.

But what could we do instead? The answer lies beneath golden arches. Let's return to our dine-and-dash analogy. Only certain restaurants experience dine-and-dash problems; many do not. Unlike most restaurants, McDonald's, Burger King, and Tim Hortons do not have a dine-and-dash problem. Why is this? They use a different payment system. In fast food restaurants you must pay *before* you eat. You cannot steal food you have already paid for; the fast-food model eliminates any Hamburglar's opportunity to steal.

De Patie's parents met with government officials to devise new policies to ensure no one else lost their child the same way. The solution was simple and did not require police action. It involved getting gas stations to implement fast food-like payment systems. They lobbied the government to pass Grant's Law, a set of amendments to the Occupational Health and Safety Regulations at gas stations and convenience stores. One of those amendments was to require all gas stations to use pre-payment systems.[51] Requiring drivers to pay before they can pump any gas removes the opportunity to gas-and-dash. The government changed occupational health and safety regulations to force place managers to change their operating practices. This has created a long-term proactive solution that does not require police intervention.

Shoplifting Videogames at Retail Stores

Videogames are another CRAVED item, particularly back before instant downloads were available. They are small, highly valuable, and enjoyable consumer goods. Thus, they have high street value and videogames sold in physical form, such as a disc or chip, come in relatively small cases. Consequently, videogames retailers have had to take precautions to avoid shoplifting. Your experience buying one was likely impacted by these place management decisions.

Try the following thought experiment. You want to buy a videogame and learn that Walmart carries it at the lowest price. Picture yourself getting in the door of the store. Now think about the exact steps you would need to take to buy the game. How would you do it?

It would look something like this. You walk to the back of the store where the electronics department is located. You browse through the aisles and see that the game is locked in a glass case against the back wall. So, you go find an employee and indicate your intent to buy the game. She goes over to the display case, unlocks it, and takes a copy of the game from the shelf. She then walks it over to the checkout in the electronics department where you pay for the game. She passes the game over a machine that de-activates the security strip attached to the packaging and then places it in a bag with your receipt and sends you on your way.

And once you get home, you will likely spend ten minutes removing the plastic packaging and adhesive strips that seal the case.

Can you think of any other item that requires this set of steps to acquire? Do you need to go through this same process to buy a notepad, garden hose, or candy? No, they let you roam around the store with a supersized shopping cart, hoping you will fill it up with as many items as possible. Once you have gathered all your goods, you take them to the front of the store to a checkout counter or self-serve checkout. So why are video games, along with a select number of electronics, different?

Because videogames fit Clarke's CRAVED criteria perfectly.[52] Not surprisingly, they rank high on the list of most shoplifted items. Traditional responses to this problem were very inefficient and ineffective. When valuable goods sat on regular shelves with no glass encasing, it was much easier for shoplifters to conceal games in their clothing, backpacks, or handbags and remove them from the store without payment. If they got caught, the store could call the police. However, shoplifting occurs at stores like Walmart each day, costing millions in taxpayer dollars per year in police response.[53]

The current payment method works because many obstacles are put in place to make shoplifting videogames much more difficult. Offenders would need to break into the locked glass cases; this is difficult to do, especially without being noticed. The excessive packaging and adhesive strips sealing the cases are also a crime prevention measure. Opening these cases takes time and makes noise; this would draw attention to anyone trying to open the case and sneak the disc into one's pocket or bag.

Also, note that the employees do not hand the game over to customers to put in their cart and continue shopping. They do not pay for the video games with their other items when they get to the front of the store. If they did this, some would try to hide the games in their clothing or handbags and walk out the door with them. Instead, people have to pay for the games on the spot in the electronics department before they get possession of them. This is similar to the fast-food payment model that prevents dine-and-dash problems. If you have paid for the video game before you get possession of it, you cannot steal it. Last, the employee also de-activated the security strip attached to the game that would have set off an alarm at the exit if it had not been de-activated.

This store design change and policy, enacted by its place manager, reduces the opportunity to steal video games. Many of the techniques described come from situational crime prevention,[54] which we discuss in chapter 10. These strategies are also not reactive thereby relying on the police to arrest shoplifters after they have been caught. Instead, installing the glass cases and changing store purchasing policies for electronics makes it difficult for any offender, no matter how motivated they are, to steal a game.

Theft of Automobiles

The Kia Boyz challenge, a TikTok trend, started a crime spree in the United States in 2021. Car thieves learned how to easily steal Kia and Hyundai vehicles by jamming a USB cable into their steering wheel columns. The thieves later posted video instructions on how to steal the cars on the social media platform, TikTok. They also posed a challenge to others to try their methods. Thefts of Kias and Hyundais skyrocketed in the United States, often doubling the auto theft rate of other vehicle makes and models.[55] The problem became so bad that some of America's largest auto insurers, refused to insure these vehicles.[56] In Canada, however, Kia and Hyundai vehicles were unaffected by the theft issue. So why was this happening?

Between 2015 and 2019, 74% of Kia and Hyundai vehicles manufactured for the United States did not have engine immobilisers, compared to 4% among other vehicle manufacturing companies.[57] Engine immobilisers, created in the 1980s, are transponder chips or key fobs built into car keys.[58] These chips and fobs are linked to electronic systems in the vehicle's engine. The engine will only start provided the transponder chip or fob is within a certain range of the vehicle and the key is in the ignition. Without the fob, the electronic system in the engine will not activate the fuel system or ignition circuit.[59] Such technology makes it much more difficult for someone to steal a car.

Initially, in the 1980s, manufacturers were reluctant to install engine immobilisers into their vehicles. Developing these innovations were costly, and they thought consumers would be more interested in improvements in comfort, safety, or speed of vehicles.[60] To compel manufacturers to integrate engine immobilisers, the UK government decided to implement a

Car Theft Index. This was an annual report detailing the make and model of the cars most at risk for vehicle theft.[61] It quickly generated widespread publicity and gave consumers more information to make purchasing decisions. This incentivized automobile manufacturers to start taking anti-theft features more seriously. Engine immobilizers became more common in the 1990s. By 1998, legislation required that all new vehicles produced in the European Union were equipped with the technology.[62] There is evidence to suggest that the technology contributed in part to the decline in vehicle theft through the 1990s and 2000s.[63] For instance, Rick Brown's review of studies on immobilizers across four countries found that 15 of the 16 studies showed reductions in vehicle theft.[64]

The Canadian Federal government required all new vehicles sold in Canada after 2007 to be equipped with engine immobilizers.[65] Thus, the viral TikTok challenge sparked no crime surge in Canada. But there remains no such requirement in the United States. Once car thieves caught on that they could steal these Kia and Hyundai vehicles with as little as a screwdriver or USB cable, it sparked a national epidemic of vehicle thefts; Kia and Hyundai vehicles became hot products.[66]

Kia and Hyundai have responded to pressures from Attorney Generals in the United States by installing software updates in vehicles and distributing steering wheel locks to affected vehicle owners.[67] However, their vehicles without engine immobilisers continue to be targeted by thieves. Their new models of vehicles, now equipped with engine immobilisers, are not targeted as readily.

Vehicle theft has been one of the most pressing crime issues around the world. Since their invention in 1886,[68] thieves have coveted automobiles and their theft has cost billions to consumers, particularly through increased insurance costs. Joyriding is the most common reason offenders steal cars, however some also do it to re-sell the vehicle itself or its parts.[69] In other cases, such as with some of the Kia and Hyundai vehicle thefts, offenders steal vehicles to use for transportation to and from other crimes.[70]

The standard response to theft of an automobile was for the police to await calls from the public when they discovered the crime. Thefts of automobiles are one of the most well-reported crimes because of reporting requirements for insurance companies.[71] Owners need to go through the correct process to obtain insurance payouts to replace their vehicles if they are not recovered. This police response is rather inefficient. Though cars used for joyriding could sometimes be found, those stolen for parts or resale were often difficult to recover, and when cars are recovered, they have often been abandoned. Thus, there is no guarantee that the police will identify who actually stole the vehicle.

Governments have adopted several strategies over the years to address the problem. We have already provided the example of engine immobilisers and Car Theft Indexes adopted in Europe and North America. There are other innovations that have helped curb vehicle crime. Steering column locks, for example, provided some crime reduction effects over 50 years ago.

In 1949, Chrysler developed the innovative key-operated ignition switch. This ensured cars could only be driven when the key was inserted into the ignition.[72] Though this deterred some offenders, others were able to circumvent the technology and hotwire vehicles. This led companies to consider further measures; that's when steering column locks came in. Manufacturers designed a pin that would lock a vehicle's steering column in place when the key was removed from the ignition. This prevented anyone from being able to turn the steering wheel. Thus, even if someone could hotwire a car, they could not steer the car. The pin would only release if the key was inserted into the ignition and turned on.

The German government was the first to require that manufacturers incorporate steering column locks into all of their cars from 1962 onward. A decade later the British and US governments followed suit.[73] They too used a grandfathering process. As such, the full effect of the policy change would take about a decade to show its impact.[74] Cars manufactured prior to the new legislation were not required to have the anti-theft devices. But as new cars with the locks were brought into the market and old cars were removed from circulation, the number of cars that were easier to steal declined. In Germany, there was an almost immediate impact. In 1963, after the first full year that the legislation had been in effect, thefts of vehicles were 20% lower than in 1960. This decline was sustained for about a decade until crime started rising again.[75] Other countries, such as England and the United States, followed suit with similar legislation in the 1970s generating mixed results.

Over time, vehicle security technology has been improving. It's difficult to say whether any single manufacturing design change has been the cause of the reduction in thefts of vehicles. This occurs because small innovations have been developed that compound over time to generate greater reductions in crime.[76] Consider how car security has evolved: Chrysler invented the key-operated ignition switch in 1949. This was followed by steering column locks. But remember, once steering column locks were incorporated, car manufacturers did not stop incorporating key-operated ignition switches. Cars were then equipped with both. Engine immobilizers have since been added. Then car alarms came onto the market. Even now, many vehicles have GPS tracking devices embedded into them. There has been a compounding effect over time. These smaller design changes have made it incrementally more difficult for someone to steal automobiles. While before offenders needed only know how to hotwire a car, now they need the skills to overcome electronic chips, alarms, and tracking devices. Governments have also added hurdles to offenders by creating centralized vehicle registration and licensing systems to track ownership and reduce illegal resale.[77]

Every year new automobiles come into the market with these improved security technologies and older cars without them are taken out of circulation. Thus, many of these beneficial outcomes can have a delayed effect. But we will only sustain these crime reductions if vehicle manufacturers continue to incorporate all of these security features into their vehicles.

When manufacturers fail to include these vehicle security features, we see the consequences, like in the Kia and Hyundai examples. One of the most important things to take away from these examples is that the police had nothing to do with these changes. This crime problem was mitigated mostly by innovations in the private sector by vehicle manufacturers to create more desirable products for their consumers.

Conclusions

We chose the examples in this chapter for two reasons. First, they demonstrate how many crime problems are often a by-product of everyday life. They can originate from non-crime sources, such as the invention of a new consumer product or changes in people's routine activities.[78] This helps explain the ebb and flow of crime trends. We began our examples with the surge in smartphone robberies and how practitioners have had to respond. But new crime trends continue to emerge as our society changes and offenders modify their behavior to adapt to them. For example, online shopping has become increasingly popular. But it too has a crime by product: porch piracy. The police are now fielding calls for stolen delivery parcels at unprecedented rates.[79]

The reasons for the new crime types, such as Apple picking and porch piracy, lead to our second important point: to reduce crime, we should not solely focus on criminal propensity. Porch piracy has not become a widespread problem because there has been an unexpected surge in criminally motivated people in society. Instead, a new crime opportunity arose that some are choosing to act on. This has been happening for decades. After all, there was no car theft before cars were invented and their introduction eventually eradicated almost all horse theft.[80] Cybercrime did not exist prior to the internet being invented. As society changes, new products come onto the market, and people spend their time engaging in different activities, crime patterns change.

As the examples illustrate, the solutions did not revolve around understanding or changing criminal propensity. Practitioners did not care why some people stole gas or smartphones and others did not, or why some people smashed their pint glasses to use as weapons in a bar brawl. Instead, they focused on eliminating (or reducing) the opportunity to do these things and who had control over those opportunities. In other words, they did not ask *why*? Instead, they asked *how*? When we understand how offenders carry out their crimes, we can often find ways to intervene in that process, leading to more permanent solutions. Understanding what creates opportunities can sometimes be the most effective way to reduce crime. Instead of putting a figurative band aid on the problem, such as using arrests as the go-to response, these solutions eliminate the opportunity to behave badly.

This is where the crime triangle comes in handy. Once we identify the opportunity, we can then assess which controllers might have the greatest ability to suppress that opportunity. Without opportunity, people cannot act on the impulse to offend, no matter how motivated they are. Too often we focus on motivation, but this limits our potential solutions. Humans are motivated to do things that will benefit them. Offenders committing street crimes in low-income neighborhoods are not much different than a banker on Wall Street who engages in insider trading. The one major difference is that the banker on Wall Street has access to insider trading opportunities that the street offender does not. He has the superficial appearance of legitimacy and easy access to his targets.[81] The rich parents involved in the college admissions scandal were given an opportunity by William Singer to get their children into prestigious universities through fraud.[82] Those in the health care sector commit fraud by exploiting the complex medical billing systems.[83] Countless people in the banking and real estate sectors exploited regulations and committed fraud leading to the 2008 recession. Why? Because they had access to opportunities.[84]

The theme of criminal opportunity will continue throughout this book, and in part 3 we discuss how opportunities are created and provide tools you can use to suppress them. Much of our discussion will revolve around identifying crime opportunities, determining who has control over them, and finding ways the controllers can act to suppress crime opportunities. For now, our goal was to get you to re-think crime and how it occurs. We hope you're with us so far. The next question is, are you willing to approach problem-solving differently? In the next chapter, we hope to convince you that small steps may be the next best way to tackle some of the most common problems.

Key Points

- Understanding how crimes are committed can lead to more effective prevention efforts than asking why crimes are committed.
- Many crime opportunities emerge from everyday processes
- Often the people or organizations who create the places and products we use influence crime opportunities.
- These same people are organizations who inadvertently create crime opportunities and are best equipped to suppress them.
- Ask: how is the crime committed?

Notes

1 Choney, S. (2013, May 13). Apple, other phone makers need to make phones harder to steal, says NY Lawman. NBC News. Retrieved from: https://www.nbcnews.com/tech/tech-news/apple-other-phone-makers-need-make-phones-harder-steal-says-flna1c9904740; Smith, G. (2013, March 7). Apple Picking: How the iPhone became an object worth killing for. Huffington Post. Retrieved from: https://www.huffpost.com/entry/apple-picking-stolen-iphones_n_2818488

2 Fox, A. (2014, January 14). Device Thefts Fueling Rise in Larcenies: New York City Became a Safer Place in the Past 12 Years, Unless you're the Owner of an iPhone or iPad. Wall Street Journal. Retrieved from: https://www.wsj.com/articles/SB10001424052702304617404579303193340022488; Padilla, R. (2014, January 13). Increased Theft of Apple Devices 'Driving Force' Behind Rise of Larcenies in New York City. MacRumors. Retrieved from: https://www.macrumors.com/2014/01/13/theft-apple-devices-rise-larcenies-new-york-city/

3 Parascondola, R. (2011, December 6). NYPD: Thefts of smartphones and iPads now more prevalent than cash as criminals turn focus on electronics. New York Daily News. Retrieved from: https://www.nydailynews.com/2011/12/06/nypd-thefts-of-smartphones-and-ipads-now-more-prevalent-than-cash-as-criminals-turn-focus-on-electronics/

4 Gentry, K. (2015). Apple Picking: The Rise of Electronic Device Thefts in Boston Subways. In V. Ceccato & A. Newton (Eds.), *Safety and Security in Transit Environments. Crime Prevention and Security Management*. Palgrave Macmillan. https://doi.org/10.1057/9781137457653_3; Smith, G. (2013, March 7). Apple Picking: How the iPhone became an object worth killing for. Huffington Post. Retrieved from: https://www.huffpost.com/entry/apple-picking-stolen-iphones_n_2818488

5 Snider, M. (2012, April 9). Smartphone thefts prompt joint effort by carriers, FCC. USA Today. Retrieved from: https://abcnews.go.com/Technology/smartphone-thefts-prompt-joint-effort-carriers-fcc/story?id=1610544

6 Clarke, R.V. (1999). *Hot products: Understanding, anticipating and reducing demand for stolen goods*. Police Research Series Paper 112. London, UK: Policing and Reducing Crime Unit. Retrieved from: https://popcenter.asu.edu/sites/g/files/litvpz3631/files/hot_products_understanding_anticipating_and_reducing_demand_for_stolen_goods_clarke_1999.pdf

7 Clarke, R.V. (1999). *Hot products: Understanding, anticipating and reducing demand for stolen goods*. Police Research Series Paper 112. London, UK: Policing and Reducing Crime Unit. Retrieved from: https://popcenter.asu.edu/sites/g/files/litvpz3631/files/hot_products_understanding_anticipating_and_reducing_demand_for_stolen_goods_clarke_1999.pdf

8 Wilkins, L.T. (1964). *Social Deviance: Social Policy, Action, and Research*. London, UK: Tavistock.

9 From page 24 of: Clarke, R.V. (1999). *Hot Products: Understanding, Anticipating and Reducing Demand for Stolen Goods*. Police Research Series Paper 112. London, UK: Policing and Reducing Crime Unit. Retrieved from: https://popcenter.asu.edu/sites/g/files/litvpz3631/files/hot_products_understanding_anticipating_and_reducing_demand_for_stolen_goods_clarke_1999.pdf

10 Luke, P. (2013, April 28). Smartphone thefts reaching 'epidemic levels' in Lower Mainland communities. The Province; Global News. Retrieved from: https://globalnews.ca/news/517414/smartphone-thefts-reaching-epidemic-levels-in-lower-mainland-communities/

11 Pereira, I. (2013, November 18). City looking to curb rising number of Apple product thefts with database. AM New York. Retrieved from: https://www.amny.com/news/city-looking-to-curb-rising-number-of-apple-thefts-with-database-1.6458803

12 Winkler, R. (2014, June 19). Apple 'Kill Switch' Appears to Reduce iPhone Robberies: Thefts Drop in New York, London and San Francisco. The Wall Street Journal. Retrieved June 11, 2018 from: https://www.wsj.com/articles/decline-in-theft-of-apple-iphones-points-to-kill-switch-1403217173

13 Winkler, R. (2014, June 19). Apple 'Kill Switch' Appears to Reduce iPhone Robberies: Thefts Drop in New York, London and San Francisco. The Wall

Street Journal. Retrieved June 11, 2018 from: https://www.wsj.com/articles/decline-in-theft-of-apple-iphones-points-to-kill-switch-1403217173
14 Winkler, R. (2014, June 19). Apple 'Kill Switch' Appears to Reduce iPhone Robberies: Thefts Drop in New York, London and San Francisco. The Wall Street Journal. Retrieved June 11, 2018 from: https://www.wsj.com/articles/decline-in-theft-of-apple-iphones-points-to-kill-switch-1403217173
15 Winkler, R. (2014, June 19). Apple 'Kill Switch' Appears to Reduce iPhone Robberies: Thefts Drop in New York, London and San Francisco. The Wall Street Journal. Retrieved June 11, 2018 from: https://www.wsj.com/articles/decline-in-theft-of-apple-iphones-points-to-kill-switch-1403217173
16 Collins, T. (2014, April 5). Samsung adding anti-theft solutions to smartphones. *Associated Press*. Retrieved June 11, 2018 from: https://www.apnews.com/031225152c6d433db20840d7fc20a4f8
17 Mlot, S. (2015, February 11). Cell phone kill switches prompt 'dramatic' drop in thefts. PC Mag. Retrieved from: https://www.pcmag.com/news/cell-phone-kill-switches-prompt-dramatic-drop-in-thefts
18 Bogart, N. (2015, June 10). Smartphone thefts drop dramatically in cities with 'kill switch' technology. Global News. Retrieved April 14, 2021 from: https://globalnews.ca/news/1824691/smartphone-thefts-drop-dramatically-in-cities-with-kill-switch-technology/
19 Bogart, N. (2015, June 10). Smartphone thefts drop dramatically in cities with 'kill switch' technology. Global News. Retrieved April 14, 2021 from: https://globalnews.ca/news/1824691/smartphone-thefts-drop-dramatically-in-cities-with-kill-switch-technology/
20 Wilkins, L.T. (1964). *Social Deviance: Social Policy, Action, and Research*. London, UK: Tavistock.
21 Woodward, N. (2009). Horse-stealing in Wales, 1730–1830. *Agricultural History Review, 57*(1), 70–108.
22 Zhai, G. & Wu, X. (2014). Defeating camcorder piracy by temporal psychovisual modulation. *Journal of Display Technology, 10*(9), 754–757. https://doi.org/10.1109/jdt.2014.2317810
23 Phau, I., Teah, M., & Liang, J. (2016). Investigating the factors influencing digital movie piracy. *Journal of Promotion Management, 22*(5), 637–664. https://doi.org/10.1080/10496491.2016.1185491
24 Linning, S.J., Carroll, T., Gerard, D., & Eck, J.E. (2024). Can the police solve all crime problems? *Public Management Magazine, 107*(1), 40–44. https://icma.org/articles/pm-magazine/can-police-solve-all-crime-problems
25 Felson, M. & Eckert, M. (2019). *Crime and Everyday Life* (6th edition). Sage Publishing. https://doi.org/10.4135/9781506394817
26 Felson, M. & Eckert, M. (2019). *Crime and Everyday Life* (6th edition). Sage Publishing. https://doi.org/10.4135/9781506394817
27 Linning, S.J. & Eck, J.E. (2021). *Whose 'Eyes on the Street' Control Crime? Expanding Place Management into Neighborhoods*. Cambridge University Press. https://doi.org/10.1017/9781108954143
28 Bowers, K. (2014). Risky Facilities: Crime Radiators or Crime Absorbers? A Comparison of Internal and External Levels of Theft. *Journal of Quantitative Criminology, 30*(3), 389–414. https://doi.org/10.1007/s10940-013-9208-z; Linning, S.J., Bowers, K., & Eck, J.E. (2024). Crime radiation theory: the co-production of crime patterns through opportunity creation and exploitation. *Crime Science, 13*, 32. https://doi.org/10.1186/s40163-024-00234-6

29 Eck, J.E., Linning, S.J., & Herold, T.D. (2023). *Place Management and Crime: Ownership and Property Rights as a Source of Social Control.* Springer Publishers. https://doi.org/10.1007/978-3-031-27693-4; Linning, S.J. & Eck, J.E. (2024). Clarifying control in criminology: A proposal for six interacting controls of crime. *Canadian Journal of Criminology and Criminal Justice, 66*(3–4), 119–141. https://doi.org/10.3138/cjccj-2024-0053

30 Clarke, R.V. & Weisburd, D. (1994). Diffusion of crime control benefits. In R.V. Clarke (Ed.), *Crime Prevention Studies* (vol. 2). Monsey, NY: Willow Tree Press; Eck, J.E., Linning, S.J., & Bowers, K. (2024). Does crime in places stay in places? Evidence for crime radiation in three narrative reviews. *Aggression and Violent Behavior, 78*(5), 101955. https://doi.org/10.1016/j.avb.2024.101955

31 BBC News (2012, November 12). Bottle Stop Campaign to head to Downing Street over glass laws. BBC News. Retrieved from: https://www.bbc.com/news/uk-england-lancashire-20300578; Design Council (2010). Using design to reduce injuries from alcohol related violence in pubs and clubs. London, UK: Design Council. Retrieved from: https://www.designcouncil.org.uk/fileadmin/uploads/dc/Documents/design-out-crime-alcohol.pdf

32 Design Council (2010). Using design to reduce injuries from alcohol related violence in pubs and clubs. London, UK: Design Council. Retrieved from: https://www.designcouncil.org.uk/fileadmin/uploads/dc/Documents/design-out-crime-alcohol.pdf

33 Design Council (2010). Using design to reduce injuries from alcohol related violence in pubs and clubs. London, UK: Design Council. Retrieved from: https://www.designcouncil.org.uk/fileadmin/uploads/dc/Documents/design-out-crime-alcohol.pdf

34 From page 3 of: Design Council (2010). Using design to reduce injuries from alcohol related violence in pubs and clubs. London, UK: Design Council. Retrieved from: https://www.designcouncil.org.uk/fileadmin/uploads/dc/Documents/design-out-crime-alcohol.pdf

35 From page 111 of: Forsyth, A.J. (2008). Banning glassware from nightclubs in Glasgow (Scotland): Observed impacts, compliance and patron's views. *Alcohol & Alcoholism, 43*(1), 111–117. https://doi.org/10.1093/alcalc/agm142

36 Hocking, M.A. (1989). Assaults in south east London. *Journal of the Royal Society of Medicine, 82*, 281–284. https://doi.org/10.1177/014107688908200512; Kershaw, C., Nicholas, S., & Walker, A. (2008, July). *Crime in England and Wales, 2007/08.* Home Office Statistical Bulletin.

37 Coomaraswamy, K.S. & Sheperd, J.P. (2003). Predictors and severity of injury in assaults with barglasses and bottles. *Injury Prevention, 9*, 81–84. https://doi.org/10.1136/ip.9.1.81

38 Clarke, R.V. (2020). Assaults with glasses in bars and clubs in Lancashire, England. In M.S. Scott & R.V. Clarke (Eds.), *Problem-Oriented Policing: Successful Case Studies* (pp. 128–136). New York, NY: Routledge. https://doi.org/10.4324/9780429457357-13

39 Design Council (2010). Using design to reduce injuries from alcohol related violence in pubs and clubs. London, UK: Design Council. Retrieved from: https://www.designcouncil.org.uk/fileadmin/uploads/dc/Documents/design-out-crime-alcohol.pdf

40 Forsyth, A.J. (2008). Banning glassware from nightclubs in Glasgow (Scotland): Observed impacts, compliance and patron's views. *Alcohol & Alcoholism, 43*(1), 111–117. https://doi.org/10.1093/alcalc/agm142

41 Musson, C. (2006, December 29). A way to curb pub violence…or a waste of time? Glass ban comes under fresh criticism as new study claims its aim to reduce attacks

in city will fail. Evening Times (Glasgow). Retrieved from: https://advance-lexis-com.proxy.lib.sfu.ca/api/document?collection=news&id=urn:contentItem:4MP6-P2M0-TWTX-41Y7-00000-00&context=1516831

42 Page 33 of: Design Council (2010). Using design to reduce injuries from alcohol related violence in pubs and clubs. London, UK: Design Council. Retrieved from: https://www.designcouncil.org.uk/fileadmin/uploads/dc/Documents/design-out-crime-alcohol.pdf

43 Page 28 of: Anderson, Z., Whelan, G., Hughes, K., & Bellis, M.A. (2009, April). *Evaluation of the Lancashire polycarbonate glass pilot project*. Centre for Public Health, Liverpool John Moores University.

44 Clarke, R.V. (2020). Assaults with glasses in bars and clubs in Lancashire, England. In M.S. Scott & R.V. Clarke (Eds.), *Problem-Oriented Policing: Successful Case Studies* (pp. 128–136). New York, NY: Routledge. https://doi.org/10.4324/9780429457357-13

45 CBC News (2006, October 4). B.C. to implement 'Grant's Law' to protect gas station workers. Retrieved from: https://www.cbc.ca/news/canada/british-columbia/b-c-to-implement-grant-s-law-to-protect-gas-station-workers-1.6161.6; Joyce, G. (2008, Jan 31). New regulations to prevent 'gas-and-dash' takes effect in B.C. Friday. The Canadian Press. Retrieved April 3, 2021 from http://proxy.lib.sfu.ca/login?url=https://www.proquest.com/wire-feeds/new-regulations-prevent-gas-dash-takes-effect-b-c/docview/360036895/se-2?accountid=13800

46 Brodsky, S.L., Bernatz, M.L., & Beidleman, W.B. (1981). The perfect crime: An investigation of the gasoline station drive-away. *The British Journal of Criminology, 21*(4), 350–356. https://doi.org/10.1093/oxfordjournals.bjc.a047253

47 Sidebottom, A., Agar, I., & Kurland, J. (2023). Do increases in the price of fuel increase levels of fuel theft? Evidence from England and Wales. *Crime Science, 12*(7), 1–7. https://doi.org/10.1186/s40163-023-00182-7

48 Meini, B. & Clarke, R.V. (2012). *Gasoline drive-offs*. Problem-Oriented Guides for Police, Problem-Specific Guides Series (No. 67). US Department of Justice: Center for Problem-Oriented Policing, Inc.

49 LaVigne, N.G. (1994). Gasoline drive-offs: Designing a less convenient environment. *Crime Prevention Studies, 2*, 91–114.

50 Meini, B. & Clarke, R.V. (2012). *Gasoline drive-offs*. Problem-Oriented Guides for Police, Problem-Specific Guides Series (No. 67). US Department of Justice: Center for Problem-Oriented Policing, Inc.

51 CBC News (2006, October 4). B.C. to implement 'Grant's Law' to protect gas station workers. Retrieved from: https://www.cbc.ca/news/canada/british-columbia/b-c-to-implement-grant-s-law-to-protect-gas-station-workers-1.6161.6; Joyce, G. (2008, Jan 31). New regulations to prevent 'gas-and-dash' takes effect in B.C. Friday. The Canadian Press. Retrieved April 3, 2021 from http://proxy.lib.sfu.ca/login?url=https://www.proquest.com/wire-feeds/new-regulations-prevent-gas-dash-takes-effect-b-c/docview/360036895/se-2?accountid=13800

52 Clarke, R.V. (1999). *Hot products: Understanding, anticipating and reducing demand for stolen goods*. Police Research Series Paper 112. London, UK: Policing and Reducing Crime Unit. Retrieved from: https://popcenter.asu.edu/sites/g/files/litvpz3631/files/hot_products_understanding_anticipating_and_reducing_demand_for_stolen_goods_clarke_1999.pdf

53 Zidar, M.S., Shafer, J.G., & Eck, J.E. (2018). Reframing an obvious police problem: Discovery, analysis and response to a manufactured problem in a small city. *Policing: A Journal of Policy and Practice, 12*(3), 316–331. https://doi.org/10.1093/police/pax085

54 Eck, J.E. & Clarke, R.V. (2019). Situational crime prevention: Theory, practice, and evidence. In M.D. Krohn, N. Hendrix, G.P. Hall, & A.J. Lizotte (Eds.), *Handbook on Crime and Deviance* (pp. 355–376). Cham: Springer. https://doi.org/10.1007/978-3-030-20779-3_18

55 Samra, M. (2023, March 21). Raoul urges Kia, Hyundai to take 'comprehensive action' over Chicago-area car thefts. Chicago Sun Times. Retrieved from: https://chicago.suntimes.com/news/2023/3/21/23651031/illinois-attorney-general-kwame-raoul-kia-hyundai-chicago-car-theft-crime

56 Valdes-Dapena, P. (2023, January 28). Some auto insurers are refusing to cover certain Hyundai and Kia models. CNN Business. Retrieved from: https://www.cnn.com/2023/01/27/business/progressive-state-farm-hyundai-kia/index.html

57 Valdes-Dapena, P. (2023, January 28). Some auto insurers are refusing to cover certain Hyundai and Kia models. CNN Business. Retrieved from: https://www.cnn.com/2023/01/27/business/progressive-state-farm-hyundai-kia/index.html

58 Southall, D. & Ekblom, P (1995). *Designing for car security: Toward a crime free car.* Crime Prevention Unit Series Paper 4. London, UK: Home Office.

59 Farrell, G. (2025). The great American car crime decline. *Security Journal, 38*(1), 1–26. https://doi.org/10.1057/s41284-024-00452-2

60 Laycock, G. (2004). The UK Car Theft Index: An example of government leverage. In M. Maxfield & R.V Clarke (Eds.), *Understanding and Preventing Car Theft* (pp. 25–44). Crime Preventions Studies, vol. 17. Cullompton, Devon: Willan Publishing; Webb, B. & Brown, R. (2017). Preventing vehicle crime. In N. Tilley & A. Sidebottom (Eds.), *Handbook of Crime Prevention and Community Safety*, 2nd ed (pp. 354–381). New York, NY: Routledge. https://doi.org/10.4324/9781315724393-16

61 Houghton, G. (1992). *Car theft in England and Wales: The Home Office Car Theft Index.* Crime Prevention Unit Series Paper 33. London, UK: Home Office.

62 Walker, A., Flatley, J., Kershaw, C., & Moon, D. (2009). Crime in England and Wales 2008/09: Findings from the British Crime Survey and police recorded crime. Home Office Statistical Bulletin 11/09, Vol. 1, London, UK: Home Office.

63 Farrell, G. (2025). The great American car crime decline. *Security Journal, 38*(1), 1–26. https://doi.org/10.1057/s41284-024-00452-2

64 Brown, R. (2015b). Reviewing the effectiveness of electronic vehicle immobilisation: Evidence from four countries. *Security Journal, 28*(4), 329–351. https://doi.org/10.1057/sj.2012.55

65 Otis, D. (2023, January 30). Kia and Hyundai vehicles in Canada not affected by U.S. theft issue, automakers say. CTV News. Retrieved from: https://www.ctvnews.ca/autos/2023/1/30/kia-and-hyundai-vehicles-in-canada-not-affected-by-u-s--theft-is.html

66 Clarke, R.V. (1999). *Hot products: Understanding, anticipating and reducing demand for stolen goods.* Police Research Series Paper 112. London, UK: Policing and Reducing Crime Unit. Retrieved from: https://popcenter.asu.edu/sites/g/files/litvpz3631/files/hot_products_understanding_anticipating_and_reducing_demand_for_stolen_goods_clarke_1999.pdf

67 Samra, M. (2023, March 21). Raoul urges Kia, Hyundai to take 'comprehensive action' over Chicago-area car thefts. Chicago Sun Times. Retrieved from: https://chicago.suntimes.com/news/2023/3/21/23651031/illinois-attorney-general-kwame-raoul-kia-hyundai-chicago-car-theft-crime

68 Mercedes-Benz Group (2025). The first automobile, 1885–1886. Retrieved from: https://group.mercedes-benz.com/company/tradition/company-history/1885-1886.html

69 Clarke, R.V. & Harris, P.M. (1992). Auto theft and its prevention. *Crime and Justice, 16*, 1–54. https://doi.org/10.1086/449203 ; Keister, T. (2007). *Thefts of and from cars on residential streets and driveways*. Problem-Oriented Guides for Police Problem-Specific Guide No. 46. US Department of Justice. Retrieved from: https://popcenter.asu.edu/sites/g/files/litvpz3631/files/sites/default/files/problems/pdfs/residentialcartheft.pdf

70 Manjoo, F. (2023, September 1). Kia and Hyundai Helped Enable a Crime Wave. They Should Pay for It. The New York Times. Retrieved from: https://www.nytimes.com/2023/09/01/opinion/kia-hyundai-tiktok.html

71 Clarke, R.V., & Harris, P.M. (1992). Auto theft and its prevention. *Crime and Justice, 16*, 1–54. https://doi.org/10.1086/449203

72 Webb, B. & Brown, R. (2017). Preventing vehicle crime. In N. Tilley & A. Sidebottom (Eds.), *Handbook of Crime Prevention and Community Safety*, 2nd ed (pp. 354–381). New York, NY: Routledge. https://doi.org/10.4324/9781315724393-16

73 Webb, B. (1994). Steering column locks and motor vehicle theft: Evaluations from three countries. *Crime Prevention Studies, 2*, 71–89.

74 Webb, B. & Brown, R. (2017). Preventing vehicle crime. In N. Tilley & A. Sidebottom (Eds.), *Handbook of Crime Prevention and Community Safety*, 2nd ed (pp. 354–381). New York, NY: Routledge. https://doi.org/10.4324/9781315724393-16

75 Webb, B. (1994). Steering column locks and motor vehicle theft: Evaluations from three countries. *Crime Prevention Studies, 2*, 71–89.

76 Farrell, G., Tseloni, A., & Tilley, N. (2011). The effectiveness of vehicle security devices and their role in the crime drop. *Criminology and Criminal Justice, 11*(1), 21–35. https://doi.org/10.1177/1748895810392190

77 Brown, R. (2015a). Crime prevention design in a vehicle registration system: A case study from Australia. *Crime Science, 4*(25), 1–10. https://doi.org/10.1186/s40163-015-0038-1

78 Felson, M. & Eckert, M. (2019). *Crime and Everyday Life* (6th edition). Sage Publishing. https://doi.org/10.4135/9781506394817

79 Stickle, B., Hicks, M., Stickle, A., & Hutchison, Z. (2020). Porch pirates: Examining unattended package theft through crime script analysis. *Criminal Justice Studies, 33*(2), 79–95. https://doi.org/10.4324/9781003240280-7

80 Walsh, D.P. (1994). The obsolescence of crime forms. *Crime Prevention Studies, 2*, 149–163; Wilkins, L.T. (1964). *Social Deviance: Social Policy, Action, and Research*. London, UK: Tavistock.

81 Benson, M.L., & Simpson, S. (2018). *Understanding White-Collar Crime: An Opportunity Perspective* (3rd ed.). New York, NY: Routledge. https://doi.org/10.4324/9781315267609

82 Kates, G. (2019, March). Lori Loughlin and Felicity Huffman among dozens charged in college bribery scheme. CBS News. Retrieved from: https://www.cbsnews.com/news/college-admissions-scandal-bribery-cheating-today-felicity-huffman-arrested-fbi-2019-03-12/

83 Benson, M.L. & Madensen, T.D. (2007). Situational crime prevention and white-collar crime. In H.N. Pontell & G. Geis (Eds.), *International Handbook of White-Collar and Corporate Crime* (pp. 609–626). Dordrecht, The Netherlands: Kluwer Academic/Plenum. https://doi.org/10.1007/978-0-387-34111-8_31; Benson, M.L., Madensen, T.D., & Eck, J.E. (2009). White-collar crime from an opportunity perspective. In S. Simpson & D. Weisburd (Eds.), *The Criminology of White-Collar Crime* (pp. 175–193). New York, NY: Springer. https://doi.org/10.1007/978-0-387-09502-8_9

84 Benson, M.L. & Simpson, S. (2018). *Understanding White-Collar Crime: An Opportunity Perspective* (3rd ed.). New York, NY: Routledge. https://doi.org/10.4324/9781315267609

6
It's the Small Wins that Count

Jerry Sternin coined the term TBU: true but useless.[1] As a field director in the non-profit organization Save the Children, the Vietnamese government asked him to address childhood malnutrition in rural villages. But they gave him six months and limited funds.[2] To prepare for the task, he read as much from malnutrition researchers as possible. There was a consensus among these researchers that four social issues caused malnutrition: poverty, bad drinking water, poor sanitation, and limited education.[3] Sternin realized that although these experts' findings were true, they were useless.

Sternin was in a difficult situation. Millions of children were malnourished and if ending poverty, purifying water, installing full-scale sanitation systems, and educating people about nutrition in the next six months was the only solution, these children would continue to suffer.[4] This gave Sternin a sense of urgency; he did not have the luxury of instigating widespread change. Though these large-scale social issues needed to be addressed, Sternin knew he would not be the one to address them. Nevertheless, he could produce meaningful change if he re-thought the situation.

Sternin began by asking: were all children malnourished? The answer was no. He conducted a nutritional survey and found another example of the rule of the few: a few children were well-nourished,[5] and these

 DOI: 10.4324/9781003430155-8

children's families had the same income levels of other villagers.[6] These families made up what Sternin refers to as *positive deviants*. They are families "whose uncommon behaviors or practices enable them to outperform or find better solutions to pervasive problems than their neighbours with whom they share the same resource base".[7] These families were proof that children could avoid malnutrition even with the same resources as the other villagers. So, he started interviewing these families.

These interviews revealed two differences. First, he found that parents of well-nourished children fed them three to five smaller meals a day.[8] This differed from most families who fed their children two larger meals per day.[9] In both cases, the children were eating roughly the same amount of food. But the malnourished children receiving two large meals were not absorbing all the nutrients from each large meal. Consuming smaller amounts of food more times throughout the day helped them absorb more nutrients.[10] Second, compared to the other villagers, the families Sternin interviewed were feeding their children different free and readily available foods: shrimp and crab. Most villagers thought that free shrimp and crab were dangerous to young children's health.[11]

With these discoveries, Sternin set up community events where the positive deviants would teach others in their village how to forage for these foods and ways to cook them.[12] The program produced quick results. Within two weeks Sternin observed mothers adopting these new practices and seeing that their children were not getting sick. This reinforced the message and even more mothers began adopting these new ways. Sternin reported that "within two years, 80% of the children participating in the project were no longer malnourished".[13] Sternin's program cost very little and began reaping rewards almost immediately. This only worked because he ignored true but useless (TBU) findings and focused on simple, actionable solutions.

Addressing widescale social issues like poverty, access to drinking water and sanitation systems, and education are still important. But they require immense co-operation between major government agencies, vast sums of money, and community buy-in. These are issues that should be pursued but addressing them overlooks urgency. Addressing poverty may reduce gun homicides, for example, but while we are waiting for this to happen, many people will die. Instead, if we break social issues down into smaller, actionable problems, we can find practical solutions. These can be solved far more quickly and may not cost as much.

Local governments are often in similar predicaments as Sternin. They are frequently expected to address the root causes of crime: poverty, substance abuse, mental illness, homelessness, and more. These are serious social issues.

Local governments often turn to police as their primary responders. But think of the scale of the issues they are expecting the police to solve. Providing mental health services widely to those in need is an immense task. Finding homes and support for unhoused people will take great resources. Helping persons with substance use disorders with recovery will not happen overnight. But, like Sternin, when an officer is called, she must respond immediately. She will not be able to eliminate poverty, treat addiction, or provide counselling to everyone in need. These are much larger societal issues that need to be tackled. The police are often tasked with short-term stabilization until such widescale changes can take place.

In his paper *Small Wins*, Karl Weick took a similar approach to Sternin advocating for practitioners to break major societal issues down.[14] To Weick, looking at issues at a massive scale blocks our ability to make headway. At large scales, there are seldom solutions. Societal issues overwhelm us. They may be helpful to special interest groups raising money, or politicians running for office, or academics writing a social treatise. But for people trying to get something done on the ground, we need to view things differently. Weick argued that:

> To recast larger problems into smaller, less arousing problems, people can identify a series of controllable opportunities of modest size that produce visible results and that can be gathered into synoptic solutions.[15]

Weick's sage advice is also a cousin of the rule of the few: both tell us to focus, look for the small manageable chunks we can solve. If we can pull apart major societal issues into its smaller problems, we can find ways to solve each problem. As Weick pointed out, solving these small problems gives us the experience and enthusiasm to tackle the next problem.

Weick and Sternin's way of thinking could help with some common issues the police are frequently called upon to answer. But many of these issues are very large in scale and research on their underlying causes is often TBU. We call this the *solutions to crime are complicated* fallacy.[16] But there is still hope. By breaking down these issues into more manageable chunks, we can start addressing small problems. Let's look at a few examples for insight.

Small Wins to Re-Think Police Calls Involving Persons with Mental Illness

The calls for police service to deal with persons with mental health issues is an ongoing issue. This can seem like an insurmountable problem. These types of calls have been increasing every year.[17] Police also spend more time, on average, tending to such calls.[18] Events involving such people are not necessarily criminal. Dealing with people with mental illness is supposed to fall within the jurisdiction of medical and social services. However, new laws that moved toward major deinstitutionalization in the 1960s led to many persons with mental illness being released back into the community with insufficient care.[19]

Some of these individuals "frequently disrupt public order" so the public often default to calling the police to handle the situation.[20] Although many of the calls are for actions that are not criminal in nature, officers often struggle to manage them effectively.[21] They tried to deal with these individuals informally but found that many mental health facilities had strict admission requirements and would often refuse to admit certain people.[22] Consequently, many officers resorted to arrest, leading to larger proportions of mentally ill people in correctional facilities.[23] In fact, some estimates are now suggesting that "the largest psychiatric inpatient facilities in the USA today are actually jails"[24] and that about one in six inmates in jail has a mental illness.[25]

Clearly, this is a major societal issue that needs to be addressed. But much like Jerry Sternin's predicament in Vietnam, no single officer or group will be able to treat the mental health problems of those in need. Yet at the same time, when an officer is called, she must do something in the short term. To an officer on the ground, providing therapy, medication, or healthcare services are TBU. So, what can we do?

We could first start by breakdown this large "umbrella" term: calls involving person with mental health issues. There is an abundance of

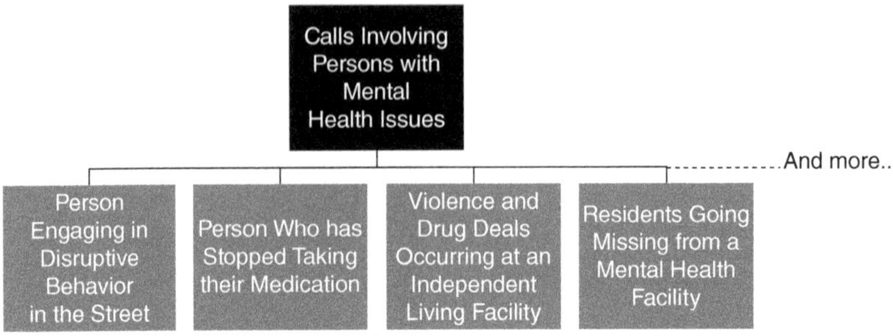

FIGURE 6.1 Examples of Police Calls for Service Involving People with Mental Illness

problems that would fit under this widespread term. For the purpose of illustration, let's consider four examples, shown in figure 6.1.

Example #1: Person Engaging in Disruptive Behavior in the Street

The first example is calls to respond to a person who is engaging in disruptive behavior in the street. A common occurrence is someone yelling in the streets. Again, while this is not inherently criminal, people do not appreciate the disruption and often call the police hoping to make the person stop. Research indicates that these types of calls tend to cluster in small areas of cities, often in city centers.[26] As mentioned before, with dwindling mental health resources and strict admissions requirements by facilities, officers often resorted to arrest to address calls for service of this type.[27]

More recently, police departments have been trying three strategies. They include: 1) *police-based specialized police response*, 2) *police-based specialized mental health response*, and 3) *mental health-based specialized mental health response*.[28] Police in Memphis, TN, developed the first strategy after the police killed a mentally ill person wielding a knife. To reduce the chances of more tragedies like this, the police department developed a Crisis Intervention Team (CIT). CIT is comprised of officers who received extra training in dealing with mentally ill persons.[29] Officers selected for the training carry out their regular patrol duties, but are the primary officers dispatched to calls involving people suspected of being mentally ill. Their job is to assure a safe outcome for the people involved. After the event, they serve as liaisons for these individuals within the mental health system.[30]

The second response—*police-based specialized mental health response*—involves the co-operation of medical and mental health services. This strategy employs mental health workers who are on-call for on-site and telephone consultations to officers.[31]

Lastly, the *mental health-based specialized mental health response* involves specific mobile units of mental health professionals who respond to calls in person when requested by the police.[32] In some cities, departments even have mobile units who patrol with officers for entire shifts. These patrol cars are dispatched specifically to calls reporting incidents with mentally ill persons and/or those exhibiting emotionally disturbed behavior.[33]

Clearly, providing mental health care to those in need is an ideal response. Officers working directly with those mental health professionals will likely lead to better responses and assistance to such individuals. For example, doctors could prescribe persons with schizophrenia medication that alleviates certain problems. However, this only works if the individuals continue to take their medication. If they do not take their medication, this creates a separate problem.

Example #2: Person Who Has Stopped Taking Their Medication

As described in the previous example, medication adherence among people with mental illness can be problematic. Many do not keep up with their medications. Some do not like taking them, some forget to take it regularly, some even sell their medications for alcohol or illicit substances.[34] Thus, working with those who have stopped taking their medication can pose an entirely different set of challenges for police.

A study in Chicago found that in nearly half of the police calls involving persons with mental illness, the individuals in question were prescribed psychiatric medication. Of those who had prescriptions, more than half of the calls involved someone who had stopped taking their medication.[35] Often, it is the same small group of people who the police respond to regarding such calls.[36]

Officers often report trying to avoid using arrests in these circumstances. The most common responses the police report using is to transport such persons to hospitals or mental health facilities. However, both of these responses only provide short-term solutions. If doctors can get patients back on their medication, the officers say it acts as a so-called "reset button" whereby the individuals become much more stable.[37] Once they are released back into the community, however, most eventually stop taking their medication again. This leads to the police being called again and the cycle starts over. Police have also reported frustrations with taking individuals to mental health clinics. These clinics usually turn patients away if they are intoxicated. If this occurs, then the transport officer is left with few options other than arrest and jail. Officers also report that while mental health facilities offer appointments with doctors, they are for appointments many months in the future.[38] This provides little support to these individuals and officers who need immediate attention.

Strategies to solve these problems are still ongoing. Two show some promise. The first involves a 'whole-of-family perspective' whereby practitioners try to get family members of the patients involved in aftercare.[39] Though mental health professionals can stabilize many patients and get them onto medications that can help normalize their symptoms, they need patients to continue taking their medication. Some believe that finding someone with a connection to the patient, such as a family member, can help with this process. Second, cities could develop mobile units of mental health professionals who tend to patients in the community, particularly in checking in to assure they are taking their medication. Some cities have mental health professionals patrol with police to help with calls involving persons with mental illness.[40] But some work may not have to be done with an officer. Checking in to see if someone has taken their medication that day, for example, could be done exclusively by mental health professionals.[41]

Example #3: Violence and Drug Deals at an Independent Living Facility

The third example—violence and drug dealing at an independent living facility—would require an entirely different response: a change in place management. Such examples are becoming more common because of the privatization of mental health services. As Gary Cordner explains:

> Many of today's community-based mental health facilities, especially group homes, are operated by private individuals or companies. To be sure, government-run mental health facilities can be

> inefficient, callous, and neglectful. However, private profit-making facilities introduce another issue—greed. Privately run facilities have an inherent incentive to cut expenses; this often translates into minimum staffing levels and low-paid staff, which in turn results in a facility that relies on the police to help manage patients/clients. As a result, police resources are wasted and people with mental illness do not get the quality of care that they deserve.[42]

This passage clearly indicates that proper place management could alleviate certain issues for police dealing with persons with mental illness. Yet, place management is seldom discussed in policing or research regarding mental health. Only a handful of examples exist, but they are showing promising results.

A case from the San Diego Police Department provides a good illustration of the third example and how effective good place management can be.[43] A low-income apartment complex in the city owned by absentee landlords was known to police and the community as a hotspot for drug dealing, prostitution, and gang activity. Although families primarily lived in the complex, the police found that an average of 2.66 calls were being generated from the property per month.

However, in early 1999 a surge in calls to an average of 12.6 per month at and around the complex became the norm. Upon investigation, the police learned that the owner had leased the property to a new landlord and its function and management had drastically changed to increase profits. The new landlord evicted all residents and converted the complex into an independent living facility for persons with mental illness. By law, such facilities were only supposed to be rented to persons who could live independently without care or supervision. These regulations were not being followed. Instead, the new landlord rented rooms to those in need of psychiatric care and medication. Moreover, he hired a property manager who was a "known felon with an extensive drug history" to manage the facility and dispense medications to its residents.[44]

Clearly the facility was violating several licensing rules, both medical and residential. The new landlord had promised the owner increased profits with less inputs by ignoring regulations and providing unsuitable living conditions to a vulnerable population.[45] To address these issues, the

San Diego Police Department partnered with community residents and threatened the owner with a civil lawsuit and injunction. They also alerted local government authorities who began inspecting the property and documenting numerous violations. This was sufficient to compel the owner to relocate the residents and sell the property to a more responsible owner. Police later reported that their calls for service at the location dropped from a high of 23 calls per month to only two, many of which were noise complaints for a new construction project that began in the area.[46]

Example #4: Residents Going Missing from a Mental Health Facility

A case from Lancashire, United Kingdom provides insight into the fourth example. Police were receiving numerous calls for mentally ill persons who were going missing from a small number of facilities. They responded by appointing liaison officers to work with the facilities and improve upon the physical features, security, and management of the places.[47] Interestingly, they also imposed a regulatory approach.[48] Specifically, they incentivized better place management by setting annual performance targets for missing persons for each facility. If a facility failed to meet them, the government would review their operating procedures and could revoke their "licenses and social service funding".[49]

Our examples demonstrate only a fraction of the many types of calls the police receive involving persons with mental illness. But they show how different small problems require different solutions. While some problems could best be solved by partnering with handlers, such as family members, others would be much better addressed through place management (see figure 6.2). Police calls for service involving persons with mental illness adhere to the rule of the few like everything else. Such calls cluster in small areas of cities.[50] The calls often involve the same few people.[51] Thus, being hyper-specific in who and what we focus on can go a long way in addressing problems.

These examples showed only one of many ways we could break the larger issue of "police calls involving persons with mental health issues" down into smaller problems in which solutions could be achieved. But this is not the only way of breaking things down. Another set of questions one could ask to break down problems is: how can we help those involved

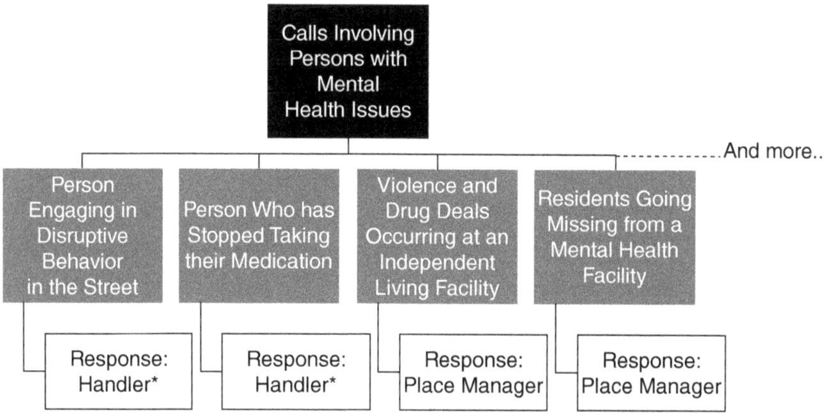

FIGURE 6.2 Responses to Police Calls for Service Involving People with Mental Illness

*NOTE: Not all mentally ill persons whose behavior falls under these examples have committed crimes. Thus, not all are offenders. We use the term "handler" simply to be consistent with the crime triangle to show the effectiveness of identifying a person with a connection to the mentally ill person who can assist them (e.g., get them to take their medication, go to appointments with mental health professionals, and so on).

with the problem and how can we prevent future people from becoming involved in the problem? We provide some examples of this in the next section to help illustrate how this can help.

Small Wins to Re-Think Homelessness

In his book, *Upstream: The Quest to Solve Problems Before They Happen*, Dan Heath describes a case study on homelessness from Rockford, Illinois. Heath was able to interview the mayor, Larry Morrissey, and some of his team who reduced homelessness in their city to "functional zero"* in less than a year.[52] Homelessness in the city had grown to epic proportions as a by-product of the 2008 recession. The economic crash eliminated thousands of jobs in a formerly prosperous city, a hub for manufacturing. The city's population plummeted as people left in search

* Heath uses the term "functional zero" because true zero is not possible. It is an unfortunate reality that new people become homeless each day. The city sought to design a system where placement could keep up with need/demand. Therefore, functional zero means the number of current homeless people is less than the number of people who are being housed through city programs.

of work elsewhere. Of those who remained, over one third of people held mortgages for homes that were now worth less than what they bought them for. Homelessness grew to the point that few held any hope that the city could come back from the crash.

Though Morrissey and his team had been trying to address homelessness for nine years, they never seemed to get ahead of it. But in 2014, he accepted the Mayor's Challenge, a federal government campaign to end veteran homelessness, from a colleague. In the months that followed, Morrissey and his team attended a training session organized by the Department of Housing and Urban Development (HUD). They reported it being a transformative experience that made them re-think solutions. They broke down their overall homelessness issues into smaller pieces and shifted their approach in each area.[53] We show this breakdown in figure 6.3.

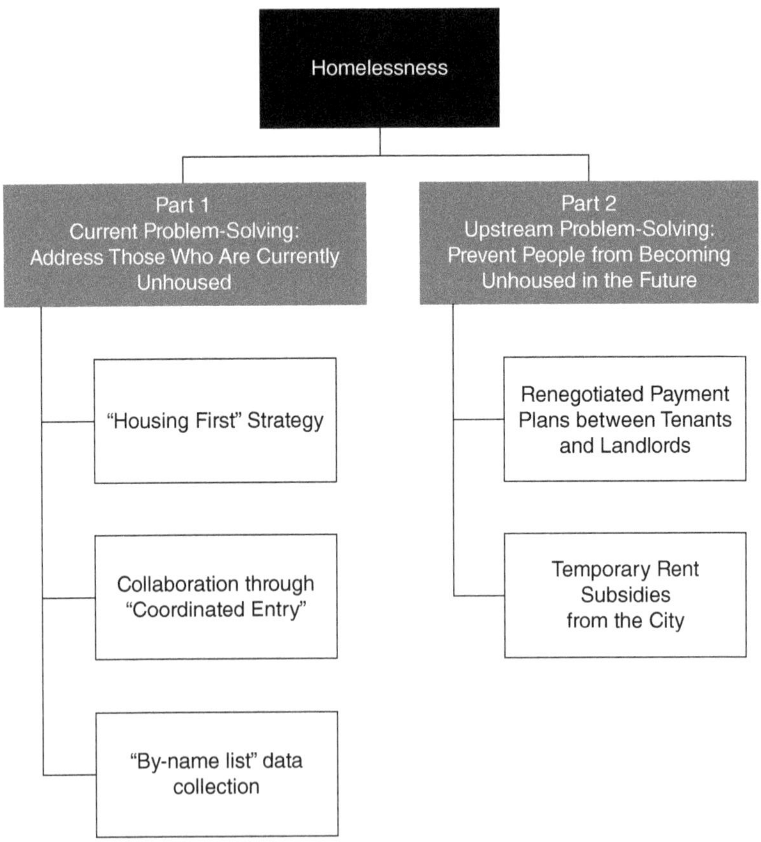

FIGURE 6.3 Re-Thinking Homelessness – A Case Study from Rockford, IL

To begin, Morrissey and his team realized they needed to separate their strategy into two parts. First, they needed to devise ways to help those who are currently homeless. Second, to maintain long-term benefit, they also needed to have ongoing programs in place to prevent people from becoming homeless in the future.

Part #1: Address Those Who Are Currently Homeless

In the currently homeless portion, they restructured three important parts of their intervention: strategy, collaboration, and data. The first involved a shift to a "housing first" strategy. Prior to their restructuring, all housing programs required unhoused people to earn their eligibility. Examples included completing substance abuse treatment, job training, or treatment for mental illness. If they could show success in this, they would then earn housing assistance. But the team realized that flipping the order of things could be more beneficial for everyone. Many people who have homes and stable lifestyles struggle to complete addiction treatment or hold a job. Having the added stress of having no home can make such problems even more difficult. So, they developed a "housing first" strategy.[54] That is, get unhoused people a home as soon as possible. With this stressor alleviated, they can then focus on completing treatment programs or getting a job, and likely with more success.

The second part of the intervention, collaboration, involved a shift to "coordinated entry".[55] Housing strategies, particularly in large cities, are complex and involve many programs. For example, a single city can have "supportive housing, transitional housing, shelters, and more" for unhoused people.[56] Each program can have different eligibility requirements and be confusing for those seeking services. With a coordinated entry approach, there was a single office where unhoused people were directed to. Using a single point of contact, that office could streamline the process and determine placement. The office could also prioritize who was in most need of the services.

The third part of the currently homeless portion involved a change in data collection. The city shifted from a "point in time" count of the unhoused population to a "by-name list".[57] In past years, the city deployed employees to conduct a census of unhoused people. They would station workers at all of the shelters in the city to count the number of people who passed through on a particular day. This approach was not ideal.

It generated little information about the individuals and how programs might be able to help them. It also did not include the people who were not present in shelters on that day nor the unsheltered people. So, the team shifted to a "by-name list". It consisted of a continually updated document with the names, histories, and last known location information of each unhoused person. The team compiled the list not only by connecting with people in shelters, but also by walking the streets and locating those who were not previously captured in their census.

These three changes had a profound impact on the city's ability to help the homeless population. Meetings between practitioners—including shelters, churches, soup kitchens, paramedics, police, and the fire department—became more productive. Instead of coming together and complaining about the seemingly unsolvable homelessness problem, they had specific people they could focus their discussions on. When housing became available, they could prioritize which unhoused person needed it most, which team member last saw the unhoused person, and who would be the best contact to work with the unhoused person to get them housing. Once conversations became about specific people, those involved could see how their efforts were benefitting specific people instead of working towards ambiguous goals. By December 2015, less than a year after they implemented their changes, Rockford housed 156 unhoused veterans and achieved functional zero.[58]

Part #2: Prevent People from Becoming Homeless in the Future

The Rockford team then began to tackle the second part of their efforts, the prevention of people becoming homeless in the future. Though housing many unhoused people was a big win for the city, there were always people at risk of becoming homeless. One of the most common ways this happens is through evictions. Rockford had one of the highest eviction rates in the country. In 2019, the city conducted a pilot program attempting to reduce evictions and ultimately keep people from becoming unhoused. They used two main approaches. The first involved a city agency acting as an intermediary between tenants and landlords if an eviction was imminent. This often involved negotiating a new payment plan for the tenant. The second was a program in which the city would provide a month or two of rent to help tenants get back on track and stay in their home. Not only did this help tenants in terms of job stability and mental well-being, but it was also more cost-effective than having to find new housing if they became unhoused. The team's preliminary figures estimated that the "pilot had decreased the number of people who became homeless due to eviction by 30%".[59]

This second part, the prevention of people becoming homeless in the future, is what Heath refers to as an upstream effort. It is an effort to stop a problem before it happens. Investing in the prevention of problems before they begin can not only be more beneficial to those entangled in the problem, but it can also be more cost effective in the long run. Thus, considering both current and upstream solutions can provide more benefit in the long-term.

Small Wins to Re-Think the Opioid Epidemic

We are beginning to see current and upstream strategies to address another common problem: opioid addiction. Recent research suggests that opioid use has been rising to staggering levels.[60] More people are using and overdosing on substances such as fentanyl and heroin. The issue is also reaching a wider demographic group. People from all ethnic groups, backgrounds, and social classes are engaging in opioid use. Moreover, individuals who are considered high-functioning members of society are also using opioids at record-setting rates. So how might we begin to address this issue?

Many opioid addiction responses fit into the current or upstream groups discussed in our previous homelessness example. That is, developing responses to help those who are currently using opioids will be very different from responses to prevent future people from becoming addicted to opioids. By breaking things down, it can make the overall goal of addressing the opioid epidemic. We limit our discussion to six examples, shown in figure 6.4. There are many more examples we could have included. For our purposes, we simply wanted to illustrate some of the smaller strategies that can be implemented that may collectively work to address the larger opioid addiction issue.

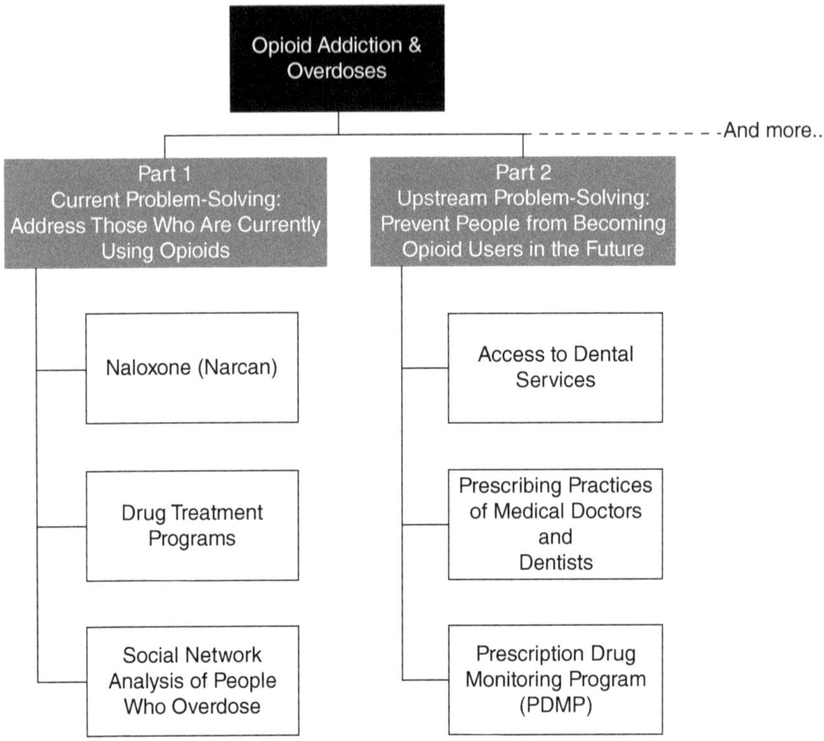

FIGURE 6.4 Re-Thinking Opioid Addiction with Current and Upstream Problem-Solving

Part #1: Address Those Who Are Currently Using Opioids

One of the most immediate responses we have developed is the medication naloxone, commonly referred to as Narcan. This is a nasal spray that can be administered by anyone to a person who has overdosed on opioids to block the effects of opioids. The treatment has saved countless lives by stabilizing those who have overdosed long enough to seek medical attention.[61] Though this medication has been instrumental in saving lives, it only provides temporary treatment. If a person survives the overdose, they can continue to use substances and may even overdose several more times. This is where more long-term treatment programs come in.

The second current response involves drug treatment programs. People can enter into drug treatment for many reasons. Some are compelled through court orders, some are pressured by family members, and others may willingly seek it out after a near death overdose experience. Voluntary, as opposed to compulsory, participation in programs is generally more effective at reducing substance use.[62] Many cities have rehabilitation clinics that can provide services to those with substance use disorders, and community programs can also offer support.

The small wins principle is at the core of many community treatment programs. As Karl Wieck describes:

> Alcoholics Anonymous has been successful in helping alcoholics, partly because it does not insist that they become totally abstinent for the rest of their lives. Although this is the goal of the program, alcoholics are told to stay sober one day at a time, or one hour at a time if temptation is severe. The impossibility of lifetime abstinence is scaled down to the more workable task of not taking a drink for the next 24 hours, drastically reducing the size of a win necessary to maintain sobriety.[63]

Though this quote is specific to Alcoholics Anonymous, many of the same principles guide Narcotics Anonymous programs. Practitioners need to make recovery manageable. If the goal seems impossible to achieve, many lose hope and struggle to continue with the program. Scaling down helps to keep people recovering from substance abuse disorder on track.

An emerging current tactic involves the identification of at-risk opioid users. This is the third example in part 1 of our figure. Researchers have been experimenting with social network analysis to provide help to people most at-risk of overdosing. Every person has a social network, that is a set of people who they are tied to. Ties can be through friendship, family, work, and so on. Some people have larger social networks that others. Certain people within your network will be closer to you than others. For example, a man's girlfriend will be closer to him than his girlfriend's best friend. Though both are in his network, the girlfriend is more closely tied to him. Researchers have applied these principles in crime research on gangs and organized crime.[64]

New researchers are experimenting with social network analysis using drug users. The idea is that when someone overdoses from opioids, the people closest in his network are likely also users who are at higher risk of overdosing as well. So, researchers have begun compiling social network data to identify these close contacts. They approach them, inform them that their friend nearly died (or did die) of an overdose and that they can provide them with help should they agree to it. Knowing someone close to you has been directly and negatively impacted is more likely to compel you to seek help. Though this technique is still in development, it is showing promise.[65] Other researchers are exploring the use of social media data to accomplish similar goals.[66]

Part #2: Prevent People From Becoming Opioid Users in the Future

Much like addressing homelessness in Rockford, addressing opioid addiction also benefits from developing upstream interventions. Even if we are able to help all current opioid users, the problem will persist because new people become addicted each day. So upstream strategies to reduce entry into the problem should also be used. There are many ways people become addicted to opioids. Again, for illustrative purposes we discuss a few examples to illustrate some smaller-scale solutions that can collectively lead to great benefit. Much like we discussed in the previous chapter, focusing on "how" as opposed to "why" may offer some insight into how we can solve the problem.

The first upstream response involves the availability of dental services. There is emerging evidence that people with dental issues seek assistance from a medical clinic, such as Urgent Care.[67] They often forgo seeing a dentist because none are practicing nearby or they do not have insurance to cover the expenses. The medical doctors who attend to these patients cannot give the patients proper treatment to fix the underlying problem. They are not trained in dentistry and thus cannot resolve the problem (e.g. removing a tooth). Often the doctors prescribe pain relieving drugs for temporary pain relief and refer the patients to a dentist. These over-the-counter medicines can range from acetaminophen (i.e., Tylenol) and nonsteroidal anti-inflammatory drugs (NSAID) to more powerful pain relievers such as oxycodone from the opioid/narcotic drug family. Yet, because of the accessibility and insurance barriers, many of these patients do not seek follow up treatment from a dentist. Once their prescription runs out, they return to a medical clinic for relief. If the doctor prescribes pain relieving drugs again and the underlying issue still remains unresolved, the patient's risk of becoming dependent on drugs increases. Many continue this cycle until doctors begin refusing to prescribe pharmaceutical pain relievers any longer. If they can no longer acquire the drugs through legitimate means, many turn to the illicit market for relief. So, one possible solution would be to focus on providing dental services to more people. This might require both an increase in the number of clinics that exist, particularly in rural areas, as well as access to insurance that helps patients cover the cost of seeing a dentist.

The second response involves the prescribing practices of dentists and medical doctors. Linked to the first response, prescribing narcotics without any treatment plan to address the underlying problem, such as the need to remove a tooth, will not solve the problem. There have also been numerous accounts of people getting injured or enduring surgery and needing pain relief as they recover. If prescriptions for the pain medication are not administered and monitored correctly, patients can become addicted. Policies and procedures have been developed over the years in the medical and dental professions to educate doctors on best practices. The American Dental Association, for example, has professional guidelines and educational resources for dentists to follow to prevent opioid abuse.[68] Thus, education and mandated policies and procedures can help address the problem.

The last example we will cover is Prescription Drug Monitoring Programs (PDMP). The idea behind these programs is to create a central state-level database that tracks information on all people who are prescribed controlled substances, such as opioids. Information can include the name of the patient, the medication prescribed and in what doses, the prescribing doctor(s), location, and so on.[69] Such programs have the potential to address two important problems. The first is doctor shopping. Some patients will see different doctors hoping to get multiple prescriptions for narcotics, particularly if they have become addicted or want to sell the pills on the streets. Seeing different doctors reduces the likelihood that the doctor would question or second-guess whether to give the prescription. But with the PDMP, doctors can look up patients to see whether any other doctors have already prescribed them controlled substances.

The second function PDMP can serve is to identify doctors who may be engaging in fraudulent practices. Though such cases are rare (remember the rule of the few rules all!), a small number of doctors have operated clinics where they prescribe unneeded narcotics. Often referred to as "pill mills", some doctors become involved in fraudulent prescribing as it can generate immense profits.[70] Thus, a PDMP can also identify doctors who are prescribing narcotics at higher-than-normal rates.

Research suggests that PDMP are not the best way to reduce substance abuse.[71] However, they may help reduce the number of people who may become addicted in the future and improve opioid prescribing.[72] Without a doctor willing to prescribe them the medication, they are less likely to consume the substances in excess and become addicted.

Why Small Wins Can Help Us Address Crime Problems

Let's revisit the theft of automobiles example we discussed in the previous chapter. We explained how measures like steering column locks and engine immobilizers effectively reduces thefts of automobiles. One reason for the success was because automotive manufacturers designed anti-theft devices to reduce a specific crime type: theft of automobiles. Instead of trying to tackle major societal issues like poverty or general theft, they broke the issue down into a specific problem. In this final section, we show you how theft of automobiles is one of many problems that falls under vehicle theft. You will see how narrowing your focus to a specific problem can generate progress.

To understand the scope of vehicle theft, we first need to define what it is. A vehicle is any machine that transports people or cargo. Thus, cars, trucks, buses, motorcycles, boats, trains, all-terrain vehicles (ATV), and snowmobiles are vehicles. That is a broad range of items, and a range that gets broader as companies develop new types of vehicles (e.g., trikes and electric scooters). Moreover, vehicle theft could involve either the taking *of* a vehicle itself or merely the removal of personal possessions *from* a vehicle.[73] Clearly, we need to break vehicle theft into solvable chunks.

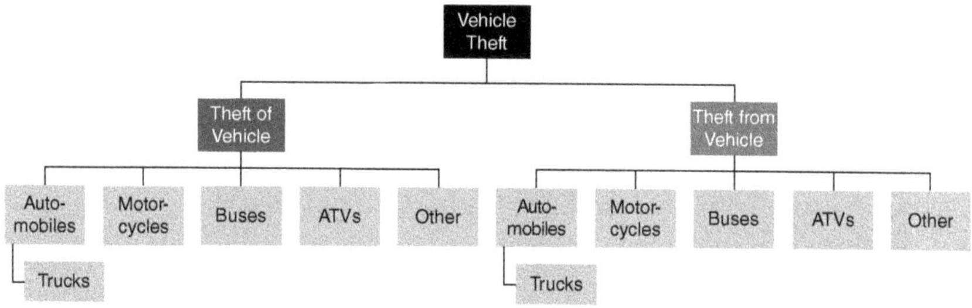

FIGURE 6.5 Types of Vehicles and Vehicle Thefts

Our first effort to break down this problem is in figure 6.5. To be most effective, crime prevention strategies must be crime type specific.[74] We can first divide the problem into two categories: theft of and theft from vehicles. Then we can subdivide each by the vehicle type. Immediately, you should intuit that some of these problems may be bigger than others. For example, theft from automobiles is probably a bigger problem than thefts from ATVs given the lack of carrying space within ATVs. If you think about where you live, you will guess that some of these problems are more likely to affect you than others.

Different problems, even if the problems appear similar, require different solutions. In the figure above we show a breakdown for thefts *of* vehicle. Different types of vehicles can require different interventions to reduce crime. What we might do to prevent thefts of automobiles will be different than what we do to reduce motorcycle thefts. The actions taken to reduce one type of vehicle theft may have no impact on another type of vehicle theft.

For example, in Germany from 1976 through 1985, the Federal government imposed helmet legislation in four stages. The intent was to get users of all motor-assisted cycles to use helmets within ten years. The original purpose of the legislation was to protect users of cycles, mopeds, and motorcycles in particular from harm if they were ever involved in a crash. But something else quite remarkable happened. The thefts of motorcycles dropped steadily for years afterwards.[75] Why did this happen?

Many offenders are opportunistic. So, if they came across an unsecure motorcycle with no one around, they would seize the opportunity to steal the bike. Before the helmet legislation, a thief on a stolen motorcycle did not stand out from legitimate riders on their motorcycles. After the helmet legislation took effect, a person operating a motorcycle without a helmet was vulnerable to police attention; helmet-less offenders had a greater risk of being caught on stolen motorcycles. Of course, a thief could wander about with a spare helmet, but this was awkward and unappealing to opportunistic offenders. So, their options became: steal a motorcycle without a helmet and risk a police stop, or stop stealing motorcycles. This explains why legislation designed to prevent motorcycle rider injuries drove down motorcycle theft. The legislation had no impact on automobile theft, or boat theft, or airplane theft. It was specific to one type of vehicle.[76]

Figure 6.6 gives only a partial view of ways we can reduce thefts of automobiles and motorcycles. We could have added additional branches in the figure denoting buses, boats, trains, ATVs, and so on. Each would have their own possible interventions as well. The point of the figure is to illustrate the different small wins that could be made if you break problems down. Perhaps you do not have enough clout to influence the manufacturing process of multi-billion-dollar automobile companies to change their product design. That's fine. Instead, you could focus on car owners and create a publicity campaign to encourage them to clean out their home garages to make room for their cars. Offenders are far less likely to steal a vehicle parked in a secure garage than one sitting unlocked on the street.

Let's turn our attention to thefts *from* vehicle. This involves offenders taking valuables—such as cellphones left behind or even car parts—from vehicles. We break this down in figure 6.7. For thefts from automobiles, car manufacturers can do far less. Once they sell their products to consumers, they have no control over how people use them. It would require a different set of responses. For instance, reminding car owners not to leave valuables, particularly in plain view, in their cars is an effective way to reduce the likelihood of theft from automobile. If an offender cannot see anything inside a car, they are less likely to break into it. So that response is on the part of the vehicle owner or user, not the manufacturer.

Another set of strategies involves the parking environment, such as parking lots and garages. Much research has gone into making parking facilities less crime prone. There are many strategies that can be used.

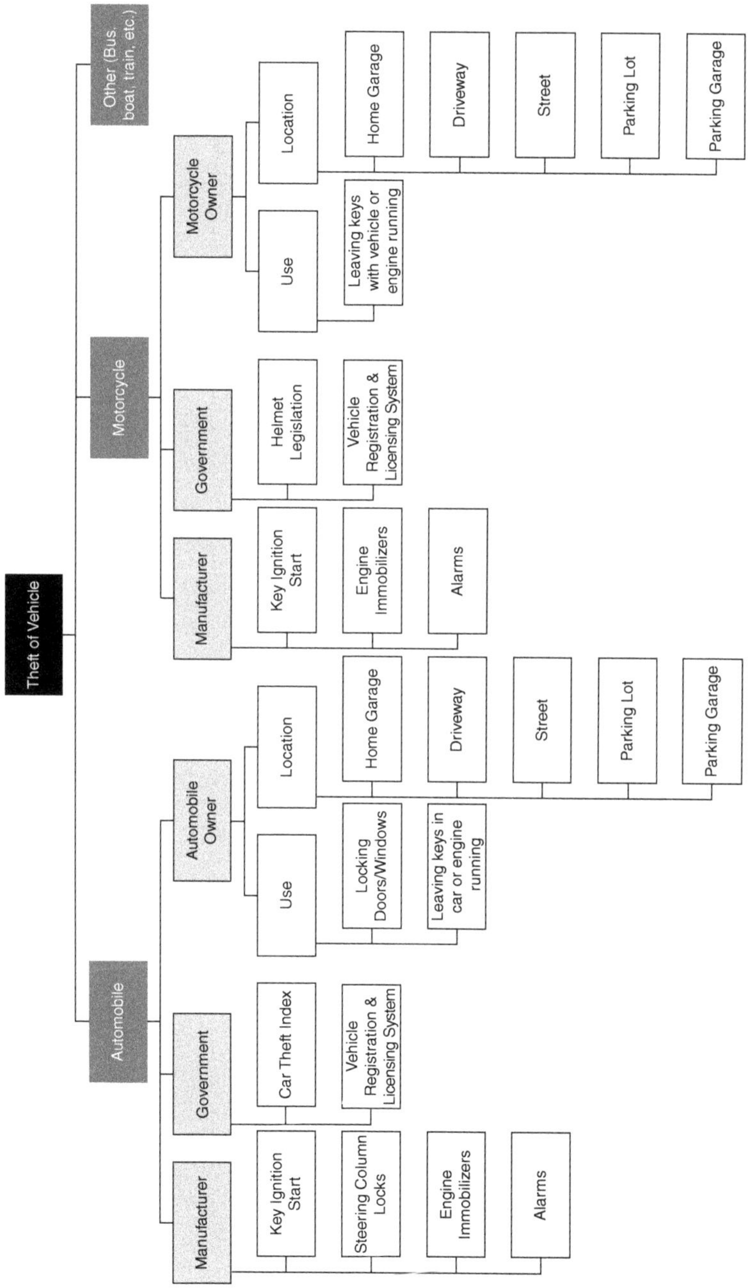

FIGURE 6.6 Breaking Down Responses to Thefts of Vehicles

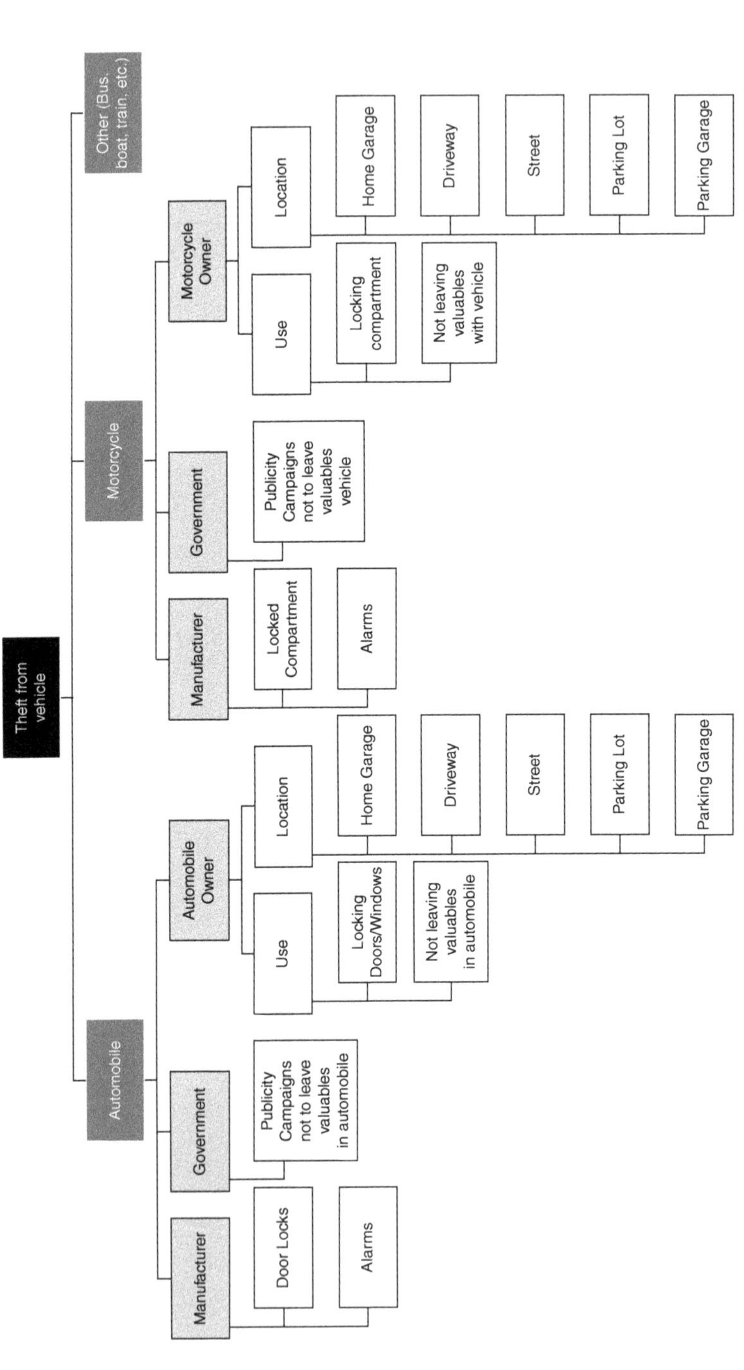

FIGURE 6.7 Breaking Down Responses to Thefts from Vehicle

For example, pay parking lots in which you must place the receipt on your dashboard showing the expiration time created crime problems. If you bought eight hours worth of parking and then put that receipt on your dash, it indicates to offenders that no one is likely to come back to the car for many hours. A simple solution to this problem was to print receipts that did not show expiration dates or times. Similarly, lots with parking attendants at kiosks when you exit were shown to decrease the incidence of thefts of automobiles but did little to prevent theft from vehicles.[77] Apps on smartphones are the newest way to avoid advertising the amount of parking time purchased.

As you can see from these examples, there are many crime problems related to vehicle theft. In fact, if we were to summarize vehicle theft it would look something like figure 6.8. Vehicle theft could be seen as an umbrella concept covering a wide range of problems across many vehicle types. We only briefly touched on problems with automobiles and motorcycles so only those are shown in detail. Again, we could have expanded this to also cover boats, planes, trains, airplanes, and so on. We also did not discuss any of the strategies used to curb joyriding or regulating automotive parts markets to reduce theft of vehicle parts.

So, the next time you think about tackling a crime issue, ask yourself, can we break it down into smaller parts? After all, which would you feel more confident in addressing: vehicle theft or reducing thefts from automobiles in one problematic parking garage? Tackling vehicle theft seems insurmountable. But addressing crime at a single, problematic parking garage may not be. As the rule of the few predicts; a tiny fraction of parking garages will experience most of the vehicle thefts. So, focusing on crime in those few problematic parking garages will have a substantial impact on vehicle theft overall. Developing many small solutions can then have a compounding effect too. For example, making parking garages more secure could reduce both actual thefts of vehicles and thefts from vehicles across multiple vehicle types. Solving smaller problems will help work towards a larger vehicle theft problem overall. Scaling down to specific problems can help us better understand problems and see simpler solutions that have long-term benefits.

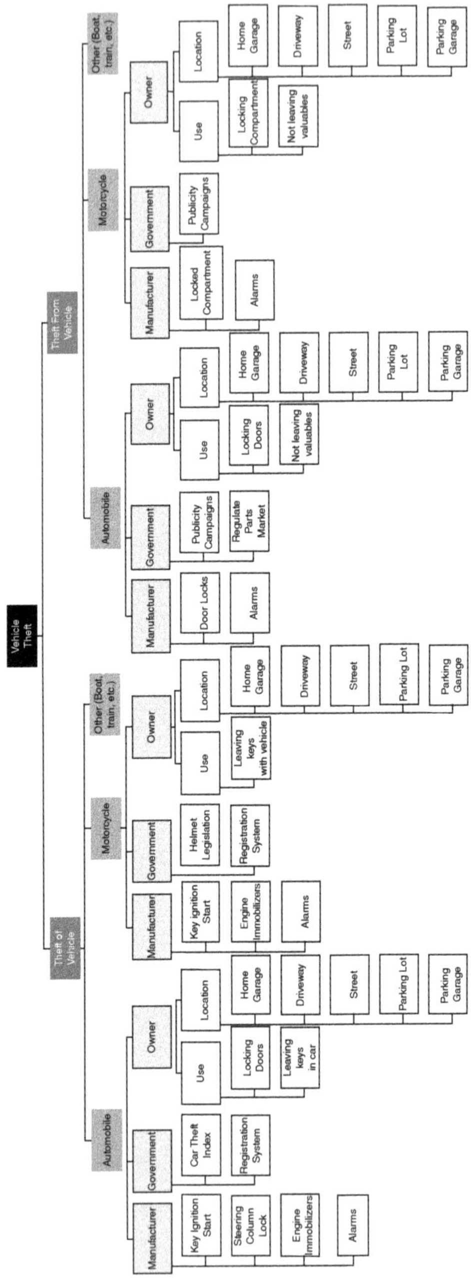

FIGURE 6.8 What Vehicle Theft Really Looks Like

Conclusions

Breaking down issues into smaller and manageable problems can not only lead to specific solutions, but they can also help us re-think problems. Achieving smaller goals can give us the momentum we need to address larger problems over time. Considering upstream causes forces us to consider why the problem exists in the first place. Considering positive deviants compels us to learn from those who have been thriving despite being in a difficult situation. As you have seen from these examples, though the police can play a role in addressing these problems, they are often not inherently police or crime problems. Moreover, the police do not always have the ability to solve them. This needs to come from a specific group of people in the community: place managers. In the next chapter, we show you the power place managers have to suppress crime on their properties. They are often an overlooked group in crime prevention. By understanding their role, you will discover they have a great deal of power to solve problems, and for the long-term.

Key Points

- Break issues down into smaller, solvable problems.
- If a few cause the most, focus on the few driving the problem.
- Avoid solutions that are TBU: true but useless.
- Consider both current and upstream problem-solving strategies.
- Ask: is there a smaller problem I can solve?

Notes

1 From page 58 of: Sternin, J. (2002). Positive deviance: A new paradigm for addressing today's problems today. *The Journal of Corporate Citizenship, 5*, 57–62. https://doi.org/10.9774/gleaf.4700.2002.sp.00007
2 Pascale, R., Sternin, J., & Sternin, M. (2010). *The Power of Positive Deviance: How Unlikely Innovators Solve The World's Toughest Problems.* Boston, MA: Harvard Business Press.
3 Sternin, J. (2002). Positive deviance: A new paradigm for addressing today's problems today. *The Journal of Corporate Citizenship, 5*, 57–62. https://doi.org/10.9774/gleaf.4700.2002.sp.00007; Sternin, J. & Choo, R. (2000, January–February). The power of positive deviancy: An effort to reduce malnutrition in Vietnam offers an important lesson about managing change. *Harvard Business Review*, 14–15.
4 Sternin, J. & Choo, R. (2000, January–February). The power of positive deviancy: An effort to reduce malnutrition in Vietnam offers an important lesson about managing change. *Harvard Business Review*, 14–15.

5 Pascale, R., Sternin, J., & Sternin, M. (2010). *The Power of Positive Deviance: How Unlikely Innovators Solve The World's Toughest Problems.* Boston, MA: Harvard Business Press.
6 Sternin, J. & Choo, R. (2000, January–February). The power of positive deviancy: An effort to reduce malnutrition in Vietnam offers an important lesson about managing change. *Harvard Business Review*, 14–15.
7 From page 58 of: Sternin, J. (2002). Positive deviance: A new paradigm for addressing today's problems today. *The Journal of Corporate Citizenship, 5*, 57–62. https://doi.org/10.9774/gleaf.4700.2002.sp.00007
8 Pascale, R., Sternin, J., & Sternin, M. (2010). *The Power of Positive Deviance: How Unlikely Innovators Solve The World's Toughest Problems.* Boston, MA: Harvard Business Press.
9 Sternin, J. & Choo, R. (2000, January–February). The power of positive deviancy: An effort to reduce malnutrition in Vietnam offers an important lesson about managing change. *Harvard Business Review*, 14–15.
10 Heath, C. & Heath, D. (2010). *Switch: How To Change Things When Change Is Hard.* New York, NY: Currency.
11 Sternin, J. (2002). Positive deviance: A new paradigm for addressing today's problems today. *The Journal of Corporate Citizenship, 5*, 57–62. https://doi.org/10.9774/gleaf.4700.2002.sp.00007
12 Pascale, R., Sternin, J., & Sternin, M. (2010). *The Power of Positive Deviance: How Unlikely Innovators Solve The World's Toughest Problems.* Boston, MA: Harvard Business Press.
13 From page 15 of: Sternin, J. & Choo, R. (2000, January–February). The power of positive deviancy: An effort to reduce malnutrition in Vietnam offers an important lesson about managing change. *Harvard Business Review*, 14–15.
14 Weick, K.E. (1984). Small wins: Redefining the scale of social problems. *American Psychologist, 39(*1), 40–49. https://doi.org/10.1037//0003-066x.39.1.40
15 From page 40 of: Weick, K.E. (1984). Small wins: Redefining the scale of social problems. *American Psychologist, 39(*1), 40–49. https://doi.org/10.1037//0003-066x.39.1.40
16 Linning, S.J., Carroll, T., Gerard, D., & Eck, J.E. (2024). Do solutions to crime need to be complicated? *Public Management, 106*(8), 36–39. https://icma.org/articles/pm-magazine/do-solutions-crime-need-be-complicated
17 Patch, P. & Arrigo, B. (1999). Police officer attitudes and use of discretion in situations involving the mentally ill: The need to narrow the focus. *International Journal of Law and Psychiatry, 22*(1), 23–35. https://doi.org/10.1016/s0160-2527(98)00014-4; Watson, A.C. & Angell, B. (2007). Applying procedural justice theory to law enforcement's response to persons with mental illness. *Psychiatric Services, 58*(6), 787–793. https://doi.org/10.1176/appi.ps.58.6.787
18 Famega, C.N., Frank, J., & Mazerolle, L. (2005). Managing police patrol time: The role of supervisor directives. *Justice Quarterly, 22*(4), 540–559. https://doi.org/10.1080/07418820500364692; Short, T.B., MacDonald, C., Luebbers, S., Ogloff, J.R., & Thomas, S.D. (2014). The nature of police involvement in mental health transfers. *Police Practice and Research, 15*(4), 336–348. https://doi.org/10.1080/15614263.2012.736717
19 Abramson, M.F. (1972). The criminalization of mentally disordered behavior: possible side-effect of a new mental health law. *Psychiatric Services, 23*(4), 101–105. https://doi.org/10.1176/ps.23.4.101; Murphy, G. (1986). Improving the police response to the mentally disabled. In *Washington, DC: Police Executive Research Forum.*

20 From page 166 of: Meehan, A.J. (1995). From conversion to coercion: The police role in medication compliance. *Psychiatric Quarterly, 66*(2), 163–184. https://doi.org/10.1007/bf02238862

21 Meehan, A.J. (1995). From conversion to coercion: The police role in medication compliance. *Psychiatric Quarterly, 66*(2), 163–184. https://doi.org/10.1007/bf02238862

22 Borum, R., Deane, M.W., Steadman, H.J., & Morrissey, J. (1998). Police perspectives on responding to mentally ill people in crisis: Perceptions of program effectiveness. *Behavioral Sciences & the Law, 16*, 393–405. https://doi.org/10.1002/(sici)1099-0798(199823)16:4%3C393::aid-bsl317%3E3.0.co;2-4; Green, T.M. (1997). Police as frontline mental health workers: The decision to arrest or refer to mental health agencies. *International Journal of Law and Psychiatry, 20*(4), 469–486. https://doi.org/10.1016/s0160-2527(97)00011-3; Teplin, L.A. & Pruett, N.S. (1992). Police as streetcorner psychiatrist: Managing the mentally ill. *International Journal of Law and Psychiatry, 15*(2), 139–156. https://doi.org/10.1016/0160-2527(92)90010-x

23 Lurigio, A.J. (2013). Forty years after Abramson: Beliefs about the criminalization of people with serious mental illnesses. *International Journal of Offender Therapy and Comparative Criminology, 57*(7), 763–765. https://doi.org/10.1177/0306624x13490142

24 From page 317 of: Reuland, M. (2010). Tailoring the police response to people with mental illness to community characteristics in the USA. *Police Practice and Research: An International Journal, 11*(4), 315–329. https://doi.org/10.1080/15614261003701723

25 Reuland, M. & Margolis, G.J. (2003). Police approaches that improve the response to people with mental illnesses: A focus on victims. *The Police Chief, 11*, 35–39. https://www.policechiefmagazine.org/police-approaches-that-improve-the-response-to-people-with-mental-illnesses-a-focus-on-victims/; Wolch, J. & Philo, C. (2000). From distributions of deviance to definitions of difference: past and future mental health geographies. *Health & Place, 6*(3), 137–157. https://doi.org/10.1016/s1353-8292(00)00019-8

26 Wood, J.D. & Beierschmitt, L. (2014). Beyond police crisis intervention: Moving "upstream" to manage cases and places of behavioral health vulnerability. *International Journal of Law and Psychiatry, 37*, 439–447. https://doi.org/10.1016/j.ijlp.2014.02.016

27 Borum, R., Deane, M.W., Steadman, H.J., & Morrissey, J. (1998). Police perspectives on responding to mentally ill people in crisis: Perceptions of program effectiveness. *Behavioral Sciences & the Law, 16*, 393–405. https://doi.org/10.1002/(sici)1099-0798(199823)16:4%3C393::aid-bsl317%3E3.0.co;2-4; Green, T.M. (1997). Police as frontline mental health workers: The decision to arrest or refer to mental health agencies. *International Journal of Law and Psychiatry, 20*(4), 469–486. https://doi.org/10.1016/s0160-2527(97)00011-3; Lurigio, A J. (2013). Forty years after Abramson: Beliefs about the criminalization of people with serious mental illnesses. *International Journal of Offender Therapy and Comparative Criminology, 57*(7), 763–765. https://doi.org/10.1177/0306624x13490142; Teplin, L.A. & Pruett, N.S. (1992). Police as streetcorner psychiatrist: Managing the mentally ill. *International Journal of Law and Psychiatry, 15*(2), 139–156. https://doi.org/10.1016/0160-2527(92)90010-x

28 Deane, M.W., Steadman, H.J., Borum, R., Veysey, B.M., & Morrissey, J.P. (1999). Emerging partnerships between mental health and law enforcement. *Psychiatric Services, 50*(1), 99–101. https://doi.org/10.1176/ps.50.1.99

29 Cordner, G. (2006). *People with Mental Illness* (1st ed.). Problem-Oriented Guides for Police Problem-Specific Guides Series No. 40; Corder, G., Scott, M.S., & Sanchez, M.J. (2022). *People with Mental Illness* (2nd ed.). Problem-Oriented Guides for Police Problem-Specific Guides Series No. 40. Retrieved from: https://popcenter.asu.edu/content/people-mental-illness-2nd-edition

30 Reuland, M. (2010). Tailoring the police response to people with mental illness to community characteristics in the USA. *Police Practice and Research: An International Journal, 11*(4), 315–329. https://doi.org/10.1080/15614261003701723

31 Reuland, M.M. (2004). *A Guide to Implementing Police-Based Diversion Programs for People with Mental Illness.* Delmar, NY: Technical Assistance and Policy Analysis Center for Jail Diversion.

32 Deane, M.W., Steadman, H.J., Borum, R., Veysey, B.M., & Morrissey, J.P. (1999). Emerging partnerships between mental health and law enforcement. *Psychiatric Services, 50*(1), 99–101. https://doi.org/10.1176/ps.50.1.99

33 Wiebe, D. (2016). *Vancouver Police Mental Health Strategy: A Comprehensive Approach for a Proportional Police Response to Persons Living With Mental Illness.* Vancouver, BC: Vancouver Police Department. Retrieved from: https://vpd.ca/wp-content/uploads/2021/06/mental-health-strategy.pdf

34 Wood, J.D. & Beierschmitt, L. (2014). Beyond police crisis intervention: Moving "upstream" to manage cases and places of behavioral health vulnerability. *International Journal of Law and Psychiatry, 37*, 439–447. https://doi.org/10.1016/j.ijlp.2014.02.016

35 Watson, A.C. & Wood, J.D. (2017). Everyday police work during mental health encounters: A study of call resolutions in Chicago and their implications for diversion. *Behavioral Science & The Law, 35*, 442–455. https://doi.org/10.1002/bsl.2324

36 Watson, A.C. & Wood, J.D. (2017). Everyday police work during mental health encounters: A study of call resolutions in Chicago and their implications for diversion. *Behavioral Science & The Law, 35*, 442–455. https://doi.org/10.1002/bsl.2324; Wood, J.D. & Beierschmitt, L. (2014). Beyond police crisis intervention: Moving "upstream" to manage cases and places of behavioral health vulnerability. *International Journal of Law and Psychiatry, 37*, 439–447. https://doi.org/10.1016/j.ijlp.2014.02.016

37 From page 449 of: Watson, A.C. & Wood, J.D. (2017). Everyday police work during mental health encounters: A study of call resolutions in Chicago and their implications for diversion. *Behavioral Science & The Law, 35*, 442–455. https://doi.org/10.1002/bsl.2324

38 Wood, J.D., Watson, A.C., & Barber, C. (2020). What can we expect of police in the face of deficient mental health systems? Qualitative insights from Chicago police officers. *Journal of Psychiatric Mental Health and Nursing, 28*, 28–42. https://doi.org/10.1111/jpm.12691

39 From page 453 of: Watson, A.C. & Wood, J.D. (2017). Everyday police work during mental health encounters: A study of call resolutions in Chicago and their implications for diversion. *Behavioral Science & The Law, 35*, 442–455. https://doi.org/10.1002/bsl.2324

40 Wiebe, D. (2016). *Vancouver Police Mental Health Strategy: A Comprehensive Approach for a Proportional Police Response to Persons Living With Mental Illness.* Vancouver, BC: Vancouver Police Department. Retrieved from: https://vpd.ca/wp-content/uploads/2021/06/mental-health-strategy.pdf

41 Wood, J.D. & Beierschmitt, L. (2014). Beyond police crisis intervention: Moving "upstream" to manage cases and places of behavioral health vulnerability. *International Journal of Law and Psychiatry, 37*, 439–447. https://doi.org/10.1016/j.ijlp.2014.02.016

42 From page 9 of: Cordner, G. (2006). *People with Mental Illness* (1st ed.). Problem-Oriented Guides for Police Problem-Specific Guides Series No. 40.
43 San Diego Police Department (2000). *The Question of Independent Living*. Submission for the Herman Goldstein Award for Excellence in Problem-Oriented Policing. Retrieved from: http://www.popcenter.org/library/awards/goldstein.cfm?browse=abstracts&year=2000
44 From page 2 of: San Diego Police Department (2000). *The Question of Independent Living*. Submission for the Herman Goldstein Award for Excellence in Problem-Oriented Policing. Retrieved from: http://www.popcenter.org/library/awards/goldstein.cfm?browse=abstracts&year=2000
45 Cordner, G. (2006). *People with Mental Illness* (1st ed.). Problem-Oriented Guides for Police Problem-Specific Guides Series No. 40.
46 San Diego Police Department (2000). *The Question of Independent Living*. Submission for the Herman Goldstein Award for Excellence in Problem-Oriented Policing. Retrieved from: http://www.popcenter.org/library/awards/goldstein.cfm?browse=abstracts&year=2000
47 Lancashire Constabulary (2004). Finding missing persons: Who's responsible for whom? Presented at the 15th Annual Problem-Oriented Policing, Conference, Charlotte, North Carolina, as cited in Cordner, G. (2006). *People with Mental Illness* (1st ed.). Problem-Oriented Guides for Police Problem-Specific Guides Series No. 40.
48 Eck, J.E. (2018). Regulation for high-crime places: Theory, evidence, and principles. *The Annals of the American Academy of Political and Social Science, 679*(1), 106–120. https://doi.org/10.1177/0002716218778764; Eck, J.E. & Eck, E.B. (2012). Crime place and pollution. *Criminology & Public Policy, 11*(2), 281–316. https://doi.org/10.1111/j.1745-9133.2012.00809.x; Farrell, G. & Roman, J. (2006). Crime as pollution: Proposal for market-based incentives to reduce crime externalities. In K. Moss & M. Stephens (Eds.), *Crime Reduction and the Law* (pp. 14–33). London, UK: Routledge. https://doi.org/10.4324/9780203696842
49 From page 37 of: Cordner, G. (2006). *People with Mental Illness* (1st ed.). Problem-Oriented Guides for Police Problem-Specific Guides Series No. 40.
50 Koziarski, J. (2021). Examining the spatial concentration of mental health calls for police service in a small city. *Policing: A Journal of Policy and Practice, 15*(2), 1011–1028. https://doi.org/10.1093/police/paaa093; Vaughan, A.D., Hewitt, A.N., Andresen, M.A., & Brantingham, P.L. (2016). Exploring the role of the environmental context in the spatial distribution of calls-for-service associated with emotionally disturbed persons. *Policing: A Journal of Policy and Practice, 10*(2), 121–133. https://doi.org/10.1093/police/pav040; Wood, J.D. & Beierschmitt, L. (2014). Beyond police crisis intervention: Moving "upstream" to manage cases and places of behavioral health vulnerability. *International Journal of Law and Psychiatry, 37*, 439–447. https://doi.org/10.1016/j.ijlp.2014.02.016
51 Watson, A.C. & Wood, J.D. (2017). Everyday police work during mental health encounters: A study of call resolutions in Chicago and their implications for diversion. *Behavioral Science & the Law, 35*, 442–455. https://doi.org/10.1002/bsl.2324 ; Wood, J.D., & Beierschmitt, L. (2014). Beyond police crisis intervention: Moving "upstream" to manage cases and places of behavioral health vulnerability. *International Journal of Law and Psychiatry, 37*, 439–447. https://doi.org/10.1016/j.ijlp.2014.02.016; Wood, J.D., Watson, A.C., & Barber, C. (2020). What can we expect of police in the face of deficient mental health systems? Qualitative insights from Chicago police officers. *Journal of Psychiatric Mental Health and Nursing, 28*, 28–42. https://doi.org/10.1111/jpm.12691

52 From page 95 of: Heath, C. (2020). *Upstream: The Quest to Solve Problems Before They Happen*. New York, NY: Avid Reader Press.
53 Heath, C. (2020). *Upstream: The Quest to Solve Problems Before They Happen*. New York, NY: Avid Reader Press.
54 From page 92 of: Heath, C. (2020). *Upstream: The Quest to Solve Problems Before They Happen*. New York, NY: Avid Reader Press.
55 From page 92 of: Heath, C. (2020). *Upstream: The Quest to Solve Problems Before They Happen*. New York, NY: Avid Reader Press.
56 From page 93 of: Heath, C. (2020). *Upstream: The Quest to Solve Problems Before They Happen*. New York, NY: Avid Reader Press.
57 From page 93 of: Heath, C. (2020). *Upstream: The Quest to Solve Problems Before They Happen*. New York, NY: Avid Reader Press.
58 Heath, C. (2020). *Upstream: The Quest to Solve Problems Before They Happen*. New York, NY: Avid Reader Press.
59 From page 96 of: Heath, C. (2020). *Upstream: The Quest to Solve Problems Before They Happen*. New York, NY: Avid Reader Press.
60 Mattson, C.L., Tanz, L.J., Quinn, K., Kariisa, M., Patel, P., & Davis, N.L. (2021). Trends and geographic patterns in drug and synthetic opioid overdose deaths — United States, 2013–2019. *Morbidity and Mortality Weekly Report, 70*, 202–207. https://doi.org/10.15585/mmwr.mm7006a4
61 Chimbar, L. & Moleta, Y. (2018). Naloxone effectiveness: a systematic review. *Journal of Addictions Nursing, 29*(3), 167–171. https://doi.org/10.1097/jan.0000000000000230
62 Werb, D., Kamarulzaman, A., Meacham, M.C., Rafful, C., Fischer, B., Strathdee, S.A., & Wood, E. (2016). The effectiveness of compulsory drug treatment: a systematic review. *International Journal of Drug Policy, 28*, 1–9. https://doi.org/10.1016/j.drugpo.2015.12.005
63 From page 42 of: Weick, K.E. (1984). Small wins: Redefining the scale of social problems. *American Psychologist, 39(*1), 40–49. https://doi.org/10.1037//0003-066x.39.1.40
64 Diviák, T. (2018). Sinister connections: How to analyse organised crime with social network analysis? *Acta Universitatis Carolinae Philosophica et Historica, 24*(2), 115–135. https://doi.org/10.14712/24647055.2018.7; Green, B., Horel, T., Papachristos, A.V. (2017). Modeling contagion through social networks to explain and predict gunshot violence in Chicago, 2006 to 2014. *JAMA Internal Medicine, 177*(3), 326–333. https://doi.org/10.1001/jamainternmed.2016.8245; Papachristos, A.V., Braga, A.A., & Hureau, D.M. (2012). Social networks and the risk of gunshot injury. *Journal of Urban Health, 89*, 992–1003. https://doi.org/10.1007/s11524-012-9703-9; Papachristos, A.V. & Wildeman, C. (2012, September 19). Social networks and risk of homicide victimization in an African American community. Available at SSRN: https://ssrn.com/abstract=2149219 or http://dx.doi.org/10.2139/ssrn.2149219; Piquette J.C., Smith C.M., & Papachristos A.V. (2014) Social Network Analysis of Urban Street Gangs. In: G. Bruinsma & D. Weisburd (Eds.), *Encyclopedia of Criminology and Criminal Justice*. Springer, New York, NY. https://doi.org/10.1007/978-1-4614-5690-2_240
65 DeMio, T. (2022, Sept. 21). Cincinnati opioid addiction response strategy focuses on those most vulnerable to overdose. Cincinnati Enquirer. Retrieved from: https://www.cincinnati.com/in-depth/news/2022/09/22/cincinnati-opioid-overdoses-addiction-hotspots-medical-response/7777018001/
66 Zhang, Y., Fan, Y., Ye, Y., Li, X., & Winstanley, E.L. (2018). Utilizing social media to combat opioid addiction epidemic: Automatic detection of opioid users from Twitter. Association for the Advancement of Artificial Intelligence: The Workshops of the Thirty-Second AAAI Conference on Artificial Intelligence, 538–545.

67 Baghaie, H., Kisely, S., Forbes, M., Sawyer, E., & Siskind, D. J. (2017). A systematic review and meta-analysis of the association between poor oral health and substance abuse. *Addiction, 112*(5), 765–779. https://doi.org/10.1111/add.13754; Paisi, M., Witton, R., & Plessas, A. (2021). Is there an association between drug use and oral health conditions? *Evidence-Based Dentistry, 22*(1), 46–47. https://doi.org/10.1038/s41432-021-0158-2
68 American Dental Association (2021). Preventing opioid abuse. Retrieved from: https://success.ada.org/en/wellness/preventing-opioid-abuse
69 Patrick, S.W., Fry, C.E., Jones, T.F., & Buntin, M.B. (2016). Implementation of prescription drug monitoring programs associated with reductions in opioid-related death rates. *Health Affairs, 35*(7), 1324–1332. https://doi.org/10.1377/hlthaff.2015.1496
70 ABC News (2020, March). 2 doctors charged in Montgomery county pill mill scheme. Retrieved May 25, 2020 from: https://6abc.com/2-doctors-charged-in-montco-pill-mill-scheme/6001195/; Department of Justice (2016, September). Alabama pill mill doctor charged with illegal prescribing and health care fraud. Department of Justice: Office of Public Affairs. Retrieved from: https://www.justice.gov/opa/pr/alabama-pill-mill-doctor-charged-illegal-prescribing-and-health-care-fraud; Eil, P. (2017, July 5). The pill mill that ravaged Portsmouth. Cincinnati Magazine. Retrieved from: https://www.cincinnatimagazine.com/features/pill-mill-portsmouth/
71 Paulozzi, L.J., Kilbourne, E.M., & Desai, H.A. (2011). Prescription drug monitoring programs and death rates from drug overdose. *Pain Medicine, 12*(5), 747–754. https://doi.org/10.1111/j.1526-4637.2011.01062.x
72 Rhodes, E., Wilson, M., Robinson, A., Hayden, J.A., & Asbridge, M. (2019). The effectiveness of prescription drug monitoring programs at reducing opioid-related harms and consequences: a systematic review. *BMC Health Services Research, 19*(1), 784. https://doi.org/10.1186/s12913-019-4642-8
73 Clarke, R.V. & Harris, P.M. (1992). Auto theft and its prevention. *Crime and Justice, 16*, 1–54. https://doi.org/10.1086/449203
74 Felson, M. and Clarke, R.V. (1998). Opportunity Makes the Thief: Practical Theory for Crime Prevention. Home Office Police Research Series, Paper 98. Retrieved from: https://popcenter.asu.edu/sites/g/files/litvpz3631/files/opportunity_makes_the_thief.pdf ; Shen, J-L. & Linning, S.J. (2025). Direct and indirect situational crime prevention: Using the COSTS criteria to improve interventions. *Security Journal, 38*, 60. https://doi.org/10.1057/s41284-025-00507-y
75 Mayhew, P., Clarke, R.V., & Elliott, D. (1989). Motorcycle theft, helmet legislation and displacement. *The Howard Journal of Criminal Justice, 28*(1), 1–8.
76 Mayhew, P., Clarke, R. V., & Elliott, D. (1989). Motorcycle theft, helmet legislation and displacement. *The Howard Journal of Criminal Justice, 28*(1), 1–8.
77 Webb, B. & Brown, R. (2017). Preventing vehicle crime. In N. Tilley & A. Sidebottom (Eds.), *Handbook of Crime Prevention and Community Safety*, 2nd edition (pp. 354–381). New York, NY: Routledge. https://doi.org/10.4324/9781315724393-16

7

The Power of Place Managers

Consider the six examples we described in earlier chapters: the Creston apartments problem, the facial glass injury problem, the gasoline drive-off problem, the Walmart problem, the smart phone robbery problem, and the Barksdale Market problem. What was the one critical factor in the solutions to these problems? Place managers did the work. In the Creston apartments problem, the apartment owners relocated tenants and demolished the building. In the facial glass injury problem, the bar owners changed how they served drinks. In the gasoline drive-off problem, the gas station owners changed how customers pay for gasoline. In the Walmart problem, the store owners established specific videogame payment policies. In the smart phone robbery problem, the product manufacturers added kill switch technologies to phones. In some cases, crime declines involved a change in ownership. At the Barksdale Market, crime declined once a new owner took over the property.

In each case, the place managers had to be replaced or prompted to act. In no case did residents' actions solve the problems and although police facilitated actions that solved the problems, the solutions only occurred when the owners acted. In this chapter we dive into place management. We explain who place managers are, where they get their powers to control crime, and how they use these powers at and around their properties.

 DOI: 10.4324/9781003430155-9

Place Managers: The Overlooked Shapers of Communities

Recall, we define the term *places* to mean property parcels.[1] These places have established boundaries and identifiable owners.[2] Property parcels have property titles, or deeds, which specify who owns the property, the legal rights given to the owner, and any restrictions that must be followed.[3] These owners are responsible for complying with local, state, and Federal rules: zoning, environmental regulations, health and safety codes, and many more. If you have ever purchased a home, you will be familiar with this. You are the place manager of your home. You would have signed legal documents specifying the boundaries of your property, what you can and cannot build on the property (e.g., residential vs. commercial building), how tall any structures can be, how close the building(s) can be to the street, and so on. This prevents people from building a 27-story high-rise on a rural lakefront property that blocks the neighbors' view. Similarly, it prevents a company from building a commercial structure, such as a chemical plant, in the middle of a suburban residential area.

The legal powers given to property owners are a bundle of rights which allow them to dictate much of what occurs on their property.[4] For instance, if you own your home, you have the right to ban other people from entering your home. You have the right to make physical changes to your home, but others do not; you could take legal action against anyone who alters your home without your consent. This can be anything from a person painting graffiti on your house to changing the locks on your doors. You, as the property owner, are the only person who has the authority to control what happens on the property that you own.[5]

Everywhere we go, we use land owned by someone else. When we shop, we tread upon a floor owned by the store's proprietor. When we drink at a bar, we sit in a room owned by the bar's owner. When we attend school, we learn in a setting owned by a school board. When we worship at a place, the building and grounds are owned by the religious institution. If we rent an apartment, we rent a unit in a building owned by the landlord. Public places are also owned, usually by a government. National parks, for example, are owned by Federal governments while local parks are usually owned by municipal governments. Even vacant buildings have owners. Though the owners have neglected the property, their names are still on the title making them legally responsible for the property. This means that all places have someone or an organization who is legally responsible for them. These people or organizations are place managers too.

Recall, that place managers are one of the three controllers in the crime triangle. The other two are handlers,[6] whose primary concern is to keep offenders out of trouble, and guardians,[7] whose primary concern is to protect targets. Place managers include everyone who has legal authority to exercise control over a place.[8] The most important place managers are owners. The owner may be a person, partnership, business, non-profit non-government organization, religious organization, college or university, or government.[9] Sometimes the owners delegate place management responsibilities to others. Store employees are an example of place managers if the owner has delegated control to them. Similarly, if someone decides to purchase an apartment building, she could hire a property management company to run the property and act as a place manager. Though she owns the property, she delegates tasks like screening potential tenants, collecting rent each month, and carrying out the maintenance to the property management company.

Place managers are primarily concerned with the smooth functioning of a place.[10] If a place manager is running a business, for example, she wants to assure that everything is operational, customers are satisfied, and profits are earned. If crime does not occur at the place, it is unlikely that the place manager will take any action to address crime. The rule of the few reminds us that most places experience no crime. So, most place managers do not concern themselves with crime prevention because they do not have to.

If crimes begin occurring at a place, the manager can do one of two things. The first and most common response is to make changes to the functioning of the place to suppress crime. For example, if thieves start trying to acquire change at a coffee shop by paying for low-value items using counterfeit $100 bills, the owner of the coffee shop can create a store policy to only accept bills of $20 or less. The second and less likely response is not to act. Some place managers do not know how to solve the problem, so they do nothing. In rare cases, a place manager might benefit from crime. Thus, he may turn a blind eye to what is happening. For example, the owner of a metal recycling center may knowingly accept stolen copper pipes and wire.[11]

Property owners can be held legally accountable for what happens on their property in civil court. For example, victims can file premise liability suits against the owners of property in which they experienced harm.[12] Similarly, prosecutors can file nuisance abatement suits against property owners whose places are being used for crime.[13] If civil lawsuits can be leveraged against property owners, then owners are considered responsible for their property under the eyes of the law. This has important implications for crime prevention. So, the next logical question to ask is, what do place managers do? And what are they responsible for? The ORCA framework has these answers.

What Place Managers Do?

All place managers enact four functions as part of the management of their property. These are specified in Tamara Madensen's ORCA framework.[14] It shows that place managers have the authority to:

Organize space
Regulate conduct
Control access
Acquire resources

The first function is the *organization of space*. All place managers control the physical setting of their places. They begin by deciding where they want their place. A prospective ice cream shop owner, for example, will likely seek out properties near beaches, swimming pools, or parks as opposed to properties in industrial areas of cities. Prospective home buyers do the same when looking for a new home. They usually consider neighborhood characteristics such as schools, nearby amenities, and duration of their commute to work. Once a place manager owns a property, she has full authority to decide its physical layout and appearance. This can include where the entrance and exit are located and the configuration of internal space. A homeowner, for example, may decide to knock out a wall between the living and dining rooms to create a more open-concept space. A bar owner can decide whether the bar should be at the front, side, or back of the establishment and where to place the dance floor or stage.[15]

Decisions about the organization of space are often used to increase profits. For example, you have probably heard that grocery stores deliberately place items like milk in the back of their stores so that you must walk past hundreds of other items that may entice you while on your quest for milk. Food manufacturers pay a premium for their products to be placed at eye-level on shelves as opposed to the top or bottom shelves that customers might overlook. These decisions influence customer behavior.

Decisions about the organization of space can also be made to influence potential criminal behavior of those who use the place too. For instance, a bar owner may purchase a bar with two bathrooms located down a dark hallway at the back of the establishment. To reduce potential harassment or feelings of unsafety for women, he could improve the lighting in the hallway and designate the bathroom closest to the public area of the bar for women and require men to use the bathroom further down the hall. A store owner can place her checkout counter near the exit so that more employees are present to stop potential shoplifters trying to make it out of the store with stolen goods.

Similarly, to reduce shoplifting, a convenience store owner could reconfigure the aisles so that employees can always see patrons (figure 7.1). This increases surveillance of the goods in the store and increases the risk that potential shoplifters will get caught if trying to steal something.

The second place management function is the *regulation of conduct*. This involves the ways place managers encourage desired behaviors and discourage unwanted behaviors.[16] For example, libraries want to encourage quiet, non-disruptive behaviors so that patrons can read or study without distraction. Sports arenas, on the other hand, play very loud music, sell alcohol, and have announcers encourage spectators to make a lot of noise to cheer on their favorite team. Similarly, nightclubs serve alcohol and play loud music to encourage their patrons to dance.

Place managers regulate conduct several ways. The most common are to establish a set of rules, post signs indicating clear expectations, and engage site users in rule maintenance. The "no shoes, no shirt, no service" is the epitome of this ORCA component. Place managers can communicate expectations they have to any place users. Sit down restaurants, for example, configure their space to signal that patrons will eat first and pay after their meal. Fast food restaurants, on the other hand, regulate conduct by requiring customers pay for their food before receiving it. Place

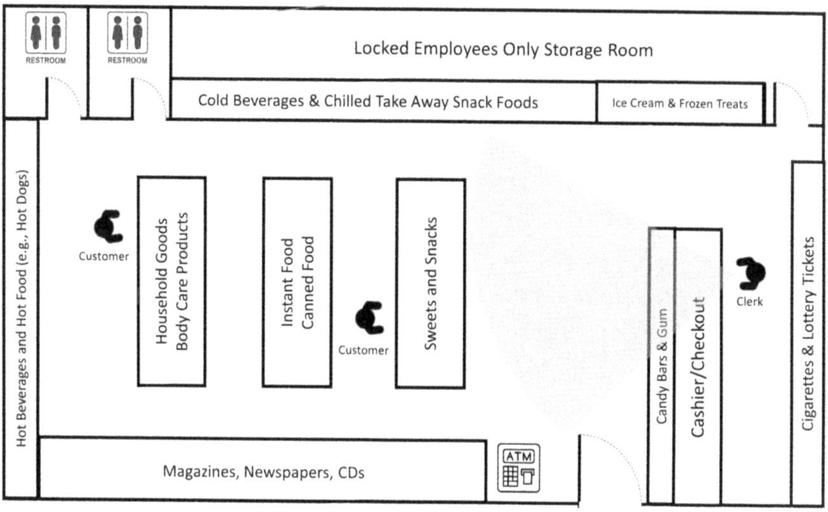

(a)

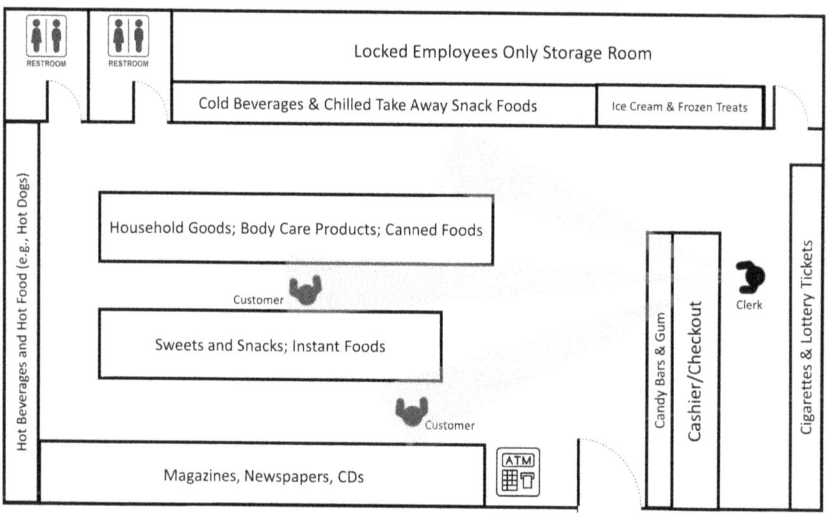

(b)

FIGURE 7.1 Change in Convenience Store Layout to Reduce Shoplifting

A Layout with many blind spots that give offenders the opportunity to stash goods in their pockets without being seen by employees.

B Reconfiguration of aisles to increase surveillance/sightlines of employees to see if patrons are trying to steal goods from shelves.

managers can also regulate the types of behavior they allow at particular times. For example, cafes can ban people from occupying tables to work on their laptops during their peak lunch or dinner hours.

Place managers can also regulate conduct to encourage desired behavior. For instance, these days you would be hard pressed to find a coffee shop that does not offer free Wi-Fi to its patrons. Why do they offer this? To encourage people to spend more time at the coffee shop on their phones or laptops. The longer they stay, the more likely they are to spend money on additional cups of coffee or food. Similarly, some casinos are known to give out free drinks to people using slot machines with hopes that they continue gambling. Some bars and night clubs provide free non-alcoholic drinks to encourage designated drivers.

Naturally, the regulation of conduct has important implications for crime prevention. You have probably seen signs on bank entrances telling you that hats, sunglasses, and facial coverings are not permitted. This is a form of conduct regulation to make bank robberies more difficult for motivated offenders. Landlords can require tenants sign a detailed lease specifying prohibited behaviors, such as illicit drug use or vandalism of the rented unit, that could result in eviction.[17] Place managers can also train employees to help with regulation. For example, bar owners can require all staff to complete training on safe serving practices and require that they stop serving alcohol to visibly intoxicated patrons. Retail stores can hire security guards and have them stand at the entrances and exits of the stores signalling to customers that crime will not be tolerated.

The third place management function is *controlling access*. Place managers "regulate who, when, and under what circumstances people can enter and use their places".[18] Business hours are a prime example of this. Retail and grocery stores welcome as many customers as possible, hoping to make profits from their purchases. But many regulate when customers can do this. Place managers can convey the control of access through advertising and marketing. For example, stores like Walmart are known to remain open 24 hours in the weeks leading up to Christmas. They advertise this widely, hoping to attract customers at all hours. Advertising can also be used to attract certain types of customers over others. For example, a bar might create a ladies night each week looking to attract female patrons as opposed to males. Night clubs might advertise country nights on Thursdays but hip-hop nights on Fridays which attracts people with different musical tastes on different days.

Place managers can also deny entry or remove people for misbehavior.[19] Denying entry involves keeping certain people off a property altogether. For example, an apartment landlord may give key fobs to tenants so that only they and their guests may enter the building. Place managers of convenience stores may limit entry to one teenager at a time to prevent teens from working together to distract store clerks while another shoplifts goods. Removing people for misbehavior could include hiring bouncers at bars to eject patrons who start fights. It could also include evictions of tenants who violate the terms of their apartment lease. Parking and towing rules are also examples. Place managers often post signage to indicate that one's vehicle will be towed if they are not authorized to park in designated areas.

The final component of the ORCA framework is the *acquisition of resources*. Eck and Madensen explain that "all places need resources to function".[20] Resources can be obtained in several ways through profits, donations, tax subsidies, and reputation. Commercial places need to generate profits to remain open. Retail stores must continually sell products to cover their rent, employee wages, and utility bills. Landlords of apartment buildings make profits through the rents collected. Non-commercial places also need to acquire resources. Municipal parks departments must lobby their local governments for a portion of the annual budget to maintain public parks. Homeowners also need to acquire resources. In Canada, for example, many homeowners create separate living suites in the basements of their homes to rent out. Money acquired from their tenants can help make the mortgage payments on their homes.

Reputation also plays a role in the amount of profits a place can make. The better the reputation, the more likely a place will get customers which earns them more profits. Universities, for example, work very hard to improve their reputation to collect additional tuition dollars from students, subsidies from governments, and donations from alumni or other donors.

The ability of a place to attract resources influences the other three ORCA components. More sales means more profit. This gives place managers more options to increase resources further. Specifically:

> A well-funded place can renovate its space, but a poorly funded place cannot. A well-funded place can hire better staff and train them so they can regulate conduct, but a poorly funded place will have more trouble with this. And a well-funded place can afford to be more exclusive than a poorly funded place.[21]

So, the acquisition of resources is a fundamental component to good place management. This final component of the ORCA framework is also critical to understanding how place managers can influence behavior not only at places, but also across larger areas, like neighborhoods.[22]

How Place Management Explains Crime Concentration

We showed in chapter 2 that crime concentrates at specific property parcels. While most places experience no crime, a tiny fraction of places experience a lot of crime, and no type of facility is exempt from the rule of the few. Some places, like bars and clubs, have a reputation for being high crime places, but they too follow the rule of the few. Most bars have no crime; a small number of bars have lots of crime. Most night clubs experience no problems; a small proportion of night clubs do.

Place management theory explains why crime is concentrated at places.[23] Although all places have managers, some managers are better than others. Most properties are managed in ways that prevent crime. But if they experience crime, their place managers adjust their practices to thwart it. The reasons are obvious; crime is costly. In contrast, a small number of places are not well-managed. Poor management creates crime opportunities that offenders exploit. The reasons for this can vary.[24] Some place managers are ignorant to the problem: an absentee landlord, for example. Some place managers do not know how to fix the problem: a novice business owner, for example. Some place managers do not care that much: the crimes are not costly to them, for example. Some place managers benefit from crime: the owner of the Barksdale Market, for example.

Among the thousands of place managers in a city, bad place management is relatively rare, regardless of the reason. But the relatively rare places with poor management generate a great deal of crime. In fact, as we noted earlier, they may generate most of the crime. This means that addressing deficiencies in place management at problem places will reap many benefits.

Place managers can create or suppress crime opportunities (we explain how in Chapter 10). Installing locked display cases for videogames in Walmart is an example of how the place manager suppressed a crime opportunity. Changing the payment structure at gasoline pumps so that customers must pre-pay is another example. Swapping out regular glass beer mugs for polycarbonate (shatter-proof) ones is another.

A question you may be wondering is if place managers only have control over what happens on their property, doesn't that mean they can only suppress crime opportunities within the boundaries of their properties? How does this help communities more widely? How does this relate to neighborhood crime? We address these questions in the next section.

Expanding Place Management into Neighborhoods

Architectural journalist Jane Jacobs is famous for her 1961 book, *The Death and Life of Great American Cities*. Even before she wrote this book, she highlighted the importance of place managers.[25] Her work inspired three principles needed to understand crime in cities:

1. Place managers, not residents, have the most power to control crime.
2. Cities change through deliberate, not natural, decisions by a few place managers and government agencies.
3. Places, not neighborhoods, are where to focus attention to create widespread change.[26]

We have discussed the first principle extensively in this book already. The legal powers given to place managers allows them to control crime, usually through suppressing crime opportunities. They are the ones who often have "eyes on the street" and intervene when unwanted behavior occurs.[27] Residents can seldom accomplish this, certainly not to the same degree as place managers.

The second and third principles provide further insight into how place managers influence larger areas, like neighborhoods. Cities are deliberate, man-made areas. They are usually founded on some basic resource (such as timber, metal, or oil); a shipping center; or human activity that creates a demand for people.[28] People are drawn to cities because of the jobs and living opportunities. But most people do not have control over the amount, location, or characteristics of these opportunities. Instead, governments or persons in the private sector create them. Private companies decide which cities to locate their offices in. Many technology companies, for example, chose to establish their headquarters in Silicon Valley, California. Detroit is known for its concentration of automobile manufacturers. Pittsburgh is known for steelmaking. Texas is known for oil and natural gas. People looking to work in these sectors often relocate to cities with abundant job opportunities. Private developers are also drawn to areas by opportunities to build office space and housing needed to support these industries.[29]

Governments also play a role in shaping city areas. They create zoning laws to organize what types of buildings can be in certain areas over others.[30] They build and maintain the roads, highways, and transit systems to allow people to move throughout the city. Governments also build incentive and disincentive structures to influence the actions of private investors. In the case of incentives, for example, they can offer tax breaks (sometimes called abatements) to property developers who are willing to invest in properties located in deteriorating areas.[31] Conversely, governments can withhold insurance for properties in declining areas. This disincentivizes financial institutions from giving out mortgages to invest in such properties.[32]

Property gives owners a great deal of power and control, and as you are probably aware, property ownership is not something that all people have. Yet again, it's another manifestation of the rule of the few. Just like the concentration of crime, there is a concentration of land ownership. A small number of people own large proportions of land. For example, Scotland has a population of nearly 5.5 million people, yet only 432 of them own half of Scotland's privately owned land area.[33] Similarly, less than 1% of England's population (roughly 25,000 people) own more than half of its land.[34] This concentration can be even greater when you move to smaller geographic areas. For instance, in the United States' Silicon Valley area, "…just 10 power brokers—a mix of technology behemoths, commercial and residential developers and one private university—own about $59.2 billion in taxable property".[35] This works out to ten owners

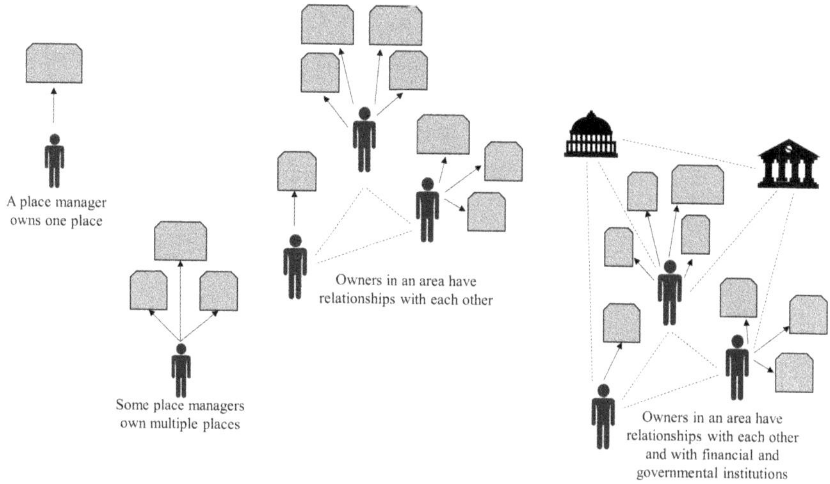

FIGURE 7.2 How Property Ownership Networks Extend Control to Larger Areas

Adapted from Linning & Eck (2021)

controlling more than 11% of all the taxable property in the county.[36] There is a concentration of land ownership among governments as well. For example, just four federal government agencies own about 28% of the land in the United States.[37] When a small number of people control many property parcels, it extends their degree of control over city areas.

There are at least four ways that the control of places can influence larger areas, such as neighborhoods.[38] We show this in figure 7.2. The first case is when a single place manager owns one property. We discussed this extensively earlier in the chapter. This represents the scenario in which the place manager engages in each of the ORCA functions to ensure the smooth functioning of their place. Most of her control is confined to the boundaries of her property parcel. As a homeowner, she can install new locks or security cameras. If she owns an apartment, she can carry out background checks on prospective tenants. If she owns commercial space, she can ask prospective business owners for references, business plans, and financial records before agreeing to lease them storefront retail space.

The second case is where place managers purchase multiple properties. They can do this with clusters of nearby land parcels, buy properties in different neighborhoods, or even different cities. This creates a concentration of ownership and thus control. This is common in all cities. For example, Troy Payne found that a small proportion of people owned multiple apartment buildings in Cincinnati, Ohio.[39] Limited liability corporations (LLCs), real estate investment trusts (REITs), and development companies often purchase clusters of properties too.

Owning multiple properties is a common practice among property developers as it extends the level of control they have over areas. In our research, for example, we have found that acquiring ownership of nearby properties was a deliberate strategy used by developers.[40] In one instance, Shannon interviewed a property developer who had been rehabilitating multiple parcels in a lower income neighborhood. He was trying to revitalize the area by fixing up multiple properties in the area. But there was a payday lending facility nearby that he felt would impinge on the potential desirability of the area. So, he purchased the property and informed the payday lending company that he would not renew their lease. This forced the payday lender to leave.

In another example, a developer told us that there was a vacant building causing problems near his properties. Several people were squatting in the building, using drugs, and creating crime problems. He did not believe the local government would solve the problem, especially not quickly. So, he decided to purchase the property himself. He proceeded to renovate it and lease the street-level storefront spaces to aspiring business owners and rent the apartment units above to tenants. He believed that ridding that building of its crime problems and transforming it into an active space made the entire street more desirable. This brought more business to that building as well as his other properties on the street.[41]

The third case is when place managers have relationships with other place managers (figure below). This extends their control even further. Our research has revealed several examples of place managers working together to create safer areas, even beyond the physical boundaries of their properties. For example, a coffee shop manager once told us that she partnered with the restaurant owner next door. The two properties sat perpendicular to one another and shared common outdoor space, often used for dining (Figure 7.3a). The place managers noted that by having different business hours, they could extend the amount of surveillance they had over the area. The coffee shop opened early, at 6:30am. Employees were instructed to be mindful of both their property and the restaurant's next door. Once the restaurant opened, their employees took

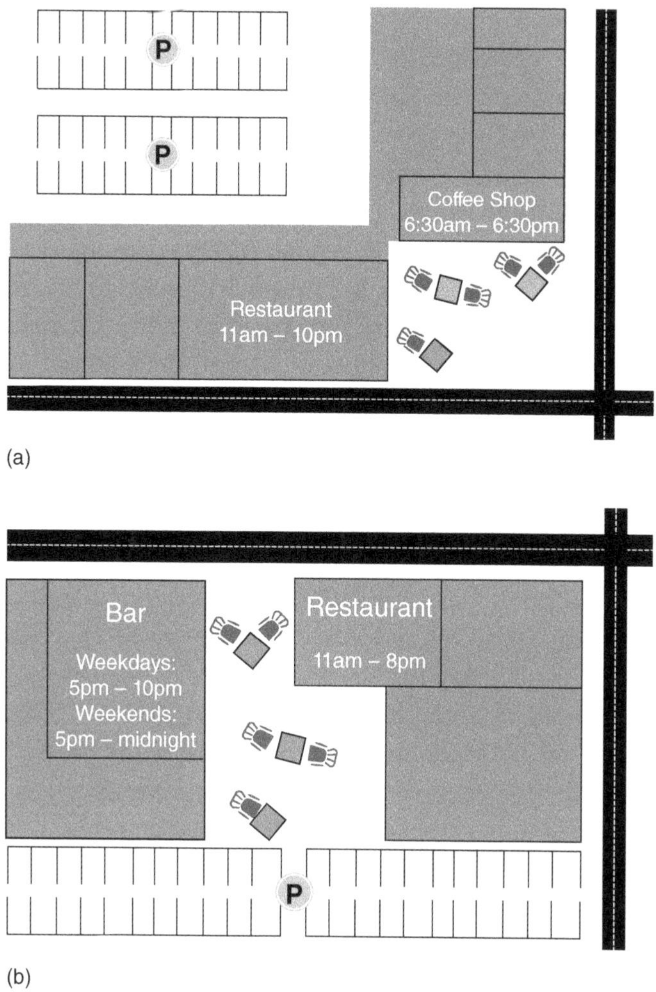

FIGURE 7.3 Place Managers Working Together to Control Space Around Their Properties

A Place managers of coffee shop and restaurant work together to increase surveillance to nearly 16 hours/day.

B Place managers of restaurant and bar work together to increase surveillance to 9 or 13 hours/day depending on day of the week.

watch of the area from 6:30pm when the coffee shop closed to 10pm when the restaurant closed.

In different example, we learned from another restaurant owner that he often worked with his next-door neighbor, a bar owner, to address crime problems (Figure 7.3b). They watched each other's properties. The restaurant owner also had security cameras installed and always operational, even after hours. From time to time, customers of the bar might experience a crime. The bar owner had gone to the restaurant owner asking to see the security footage. They worked together, along with the police, to identify the offender through the footage.[42]

These are small-scale examples of place managers working together. However, this can also happen at a much larger scale. Business Improvement Districts (BIDs), for example, are designated areas whereby business owners must pay additional tax to fund projects within the district's boundaries.[43] This money funds a local group who then re-invest in the district. Their services can range from maintenance and landscaping of shared space, to addressing problems of litter or graffiti and sponsoring prosocial activities.[44] Often BIDs hire designated hosts or ambassadors as visible representatives of the BID who carry out these activities. In fact, they often extend the place management control of the business owners in the BID. We have personally attended BID meetings where we have witnessed these groups organizing common space, regulating conduct on the streets, and trying to draw additional people (e.g., customers, investors) to the area. If a problem arose with one of the businesses, members of the BID would apply informal pressure on the owner to fix the problem. For example, they might persuade the owner of a convenience store to curb sales of chilled single servings of beer or high alcohol beers. If the owner does not comply, the BID can seek help from the city, which makes up the final way control is exercised.

The fourth case shows that control is spread the widest through relationships between place managers and "the small number of financial and governmental institutions who finance and regulate place ownership".[45] Though property owners can enjoy a host of powers over their properties, governments can still influence some of their decision-making processes. Building codes, for example, restrict how tall a building could be constructed by a developer. Zoning laws dictate whether a developer can build a commercial or residential structure. Fire codes limit the number of occupants a night club can have inside at any given time. Liquor boards restrict the age of people that a bar or restaurant can serve alcohol to. Private institutions, such as financial organizations, can also influence the actions of place managers. Banks, for example, can deny someone a business loan if their business plan seems undependable. Similarly, insurance companies can deny coverage or raise premiums if a property owner has not kept the electrical wiring in his property up to code.[46]

These examples demonstrate the economic incentive place managers have to adhere to government codes and regulations, along with the policies of financial institutions. This gives a certain level of control to governments and financial agencies even if they are not the outright owners of these properties. It also means that "these entities can control larger areas by influencing the decisions of each property owner within the area".[47] This means that control of wider areas comes from controlling individual property parcels. Because there is a concentration of property ownership, a small number of people are the ones controlling larger areas. So, when you are confronted with a problem in your neighborhood, one of the first things to consider is who might *own* the problem. As the evidence shows, it will likely be one of a small number of people in the area. He also may not be a resident of the area. But his ability to implement meaningful change in the area could be greater than anyone else's. In Part 3, particularly in chapter 10, we provide the techniques place managers can use to solve crime problems.

Integrating Place Managers into Crime Prevention Strategies

Though we have hopefully convinced you of the importance of place managers by now, we find the idea can initially be difficult for some to accept. The idea of working with community residents is so ingrained in our way of operating that it is difficult to consider placing such emphasis on another group. We wanted to provide some parting thoughts to help with this transition.

Although property ownership gives much power and control to owners, this power is neither positive nor negative. Power is not inherently good nor bad. It simply means you can enact change. How someone with power decides to use it can dictate whether it is positive or negative. So, we are not saying that property owners are good or bad. Instead, our intent was to show the extent to which property owners can influence cities and the areas within them.

Most property owners use their powers in positive or neutral ways. They comprise the larger portion of the rule of the few. Place managers are interested in the smooth functioning of their place and as we have shown, most do not contribute to any crime problems. Recall, crime data consistently show that most places are on the handle of the hockey stick; they experience no crime. So, most property owners are doing their part in keeping their places free of crime. These people are your allies in solving community problems. They are often highly motivated to keep the community safe. Feeling unsafe often deters customers from shopping at a store or eating at a restaurant.[48] Fewer customers means fewer profits, so most business owners want to keep their places crime-free. Similarly, if you own a home, you are a place manager, and we suspect that you are motivated to keep up your property. You also expect your neighbors to do the same. This makes your community a pleasant place to live and helps maintain or increase the value of your home.

That said, you are going to have problems with a few place managers. The good news is, per the rule of the few, this will be a small number of people. If a place has crime, simply bringing it to the attention of the owner could be enough to compel her to act. For example, we have seen examples where children inherit apartment buildings that were owned and managed by their now deceased parents. Having no experience in property management, they may decide to hire a management company to oversee the building's operations. Sometimes the management company does not do its due diligence and crime starts to occur unbeknownst to the owner who assumes the management company is handling things properly. Often when the problems are brought to the attention of the owners, they solve the problems by hiring a new property management company.

In the rarest of circumstances, you may have to deal with a place manager who knows about the crime problem(s) but chooses not to act. Perhaps he receives benefit from the crimes, such as money from the offenders to carry out their operations on his property.[49] In these cases, you can impose more drastic civil measures such as premise liability suits,[50] nuisance abatement suits,[51] or criminal ones. We cover this more extensively in chapter 11 when discussing how to compel uncooperative place managers to act.

To reduce crime, it is always important to remember the rule of the few; only a tiny fraction of place managers will have places with a lot of crime. Most place managers are interested in having safe, economically prosperous areas as much as everyone else.[52] Not only do they want this for the sake of operating in a desirable area, but they have economic incentives to ensure their places are safe. Thus, while community meetings with residents are important so that you can understand their concerns, do not forget about this other group within the community. Place managers are the ones who can enact most solutions.[53] But they are often busy running their businesses and may not have time to attend these meetings. You may need to seek them out. Moreover, be very intentional in who you seek out. If there is a problem in a local apartment building, for example, you may not need to meet with all apartment building owners in the neighborhood. You may only need to meet with that one apartment's owner. Forming a partnership with that one person can have powerful results. In Part 3, we provide guidance on how to partner with such place managers and what they can do to affect meaningful change to create safer communities.

Key Points

- A few place managers have the power to influence crime opportunities, while most community members have little ability to reduce crime
- Place managers are the most powerful actors because they can influence all components in the crime triangle
- Place managers have legal authority to organize space, regulate conduct, control access, and acquire resources on their property
- Ask: who is the place manager of the property experiencing the problem?

Notes

1 Madensen, T.D. & Eck, J.E. (2012). Crime places and place management. In F.T. Cullen & P. Wilcox (Eds.), *The Oxford Handbook of Criminological Theory* (pp. 1–18). Oxford University Press. https://doi.org/10.1093/oxfordhb/9780199747238.013.0029

2 Eck, J.E., Linning, S.J., & Herold, T.D. (2023). *Place Management and Crime: Ownership and Property Rights as a Source of Social Control.* Springer Publishers. https://doi.org/10.1007/978-3-031-27693-4

3 Linning, S.J. & Eck, J.E. (2021). *Whose 'Eyes on the Street' Control Crime? Expanding Place Management into Neighborhoods.* Cambridge University Press. https://doi.org/10.1017/9781108954143; Felson, M. & Eckert, M. (2017). *Introductory Criminology: The Study of Risky Situations.* Routledge. https://doi.org/10.4324/9781315618739
4 Honore, A.M. (1961). Ownership. In A.G. Guest (Ed.), *Oxford Essays in Jurisprudence* (pp. 370–375). Oxford University Press; Johnson, D.R. (2015). Reflections on the bundle of rights. *Vermont Law Review, 32*(2), 247–272; Merrill, T.W. & Smith, H.E. (2010). *Property.* Oxford University Press.
5 Eck, J.E., Linning, S.J., & Herold, T.D. (2023). *Place Management and Crime: Ownership and Property Rights as a Source of Social Control.* Springer Publishers. https://doi.org/10.1007/978-3-031-27693-4
6 Felson, M. (1986). Routine activities, social controls, rational decisions, and criminal outcomes. In D. Cornish & R.V. Clarke (Eds.), *The Reasoning Criminal: Rational Choice Perspectives On Offending* (pp. 119–128). New York, NY: Springer-Verlag.
7 Hollis, M., Felson, M. & Welsh, B. (2013). The capable guardian in routine activities theory: A theoretical and conceptual reappraisal. *Crime Prevention and Community Safety,* 15, 65–79. https://doi.org/10.1057/cpcs.2012.14; Reynald, D.M. (2009). Guardianship in action: Developing a new tool for measurement. *Crime Prevention and Community Safety, 11*(1), 1–20. https://doi.org/10.1057/cpcs.2008.19
8 Eck, J.E. & Madensen, T.D. (2018). Place management. In G.J.N. Bruinsma & S.D. Johnson (Eds.), *The Oxford Handbook of Environmental Criminology* (pp. 629–663). Oxford University Press. https://doi.org/10.1093/oxfordhb/9780190279707.013.22
9 Eck, J.E., Linning, S.J., & Herold, T.D. (2023). *Place Management and Crime: Ownership and Property Rights as a Source of Social Control.* Springer Publishers. https://doi.org/10.1007/978-3-031-27693-4
10 Eck, J.E., Linning, S.J., & Herold, T.D. (2023). *Place Management and Crime: Ownership and Property Rights as a Source of Social Control.* Springer Publishers. https://doi.org/10.1007/978-3-031-27693-4; Eck, J.E. & Madensen, T.D. (2018). Place management. In G.J.N. Bruinsma & S.D. Johnson (Eds.), *The Oxford Handbook of Environmental Criminology* (pp. 629–663). Oxford University Press. https://doi.org/10.1093/oxfordhb/9780190279707.013.22
11 Eck, J.E. & Madensen, T.D. (2018). Place management. In G.J.N. Bruinsma & S.D. Johnson (Eds.), *The Oxford Handbook of Environmental Criminology* (pp. 629–663). Oxford University Press. https://doi.org/10.1093/oxfordhb/9780190279707.013.22
12 Eck, J.E. (1997). Do premise liability suits promote business crime prevention? In R.V. Clarke & M. Felson (Eds.), *Business and Crime Prevention* (pp. 125–150). Monsey, NY: Criminal Justice Press.
13 Smith, M.J. & Mazerolle, L. (2016). *Using Civil Actions Against Property To Control Crime Problems.* Response Guide Series; Problem-Oriented Guides for Police (No. 11). Center for Problem-Oriented Policing. Retrieved from: https://popcenter.asu.edu/sites/g/files/litvpz3631/files/civil_actions_against_properties.pdf
14 Madensen, T.D. (2007). *Bar Management and Crime: Towards a Dynamic Theory of Place Management and Crime Hotspots.* Unpublished doctoral dissertation, University of Cincinnati.
15 Eck, J.E., Linning, S.J., & Herold, T.D. (2023). *Place Management and Crime: Ownership and Property Rights as a Source of Social Control.* Springer Publishers. https://doi.org/10.1007/978-3-031-27693-4; Eck, J.E. & Madensen, T.D. (2018). Place management. In G.J.N. Bruinsma & S.D. Johnson (Eds.), *The Oxford Handbook of Environmental Criminology* (pp. 629–663). Oxford University Press. https://doi.org/10.1093/oxfordhb/9780190279707.013.22

16 Eck, J.E., Linning, S.J., & Herold, T.D. (2023). *Place Management and Crime: Ownership and Property Rights as a Source of Social Control.* Springer Publishers. https://doi.org/10.1007/978-3-031-27693-4; Eck, J.E. & Madensen, T.D. (2018). Place management. In G.J.N. Bruinsma & S.D. Johnson (Eds.), *The Oxford Handbook of Environmental Criminology*, (pp. 629–663). Oxford University Press. https://doi.org/10.1093/oxfordhb/9780190279707.013.22
17 Campbell DeLong Resources, Inc. (2000). Keeping illegal activity out of rental property: A police guide for establishing landlord training programs. NCJ 148656 (Washington, DC: US Department of Justice, Bureau of Justice Assistance).
18 From page 639 of: Eck, J.E. & Madensen, T.D. (2018). Place management. In G.J.N. Bruinsma & S.D. Johnson (Eds.), *The Oxford Handbook of Environmental Criminology* (pp. 629–663). Oxford University Press. https://doi.org/10.1093/oxfordhb/9780190279707.013.22
19 Linning, S.J. & Eck, J.E. (2024). Clarifying control in criminology: A proposal for six interacting controls of crime. *Canadian Journal of Criminology and Criminal Justice, 66*(3–4), 119–141. https://doi.org/10.3138/cjccj-2024-0053
20 From page 640 of: Eck, J.E. & Madensen, T.D. (2018). Place management. In G.J.N. Bruinsma & S.D. Johnson (Eds.), *The Oxford Handbook of Environmental Criminology* (pp. 629–663). Oxford University Press. https://doi.org/10.1093/oxfordhb/9780190279707.013.22
21 From page 640 of: Eck, J.E. & Madensen, T.D. (2018). Place management. In G.J.N. Bruinsma & S.D. Johnson (eds.), *The Oxford Handbook of Environmental Criminology* (pp. 629–663). Oxford University Press. https://doi.org/10.1093/oxfordhb/9780190279707.013.22
22 Linning, S.J. & Eck, J.E. (2021). *Whose 'Eyes on the Street' Control Crime? Expanding Place Management into Neighborhoods.* Cambridge University Press. https://doi.org/10.1017/9781108954143
23 Eck, J.E., Linning, S.J., & Herold, T.D. (2023). *Place Management and Crime: Ownership and Property Rights as a Source of Social Control.* Springer Publishers. https://doi.org/10.1007/978-3-031-27693-4
24 Eck, J.E. & Madensen, T.D. (2018). Place management, guardianship, and the establishment of order. In D.S. Nagin, F.T. Cullen, & C.L. Jonson (Eds.), *Deterrence, Choice, and Crime: Contemporary Perspectives* (pp. 269–296). Routledge. https://doi.org/10.4324/9781351112710-10
25 Jacobs, J. (1956, June). The missing link in city redevelopment. *Architectural Forum: The Magazine of Building, 104*(6), 132–133; Jacobs, J. (1958). Downtown is for people. In W.H. Whyte Jr. (Ed.), *The Exploding Metropolis* (pp. 140–168). New York.
26 Linning, S.J. & Eck, J.E. (2021). *Whose 'Eyes on the Street' Control Crime? Expanding Place Management into Neighborhoods.* Cambridge University Press. https://doi.org/10.1017/9781108954143
27 From page 35 of: Jacobs, J. (1961). *The Death and Life of Great American Cities.* Vintage.
28 O'Flaherty, B. (2005). *City Economics.* Cambridge, MA: Harvard University Press.
29 Linning, S.J. & Eck, J.E. (2021). *Whose 'Eyes on the Street' Control Crime? Expanding Place Management into Neighborhoods.* Cambridge University Press. https://doi.org/10.1017/9781108954143
30 Glotzer, P. (2020). *How The Suburbs Were Segregated: Developers and the Business of Exclusionary Housing, 1890–1960.* New York: Columbia University Press.
31 Moskowitz, P.E. (2017). *How to Kill a City: Gentrification, Inequality, and the Fight for the Neighborhood.* Nation Books.
32 Rothstein, R. (2017). *The Color of Law: A Forgotten History of How Our Government Segregated America.* New York: Liveright Publishing.

33 Hunter, J., Peacock, P., Wightman, A., & Foxley, M. (2013). 432:50 – Towards a comprehensive land reform agenda for Scotland. A briefing paper for the House of Commons Scottish Affairs Committee.

34 Evans, R. (2019, April 17). Half of England is owned by less than 1% of the population. The Guardian. Retrieved from: https://www.theguardian.com/money/2019/apr/17/who-owns-england-thousand-secret-landowners-author

35 Castaneda, L. (2019, November 4). Who owns Silicon Valley? Reveal News. Retrieved June 13, 2021 from: https://revealnews.org/article/who-owns-silicon-valley/

36 Castaneda, L. (2019, November 4). Who owns Silicon Valley? Reveal News. Retrieved June 13, 2021 from: https://revealnews.org/article/who-owns-silicon-valley/

37 Vincent, C.H., Hanson, L.A., & Bermejo, L.F. (2020, February 21). Federal land ownership: Overview and data. Congressional Research Services Report R42346, version 16.

38 Linning, S.J. & Eck, J.E. (2021). *Whose 'Eyes on the Street' Control Crime? Expanding Place Management into Neighborhoods*. Cambridge University Press. https://doi.org/10.1017/9781108954143

39 Payne, T.C. (2010). *Does changing ownership change crime? An analysis of apartment ownership and crime in Cincinnati*. Unpublished PhD dissertation, University of Cincinnati, School of Criminal Justice.

40 Linning, S.J. (2019). *The Neo-Jacobian perspective of place and neighborhood crime: A case study of property management, redevelopment, and crime in Walnut Hills, Cincinnati, Ohio*. Unpublished doctoral dissertation, University of Cincinnati; Linning, S.J. & Eck, J.E. (2021). *Whose 'Eyes on the Street' Control Crime? Expanding Place Management into Neighborhoods*. Cambridge University Press. https://doi.org/10.1017/9781108954143

41 Linning, S.J. (2019). *The Neo-Jacobian perspective of place and neighborhood crime: A case study of property management, redevelopment, and crime in Walnut Hills, Cincinnati, Ohio*. Unpublished doctoral dissertation, University of Cincinnati; Linning, S.J. & Eck, J.E. (2021). *Whose 'Eyes on the Street' Control Crime? Expanding Place Management into Neighborhoods*. Cambridge University Press. https://doi.org/10.1017/9781108954143

42 Linning, S.J. (2019). *The Neo-Jacobian perspective of place and neighborhood crime: A case study of property management, redevelopment, and crime in Walnut Hills, Cincinnati, Ohio*. Unpublished doctoral dissertation, University of Cincinnati.

43 Cook, P.J. & MacDonald, J. (2011). Public safety through private action: an economic assessment of BIDS. *The Economic Journal, 121*(552), 445–462. https://doi.org/10.1111/j.1468-0297.2011.02419.x

44 Manshel, A. (2020). *Learning from Bryant Park: Revitalizing Cities, Towns, and Public Spaces*. New Brunswick, NJ: Rutgers University Press. https://doi.org/10.36019/9781978802544

45 From page 66 of: Linning, S.J. & Eck, J.E. (2021). *Whose 'Eyes on the Street' Control Crime? Expanding Place Management into Neighborhoods*. Cambridge University Press. https://doi.org/10.1017/9781108954143

46 Sampson R., Eck, J.E., & Dunham, J. (2010). Super controllers and crime prevention: A routine activity explanation of crime prevention success and failure. *Security Journal, 23*(1), 37–51. https://doi.org/10.1057/sj.2009.17

47 From page 48 of: Linning, S.J. & Eck, J.E. (2021). *Whose 'Eyes on the Street' Control Crime? Expanding Place Management into Neighborhoods*. Cambridge University Press. https://doi.org/10.1017/9781108954143

48 Jacobs, J. (1961). *The Death and Life of Great American Cities*. Vintage.

49 Eck, J.E. & Madensen, T.D. (2018). Place management, guardianship, and the establishment of order. In D.S. Nagin, F.T. Cullen, & C.L. Jonson (Eds.), *Deterrence, Choice, and Crime: Contemporary Perspectives* (pp. 269–296). Routledge. https://doi.org/10.4324/9781351112710-10
50 Eck, J.E. (1997). Do premise liability suits promote business crime prevention? In R.V. Clarke & M. Felson (Eds.), *Business and Crime Prevention* (pp. 125–150). Monsey, NY: Criminal Justice Press.
51 Smith, M.J. & Mazerolle, L. (2016). *Using civil actions against property to control crime problems.* Response Guide Series; Problem-Oriented Guides for Police (No. 11). Center for Problem-Oriented Policing. Retrieved from: https://popcenter.asu.edu/sites/g/files/litvpz3631/files/civil_actions_against_properties.pdf
52 Mallach, A. (2019). Addressing problem rental housing. In A. Mallach, J. Bacher, & M.B. Williams (Eds.), *Vacant and Problem Properties: A Guide to Legal Strategies and Remedies* (pp. 123–162). American Bar Association.
53 Eck, J.E., Linning, S.J., & Herold, T.D. (2023). *Place Management and Crime: Ownership and Property Rights as a Source of Social Control.* Springer Publishers. https://doi.org/10.1007/978-3-031-27693-4

PART 3
WHAT'S YOUR PROBLEM?

So far, we have given you new ways to think about crime. Part 1 showed that: crime is highly concentrated, particularly at places; communities are made up of more than just residents; and arrests will not reduce crime as much as you think because they are a means not an end. Part 2 explained that: crime is often the by-product of everyday life; to solve crime problems, we need to break them down into more manageable pieces; and the best people to tackle many crime problems are place managers.

Typically, when we think about crime, we assume the police should be the ones to deal with it. But, as we have shown, the standard police responses seldom reduce crime. The standard police response is not worthless: it can rescue people in emergencies, provide a feeling of safety, and support justice. As important as these outcomes are, they seldom prevent much crime. Breaking up a fight addresses that incident, but is unlikely to prevent other fights if the situation that leads to fights remains. A passing patrol car may assure pedestrians that they are safe, but they were probably safe already. Arresting the person who committed a burglary can lead to justice, but unless something is done to make burglaries difficult, burglaries will continue.

The standard police response is incident-based. Someone calls the police and the police come and deal with that incident. If everything goes well – the caller and others involved are cooperative and the police are competent – the police response may address the immediate needs. We have seen, however, that incidents cluster. Clustering is a sign that

DOI: 10.4324/9781003430155-10

something is going on to cause multiple incidents with something in common. Handling each incident as if they are unconnected just assures that each incident is handled, but more will arise. So, people will continue calling the police.

Good and just incident handling does not identify and solve the underlying problem any more than swift ambulance services stop car crashes and their associated injuries. If we are hurt in a car crash, we want emergency medicine, and we want it now. But as fast and capable as emergency medical technicians are, they cannot prevent more car crashes in a car crash hot spot. Someone has to fix the car crash problem. The police response to incidents is the same.

Dentists routinely detect and fill cavities. If the cavities are the result of consuming too much sugar and not brushing teeth, repairing a tooth does not prevent the next tooth from needing repair. That is why our dentists give us dietary and mouth hygiene advice. They know that merely responding to a tooth incident will not fix the cavity problem that brought you into their offices. You have to fix the cause of the problem. The same is true of police handling calls from the public; responding to calls must be done well, but we should never assume that call response alone will prevent much. That is, unless the call handling leads to actual problem solving.

You may get our belabored point but have some important questions: What exactly is a problem? How do crime problems come to exist in the first place? What specific actions could people take to reduce crime? What if the people responsible for fixing crime problems are reluctant to act? In this part of the book, we answer these questions. Once equipped with the knowledge contained in these five chapters you can start problem-solving yourself.

In the next chapter, we dive further into the concept of problems. We provide guidance on what constitutes a problem. Though we told you to break major societal issues down into small solvable problems, you still need to understand what differentiates them from one-off troublesome events. You also need to decide which types of problems are most worth pursuing to reap the greatest benefits. We follow this up in chapter 9 with an explanation of why crime problems arise in the first place. We outline the three related explanations for crime. Not only do they show what it takes for a crime to occur, they can also explain where and when most crimes happen and why. Chapter 10 dives into the steps you can take to intervene in the crime process. We give you dozens of practical tools to block or reduce crime opportunities.

In chapters 11 and 12, we address two common criticisms of the tools we describe: dealing with uncooperative place managers and displacement. The first criticism raises the concern that while place managers can solve crime problems, some place managers will not engage in crime prevention. When this happens, are we out of luck? We show you that there are some alternatives, such as using super controllers. For the second criticism—displacement—most people assume that if we make crime more difficult to commit at once place, then offenders will just go somewhere else to carry out their crimes. This is another common, but faulty, assumption about crime. We will explain why it is not as likely as you think and how additional beneficial effects can even be observed when we use situational interventions.

Together these chapters provide a comprehensive explanation for crime problems, how you should think about them, and what you can do to proactively address them. So, let's get started!

8
What is a Problem?

People tend to make one of two mistakes when thinking about problems: they either make them too big or too small. We provided several examples of big problems in chapter 6: poverty, homelessness, mental illness, and the opioid epidemic. These cannot be solved quickly or with assurance of success. Or people focus on small problems: a man yelling in the street, a noise complaint, or a burglar alarm that needs tending to. We can address these quickly, but more of them tend to pop up.

Most people overlook the middle-sized problems. These are Goldilocks problems. They take more effort to solve than the tiny ones, but they are solvable, unlike big problems. When they are solved, the solution prevents more tiny problems from recurring. To understand Goldilocks problems, you need to understand the two extremes. So, we begin with the big and the small, which we will rename to keep things straight. Then, we explain the middle range problems you should look for to focus your response.

Where to Focus Your Problem-Solving Efforts

Rather than use the word *problem* to mean everything that troubles us, lets separate trouble into three categories: 1) major societal issues; 2) problems; or 3) immediate troublesome events. The inverted triangle illustrates the categories (figure 8.1).

DOI: 10.4324/9781003430155-11

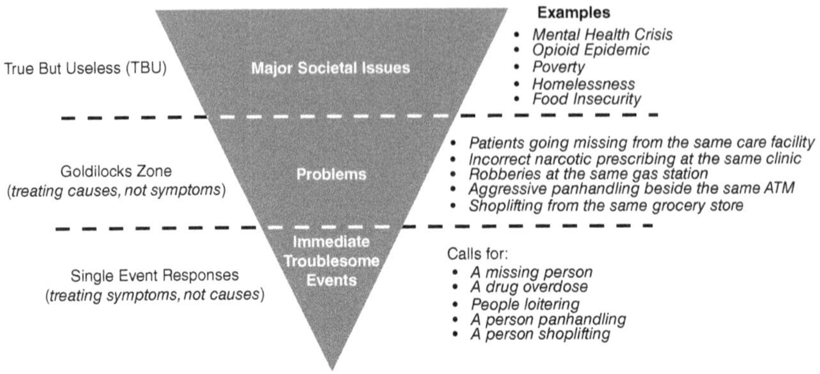

FIGURE 8.1 Engage with the Goldilocks Zone for Solutions

Figure modified from Linning et al. (2024)

Major societal issues are massive. They span countries and often the globe. They last years, decades, and centuries. They are unspecific. They include issues such as poverty, homelessness, and mental illness. Police and local governments are not going to solve major societal issues in their next 8-, 10- or 12-hour workday.

Crime is a social issue. These issues need to be addressed, but there will be no single solution. We chip away at social issues, making them less pervasive and serious. But we do not solve them, usually. The chipping processes takes widespread co-operation from many organizations consuming immense resources over many years. Recall, these major societal issues are what cause people to believe in the *solutions to crime are complicated* fallacy.[1] Again, these are what Jerry Sternin refers to as "TBU: true but useless!"[2] It is TBU to say that a street corner with many shootings and several killings is due to poverty and racism. No local organization, or group of organizations, will reduce the shootings and killings on that corner by focusing on TBU issues. Police officers, social workers, and community organizers do not have the resources, time, or know how. Even if they did, their efforts would take years: years in which the corner would have more shootings and killings in the meantime. While we are waiting for the solutions to major social issues, we need to do something that provides tangible results within months.[3]

At the other extreme are immediate troublesome events. These events are short—seconds, minutes, or hours—and extremely local. A shooting takes seconds and is confined to a small space (people a block away may be unaware of it). Shootings are also highly specific: a gunshot is different from a wounding, which is different from a homicide.

These events need to be addressed, which is one of the reasons we have policing services. It's the troublesome events that police primarily respond to. These events include anything from loud music to a missing person, to a car crash, to a killing. Many are one-off events that do not need to be tended to beyond the initial call. If the loud music turned out to be caused by a new resident in an apartment complex who bought a new sound system and did not realize its power, simply talking to him may resolve the issue. Similarly, worried parents who have not been able to locate their toddler may call the police for assistance. If it turned out the child simply crawled under her bed and fell asleep, this is not an overt problem that warrants innovative problem-solving efforts to prevent future incidents. If the car crash was simply the result of a driver being momentarily distracted by their child in the backseat, no action beyond tending to the scene is needed.

The public, elected officials, government administrators, and the press seem to vacillate between the hyper-local harmful event and extremely general social issues. We hear of the death of a child from a stray bullet and grieve for the child and her loved ones. There is an immediate and justified search for the culprit and then there is the editorial decrying the decline in family values, increased income inequality, the prevalence of guns, the lack of organization in communities, or some other social issue. Neither the apprehension of the shooter nor the pleas to alter economic, social, or moral conditions will prevent another child from being shot in the next year. To make real headway against harmful events we need to focus on the middle.

Extreme thinking inhibits solving other problems. Consider a car crash. The first reaction is to save the people involved. Then there is the search for the person responsible. Both are decent reactions. If the crash was horrific, then we hear palavering about drivers in general—they are untrained, they are drunk, they are texting. Any or all of these may be true in general, but this switch to generalities seldom saves lives. To save lives, one must become more specific than the social issue but more general than the specific event.

So, what are these middle-level, Goldilocks Zone problems? When we refer to problems, we mean a collection of unwanted or harmful events that need solving. Problems are patterned; they are not random. So, they must recur and will do so in a predictable manner. If there is no pattern, there is nothing to be solved or prevented. You cannot intervene in a random event. The patterns themselves reveal the true causes of problems. Problems are troublesome circumstances bigger than individual events, but smaller than bad socio-economic conditions. We have described several examples in earlier chapters.

Our discussion of residents going missing from a mental health facility, in chapter 6, is one example.[4] This was a recurring problem that could be traced back to one facility. Similar facilities were not calling the police for assistance to locate missing residents. Initially, the first call or two to the police about missing persons likely seemed like immediate troublesome events. But as they continued to occur, the police noticed a pattern was present. Indeed, there was. The calls kept coming from the same facility. The police consulted with the facility and realized that the security practices at that specific facility were insufficient. Compelling the place manager to change their security practices addressed the problem.

Let's return to the car crash example from chapter 1 as another illustration of a problem. Crashes can happen for many reasons. Again, if the crash was a one-off event caused by the driver being distracted by their child in the backseat there probably isn't much else we can do about what happened. If, however, the crash occurred because one of the tires burst on the vehicle, you may want to look at the brand and model of tires to see if there have been multiple crashes linked to product failures. If this is the case, efforts to get the tire manufacturer to improve the design or materials of the product could solve your problem. If the crash occurred because the driver was distracted while texting, you should look to see if this was a common factor in other crashes. If so, a "no texting while driving" campaign could raise awareness of the problem. Similarly, creating a traffic law that permits the police to issue fines for drivers distracted on their phones while driving could deter some from engaging in the behavior.

But if the crash was one of several at the same location, you may want to look at the road conditions at that place. Our example from chapter 1 occurred in the early 2000s in Cincinnati, Ohio.[5] There were several small stretches of road that experienced multiple serious traffic crashes. The primary reason for the crashes was that drivers seemed to have lost control of their vehicles, particularly in bad weather. The Cincinnati Police Department consulted with the City of Cincinnati Traffic Engineering Department to determine if anything about the road could be changed to improve driving conditions. They determined that loss of traction, particularly in one of the curves in the road, was often to blame. Finding a way to increase the coefficient of friction on the road, especially in the rain, could reduce the problem. The traffic department used diamond grinding procedures to create a rougher surface on the stretch of road that experienced the accidents. No vehicle-related fatalities have been reported at the locations where the traffic department used diamond grinding procedures.

The Cincinnati car crash example provides a good example of getting past symptoms and instead getting to the cause of the problem. The car crashes were a symptom of the cause: poor road conditions in wet weather. Sending police and ambulances to car crashes is needed, but it merely addresses the symptoms of the problem. Increasing the coefficient of friction on the street addresses the cause. Motorists are less likely to skid on wet pavement.[6]

Treating Symptoms Versus Causes

Focusing on causes is not just effective for solving crime problems, it works for all problems. One night in the 1960s, pediatrician Dr. Henri Breault came home from work in a terrible mood. He had recently become the Chief of Pediatrics at the Hotel-Dieu Grace Hospital in Windsor, Ontario, Canada and was dealing with a troubling problem. Children were being admitted to the hospital at staggering rates for accidental poisonings. There were approximately 1,000 child poisonings in Canada per year. Often, the children had consumed common household substances, such as aspirin, found in easy-to-open pill bottles. The standard response was to rush children to the hospital and have their stomachs pumped. Though this worked fairly well, about 100 children still died per year and those who survived had to endure a traumatizing hospital experience.[7]

Breault was at a breaking point and confided in his wife. In an interview she recalls him saying, "You know, I've had it! I am tired of pumping children's stomachs when they're taking pills that they shouldn't be having! I've got to do something about it." This launched a comprehensive public health campaign attempting to reduce the problem. Breault knew that he could not change the children's behavior. Most were so young that they did not understand the danger they were putting themselves in by ingesting things they were findings around the home. So, he tried educating parents instead. However, the health education attempts failed to reduce the number of poisonings. They were unsuccessful in getting people to store dangerous substances out of the reach of children. Not everyone would participate in the program, some would forget to use the lessons on a regular basis, and so on.[8]

Breault decided he needed to intervene in the processes that allowed these substances to enter the children's mouths. He realized the best way to address the problem was to create a physical barrier that a child could not overcome. That is, if a child cannot open a pill bottle to begin with, there will be no pills for her to accidentally ingest.[9] In essence, he looked for *upstream* solutions to the problem.[10]

So, Breault teamed up with Peter Hedgewick, president of International Tool Limited (ITL) Industries, to create a child-resistant bottle cap. The caps require the strength and manual dexterity of an adult to open. They released the "Palm N Turn" bottle cap in 1967. Once the government of Ontario made the caps mandatory, local child poisonings dropped over 90 percent. All governments in North America quickly followed suit, resulting in further declines in poisonings.[11]

Finding the Goldilocks zone to focus on gives us the best perspective to solving a problem. Immediate troublesome events are often the most visible. In the example above, these were the poisoned children coming into the emergency room. But many immediate troublesome events are often symptoms of a larger problem. Easy access to poisonous materials was the cause. Children ingesting the substances and being poisoned was the symptom of the larger problem. Ongoing car crashes at the same location are likely the symptom of poor road conditions at that location.[12] Patients repeatedly going missing from a specific mental health facility is a symptom of inadequate security procedures at that facility.[13] Some drug overdoses are a symptom of poor prescribing procedures in the medical and dental fields.[14] Gasoline drive-offs are the symptom of pump-before-you-pay payment systems.[15] Glassings are a symptom of "serving a mind-altering substance in a potential weapon".[16] And so on.

Standard responses to these immediate troublesome events are usually reactive and only treat symptoms.[17] Tending to those involved in car crashes does not prevent future crashes from occurring. Responding to drug overdoses and administering Narcan does not prevent the person, or others, from overdosing in the future. Recording and reporting the license plates of cars whose drivers gas-and-dash does not guarantee the police will apprehend the suspect, nor prevent others from committing the same crime. Arresting assailants and performing reconstructive facial surgery on those who are victims of glassings does not prevent such events from happening again.

Think of these immediate troublesome events as houses that are on fire. Each time one ignites, we can call the fire department. They can arrive in record time and spend time putting out the fire using refined firefighting techniques. But even if they are successful, people may have gotten injured, and the house, along with possessions inside, may have been damaged. Plus, success has no bearing on preventing any other houses from going up in flames. Yet our go-to response may be to hire more firefighters, to increase their funding for better equipment, and so on. After all, if there is a fire, we call the experts on fires, right? But often the best firefighters can do is react and address symptoms. We need to address the underlying cause. Usually this will not involve the firefighters themselves, except maybe if they are in a consulting role.

How else could we solve fire problems? We could ask that construction companies use specific building materials that are more flame retardant. If they do not voluntarily comply, governments could pass legislation to require it. Property owners could be required to maintain a certain standard in their buildings, such as the quality of the electrical systems. They could also require all tenants to sign detailed leases outlining prohibited practices. For example, they may not be allowed to have a grill on their balconies. Similarly, landlords could forbid tenants from using fryers that are likely to start grease fires, or from smoking indoors. Property owners could frequently water the grounds around the property to reduce chances of fire. What is the common theme running through these alternative examples? They do not involve government agencies treating symptoms (i.e., the fire department responding to calls). They highlight ways place managers can suppress conditions that make fires more likely.

Addressing crime problems works much the same way. The police, like firefighters, react to immediate troublesome events. Most of the tools at their disposal to respond, are reactive and only treat symptoms. Though the police can be gatekeepers to identify recurring patterns, they often are not the ones who can treat the sources of the problems.

Say CHEERS to Your Problems!

We have advocated for focusing on problems, but how do you know when you have a problem? One way to identify crime problems is to use a modification of the CHEERS criteria, developed by John and crime scientist Ronald Clarke.[18] CHEERS is an acronym that represents the six components of crime problems (table 8.1).

First, the concern being described must occur in the community. It cannot be a concern solely for local government administrators, such as police officers not wearing their hats. Second, there must be something harmful happening: death, injury, taking or destroying something that belongs to someone else, or even fear of using public space. It cannot be just a state of being, such as homelessness or something that makes people uncomfortable, such as teenagers standing on a street corner as you pass by. Third, there must be some expectation among some members of the public that local government must be involved. Fourth, all problems involve events, such as break-ins, threats, or transactions. It cannot be general states such as poverty or racism, or other general conditions like stupidity or declining morals. Fifth, the events need to repeat or have a high likelihood of repeating. If something is unlikely to recur (like a meteor strike), then there are no future events to prevent. Finally, these events that repeat must have something in common, a basis of similarity that indicates a common set of causes. They cannot be an arbitrary set of unconnected, albeit unfortunate, events.

Anything that does not meet all six CHEERS criteria is not a crime problem, in the technical sense. But if all six criteria are met, you can consider it a crime problem and begin your problem-solving process to understand why crime is occurring. The next question you might ask is: how can you solve problems? We answer this in chapter 10. We will give you a set of problem-solving tools to choose from. But to understand which tools are best for different problems, you need to understand why most crime problems arise in the first place. That is the topic of the next chapter.

Table 8.1 Use the CHEERS Criteria to Identify Crime Problems

Criteria	Must	Cannot	Good Example	Bad Example
Community	The difficulty must affect the community/public	It cannot just be a concern to the police	Break-ins to cars parked along a street block	Police cars scraping each other in the police station parking lot
Harm	There must be a tangible harm	Cannot just be a dislike	Death; injury; theft; psychological trauma	Discomfort with teenagers on sidewalk
Expectation	Some in the public must see this as something for the local government to handle	Cannot be something completely outside local government mandate	Traffic crashes; burglaries; and fights	A pandemic
Event	Discrete incidents make up the problem	Cannot be a general state	A prostitution transaction; a terrorist bombing	Homelessness (is a state, not an event)
Repeat	Events must recur, or are likely to	Cannot be a singular event with little chance of recurring	A building with frequent burglaries; reports of aggressive panhandling at an ATM	A train derailment with injuries; a bridge collapse
Similarity	Events must share important characteristics	Cannot be an arbitrary collection of unlinked events	Crimes occurring at the same address; shootings between two rival gangs; wallet thefts from elderly men	A car crash, burglary, report of a loud teen party, and theft all in the same week on the same block

From Linning et al. (2024); modified from Clarke and Eck (2003)

Key Points

- Problems are a collection of repeated, unwanted, or harmful events that need solving.
- Address problems instead of major social issues or immediate troublesome events.
- To identify problems, say CHEERS!
- Ask: what is the cause of the problem (as opposed to the symptom)?

Notes

1 Linning, S.J., Carroll, T., Gerard, D.W., & Eck, J.E. (2024). Do solutions to crime need to be complicated? *Public Management, 106*(8), 36–39. https://icma.org/articles/pm-magazine/do-solutions-crime-need-be-complicated

2 From page 58 of: Sternin, J. (2002). Positive deviance: A new paradigm for addressing today's problems today. *The Journal of Corporate Citizenship, 5*, 57–62. https://doi.org/10.9774/gleaf.4700.2002.sp.00007

3 Linning, S.J., Carroll, T., Gerard, D.W., & Eck, J.E. (2024). Do solutions to crime need to be complicated? *Public Management, 106*(8), 36–39. https://icma.org/articles/pm-magazine/do-solutions-crime-need-be-complicated

4 Lancashire Constabulary (2004). Finding missing persons: Who's responsible for whom? Presented at the 15th Annual Problem-Oriented Policing, Conference, Charlotte, North Carolina, as cited in Cordner, G. (2006). *People with Mental Illness* (1st ed.). Problem-Oriented Guides for Police Problem-Specific Guides Series No. 40.

5 Corsaro, N., Gerard, D.W., Engel, R.S. & Eck, J.E. (2012). Not by accident: An analytical approach to traffic crash harm reduction. *Journal of Criminal Justice, 40*, 502–514. https://doi.org/10.1016/j.jcrimjus.2012.08.003

6 Corsaro, N., Gerard, D.W., Engel, R.S. & Eck, J.E. (2012). Not by accident: An analytical approach to traffic crash harm reduction. *Journal of Criminal Justice, 40*, 502–514. https://doi.org/10.1016/j.jcrimjus.2012.08.003

7 Dimopoulos, L. (2020, August 6). Dr. Henri Breault – Child Proof Safety Caps. The Drive Magazine. Retrieved from: https://thedrivemagazine.com/posts/henri-breault/

8 Dimopoulos, L. (2020, August 6). Dr. Henri Breault – Child Proof Safety Caps. The Drive Magazine. Retrieved from: https://thedrivemagazine.com/posts/henri-breault/

9 Dimopoulos, L. (2020, August 6). Dr. Henri Breault – Child Proof Safety Caps. The Drive Magazine. Retrieved from: https://thedrivemagazine.com/posts/henri-breault/

10 Heath, C. (2020). *Upstream: The Quest to Solve Problems Before They Happen*. New York, NY: Avid Reader Press.

11 Dimopoulos, L. (2020, August 6). Dr. Henri Breault – Child Proof Safety Caps. The Drive Magazine. Retrieved from: https://thedrivemagazine.com/posts/henri-breault/

12 Corsaro, N., Gerard, D.W., Engel, R.S. & Eck, J.E. (2012). Not by accident: An analytical approach to traffic crash harm reduction. *Journal of Criminal Justice, 40*, 502–514. https://doi.org/10.1016/j.jcrimjus.2012.08.003

13 Lancashire Constabulary (2004). Finding missing persons: Who's responsible for whom? Presented at the 15th Annual Problem-Oriented Policing, Conference, Charlotte, North Carolina, as cited in Cordner, G. (2006). *People with Mental Illness* (1st ed.). Problem-Oriented Guides for Police Problem-Specific Guides Series No. 40.

14 American Dental Association (2018, March 26). American Dental Association announces new policy to combat opioid epidemic: Policy supports mandates on opioid prescribing and continuing education. Retrieved from: https://www.ada.org/about/press-releases/2018-archives/american-dental-association-announces-new-policy-to-combat-opioid-epidemic ; Roberts, R.M., Bohm, M.K., Bartoces, M.G., Fleming-Dutra, K.E., Hicks, L.A., & Chalmers, N.I. (2020) Antibiotic and opioid prescribing for dental-related conditions in emergency departments: United States, 2012 through 2014. *Journal of American Dental Association, 151*(3), 174–181. https://doi.org/10.1016/j.adaj.2019.11.013

15 Meini, B. & Clarke, R.V. (2012). Gasoline drive-offs. Problem-Oriented Guides for Police Problem-Specific Guides Series No. 67. Retrieved from: https://popcenter.asu.edu/sites/default/files/problems/PDFs/gas_drive_offs.pdf

16 Design Council (2010). Using design to reduce injuries from alcohol related violence in pubs and clubs. London, UK: Design Council. Retrieved from: https://www.designcouncil.org.uk/fileadmin/uploads/dc/Documents/design-out-crime-alcohol.pdf

17 Linning, S.J., Carroll, T., Gerard, D.W., & Eck, J.E. (2024). Do solutions to crime need to be complicated? *Public Management, 106*(8), 36–39. https://icma.org/articles/pm-magazine/do-solutions-crime-need-be-complicated

18 Clarke, R.V. & Eck, J.E. (2003). Become a problem-solving crime analyst in 55 steps. Jill Dando Institute of Crime Science, University College London. Retrieved from: https://popcenter.asu.edu/sites/g/files/litvpz3631/files/library/reading/PDFs/55stepsUK.pdf

9
How Do Crime Problems Arise?

In the late 1970s, four crime scientists, Marcus Felson, Paul and Patricia Brantingham, and Ronald Clarke, decided to answer this question.[1] Oddly, most criminologists ignored this question. Criminologists traditionally focused on criminal propensity: asking why some people offend while others do not. Often, they attributed poor societal conditions to greater motivation for crime. But this only told a tiny part of the story. The four crime scientists believed we should re-think crime and our efforts to reduce it. Instead of asking *why* someone would commit a crime, they began studying *how* crimes occur. Their studies kept revealing a trend: opportunities for crime drive crime. When crime opportunities are abundant, many people exploit them. This led to three fundamental questions in crime science: how do crime opportunities arise? How do offenders find crime opportunities? How do offenders decide which opportunities to exploit?

Crime science is the study of crime events and crime processes as opposed to people's propensities for crime.[2] It is concerned with *how* offenders make use of their environments, leading to crime events. Unlike standard criminology, crime science does not focus on large - scale social issues and deep-seated personal difficulties that might lead someone to commit crime. Crime scientists consider criminal propensity a given; people vary in their willingness to engage in misbehavior, with most

 DOI: 10.4324/9781003430155-12

people unwilling to do so under most circumstances. If conditions for crime exist, someone is bound to exploit them. Therefore, crime scientists look for ways to alter or eliminate the conditions that create crime. Crime scientists call these conditions crime opportunities.

Crime scientists' studies show opportunities for crime drive crime.[3] Remember the gasoline drive-off example in chapter 5? It illustrates the importance of opportunities. Before gas stations created pay-before-you-pump systems, the conditions of a gas station made it easy to steal gasoline.[4] So, many people stole gas. Did poverty, racism, broken homes, patriarchy, or other social conditions push people from paying for gas to stealing it? Did they grow up in a gas-drive-off culture? Were they born with a gas-drive-off gene?

Crime scientists argue that trying to answer these *why* questions won't help reduce gasoline theft. Their studies showed that when gas stations switched to pay-first gas pumps, gasoline drive-offs stopped.[5] Regardless of *why* people were stealing gasoline, the gasoline thieves stopped stealing gas. They stopped not because of large-scale social change, but because we removed the opportunity to steal gas.

If opportunity, rather than propensity, is a strong driver of crime, then we have a practical approach to solving crime problems: block crime opportunities.[6] But in order to know how to block crime opportunities (discussed in chapter 10), you need to understand how crime opportunities arise. Crime scientists have developed three inter-linked explanations for this.

Explanation #1: Everyday Routines Create Crime Opportunities

By the late 1970s crime was increasing in Western nations at unprecedented rates, but criminologists could not explain why. Lawrence Cohen and Marcus Felson pointed out that many of the factors criminologists thought caused crime were moving in the opposite direction.[7] Unemployment was decreasing. Wages were increasing. Education rates were increasing. So how could crime be skyrocketing while the factors criminologists claim cause crime were not? Cohen and Felson proposed that people's everyday routines had changed. The changes in these routines opened up new opportunities for crime.

Rather than try to explain offenders' propensities, Cohen and Felson explained crime events. They pointed out that a crime can only occur when a willing offender encounters a suitable target in the absence of a capable guardian.[8] If this sounds familiar, it should. It is the original incarnation of the crime triangle we presented in chapter 2.[9] The explanation has evolved over time to include controllers: handlers, guardians, and managers.[10] So, what does this have to do with people's routines? The original premise of Cohen and Felson's argument is that the routine activities we engage in impact how often offenders and targets come in contact with each other. This increases the likelihood that crime will occur.

Prior to World War II, the nuclear family consisted of a husband and wife, who usually married young and who typically had children. The husband was the one who left during the day for work while the wife stayed home to take care of the children. Wages were low compared to the cost of living so few regularly engaged in many leisure activities outside of the home. Moreover, far fewer workers were unionized so employment benefits such as paid vacation were less common. This had important implications for crime patterns. It meant that many people occupied homes during the workday, thus increasing guardianship to protect against crimes such as residential burglaries. In the evenings many stayed home, thus reducing their likelihood of encountering motivated offenders. This meant that crimes such as assault and robbery were less likely because fewer suitable targets were wandering about in society.

But a great deal shifted during and after World War II. Women entered the workforce at unprecedented rates, workers began unionizing, and wages rose. It meant that more people were at work during the day, people had more money to engage in leisure activities after work, and people had several weeks of paid vacation to take advantage of.

What did this all mean for crime? Cohen and Felson argued that these changes to people's routine activities created more conditions where motivated offenders and suitable targets crossed paths in the absence of capable guardianship; it created more crime opportunities.[11] More homes were left unguarded as both the husband and wife went to work during the day. Census data showed that between 1960 and 1971, the number of homes that were unoccupied between 8am and 4pm increased anywhere from 10% to 58% depending on the hour of day. More homes were also left unguarded as more people began earning disposable income that allowed them to partake in entertainment activities outside the home on evenings and weekends or for longer periods on vacation. Once out at events or out travelling, this simultaneously increased people's likelihood of coming into contact with a motivated offender. So, it made sense that crimes like robbery and assault also increased.[12]

Technological advancements also played a role. With increased disposable income, more people were buying material goods, such as electronics. Those goods were also becoming smaller and lighter, making them easier to steal. For instance, Cohen and Felson looked up the weights of televisions in Sears catalogues.[13] The lightest televisions in the 1960s were 38lbs, but by the 1970s they were 15lbs. This made them easier for burglars to steal.

As Felson reflected:

> It no longer made sense to understand crime in terms of bad people while ignoring where people are, what they are doing, where their property is located, who they are with and whether offending and victimisation were likely.[14]

Instead of focusing on propensity for crime, Felson suggested that we could reduce crime by removing opportunities for crime. Like the examples provided in chapter 5, this was the original work showing us that crime is often the by-product of everyday activities.[15]

Routine activity explanation evolved. Felson augmented his theory of everyday routines when he added the concept of handlers: people who are emotionally attached to offenders and who try to keep them out of trouble (e.g., parents, teachers, coaches, and others).[16] John made places more prominent and added place managers to the explanation.[17] To help guide police and other crime preventers, John summarized routine activity theory as a set of triangles (recall from chapter 2).[18]

The routine activity explanation, and its triangles, is a useful crime prevention tool because it underscores the importance of paying attention to more than the offender (places and victims/targets matter, too). It also highlights the need to examine everyday conditions to determine how they facilitate or block crime. The routine activity explanation shows how opportunities arise—through every day legal activities. But how do offenders find these opportunities? The answer lies in crime pattern theory.

Explanation #2: How Offenders Find Crime Opportunities

At the same time that Cohen and Felson were developing their routine activities explanation, Paul and Patricia Brantingham were zeroing in on an explanation for how offenders find crime opportunities. Paul had earned a law degree and Patricia had degrees in mathematics and urban planning, so they were not as heavily influenced by standard criminology. In the 1970s Patricia was particularly inspired by the work of urban planner Kevin Lynch. Lynch's book *The Image of the City* argued that people's activities are at the mercy of how urban planners organize cities.[19] This means that people's behavior and where they spend most of their time is quite predictable. The Brantinghams realized that Lynch's ideas could help develop an explanation for when and where offenders find crime opportunities.

The Brantinghams point out that offenders behave just like us, most of the time.[20] Even the most prolific offenders, people who commit hundreds of crimes per year, spends most of their time engaging in non-criminal activities. Like us, they sleep several hours a day. Like us, they shop for food and clothing. Like us, they like to see movies and attend concerts or sporting events, and so on. Many offenders even have day jobs, again just like us. Thus, offenders engage in many of the same activities at the same places as we do. This means offenders are also at the mercy of how urban planners and developers have built cities. All these things have important implications for where, when, and how offenders commit their crimes. Like Cohen and Felson point out, they are linked to our everyday routines.[21] So how does this work?

The Brantinghams explain that everyone has the following elements in their lives: activity nodes, paths, an activity space, and an awareness space.[22] *Activity nodes* are the places where we spend our time (the black dots in figure 9.1). For most people this includes their home, their workplace or school, the places they shop, the places they go for entertainment, and so on. Then we have the *paths* we use to move to and from these places (the arrows in figure 9.1). These include our standard route

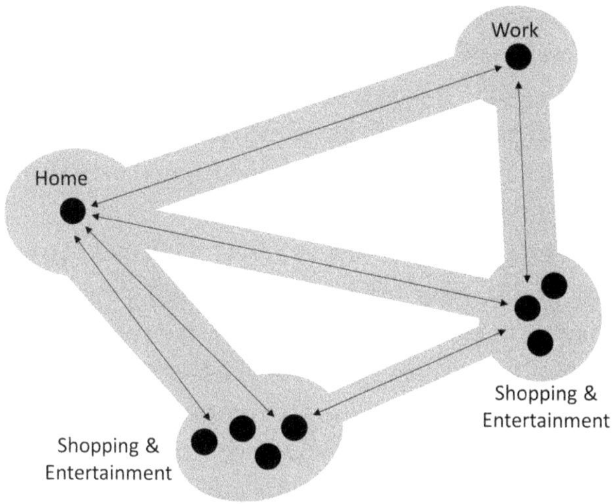

FIGURE 9.1 How Offenders Find Crime Opportunities

Adapted from Brantingham & Brantingham (1981)

to work, the running trail we always use, the streets we take to everyday shopping and entertainment.

We choose paths that take the least amount of time or impose the least amount of frustration. It's likely you do this all the time without realizing it. Take a minute to think about your paths. Do you take the same route to work every time? Why? It's likely you tried out a few different routes but settled on one that takes the least amount of time or has the least frustrating traffic. You likely even do this when travelling to places you are less familiar with. For example, people tend to select the suggested route on Google Maps that will take them the least amount of time. Because of this, our movement patterns are very predictable. In fact, it's another manifestation of the rule of the few. We spend the majority of our time at a small number of places and along a few well-worn routes.

Activity space is the collection of all places and paths where we spend our time. Your *awareness space* is made up of all the places within a city we have some knowledge about (the grey area in the figure).[23] For example, you may be aware of the few stores in the strip mall containing the closest driver's licensing office to your home. You may seldom go to these places because you need only renew your license every few years, but you are still aware of the area, nonetheless. Similarly, the blocks adjacent to your main activity nodes and paths are also likely part of your awareness space. For example, if a traffic congestion forces you to take a detour from your regularly traveled path, you will get some exposure to these nearby areas, but you would not travel further from your original path than you had to. These areas are all part of your awareness space.

Because offenders are just like us, their movement patterns can be characterized by the same elements that could describe you and us. Offenders have homes, workplaces, schools, restaurants, and shops just like us, and they, too, like to spend the least amount of time travelling to and from these nodes. This is why many people opt to take highways whenever possible (and not gridlocked with traffic) as opposed to side roads with four-way stops, speed humps, and multiple traffic lights to slow them down.[24]

We can then use this information in combination with the routine activities approach to understand where and when crimes occur. Recall that most crimes can only happen when a motivated offender and suitable target come into contact with one another in the absence of a guardian.[25] So, crimes are more likely at places where offenders and victims cross paths. A crime is much more likely to occur at an activity node shared by an offender and a victim; a crime would not happen at an activity node that an offender does not frequent.[26]

A game of connect the dots helps illustrate how offenders' searches yield crime patterns. In figure 9.2, we have three types of dots: black dots are where victims or offenders live; grey dots are places where offenders or victims go for work, play, shopping, or other activities; and the mini blasts are crime sites. Figure 9.2 has two types of connectors of these dots—thick for offenders and thin/dashed for victims. These connectors represent travel paths. In reality, such paths will be bent and wavy as our two actors move along streets. We straightened out their paths to keep things simple.

Let's begin with the offender at home. Our offender has three other places he visits. If he spots a likely target that appears vulnerable, he preys upon it (but we are getting ahead of ourselves). Our three possible victims also have homes and paths they routinely follow to their activity nodes. The crime sites sit where the paths or nodes of offenders overlap with the

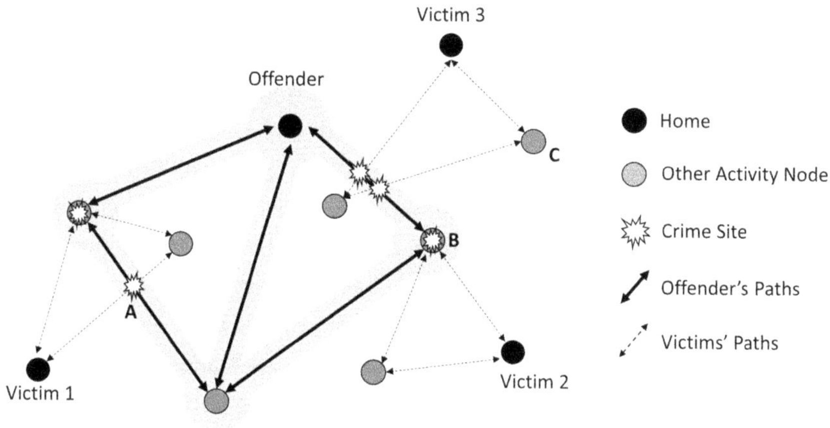

FIGURE 9.2 Where Will Crimes Occur?

paths and nodes of victims. Consider some examples. Point A denotes a crime where the offender and victim 1 cross paths while the offender is enroute to one of his nodes. If the victim is alone at night and visibly intoxicated, for example, the offender may choose to rob him as he is passing through the area on his way to a movie theatre. Point B shows a node that the offender and victim 2 share. This could be a gym, for example. If the victim leaves his valuables in a locker but does not place a lock on it, the offender may steal the contents of the locker if he discovers them while also using this place.

Point C showcases another important concept from the Brantinghams' theory. This is a place that would experience no crime, at least at the hands of the offender in the figure; the place is not within his awareness space, he spends no time there. Point C might have the most lucrative crime opportunities of all places in the figure. But our offender is ignorant of this fact, so he will not exploit it. If other offenders are equally ignorant, the place will stay crime-free.

The Brantinghams' theory dovetails with the routine activities explanation. Motivated offenders and victims need to come into contact with one another for a crime to occur. If an offender encounters a victim by chance—one or both of them is not following their routines—then the police will record a one-off event, seemingly unconnected to other crimes. But when offenders' routines and victims' routines repeatedly converge, crime patterns appear. Years ago, retired people in the United States always received a Social Security check from the federal government on the same day of the month. This created a nationwide routine. Some of these people had to walk to their post office to fetch their check. Offenders learned about this routine (it was not much of a secret). You can imagine the result. Changes in how the Social Security Administration sends payments to retired people (e.g., direct deposit) changed the victims' routines and reduced the robberies.[27] Robbery patterns also arise in situations among people who routinely take their paychecks to payday lenders for quick cashing. Pickpocketing at transit stations is another example of this. This convergence will happen in predictable places because offenders and targets have predictable movement patterns. Places that bring more people together are at greater risk of having crime.

The Brantinghams also distinguished between two types of places that experience crime: crime generators and crime attractors.[28] Crime generators are places that bring people together for purposes other than crime. But because they create opportunities for offending, we see more crime at these locations. Sports stadiums and shopping malls are prime examples. Many offenders use these places for conventional activities like the rest of us. They too want to see their favorite sports team beat a rival or go purchase new clothing. But in the process of engaging in these conventional activities, they may chance upon crime opportunities they can exploit. For example, Nancy may leave her purse in her cart when she turns to look at an item on a high shelf. If Nancy does this as Melvin passes by, Melvin may decide to swipe her purse. Our motivated offender, Melvin, did not set out to commit a crime at that time or place, but he was ready when the place and victim created a momentary opportunity too good to pass up.

Crime attractors are places known to offenders for having good crime opportunities. So, offenders deliberately travel to these places to commit crimes. Bars with poor management are a good example of this. If a minor wants to consume alcohol and learns of a bar that does not regularly check patrons' identification, she may travel to this place deliberately. Similarly, people seeking an encounter with a sex worker will travel to locations where sex workers are known to wait for customers.[29]

Note that some places can be both crime generators and crime attractors. Melvin may not have gone to the store to steal Nancy's purse. In contrast, Marvin goes to this store a lot because there are often easy shoplifting opportunities created by the tight aisles, high shelves, and few employees. A poorly managed bar could be an attractor to a minor looking to consume alcohol. But it could also be a location with many assaults if management does not stop serving visibly intoxicated patrons. The customers may not have intended to get into any trouble when they decided to go there that day, but assaults could occur if patrons get rowdy throughout the night.

The Brantinghams' explanation provided the next step after the routine activities explanation to identify the likely places that offenders and targets/victims would come in contact. The routine activity explanation spoke about how crime opportunities can arise from mundane activities by people. It explains the *supply* of crime opportunities. In contrast, the Brantinghams' explanation describes how offenders find opportunities created by people's routines and the places they visit. Some offenders deliberately seek out crime opportunities. But other offenders are more opportunistic; they do not seek out opportunities but will exploit an opportunity should one present itself. Thus, the Brantinghams explained the *demand* for crime opportunities. In economics, when supply meets demand, a market arises. With crime, when opportunity supply meets opportunity demand, a crime pattern arises.

But a final piece of the puzzle is missing: the two explanations only show possible victims bumping into possible offenders. The offender still has to make a choice to commit a crime. A motivated offender could come into contact with many targets at an activity node, but they seldom victimize all of them. Certain decision-making processes go into the commission of a crime. This is where the rational choice perspective came in to complete the crime science explanation.

Explanation #3: How Offenders Choose Targets and Commit Crime

Everyday routines expose potential targets. Offenders' routines bring targets to their attention. The two explanations we just described leave us with the possible offenders standing very near to their possible crime targets—a person, building, or stuff—but nothing is happening, so far. The possible offenders need to make a choice: actually, a series of choices.

The first choice is whether to exploit their unprotected target. If the choice is yes, the possible offenders move toward becoming actual offenders and they have more choices to make if they want to be successful. In the 1970s, criminologists fixated on social influences on offenders' behavior and avoided discussing offenders' choices. Economists were happy to discuss them but reduced them down to benefits and costs. The criminologists' views did not put policy options on the table, and the economists' views served up a meager meal of certain punishment.

Ronald Clarke and Derek Cornish found a productive alternative: the rational choice perspective.[30] Both received their degrees in psychology and early in their careers studied delinquent youth. They discovered that traditional psychological and sociological theories of crime failed to explain youth delinquency.[31] Frustrated, they developed the rational choice perspective to understand how offenders decide when, where, and how to commit crimes.

Rationality is the quality of making decisions using facts or logic. Economists often assume that when someone makes a rational choice, they weigh all the costs and benefits of their options and then make the very best choice. In short, economists believe people, including offenders, make optimal choices, usually. In the 1950s, however, Herman Simon challenged this view and developed the concept of bounded rationality.[32]

Bounded rationality recognizes that in the real world, we often have to make decisions under imperfect circumstances. Bounded rational decision makers do not optimize; they do not seek the best outcome or avoid the worst. Instead, they look for good enough outcomes using mental shortcuts and intuition (e.g., see United States Marine Corps, n.d.).[33] In recent years, the field of behavioral economics has pursued Simon's ideas and challenged the simplistic standard economic assumptions. But this occurred after Cornish and Clarke started examining how real offenders make real decisions. Cornish and Clarke assumed offenders make decisions like everyone else.

We mostly make boundedly rational decisions because of a number of constraints. For example, we seldom have the mental capacity to understand all of the pertinent information that would help us make the decision. We never know all the pertinent facts. We usually have difficulty seeking out the relevant information and we have too little time to seek all the information, process it, and arrive at the optimal decision. Instead, we make good enough decisions and hope for the best.

You have likely experienced this when taking your vehicle into an automotive repair show. Sometimes, the mechanic will call you after discovering that a part in your car is about to fail and should be replaced. You likely do not have any idea of what a reasonable estimate for parts and labour would be to replace it and do not have the time to research it for hours or get estimates from other repair shops. So, if the estimated price for the repair is not astronomical, you will likely make the decision in the moment to give them permission to proceed. You need your car back as soon as possible, so you make the decision based on the information you have. You may have increased the chances of making the right choice when you selected the mechanic: asking trusted friends or searching ratings on the internet.

But even choosing the mechanic was probably a boundedly rational decision. You probably did not list all possible mechanics along with all relevant information, assessing each and then choosing the very best. You made a good-enough search in the time you had and then made a bounded decision. You probably gave attention to how much mechanics charge: the cost of repairs. You probably attended to how far away mechanics are from your home: the effort of repairs. You probably looked for signs that the mechanic would do a bad job or cheat you: the risk of repairs.

These considerations will be important in the next chapter when we discuss ways to reduce unwanted, criminal, behavior. When an action or behavior takes a lot of effort or is risky, fewer people are inclined to engage in it. Conversely, if a behavior brings about some kind of reward, especially in the short term, we are more likely to do it, and if the behavior is provoked or encouraged somehow, we are also prone to engaging in it. Lastly, if we can come up with excuses to justify our behavior, we are more likely to do it.

To illustrate, consider the example of a voluntary 401(k) retirement plan offered by an employer. Such plans are considered major perks for employees who can have income deducted pre-tax and invested for retirement. In some plans only the employee contributes, but in other plans the employer will match the employee's contribution. There are many benefits for employees to contribute to these plans, and few risks; the investment options provided are usually low risk. Yet, many employees do not take advantage of this perk. Why might that be? Would it not be rational for anyone with access to a 401(k) and employer match to use it to their advantage?

The five factors that influence our behavior play into employees' decision-making processes to participate or not. Though these plans can reap great rewards, those rewards are not seen until many decades later. Some people might want the extra cash in the short term, as opposed to more money in the long term. Similarly, these programs can be a hassle to set up, and involve decisions about convoluted financial investments to choose from. Thus, some may not want to put in the effort to get things in place. Further, some employers may simply provide a pamphlet about the plan at the time of hiring with no follow up to get the plan started. This provides little provocation to take action and many people can easily come up with excuses, such as "I don't have the time", for not getting their plan set up.

We suspect many of you have experienced the dreaded decision-making and action (or lack thereof) of retirement planning. If not, you have still encountered these factors in other areas of your life. Shopping decisions are a perfect example. In short, these are common factors that impact human decision-making. As the Brantinghams point out, crime and the actions of offenders work much the same. But many people have a hard time believing that offenders think and behave rationally. Why would engaging in highly risky activities, such as crime, be rational? They could get hurt. They could get caught and go to jail. They could lose their reputation, and so on. In addition, many of the supposed benefits of crime are lost on the average person. Serial killer Jeffery Dahmer's desire to eat his victims hardly seems rational. The same thing applies to terrorists to who sacrifice their own lives as part of their attack.

But there are two different kinds of rationality that are important for crime. Most people think of rationality in terms of outcomes. They consider whether a person's end goal is rational. We can refer to this as *ends rationality*. Wanting a higher income is ends rational because it is socially acceptable. Wanting to murder someone is ends irrational and not socially acceptable. Ends rationality might be useful for forming judgements about people, but it is less useful for preventing bad choices.

Therefore, crime scientists argue it is more useful to focus on *means rationality*. That is, looking at the processes offenders use for achieving their outcomes. If an offender followed procedures that improved his or her success at achieving his or her desired outcomes, then we consider such a person *means* rational. This kind of rationality is most important for crime prevention; if we understand how offenders commit crimes, we can design interventions that thwart their actions. Again, the gasoline drive-off example we provided is an example of this. We did not need to understand the ends rationality of every person who decided to steal gas. To reduce crime, we only needed to understand the means they used to carry out their crime.

For any crime, no matter how simple, there are several steps the offender must take, if he wants to be successful. Each step involves a set of decisions and different sets of steps are needed for different crime types. A burglar looking for a home to break into, for example, might case different residential neighborhoods, look for homes that are unoccupied and with bushes and other shrubbery that would block anyone from seeing him breaking in. Just as important, he would avoid homes that appear occupied, have a burglar alarm or dog, and that have nosey neighbors on the lookout. This sequence of steps would be very different for an offender looking to steal a car, sell drugs, or commit a sexual assault or commercial burglary.

Crime scientists refer to sequences of decision steps as scripts. Derek Cornish introduced scripts into crime science by adapting the ideas from cognitive sciences.[34] A script is a sequence of actions. Some have likened it to a cartoon strip.[35] If a person has a script, they no longer make conscious decisions about each action in the sequence, they choose the script and follow it.

We all use scripts in our everyday lives. When you commute to work or school, you get into your car and go into autopilot to drive there or take the same transit line. If you are a university student, you take a seat in a classroom and know to stop talking once the professor starts her lecture. If you go to a fast-food restaurant, you know that script too. You walk in, order your food, pay for your food, then take it to a table of your choosing and start eating. Conversely, if you go to a sit-down restaurant, you know to wait for the host to seat you. You then order your food, eat it, and pay after the meal.

Because offenders are just like us, they, too, use scripts. Once an offender understands the script, and has some practice, he does not have to think a great deal about each crime (at least as long as things go right). A script, therefore, is much like a recipe. It might take some practice to learn the recipe, but once you do, you can reliably create the dish.

Like recipes, scripts can be quite general, or very specific. Consider an example of a specific script based on an interview of a bank robbery by two detectives. The robber had been released from prison and detectives were interested in how he thought about his crimes and the procedures he followed (they were not trying to convict him of any new crime). This robber had been quite successful, for a while, in part, because he once worked in a bank and knew their procedures. One of the reasons for this was he had a meticulously developed script. He was caught when one day he failed to follow his script.

As you can see from table 9.1, this robber is very means rational. Based on his experiences as a bank employee and from his first robberies, he knew what worked and what increased his risk of getting caught. He was once chased by a male teller, despite the bank's explicit employee instructions not to chase. Therefore, this robber assumes male tellers are less likely to follow bank rules than female tellers, so he avoids robbing banks with male tellers. He knows a common baseball hat will hide his face from overhead cameras, but will not draw suspicion. He knows that he is very nervous before a robbery, so he takes a predetermined amount of vodka: enough to calm him, but not enough to impair judgement.

There are two reasons for scripts. First, the offender does not have to start from scratch with each crime. It simplifies decision-making. A sequence of decisions is collapsed into a single script. Information gathering and thinking costs are reduced. Our bank robber did not have to make all his decisions repeatedly. By creating a script, he only had to decide to commit the crime. The rest was semi-automatic. But he also built-in points for bailing out so he did not have to make careful and time-consuming assessments (e.g., if I see X, Y, or Z, I leave).

Table 9.1. A Bank Robber's Script

Step	Explanation	Purpose
Search for targets	Go to city other than where the last robbery took place	Identify possible locations
Refine targets	Reject bank branches that fail to meet specific requirements	Identify specific target
Check equipment	Go check for clothing, note, and other equipment; wear baseball hat and non-descript clothing	Make sure everything is in order
Reduce stress	Take measured dose of alcohol	Reduce chances of failure due to nervousness, but retains ability to think clearly
Last minute surveillance	Make sure nothing new is in the way: parking area is clear, no police, etc.	Gives opportunity to call it off
Enter bank	Last check—leave if male teller is present or unexpected problems develop	Last chance to call it off
Stand in line	Wait for teller	Hides his intentions by imitating legitimate customers
Hand tellers note and demand money	Note explains he has a gun, or someone across the street has a rifle and scope. Demands only bills from drawers without dye packs	He carries no weapons to reduce risk of a large sentence and of hurting anyone
Take back note	Demand the teller hand back the note	Reduces evidence available for police
Walk out	Go to car outside of surveillance camera range	Does not draw attention to himself or his vehicle
Change clothes	Hat and shirt	Reduces chances of being identified
Drive away	Follow speed limit and other traffic rules	Reduces chances of being identified

We do the same when we commute to work or school. After the first couple of trips, most of the route becomes automatic. We no longer choose where to turn, we do so automatically unless something goes wrong (traffic congestion, for example, or construction on the road creates a detour). We might not remember anything about the trip from the time we left home to the time we arrive because our minds only pay attention to abnormalities.

Second, some processes cannot be done without taking specific steps. If someone wants to rob a bank, he needs to find one first. If the bank robber wants to use a gun, he needs to find one. If he wants to enter the bank, he needs to step through the door. Some steps come prepackaged with the script. Consider the robber who does not want to pass notes or threaten a room full of customers. What script could she choose? She could decide to confront the bank manager when he arrives for work and take the cash before the bank opens. If she wants to do that, there are some obvious things she needs to do. First, she needs to find out when the bank opens. Second, she needs to discover the basic opening procedures. There are many other considerations. In addition, failure to take these steps—not building them into the script—can end in failure.

Bringing the Three Explanations Together

At the beginning of this chapter, we listed the three questions that guide crime science research: How do crime opportunities arise? How do offenders find crime opportunities? How do offenders decide which opportunities to exploit? Together, the three crime science explanations provide answers to these questions. The routine activities explanation shows how everyday routines create crime opportunities. The crime pattern explanation shows how offenders find crime opportunities, both opportunistically and deliberately. The rational choice explanation shows how offenders choose which crime opportunities to act on and how they exploit them.

Knowing the answers to these three questions helps develop effective crime prevention strategies. Each decision offenders make before, during, and after they commit their crimes provides an opportunity for intervention. If we know the script, we can take countermeasures. In short, we can take the five factors that influence behavior—effort, risk, reward, provocations, and excuses—and use them to disrupt parts of an offender's script. If we increase the effort or risk involved in committing the crime, for example, many will not offend. So how do we do this exactly? Ron Clarke developed a framework based off on his rational choice perspective to do just this. We walk you through it all in the next chapter.

Key Points

- Our routine activities create crime opportunities
- Crime occurs at predictable places
- Offenders are reasonably rational in selecting and exploiting crime opportunities
- Ask: how do crime events occur?

Notes

1 Wortley, R., Sidebottom, A., Tilley, N., & Laycock, G. (2018). What is crime science? In R. Wortley, A. Sidebottom, N. Tilley, & G. Laycock (Eds.), *Routledge Handbook of Crime Science* (pp. 1–29). Routledge. https://doi.org/10.4324/9780203431405-1

2 Clarke, R.V. (2004). Technology, criminology and crime science. *European Journal on Criminal Policy and Research, 10*(1), 55–63. https://doi.org/10.1023/b:crim.0000037557.42894.f7 ; Wortley, R., Sidebottom, A., Tilley, N., & Laycock, G. (2018). What is crime science? In R. Wortley, A. Sidebottom, N. Tilley, & G. Laycock (Eds.), *Routledge Handbook of Crime Science* (pp. 1–29). Routledge. https://doi.org/10.4324/9780203431405-1

3 Mayhew, P., Clarke, R.V.G., Sturman, A., & Hough, J.M. (1976). *Crime as opportunity*. Home Office Research Study No. 34. Retrieved from: https://popcenter.asu.edu/sites/g/files/litvpz3631/files/2025-02/124-mayhew_et_al-crime_as_opportunity.pdf

4 Meini, B. & Clarke, R.V. (2012). Gasoline drive-offs. Problem-Oriented Guides for Police Problem-Specific Guides Series No. 67. Retrieved from: https://popcenter.asu.edu/sites/default/files/problems/PDFs/gas_drive_offs.pdf

5 Meini, B. & Clarke, R.V. (2012). Gasoline drive-offs. Problem-Oriented Guides for Police Problem-Specific Guides Series No. 67. Retrieved from: https://popcenter.asu.edu/sites/default/files/problems/PDFs/gas_drive_offs.pdf

6 Felson, M. & Clarke, R.V. (1998). *Opportunity makes the thief*. Police Research Series Paper 98, 1–36. https://popcenter.asu.edu/sites/g/files/litvpz3631/files/opportunity_makes_the_thief.pdf

7 Cohen, L.E. & Felson, M. (1979). Social change and crime rate trends: A routine activity approach. *American Sociological Review, 44*(4), 588–608. https://doi.org/10.2307/2094589

8 Cohen, L.E. & Felson, M. (1979). Social change and crime rate trends: A routine activity approach. *American Sociological Review, 44*(4), 588–608. https://doi.org/10.2307/2094589

9 Clarke, R.V. & Eck, J.E. (2005). *Crime analysis for problem solvers in 60 small steps*. US Department of Justice. Retrieved from: https://portal.cops.usdoj.gov/resourcecenter/RIC/Publications/cops-w0047-pub.pdf; Eck, J.E. (2003). Police problems: The complexity of problem theory, research, and evaluation. *Crime Prevention Studies, 15*, 79–114.

10 Eck, J.E., Linning, S.J., & Herold, T.D. (2023). *Place Management and Crime: Ownership and Property Rights as a Source of Social Control*. Springer Publishers. https://doi.org/10.1007/978-3-031-27693-4; Felson, M. (1986). Routine activities, social controls, rational decisions, and criminal outcomes. In D. Cornish & R.V. Clarke (Eds.), *The Reasoning Criminal: Rational Choice Perspectives on Offending* (pp. 119–128). New York, NY: Springer-Verlag; Hollis, M., Felson, M. & Welsh, B. (2013). The capable guardian in routine activities theory: A theoretical and conceptual reappraisal. *Crime Prevention and Community Safety, 15*, 65–79. https://doi.org/10.1057/cpcs.2012.14

11 Cohen, L.E. & Felson, M. (1979). Social change and crime rate trends: A routine activity approach. *American Sociological Review, 44*(4), 588–608. https://doi.org/10.2307/2094589

12 Cohen, L.E. & Felson, M. (1979). Social change and crime rate trends: A routine activity approach. *American Sociological Review, 44*(4), 588–608. https://doi.org/10.2307/2094589

13 Cohen, L.E. & Felson, M. (1979). Social change and crime rate trends: A routine activity approach. *American Sociological Review, 44*(4), 588–608. https://doi.org/10.2307/2094589

14 From page 87 of: Felson, M. (2017). The routine activity approach. In R. Wortley & M. Townsley (Eds.), *Environmental Criminology and Crime Analysis* (pp. 87–97). New York, NY: Routledge.

15 Felson, M. & Eckert, M. (2018). *Crime and Everyday Life* (6th edition). Sage Publishing.

16 Felson, M. (1986). Routine activities, social controls, rational decisions, and criminal outcomes. In D. Cornish & R.V. Clarke (Eds.), *The Reasoning Criminal: Rational Choice Perspectives on Offending* (pp. 119–128). New York, NY: Springer-Verlag.

17 Eck, J.E. (1994). *Drug markets and drug places: A case-control study of the spatial structure of illicit drug dealing*. Doctoral dissertation, University of Maryland, College Park.

18 Eck, J.E. (2003). Police problems: The complexity of problem theory, research, and evaluation. *Crime Prevention Studies, 15*, 79–114.

19 Lynch, K. (1960). *The Image of the City*. Cambridge, MA: The MIT Press.

20 Brantingham, P.L. & Brantingham, P.J. (1981). Notes on the geometry of crime. In P.J. Brantingham & P.L. Brantingham (Eds.), *Environmental Criminology* (pp. 27–54). Prospect Heights, IL: Waveland Press; Brantingham, P.L. & Brantingham, P.J. (1993). Environment, Routine, and Situation: Toward a Pattern Theory of Crime. In M. Felson & R.V. Clarke (Eds.), *Routine Activity and Rational Choice* (pp. 259–294). Transaction. https://doi.org/10.4324/9781315128788-12

21 Cohen, L.E. & Felson, M. (1979). Social change and crime rate trends: A routine activity approach. *American Sociological Review, 44*(4), 588–608. https://doi.org/10.2307/2094589

22 Brantingham, P.L. & Brantingham, P.J. (1981). Notes on the geometry of crime. In P.J. Brantingham & P.L. Brantingham (Eds.), *Environmental Criminology* (pp. 27–54). Prospect Heights, IL: Waveland Press; Brantingham, P.L. & Brantingham, P.J. (1993). Environment, Routine, and Situation: Toward a Pattern Theory of Crime. In M. Felson & R.V. Clarke (Eds.), *Routine Activity and Rational Choice* (pp. 259–294). Transaction. https://doi.org/10.4324/9781315128788-12

23 Brantingham, P.L. & Brantingham, P.J. (1981). Notes on the geometry of crime. In P.J. Brantingham & P.L. Brantingham (Eds.), *Environmental Criminology* (pp. 27–54). Prospect Heights, IL: Waveland Press; Brantingham, P.L. & Brantingham, P. J. (1993). Environment, Routine, and Situation: Toward a Pattern Theory of Crime. In M. Felson & R.V. Clarke (Eds.), *Routine Activity and Rational Choice* (pp. 259–294). Transaction. https://doi.org/10.4324/9781315128788-12
24 Brantingham, P.L. & Brantingham, P.J. (1981). Notes on the geometry of crime. In P.J. Brantingham & P.L. Brantingham (Eds.), *Environmental Criminology* (pp. 27–54). Prospect Heights, IL: Waveland Press; Brantingham, P.L. & Brantingham, P.J. (1993). Environment, Routine, and Situation: Toward a Pattern Theory of Crime. In M. Felson & R.V. Clarke (Ed.), *Routine Activity and Rational Choice* (pp. 259–294). Transaction. https://doi.org/10.4324/9781315128788-12
25 Cohen, L.E. & Felson, M. (1979). Social change and crime rate trends: A routine activity approach. *American Sociological Review, 44*(4), 588–608. https://doi.org/10.2307/2094589
26 Brantingham, P.L. & Brantingham, P.J. (1981). Notes on the geometry of crime. In P.J. Brantingham & P.L. Brantingham (Eds.), *Environmental Criminology* (pp. 27–54). Prospect Heights, IL: Waveland Press; Brantingham, P.L. & Brantingham, P. J. (1993). Environment, Routine, and Situation: Toward a Pattern Theory of Crime. In M. Felson & R.V. Clarke (Eds.), *Routine Activity and Rational Choice* (pp. 259–294). Transaction. https://doi.org/10.4324/9781315128788-12
27 Armey, L.E., Lipow, J., & Webb, N.J. (2014). The impact of electronic financial payments on crime. *Information Economics and Policy, 29*, 46–57. https://doi.org/10.1016/j.infoecopol.2014.10.002; Wright, R., Tekin, E., Topalli, V., McClellan, C., Dickinson, T., & Rosenfeld, R. (2017). Less cash, less crime: Evidence from the electronic benefit transfer program. *Journal of Law and Economics, 60*, 361–383. https://doi.org/10.1086/693745
28 Brantingham, P.L. & Brantingham, P.J. (1995). Criminality of place: Crime generators and crime attractors. *European Journal on Criminal Policy and Research, 3*(3), 5–26. https://doi.org/10.1007/bf02242925
29 Brantingham, P.L. & Brantingham, P.J. (1995). Criminality of place: Crime generators and crime attractors. *European Journal on Criminal Policy and Research, 3*(3), 5–26. https://doi.org/10.1007/bf02242925
30 Clarke, R.V. & Cornish, D.B. (1985). Modeling offenders' decisions: A framework for research and policy. In M. Tonry & N. Morris (Eds.), *Crime and Justice: An Annual Review of Research* (vol. 6, pp. 147–185). Chicago, IL: University of Chicago Press.
31 Cornish, D.B. & Clarke, R.V. (1975). *Residential treatment and its effects on delinquency* (No. 32). Her Majesty's Stationery Office.
32 Simon, H.A. (1957). *Models of Man: Social and Rational. Mathematical Essays of Rational Human Behavior in Society Setting*. New York, NY: Wiley.
33 United States Marine Corps (n.d.). *Decision Making B2B0237XQ Student Handout.* Retrieved from: https://www.trngcmd.marines.mil/Portals/207/Docs/TBS/B2B0237XQ%20Decision%20Making.pdf?ver=2017-01-27-145646-543
34 Cornish, D.B. (1994). The procedural analysis of offending and its relevance for situational prevention. In R.V. Clarke (Ed.), *Crime Prevention Studies* (vol. 3). Monsey, NY: Criminal Justice Press.
35 Nisbett, R.E. & Ross, L. (1980). *Human Interference: Strategies and Shortcomings of Social Judgement*. Englewood Cliffs, NJ: Prentice-Hall.

10

How Do We Fix Problems?

In the last chapter we explored three inter-linked explanations for how crime problems arise. We hinted that Ron Clarke developed a corresponding framework, based on these explanations, that can help you tackle crime. In this chapter, we show you how to put the explanations to use. Clarke's framework, called situational crime prevention, capitalizes on the psychology of human behavior.[1] Situational crime prevention suggests that we can change environments to reduce crime opportunities. This discourages people from offending. Five factors—effort, risk, reward, provocations, and excuses—tend to drive behavior, both criminal and non-criminal.[2] That is, if crime takes too much effort or incurs too much risk to carry out, fewer people will do it. Conversely, if a crime provides little reward, people are not provoked to act, or cannot excuse or justify their delinquent actions, fewer people will do it.[3]

These five factors influence us every day. They apply both to legitimate and offending behavior. Owners of places we commonly use work to manipulate these factors knowing that they will influence where we spend our time, what we eat, what we buy, and so much more. Casinos, for example, give out free alcoholic beverages to gamblers hoping they stay longer, and not to mention lowering their inhibitions. They also remove clocks and windows from the main areas hoping people will lose track of time. This keeps them gambling. Another tactic is to require gamblers use

 DOI: 10.4324/9781003430155-13

chips instead of money. This makes losses feel less painful because they are not putting real money on the table. This is a similar tactic that credit card companies capitalize on. It's much easier to charge something to a credit card and feel the pain weeks later when you get the bill than to hand over physical cash and feel the immediate pain of receiving much less back in change. So, you end up spending more, on average, when you use a credit card rather than cash.[4]

Online places work the same way. Amazon's one-click shopping and same day Prime shipping, for example, makes it more likely that you are going to buy products.[5] Their platform makes buying easy and you don't need to leave your house to get the products you want. Both business decisions reduce customer effort to acquire products. Many internet forums offer users access to exclusive parts of the website once users have posted a certain number of comments. These rewards encourage the forum's desired behavior: get users to spend as much time on the forum as possible.

Buying as much as possible not only works online but is also typical of your grocery store. Grocery stores want one thing from you: to buy as much as possible every time you go there. How do they encourage this desired behavior? They manipulate the environment.[6] They place essentials like milk and eggs at the back of the store to force you to walk past hundreds of other items. They want items that you never intended to buy before you entered the store to catch your eye so you buy them as well. They also place their higher-priced, name-brand items on shelves at eye-level so you will be more likely to buy them instead of cheaper options. They place frivolous goods, like junk food, near checkouts, hoping you will impulse buy them. All these design features provoke you to buy more.[7] Some stores even create confusing or forced-path layouts hoping you stay longer, see more items, and purchase more. Be honest, did you really need that 100-pack of tealights the last time you visited Ikea?

Some drug dealers use the same tactics to increase their sales. On the streets, it's referred to as *heroin marketing*. Drug markets locate on busy streets that are easy to enter and exit on foot or by car. Like grocery stores, some dealers give out free samples, especially of opioid-based drugs like fentanyl, which create a greater chance of you becoming addicted and a repeat customer. Some also brand their product so you know which one to buy. Dealers supply low-priced needles, so you can quickly use their product, and often offer a variety of drugs. Their drug market is convenient one-stop shopping. No need to go anywhere else.

But just as casinos, credit card companies, stores, and drug dealers use situational cues to encourage desired behavior, we can use situational cues to discourage unwanted behavior. Place managers, and others, can manipulate situations to supress harmful acts. For example, to reduce the number of traffic crashes, car manufacturers created Brake Transmission Shift Interlocks (BTSI) that prevent operators from putting a car in gear without having their foot on the brake. To reduce speeding in parking lots, property owners install speed bumps. Traffic islands can prevent unwanted left turns. Adding fencing to those islands can prevent jay walkers from crossing busy streets. Airports install seating with arm rests to keep people from sleeping, thereby allowing more people places to sit. In a recent widespread example, shutting down all non-essential businesses during the initial weeks of the Covid-19 pandemic drastically reduced the frequency with which people came into contact with one another.[8]

None of these examples involve drastic changes in propensity to engage in the behaviors. Instead, they involved changing situations or cues that make desired behaviors easier and undesired behaviors more difficult to carry out. Billions of people were highly motivated to continue their everyday activities during the Covid-19 pandemic. But the potential harms that could come from such behaviors prompted governments around the world to temporarily change our environment. These situational changes forced us to refrain from certain behaviors, like going dancing in crowded night clubs, and engage in others, like binge watching Netflix at home. Our routine activities were confined mostly to our homes no matter how motivated we were to leave them.

You may have detected a theme running through the theories we have described; offenders behave much like we do. Most of the time they engage in lawful behavior. They, too, have routines. They, too, make choices using the same criteria: effort, risks, rewards, provocations, and excuses. We are not claiming there are no differences. That is why we qualified the statement with "much like" rather than "exactly like". The outcomes of actions make the difference, but the processes leading to the outcomes are very familiar because they are the same processes used. We do not draw this parallel between unlawful and lawful behavior, between offenders and us, to inspire you to be sympathetic toward offenders. You can feel sympathy, or anger, or be indifferent toward the plight of offenders. We draw this parallel for very practical reasons. Because we and offenders approach the world similarly, we can develop insights into how offenders behave. With these insights, we can create effective crime prevention interventions.

Situational crime prevention looks at the world through the offenders' eyes and crafts solutions to defeat offending. Situational crime prevention is the subject of this chapter. We show how manipulating social and physical environments can reduce crime.

Situational Crime Prevention

In the previous chapter, we introduced Ronald Clarke, the co-creator of the rational choice perspective on crime.[9] His interest in choices was practical. He developed a widely used and tested approach to reducing crime: situational crime prevention. Since Clarke first described it,[10] situational crime prevention has been successfully applied to a wide range of criminal behavior: burglaries,[11] shoplifting,[12] violence,[13] terrorism,[14] animal poaching and smuggling,[15] and cybercrime,[16] to list a few.

Clarke's crime solutions influence offenders' behavior by altering the situations that tempt them. Clarke's approach does not require catching offenders to either scare them into behaving right or to assist them with finding the right path in life. It requires changing situations that encourage offenders to offend to situations that block (or diminish) offenders' ability or willingness to offend.

Clarke built situational crime prevention on the foundation of his rational choice perspective.[17] He maintained that offenders look for tempting situations. They assess the risk of getting caught for committing a crime, the effort such a crime will take to be successful, and the reward they will get from the crime. Some situations communicate a lot of risk and effort, and little reward. This is where crime is unlikely. Other situations communicate low risk, easy and rewarding situations to offenders. This is where crime is likely. Consequently, Clarke suggested that the most direct method to reduce crime is to identify situations that communicate that crime is easy, riskless, and rewarding and then change them so that they communicate the opposite.[18]

Situational crime prevention focuses on offenders but puts the preventive action outside of the offender. Offenders look at situations and decide whether to commit crimes. Situational crime prevention changes the situation so when potential offenders experience it, they behave like the rest of us. Therefore, we must look at situations through offenders' eyes.[19] How we perceive a situation is not relevant for crime prevention. We need to see opportunities like a thief if we want to defeat the thief.

Situations are small. A store on a street is a different situation than a bar on the same street. The apartment unit near the stairwell is a different situation than the unit in the middle of the hall. The apartment unit on the first floor is a different situation than the unit on the top floor.[20] Potential offenders notice these different situations and make choices based on the differences. If we want to keep offenders from making bad choices, we need to notice these differences too.[21]

Situations change—a convenience store at noon is not the same situation as the same store at midnight, the restaurant when open is not the same situation as it is when closed, the house when occupied is not the same situation as when its empty. The streets around a sport stadium hosting a game are not the same situation as the same streets around the same stadium when no teams are playing. Therefore, situational crime prevention aims to signal offenders right around the time the situation might tempt them.[22] Warnings weeks in advance and miles away are usually irrelevant to offenders; only the law-abiding notice these signals.

This implies applying five core principles of situational crime prevention.[23] These principles can be summarized by Shen and Linning's acronym COSTS: **C**rime-specific, **O**ffender's perspective, **S**ituation modification, **T**ime, and **S**pace.

Crime-specific means we need to address specific crime opportunities (e.g., burglaries of ground floor apartment units) instead of broad categories (e.g., burglaries). No single strategy works for all or most crime types. This relates to our discussion in chapter 6 about breaking down problems into more manageable parts with respect to vehicle theft. *Offender's perspective* means we need to understand how offenders perceive situations.[24] Our perceptions of crime opportunities do not matter because we are not the ones committing crimes. *Situation modification* means we need to alter the environmental characteristics and cues that encourage crime, not people's propensities for crime.[25] *Time* and *space* refer to intervening close to when and where offenders will act, not months or years earlier or miles away from the crime site.[26]

Do you recall from the last chapter, the five choice criteria that are influential to our behavior? They are effort, risk, reward, provocations, and excuses.[27] We talked about how these criteria influence an employee's decision to participate in retirement plans through their employers. If you found that few employees were taking the time to enroll in the program, certain steps could be taken to change behavior. Specifically, we could reverse engineer some or all of these five criteria to increase employee participation. For instance, the employers could reduce the effort by creating a simpler enrollment system. Similarly, the employer could increase rewards by offering to match the employee contribution amount. The employer could also mention the percentage of employees who have enrolled in the program to provoke others to join, and so on. In sum, the employer can find ways to promote desired behaviors and discourage unwanted ones.

Clarke used these same criteria to address crime.[28] He incorporated these five criteria into an effective crime prevention strategy (table 10.1). If a crime is easy to commit, we should increase the required effort. This makes the crime less enticing to offenders. If little risk comes from committing the crime, usually risk in getting caught, offenders are more likely to offend. Similarly, if a crime brings high rewards to offenders, we must look for ways to make it less rewarding, and so on.

Note that you do not need to reverse all five criteria to reduce crime. Often, you need only change one of them. Clarke offers five ways you can

Table 10.1 Situational Crime Prevention Considers Offenders' Choices

Offender Choice Criteria	What to Do About It?
Effort—if it is easy to do, they'll do it	Increase the effort
Risk—if it has limited or manageable risk, they'll do it	Increase the risk
Reward—if it is useful, profitable, or gratifying, they'll do it	Decrease the reward
Provocations—if enticed or provoked, they'll do it	Decrease provocations
Excuses—if the action can be justified, they'll do it	Decrease excuses

influence each of these five choice criteria, leading to an elegant 25 techniques of crime prevention. Not all will be relevant to any given problem. Instead, you can use the techniques like a menu of options to choose from. But you will ultimately be the problem-solver who deduces which technique(s) are the most useful for the present situation.

Making Crime More Effort

Let's consider each of the criteria and dig into the full range of situational techniques they provide. We will start with effort (table 10.2). We want to make possible offenders believe that a crime is simply too hard to successfully pull-off.

Target hardening creates barriers and other obstructions. Even if they do not completely prevent access, they slow people down. Door and window locks are the most common examples. Retail stores are also known to use glass display cases to protect more valuable goods such as jewellery, electronics, video games, razor blades, and cigarettes. You may have also seen products, like electronics, secured to display tables with a cable. Steering column locks and electronic immobilizers in cars also fit. These are all examples of target hardening.

Controlling access regulates who gets into a place and who gets excluded. Some places are closed to the general public and place users must show identification demonstrating they have permission to enter. Bars and

Table 10.2 Situational Crime Prevention Criterion 1: Increase Effort

Increase Effort	Examples
Target Harden	Locks; fences; windows; barricades; glass display cases; computer passwords; multi-factor authentication
Control Access	Checking ID at entrance; fewer curb cuts; fewer doors
Screen Exits	Check people leaving; pay booths
Deflect Offenders	Rail bumps (against skateboarders); one-way streets; helping stadium crowds exit area quickly
Control Tools	Reducing availability of spray paints; pseudoephedrine restrictions; screening luggage in airports; replacing traditional glasses with poly-carbonate glassware in bars

nightclubs check identification because they are not allowed to admit minors onto their premises. Public places, too, use access control. To get on board an airplane you must show picture identification and a boarding pass. Parking garages require you to obtain a ticket upon entry. To reduce shoplifting, some stores prohibit more than two or three juveniles inside at one time; each juvenile in a group can come in and shop, but not all at once. Blocking the secondary door at the few bars experiencing bag thefts and locking dumpster wheels at churches to prevent theft in chapter 1 are also examples of controlling access. When builders had to install external fire escapes on multistory buildings, they made it easy for offenders to enter upper stories. So, builders outfitted the escapes with a pully-counter weight so that it did not reach the ground, but during a fire, the weight of the people fleeing would lower the escape to the ground. Finally, it is easy to overlook one of the most common access controls, opening and closing hours. Banks are open only a few hours every day, thereby restricting access at other times. An outside ATM machine, however, is accessible every day all day.

Screening exits puts the prevention where offenders leave the situation. For example, the parking attendant looks at your ticket and asks for payment.[29] You cannot just leave. High security facilities check people out, but so do grocery stores and libraries. As you have probably experienced, some places control entrances but not exits (airports, for example); some control exits but not entrances (most stores, for example); and some places control both (some parking garages, for example).

Deflecting offenders occurs when prevention makes it harder for the offender to find or use the potential crime site, and when prevention distracts offenders' attention from the possible crime site to some other situation where crime is unlikely. In the late 1980s, the Los Angeles Police used barricades to make it harder for gang members to conduct drive - by shootings. The police realized that offenders would find such shootings more difficult and dangerous if they had to turn around at the end of the block and drive back past the crime scene.[30] Street configuration is not something a place manager can implement, usually. But place managers can organize their locations to deflect some types of offenders. The most common deflection application is the provision of separate toilet facilities for men and women, making sexual assault more difficult. To steer skateboarders from public areas where they might collide with pedestrians and cars, cities erect skateboard parks.

Controlling tools makes it harder for offenders to exploit a situation by restricting the devices offenders use to make crime easy. Airport security checks your luggage for weapons so that you cannot take anything dangerous onto an airplane.[31] This makes hijacking more difficult. College instructors sometimes ban electronic devices with internet connections from exam rooms to make cheating more difficult.[32] Laws to control the purchase of precursor chemicals for illegal drug manufacturing, to curb the sales of spray paint to prevent graffiti, or to prohibit firearms in bars to prevent shootings are all directed at tool control. Replacing traditional glasses that can be used as a weapon when broken with shatter-proof polycarbonate glassware in bars is another example.[33]

Making Crime Riskier

Let's turn our attention to the second-choice criteria: risk. To prevent crime, we want to *increase risk* of getting caught (table 10.3). Techniques in this category make offenders feel they are unlikely to get away with crime; they will be noticed, swiftly caught, and punished. Often the risk is of receiving a legal penalty. However, for some offenders, just being known to their friends as an offender is a risk, even if there are no formal

Table 10.3 Situational Crime Prevention Criterion 2: Increase Risk

Increase Risk	Examples
Extend Guardianship	Encouraging students to protect each other; cocoon neighborhood watch; announcements to lookout for suspicious activities
Assist Natural Surveillance	Improve lighting; increase sight lines; encouraging reporting of bad behavior
Reduce Anonymity	Greeters at banks and stores; showing identification at entry; sign in sheets; employee name tags and badges; logins on computers
Use Place Managers	Employee training; assigning prevention responsibilities
Strengthen Formal Surveillance	Security guards; alarms; actively monitored security cameras

legal sanctions. Again, it's how the potential offender feels about being caught that matters.

Extending guardianship improves watching. If offenders feel they are being watched, or if they are uncertain about others spotting them, they may refrain from crime. Airports often play announcements over their intercoms asking people to report suspicious activities. These announcements are designed to heighten guardianship in the airport and communicate to any offenders that many people may be watching and the risk of detection is higher. Any sign that asks place users to be alert to crime serves this purpose. In the United Kingdom, some police services use neighborhood cocoon watch. Following a burglary, police notify everyone living around the burgled residence that a nearby crime has occurred. Residents are asked to keep an eye out for the burglars' return: either to the site of the original burglary or to nearby homes. If the offender lives nearby, they are likely to hear about this request.[34] A crime consultant friend of John's told him about a bar in the Midwest that posted pictures of banned former patrons at the bar's entrance. The poster offered a free drink to anyone who reported one of these miscreants to the staff.

Assisting natural surveillance enhances people's ability to watch. Removing sight obstructions to watching or adding lighting are common examples. Replacing a solid wall with a wall containing decorative holes or glass panels allows surveillance of activities from either side.

Reducing anonymity makes offenders aware that they have been noticed. A robbery detective once told us that two bank branches next to each other had very different robbery experiences. The branch where the manager greeted every customer and asked them how they could be helped had no robberies. The neighboring bank did not greet customers and had several robberies. Showing identification upon entry—part of access control—reduces anonymity as well. The bar that displayed pictures of banned patrons was reducing anonymity as it extended guardianship. Many of these techniques come in packages, as you may have guessed.

Using place managers was a common theme throughout part 1 and 2 of this book. By virtue of owning or managing property, place managers can implement many of the techniques we are describing in this chapter.[35] Employees not only carry out their routine job responsibilities, but they can also watch patrons. Store clerks stocking shelves can spot shoplifters in the act. Doormen in apartment buildings can keep would-be burglars out of the building. Having two cashiers working in convenience stores and gas stations, particularly at night, may deter robbers. Often people who operate places do little to enhance this watching. But they could. Training employees in how to watch and greet people is one way. Making watching an explicit part of their job is another, and increasing the number of employees moving around with customers is another. The recent surge in shoplifting may be partially due to retail stores doing the opposite: reducing employees, discouraging employees from talking to patrons, and relying on electronic substitutes for people—such as self-checkouts.[36]

Strengthening formal surveillance requires designating personnel or equipment to watch for crime. Hiring security guards is one example, as is the use of closed-circuit television (CCTV) security cameras. Asking the bartender to be on the lookout for bad behavior is a form of place management. If the bar owner hires a bouncer, she is strengthening formal surveillance.

Making Crime Less Rewarding

Next, there are three offender choice criteria that we want to reduce to prevent crime. The first involves *decreasing rewards* (table 10.4). Applying these techniques makes offenders think they will get too little benefit for

Table 10.4 Situational Crime Prevention Criterion 3: Decrease Reward

Decrease Reward	Examples
Conceal Targets	Lock possessions out of sight in car trunk; lock possessions in a locker at the gym; display only one shoe in a store display
Remove Targets	Do not bring valuables to the gym; no narcotics on premises at pharmacies
Identify Property	Put your name or identification on your possessions; identification tags on pets
Disrupt Markets	Restrictions on used phone sales; regulation of pawn shops; metal recyclers and car dealerships
Deny Benefits	Exploding ink tags; separating product components before sale; kill switch technology in smartphones; graffiti clean up

their risk and effort. There are five ways crime preventers can manipulate offenders' perceptions of reward.

Concealing targets makes it less likely the offenders will notice a target and be tempted to take, destroy, or harm it. Hiding valuables is a common prevention tactic in many settings. Campaigns to have motorists lock valuables in their vehicle's trunk not only hardens these targets, but they make it more difficult for offenders to detect there are interesting targets worth taking. Homes in neighborhoods with few entrances (e.g., gated communities) have fewer burglaries than homes in neighborhoods with many entrances. The targets are better concealed in the first case than in the second.

Removing targets goes a step further. In cowboy movies, gamblers leave their cash on the table, inviting thefts and gunplay. In contrast, casinos use poker chips which removes the opportunity to steal cash off tables. Rather than giving offenders easy access to cash on the table, the casino secures it far away. Bus drivers used to make change, but this attracted robbers. Consequently, bus systems no longer allow drivers to make change and cash is in a secured box inaccessible to the driver and potential thieves. The increasing use of credit cards and other non-cash payment systems extend this idea. Pharmacies that do not store narcotics on site (or limit the amount of narcotics they have in-stock) eliminate a desirable product that drug users may try to commit robbery for.[37] Removing targets not only reduces theft and robbery by customers but can also reduce employee theft.

Identifying property reduces its value to the thief, particularly if they want to resell it. This is another widely used crime prevention technique: farmers and herders have marked their livestock for centuries to reduce theft. Companies routinely put inventory control labels on computers and other easily stolen and valuable office products. Pet owners install chips in their pets that identify the animal and the owner. Property registration with local government reduces fraudulent sales of land. In Maine, all lobstermen have their own special markings for their trap's buoys. State law prohibits anyone except the owner from handling the buoy or attached trap. This reduces theft of lobsters by other fishermen. The ability to track electronic devices is also a form of property marking. Property marking works best when the markings are visible to potential offenders, and the offenders understand the implications of markings. The clueless Maine tourist who knows nothing about the markings would not be deterred.

Disrupting markets prevents crime by making it difficult for a thief to resell their ill-gotten gains. This is the principal reason governments regulate pawnshops, metal recyclers, and car dealerships. The advent of internet sites for selling second-hand goods has created additional markets for stolen goods, so law enforcement agencies have attempted to get the sites to police themselves and thus reduce the access of thieves to their customers. Shutting down the Barksdale Market (chapter 5) eliminated the market for shoplifting goods at nearby businesses.

Denying benefits reduces the principal enticement to commit a crime. Some retail stores may only display the box, packaging, or parts of a product on the sales floor. For example, a shoe store may have a wall of left shoes for customers to examine. When a customer wants a pair of shoes, they ask an employee to fetch a pair in the right size. Ink tags that deface clothing prevent shoplifting by making the stolen clothes worthless. Refusals to bargain with kidnappers, when broadcast in advance of a kidnapping, operate under this principle. Rapid graffiti cleanup denies spray painters the glory of displaying their works. The kill switch technology in cellphones we discussed in chapter 5 renders them useless; a phone you cannot use is neither fun nor valuable.

Reducing Provocations for Crime

The next set of techniques involves decreasing provocations (table 10.5). Many situations provoke bad behavior. By provocations, we are not talking about unhappy and distressing life experiences in general. We are referring to conditions at specific times and places that stimulate people to act badly. The techniques in this set are used to change settings by removing or reducing provocations.

Reducing frustration and stress can be important. When many people gather to get a service (e.g., to renew their driver's license, buy a movie ticket, board a plane), they can jostle each other and argue over who has priority. For this reason, place managers often use lines. Adding barricades, even flimsy ones such as ropes, helps reduce line cutting and associated conflict. Adding more service agents speeds lines up and reduces frustration and conflict. Making it quick and easy for customers to pay

Table 10.5 Situational Crime Prevention Criterion 4: Decrease Provocations

Decrease Provocations	Examples
Reduce Frustrations & Stress	Create short and orderly lines; advance ticket sales; create cool, uncrowded environments
Avoid Disputes	Make rules clear and unambiguous; make prices clear
Reduce Emotional Arousal	Keeping sex offenders away from children; keeping rival fans apart during sporting events
Neutralize Peer Pressure	Hold group responsible for actions of members; banning teenage drivers from having teenage passengers
Discourage Imitation	Restricting information on how crimes are committed; rapid repair to combat vandalism

for goods can reduce some forms of shoplifting. Decorations and music choices can reduce or exacerbate frustration. In bars, crowding, heat, and noise can increase violence, so reducing crowding, increasing cooling, and noise reduction can reduce violence.[38] Increasing the certainty people will get the service also reduces frustration. Selling tickets to assigned seats online assures people waiting to enter the concert venue that they will get their seat and do not have to push. This is also a way of avoiding disputes.

Avoiding disputes among people in places, or between place managers and patrons is another way to reduce crime. When customers know the prices for goods and services in advance, there will be fewer conflicts when it is time to pay. Announcing rule changes well in advance of their being enforced helps avoid disputes over the rules when they are operational. Providing neutral third parties to settle disputes—like referees in a hockey game—can help keep conditions running smoothly.

Reducing emotional arousal reduces crime. Training staff on how to calm patrons in distress, rather than add to their distress, can reduce trouble. Bar bouncers who know how to calm intoxicated patrons may be more effective than bouncers who rely solely on brawn. Court orders for released sexual offenders to stay away from children reduces impulses to offend.

Neutralizing peer pressure can be useful when potential offenders come in groups. We mentioned stores that prohibit large numbers of juveniles into stores when we introduced access controls, and in chapter 2 we described shopping malls that require that juveniles be accompanied by adults. In addition to the direct crime prevention these measures accomplish, they also can inhibit peer pressure by reducing the number of peers or by inserting an adult who can deflect the pressure. On occasion counter-messaging can help. If individuals in a group believe, mistakenly, that others in the group like misbehaving, they will misbehave even though no one in the group wants to. This is called pluralistic ignorance.

Discouraging imitation stymies the copying of offending. Reducing publicity about crimes, refusing to provide details on how the crime was accomplished, and demonstrating that the crime was unsuccessful are all methods that attempt to discourage imitation. This is commonly used in the aftermath of mass shootings and terrorist attacks with hopes of reducing the likelihood that others will mimic the crimes.

Removing Excuses for Crime

The final set of techniques involves *decreasing excuses* (table 10.6). People use all sorts of excuses to justify crimes. Though criminologists and the news media seem fascinated with the excuses offenders give for their bad behavior, those of us who want to prevent crime have little interest in excuses after the crime has been committed. Rather, we are interested in

Table 10.6 Situational Crime Prevention Criterion 5: Decrease Excuses

Decrease Excuses	Examples
Set Rules	Lease provisions about noise, guests, etc.; trespass warnings
Post Instructions	Signage describing rules or issuing reminders to not leave valuables visible in cars
Alert Conscience	Automatic speed monitors; warnings of children present; "texting annoys other movie goers" messages; "shoplifting raises the price to consumers" signs
Assist Compliance	Providing bags for dog crap; installing trash bins, particularly in high traffic areas; emptying public trash bins regularly
Control Drugs & Alcohol	Banning alcohol; charging high prices for alcohol; only allowing place users to consume alcohol sold on premises

excuses that offenders tell themselves before the crime: their rationalizations. Situations can suggest excuses: "I didn't know" or "doesn't everyone do this?" If we can remove excuses, then it is possible that the person will not offend.

Setting rules is one of the most common situational prevention techniques. It is often used with other situational techniques. Many places have obvious rules. Sometimes place managers post these on walls. Other times they are part of written agreements and contracts, such as apartment leases. And in many circumstances, there are informal rules encouraged by place managers. If rules are obvious, it is hard for an offender to claim they do not know. Banks, for example, might post rules telling patrons they must remove their hats and sunglasses upon entry. This makes it more difficult for a robber to hide from overhead security cameras (thus removing anonymity).

Posting instructions show people how to behave rather than telling them what not to do. Here too, the idea is to deny offenders the ability to claim they did not know what to do. The Transportation Security Administration (TSA), for example, gives instructions on how to pack luggage, as well as what not to bring on flights. Signs helping people move through a building remove the excuse of "I was lost".

Alerting conscience reminds potential offenders that some behaviors are harmful. Signs reminding place users about the consequences to victims try to alert conscience. For example, many retail stores will post signs telling patrons that shoplifting is a crime and that it raises the price of goods for all consumers. Signs near schools alerting drivers of children crossing alert conscience. Electronic signs along roadways that display a driver's speed and flash when the driver exceeds the speed limit are alerting conscience.

Assisting compliance makes it easy for potential offenders to choose the appropriate action. Making checkout procedures quick and easy can reduce some shoplifting. A case study of a litter problem along a walking path near a high school found that placing trash bins along the path reduced most of the littering problem. Many had blamed the problem on teenagers who were perceived to "not care" about the area. Instead, people simply had no place to discard their trash. Once the city installed litter bins, most people who walked along the path discarded their trash in the

Table 10.7 The 25 Techniques of Situational Crime Prevention

Increase Effort	Increase Risk	Decrease Rewards	Decrease Provocations	Decrease Excuses
Target Harden	Extend Guardianship	Conceal Targets	Reduce Frustrations & Stress	Set Rules
Control Access	Assist Natural Surveillance	Remove Targets	Avoid Disputes	Post Instructions
Screen Exits	Reduce Anonymity	Identify Property	Reduce Emotional Arousal	Alert Conscience
Deflect Offenders	Use Place Managers	Disrupt Markets	Neutralize Peer Pressure	Assist Compliance
Control Tools	Strengthen Formal Surveillance	Deny Benefits	Discourage Imitation	Control Drugs & Alcohol

bins. In public parks, it's common to see dog poop bag dispensers. These remove the excuse that "I did not have anything with which to clean up after Rover".

Controlling drugs and alcohol is the last situational technique we will consider. A sports stadium may prohibit fans from bringing alcohol inside. Although the stadium probably sells alcohol, the cost and lines help limit consumption, intoxication, and resulting fights. Bars can regulate the number of drinks served to patrons. Businesses prohibit drug use by employees because drug use may increase the risk of injury, reduce productivity, and lead to other criminal behaviors at the business.

The last five tables provided five techniques of situational crime prevention that one could use to increase effort and risk, or decrease rewards, provocations, or excuses. These 25 techniques are often summarized together, as seen in table 10.7. You can think of this table like a menu. You will never use all techniques simultaneously to solve your problem. But you will be able to find a few that can guide your prevention efforts.

Evidence That Situational Crime Prevention Works

Since Clarke first created situational crime prevention, several researchers have evaluated whether its techniques reduce crime. The systematic reviews of place-based SCP techniques suggest that they are effective at reducing crime.[39] In the most recent systematic review, John Eck and Rob Guerette identified 149 evaluations of SCP applied at various places.[40] These included public, residential, transportation, recreation, and retail places. Overall, 77% of place-based interventions effectively reduced crime. Of the interventions at 52 public places (e.g., sidewalks, streets, parks), 62% reduced crime. When examining 39 interventions at residential places, 77% reduced crime. When they looked at the 25 place-based interventions at retail places, 88% reduced crime. There was an 88% success rate at the 26 transportation places they evaluated. Finally, of the 7 interventions at recreational places, 100% effectively reduced crime. Overall, there is strong evidence that place-based interventions can suppress crime.

Putting Situational Crime Prevention to Use

The techniques we described above overlap, as some of the examples demonstrate. The purpose of this classification scheme is not to create a typology to organize prevention for only research purposes. Instead, Clarke designed it to assist decision makers and allow them to easily consider a wide range of alternative techniques. Further, many of the techniques work best in combination. Setting rules is often required for other techniques to work—it is difficult to control access or screen at exits without rules to guide place users, for example. Surveillance reinforces rules; a rule that is not enforced will provide limited protection. Our Walmart videogame purchasing example from chapter 5 illustrates this well. The games are in a locked glass display case (target hardening); have anti-theft strips that would set off an alarm at the door if it's not de-activated (strengthen formal surveillance); and require an employee to retrieve it and process your payment immediately (use place managers). Thus, people looking to prevent crime need to analyze the problem and identify the relevant situational crime prevention techniques that are most likely to solve the problem.

Another detail worth noting is who is in the best position to carry out these techniques. As you may have noticed from the examples, the police do not play a very big part. The techniques are not dependent on arrest or much by way of punishment. Instead, place managers are the key players. In fact, place managers can implement at least 23 of the 25 techniques in certain conditions.[41] Just as place managers of casinos, grocery stores, online stores, and internet forums at the beginning of our chapter were able to influence place user behavior, place managers can alter environments to make them less conducive to crime. The only techniques that place managers may not be able to implement on their own are *disrupting markets* and *discouraging imitation*. We are not saying that these techniques are only applicable to places—they are applicable to many circumstances that are not places, such as computer security. Rather, these techniques provide place managers with a broad range of options.

Further, place managers must explicitly cooperate—if not act themselves—to implement most of these techniques at places. This has important implications for policing. First, police can encourage place managers to use these techniques, but the police themselves cannot design, organize, or operate a place to which they have no legal right. The police need to have place managers as willing partners, or they need to find ways to compel place managers to act.

Second, this means many people in the community have the ability to reduce crime. When we re-think communities—as described in chapter 7—to include the property and business owners, developers, financiers, and so on, it opens up many possibilities. It's time to harness the power of place management and work towards sustainable solutions. This might seem easy, particularly if the place managers are willing to put in the work and effort. But what if the place manager is not on board? Are we out of luck? Not necessarily.

Key Points

- To reduce bad behavior, change situations that tempt people to behave badly
- To reduce bad behavior, make the behavior more effort or riskier to carry out
- To reduce bad behavior, reduce the rewards, provocations, or excuses for the behavior
- Ask: how can we reduce crime opportunities?

Notes

1 Clarke, R.V. (1980). Situational crime prevention: Theory and practice. *British Journal of Criminology, 20*, 136–147. https://doi.org/10.1093/oxfordjournals.bjc.a047153; Clarke, R.V. (1995). Situational crime prevention. *Crime and justice, 19*, 91–150. https://doi.org/10.1086/449230; Clarke, R.V. (2011). Situational crime prevention. In R. Wortley, L. Mazerolle, & S. Rombouts (Eds.), *Environmental Criminology and Crime Analysis* (pp. 178–194). New York, NY: Routledge.
2 Eck, J.E., & Clarke, R.V. (2019). Situational crime prevention: Theory, practice, and evidence. In M.D. Krohn, N. Hendrix, G.P. Hall, & A.J. Lizotte (Eds.), *Handbook of Crime and Deviance* (2nd ed., pp. 355–376). Springer International Publishing. https://doi.org/10.1007/978-3-030-20779-3_18
3 Eck, J. E., & Clarke, R. V. (2019). Situational crime prevention: Theory, practice, and evidence. In M. D. Krohn, N. Hendrix, G. P. Hall, & A. J. Lizotte (Eds.), *Handbook of Crime and Deviance* (2nd ed., pp. 355–376). Springer International Publishing. https://doi.org/10.1007/978-3-030-20779-3_18
4 Prelec, D. & Simester, D. (2001). Always Leave Home Without It: A Further Investigation of the Credit-Card Effect on Willingness to Pay. *Marketing Letters, 12*, 5–12. https://doi.org/10.1023/A:1008196717017
5 Unal, M. & Park, Y. (2023). Fewer clicks, more purchases. *Management Science, 69*(12), 7317–7334. https://doi.org/10.1287/mnsc.2023.4716
6 Ebster, C. & Garaus, M. (2015). *Store Design and Visual Merchandising: Creating Store Space That Encourages Buying* (2nd edition). Business Expert Press.
7 Ebster, C. & Garaus, M. (2015). *Store Design and Visual Merchandising: Creating Store Space That Encourages Buying* (2nd edition). Business Expert Press.
8 Murphy, C., Lim, W.W., Mills, C., Wong, J.Y., Chen, D., Xie, Y., & Donnelly, C.A. (2023). Effectiveness of social distancing measures and lockdowns for reducing transmission of COVID-19 in non-healthcare, community-based settings. *Philosophical Transactions of the Royal Society A, 381*(2257), 20230132. https://doi.org/10.1098/rsta.2023.0132
9 Clarke, R.V. & Cornish, D.B. (1985). Modeling offenders' decisions: A framework for research and policy. In M. Tonry & N. Morris (Eds.), *Crime and Justice: An Annual Review of Research* (vol. 6, pp. 147–185). Chicago, IL: University of Chicago Press.
10 Clarke, R.V. (1980). Situational crime prevention: Theory and practice. *British Journal of Criminology, 20*, 136–147. https://doi.org/10.1093/oxfordjournals.bjc.a047153; Clarke, R.V. (1995). Situational crime prevention. *Crime and justice, 19*, 91–150. https://doi.org/10.1086/449230
11 Bowers, K. & Johnson, S.D. (2017). Burglary prevention in practice. In N. Tilley & A. Sidebottom (Eds.), *Handbook of Crime Prevention and Community Safety*, 2nd ed (pp. 319–353). New York, NY: Routledge. https://doi.org/10.4324/9781315724393-15
12 Hayes, R., Downs, D.M., & Blackwood, R. (2012). Anti-theft procedures and fixtures: a randomized controlled trial of two situational crime prevention measures. *Journal of Experimental Criminology, 8*, 1–15. https://doi.org/10.1007/s11292-011-9137-5
13 Clarke, R.V. (2020). Assaults with glasses in bars and clubs in Lancashire, England. In M.S. Scott & R.V. Clarke (Eds.), *Problem-Oriented Policing: Successful Case Studies* (pp. 128–136). New York, NY: Routledge. https://doi.org/10.4324/9780429457357-13
14 Freilich, J.D., Gruenewald, J., & Mandala, M. (2019). Situational crime prevention and terrorism: An assessment of 10 years of research. *Criminal Justice Policy Review, 30*(9), 1283–1311. https://doi.org/10.1177/0887403418805142; Clarke, R.V. & Newman, G.R. (2006). *Outsmarting the Terrorists*. Praeger Security International. https://doi.org/10.5040/9798400694684
15 Lemieux, A.M. (2014). *Situational Prevention of Poaching*. London: Routledge.

16 Ho, H., Ko, R., & Mazerolle, L. (2022). Situational crime prevention techniques to prevent and control cybercrimes: A focused systematic review. *Computers & Security, 115*, 102611. https://doi.org/10.1016/j.cose.2022.102611

17 Clarke, R.V. & Cornish, D.B. (1985). Modeling offenders' decisions: A framework for research and policy. In M. Tonry & N. Morris (Eds.), *Crime and Justice: An Annual Review of Research* (vol. 6, pp. 147–185). Chicago, IL: University of Chicago Press.

18 Clarke, R.V. (1980). Situational crime prevention: Theory and practice. *British Journal of Criminology, 20*, 136–147. https://doi.org/10.1093/oxfordjournals.bjc.a047153; Clarke, R.V. (1995). Situational crime prevention. *Crime and Justice, 19*, 91–150. https://doi.org/10.1086/449230; Clarke, R.V. (2011). Situational crime prevention. In R. Wortley, L. Mazerolle, & S. Rombouts (Eds.), *Environmental Criminology and Crime Analysis* (pp. 178–194). New York, NY: Routledge; Clarke, R.V. & Eck, J.E. (2003). *Become a problem-solving crime analysis in 55 small steps*. Jill Dando Institute of Crime Science; University College London. Retrieved from: https://popcenter.asu.edu/sites/g/files/litvpz3631/files/library/reading/PDFs/55stepsUK.pdf; Eck, J.E. & Clarke, R.V. (2019). Situational crime prevention: Theory, practice, and evidence. In M.D. Krohn, N. Hendrix, G.P. Hall, & A.J. Lizotte (Eds.), *Handbook of Crime and Deviance* (2nd ed., pp. 355–376). Springer International Publishing. https://doi.org/10.1007/978-3-030-20779-3_18

19 Ekblom, P. (1997). Gearing up against crime: A dynamic framework to help designers keep up with the adaptive criminal in a changing world. *International Journal of Risk, Security, and Crime Prevention, 2*(4), 249–265.

20 Robinson, M.B. (1997). Environmental characteristics associated with residential burglaries of student apartment complexes. *Environment and Behavior, 29*(5), 657–675. https://doi.org/10.1177/0013916597295004

21 Felson, M. & Clarke, R.V. (1998). Opportunity makes the thief. *Police research series, paper, 98*(1–36), 10. Retrieved from: https://popcenter.asu.edu/sites/g/files/litvpz3631/files/opportunity_makes_the_thief.pdf

22 Shen, J-L. & Linning, S.J. (2025). Direct and indirect situational crime prevention: Using the COSTS criteria to improve interventions. *Security Journal, 38*, 60. https://doi.org/10.1057/s41284-025-00507-y

23 Eck, J.E. & Clarke, R.V. (2019). Situational crime prevention: Theory, practice, and evidence. In M.D. Krohn, N. Hendrix, G.P. Hall, & A.J. Lizotte (Eds.), *Handbook of Crime and Deviance* (2nd ed., pp. 355–376). Springer International Publishing. https://doi.org/10.1007/978-3-030-20779-3_18; Felson, M. & Clarke, R.V. (1998). Opportunity makes the thief. *Police research series, paper, 98*(1–36), 10. Retrieved from: https://popcenter.asu.edu/sites/g/files/litvpz3631/files/opportunity_makes_the_thief.pdf; Shen, J-L. & Linning, S.J. (2025). Direct and indirect situational crime prevention: Using the COSTS criteria to improve interventions. *Security Journal, 38*, 60. https://doi.org/10.1057/s41284-025-00507-y

24 Cornish, D.B. & Clarke, R.V. (2003). Opportunities, precipitators and criminal decisions: A reply to Wortley's critique of situational crime prevention. *Crime Prevention Studies, 16*, 41–96.

25 Clarke, R.V. (2017). Situational crime prevention. In R. Wortley & M. Townsley (Eds.), *Environmental Criminology and Crime Analysis* (2nd ed, pp. 286–303). Routledge.

26 Clarke, R.V. (2017). Situational crime prevention. In R. Wortley & M. Townsley (Eds.), *Environmental Criminology and Crime Analysis* (2nd ed, pp. 286–303). Routledge.

27 Clarke, R.V. (1995). Situational crime prevention. *Crime and Justice, 19*, 91–150. https://doi.org/10.1086/449230

28 Clarke, R.V. (1995). Situational crime prevention. *Crime and Justice, 19*, 91–150. https://doi.org/10.1086/449230

29 Clarke, R.V. (2002). *Thefts of and from cars in parking facilities*. US Department of Justice, Problem-Oriented Guides for Police, Guide No. 10. Retrieved from: https://popcenter.asu.edu/sites/default/files/theft_of_and_from_cars_in_parking_facilities.pdf

30 Lasley, J.R. (1998). *Designing Out Gang Homicides and Street Assaults*. Washington, DC: National Institute of Justice.

31 Clarke, R.V. & Newman, G.R. (2006). *Outsmarting the Terrorists*. Praeger Security International. https://doi.org/10.5040/9798400694684

32 Hodgkinson, T., Curtis, H., MacAlister, D., & Farrell, G. (2016). Student academic dishonesty: The potential for situational prevention. *Journal of Criminal Justice Education, 27*(1), 1–18. https://doi.org/10.1080/10511253.2015.1064982

33 Clarke, R.V. (2020). Assaults with glasses in bars and clubs in Lancashire, England. In M.S. Scott & R.V. Clarke (Eds.), *Problem-Oriented Policing: Successful Case Studies* (pp. 128–136). New York, NY: Routledge. https://doi.org/10.4324/9780429457357-13

34 Bowers, K.J. & Johnson, S.D. (2005). Domestic burglary repeats and space-time clusters: The dimensions of risk. *European Journal of Criminology, 2*(1), 67–92. https://doi.org/10.1177/1477370805048631; Forrester, D., Chatterton, M., & Pease, K. (1988). *The Kirkholt Burglary Prevention Project, Rochdale*. Crime Prevention Unit Paper, No. 13. London, UK: Home Office.

35 Eck, J.E., Linning, S.J., & Herold, T.D. (2023). *Place Management and Crime: Ownership and Property Rights as a Source of Social Control*. Springer Publishers. https://doi.org/10.1007/978-3-031-27693-4

36 Taylor, E. (2016). Supermarket self-checkouts and retail theft: The curious case of the SWIPERS. *Criminology & Criminal Justice, 16*(5), 552–567. https://doi.org/10.1177/1748895816643353

37 La Vigne, N. & Wartell, J. (2015). *Robbery of Pharmacies*. US Department of Justice, Problem-Oriented Guides for Police, Guide No. 73. Retrieved from: https://popcenter.asu.edu/sites/default/files/sites/default/files/problems/PDFs/robbery_of_pharmacies.pdf

38 Graham, K. & Homel, R. (2008). *Raising the Bar: Preventing Aggression in and Around Bars, Pubs and Clubs*. Cullompton, UK: Willan; Townsley, M. & Grimshaw, R. (2013). The consequences of queueing: Crowding, situational features and aggression in entertainment precincts. *Crime Prevention and Community Safety, 15*(1), 23–47. https://doi.org/10.1057/cpcs.2012.12

39 Eck, J.E. (2002). Preventing crime at places. In L.W. Sherman, D.P. Farrington, B. Welsh, and D.L. Mackenzie (Eds.), *Evidence-Based Crime Prevention* (pp. 241–294). New York: Routledge. https://doi.org/10.4324/9780203166697_chapter_7; Guerette, R.T. (2009). The pull, push, and expansion of situational crime prevention evaluation: An appraisal of thirty-seven years of research. *Crime Prevention Studies, 24*, 29–58; Eck, J.E. & Guerette, R.T. (2012). Place-based crime prevention: Theory, evidence, and policy. In B.C. Welch & D.P. Farrington (Eds.), *The Oxford Handbook of Crime Prevention* (pp. 354–383). Oxford University Press. https://doi.org/10.1093/oxfordhb/9780195398823.013.0018

40 Eck, J.E. & Guerette, R.T. (2012). Place-based crime prevention: Theory, evidence, and policy. In B.C. Welch & D.P. Farrington (Eds.), *The Oxford Handbook of Crime Prevention* (pp. 354–383). Oxford University Press. https://doi.org/10.1093/oxfordhb/9780195398823.013.0018

41 Eck, J.E., Linning, S.J., & Herold, T.D. (2023). *Place Management and Crime: Ownership and Property Rights as a Source of Social Control*. Springer Publishers. https://doi.org/10.1007/978-3-031-27693-4

11

WHAT IF PLACE MANAGERS DO NOT COOPERATE?

In the previous chapter we showed you what place managers can do to reduce crime at their places. Most place managers carry out the necessary situational changes on their properties to keep crime at bay. Other place managers will work to address crime problems when the issues are brought to their attention.[1] But as the rule of the few dictates, a small number of place managers have most of the high crime places. What if they refuse to do anything about it? When place managers are uncooperative, are you just out of luck? Some people say yes. They think that it's only up to the police to address and if the police can't do anything about it, there are no other options. We call this the *police can solve all crime problems* fallacy.[2] But crime scientists have demonstrated otherwise; there are other options. An example from Chula Vista, California provides a great illustration.[3]

Chula Vista's motels were often magnets for crime (more than 930 calls for police service in the year 2000 alone). Problems included drug use, prostitution, refusals of guests to leave, and disputes over payment. Eventually business associations asked the city to make improvements to address the crime and disorder problems associated with motels. The police analyzed data, conducted interviews of owners and guests, and completed environmental assessments of the motels. Crime analysts discovered that the number of calls for service per room for any given motel varied greatly.

 DOI: 10.4324/9781003430155-14

Once again, the rule of the few showed up; only a small number of motels generated a majority of the calls for service. The city had 27 motels and only five motels generated more than 50% of all calls for service.[4]

The conclusion the police drew was that some of the high crime motels were suffering from poor place management. Several issues that these few "problem motels" experienced could be traced back to poor management decisions, such as not installing proper locks, failing to specify prices when guests checked in, and so on. So instead of endlessly patrolling motels to crackdown on motel patrons, the police worked with city council to craft legislation to regulate motels.

The city council passed an ordinance that held motel owners accountable for how many calls for service their properties generated. The city set a performance standard of 0.61 calls for service per room per year. They derived this standard by identifying the median calls for service-per-room from the previous year (i.e., the annual total number of calls for service for a property divided by the motel's number of rooms). Motels operating with fewer calls per room per year than that limit were given a license to operate for a year. Those with calls exceeding the limit had to enter into a legally binding agreement to address the problems. If the motel did not comply with the agreement, it would be denied a permit to operate. One motel closed and several had to agree to extensive changes.

Once the ordinance was fully operational, calls for service to motels declined by 53%. But among the high calls for service motels, calls for violent and property crimes collectively declined by 70%.

A strength of this approach is that it did not disrupt operations of any low-call motels. Place managers who were running low-crime establishments were unaffected by the ordinance. But the high crime motels had to make changes or risk losing their permit to operate. The example also illustrates that there are organizations, agencies, or people other than police who can compel place managers to act. In this example, the city council used a legal lever with their ordinance to get place managers to address crime problems.[5]

But the idea of finding other people or organizations to compel place managers to act is not new. It comes from a novel idea introduced to police and researchers by Rana Sampson, a former New York City Police Department sergeant, lawyer, and campus police Chief.

Using Super Controllers to Motivate Action

By the early 2000s, Sampson had trained thousands of police officials across agencies throughout North America. She listened to officers describe their experiences dealing with place managers, handlers, and guardians. She realized that there was another set of actors who can place pressure on controllers to act: super controllers.

Super controllers build on the crime triangle we introduced in chapter 2.[6] The inner triangle, you will remember, shows the elements necessary for a crime to occur: offenders, targets, and places. If any one of these elements is missing, a crime cannot occur. The outer triangle depicts the elements sufficient for prevention. We call these controllers. They can exert protective measures over situations and block crimes from happening.

Sampson suggested we should consider a third triangle that describes who influences the controllers (figure 11.1). That outermost triangle consists

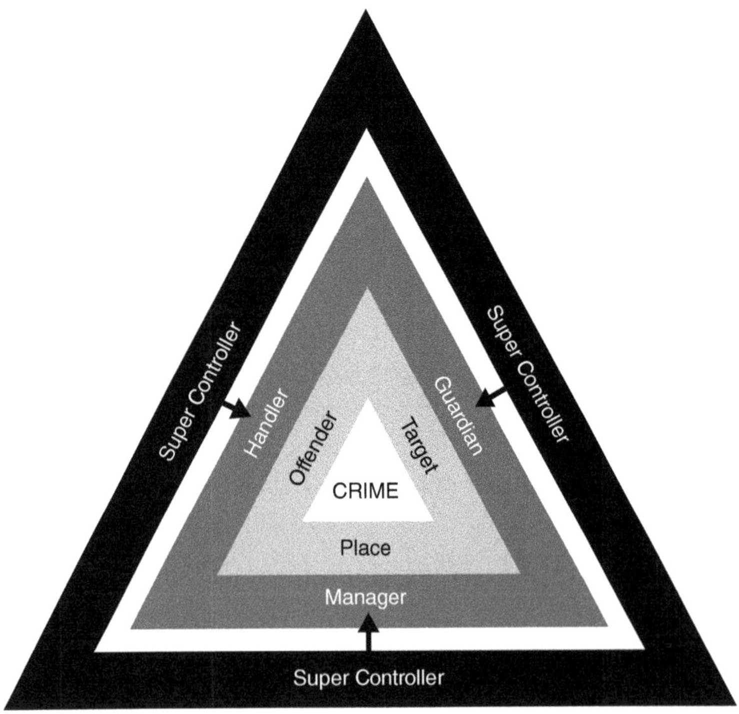

FIGURE 11.1 Adding Super Controllers to the Crime Triangle

Adapted from Sampson, Eck, & Dunham (2010)

of *super controllers*.[7] Super controllers directly influence controllers (handlers, guardians, or managers), but do not have direct influence on targets, offenders, or places. So, super controllers influence the direct causes of crime by influencing controllers. Super controllers only influence controllers, and controllers only influence the elements for crime in the innermost triangle.

Sampson and her colleagues, including John, identified ten types of super controllers in three categories (table 11.1).[8] Formal super controllers have some legally enforceable relationship with the controllers. An organizational super controller typically employs the controller and exercises authority through the organization. A bank branch manager (place manager), for example, is employed by the bank (super controller) which hired her and gives her directions. The super controller might have a contractual relationship. An apartment building owner (super controller) may contract the operations of the apartment complex to a management firm (place manager).

Financial super controllers include banks that lend controllers money, insurance companies that insure the controller's property and operations, and other institutions that deal with money. They can heavily influence place managers' decision-making. To illustrate, recall our glassing example from chapter 5.[9] One criticism of using polycarbonate glasses in bars was the additional cost the businesses would have to take on to replace all of their glassware. But insurance companies have a vested interest in minimizing glassings. They want to avoid payouts from lawsuits. So, the insurance companies (super controller) could offer discounts to business owners (place manager) on their liability insurance premiums to help offset the cost.

A regulatory super controller is a government agency that scrutinizes the controller's action. Bars, nursing homes, mental health facilities, banks, and most other businesses have some sort of regulatory agency (some have several) whose job it is to make sure the business operates within specified rules. For example, a liquor board (super controller) tells bar owners (place managers) who sell liquor the rules and regulations that must be followed or they will revoke their liquor licenses. This could include forbidding the sale of alcohol to minors or requiring the use of polycarbonate glassware in bars. The liquor board never actually deals with the minors trying to purchase alcohol or the unruly intoxicated people. They simply tell the place manager she cannot sell to minors and must use safe serving practices to reduce rowdy patrons and assaults. Courts

Table 11.1 Types of Super Controllers

Formal	Organizational Contractual Financial Regulatory Courts	*The controller has some obligation or responsibility to the super controller that is legally enforceable. The super controller can identify and single out non-compliant controllers from compliant controllers.*
Diffuse	Political Markets Media	*The super controller can influence the general situation within which the controller operates through publicity, legislation, or economics. The super controller cannot differentiate among compliant and non-compliant controllers.*
Personal	Groups Family	*The controller has some social or personal obligation or responsibility to the super controller but it is not legally enforceable. The super controller can identify and single out non-compliant controllers.*

Adapted from Sampson, Eck, & Dunham (2010)

can enforce rules and penalize rule violations. So, for example, a landlord can be sued in many US states by victims of crime on his property, if the victim can show negligence in not preventing a foreseeable crime risk.[10]

Diffuse super controllers have less direct power but can influence controllers. Political super controllers include city councils, state representatives, mayors, governors, city or county managers/administrators, and other elected or high-level appointed officials. Their power comes from their ability to put a spotlight on bad behavior (e.g., through public hearings or speeches), threatening to establish rules that regulate controllers; or pressuring regulatory agencies to increase scrutiny of controllers. Markets can be used to make bad controller behavior economically costly. For example, the San Francisco Department of Health requires that all establishments that serve food to the public display a placard indicating the quality of the facility's food handling practices.[11] The Department of Health (super controller) has no immediate control over food handling practices. But requiring restaurants to display the placard incentivizes restaurant owners (place managers) to engage in safe food handling to avoid losing customers. Remember, place managers are highly motivated to maintain their place's reputation to continue acquiring resources. The media gains its power as a super controller through its ability to embarrass. Increasingly, bloggers and social media influencers are stepping into this role. Generally, diffuse super controllers have difficulty singling out poor-performing controllers from the many well-performing controllers. The bad publicity, economic costs, or political consequences often fall across all the controllers. This is very different from formal super controllers, who usually can single out the poor-performing controllers.[12]

The last category is personal super controllers. These super controllers depend on a social bond through peer pressure or family. They do not have any legal authority over controllers. Ostracism is the most extreme sanction personal super controllers can muster.[13] Community groups could decide to boycott a store, for example. Individual controllers can be singled out, as is the case with formal super controllers.[14]

We have intentionally used examples from place management to illustrate these types, but the theory of super controllers extends to guardians and handlers too. In chapter 13, we provide an example of a super controller influencing a gang leader who served as a handler for gang members.

Also, we have described each type of super controller as if they operate alone. In reality, super controllers operate in networks, and engaging one may trigger others to become involved. Imagine, for example, a police official trying to reduce crime in and around an apartment building. The landlord (the place manager) agrees to fix the broken lighting and enforce lease provisions, but never quite gets around to doing these and other things that could prevent crime. The police describe the situation to a city council committee during budget hearings. A reporter for a local news station, covering the hearings, develops and broadcasts an evening news story. The landlord's banker, hearing the news, worries that it might not be in the bank's interest to renew loans to the landlord. The public housing authority had certified the apartment building as suitable for low-income clients needing rental assistance. The news and city council's concern create alarm at the housing authority who then pressure the landlord to improve living conditions or risk decertification. As a third of the landlord's renters have subsidized rents, this creates additional pressure on the landlord to address crime. The landlord, who believed she could superficially comply with the police requests, now faces greater pressure. She has several choices: ignore the financial risks and continue to stonewall; fix the apartment building so it meets public housing and police criteria; or sell the building.

Super controllers and controllers are embedded in a web of relationships. This web helps most controllers supress crime at their places. But the few controllers not embedded in web of effective super controllers have less incentives to supress crime. Rana Sampson's idea was that the police seek out relevant super controllers. Though super controllers could be used when dealing with reluctant or recalcitrant guardians and handlers, super controllers are most useful when dealing with uncooperative place managers. This is because the ownership of places embeds a person or organization in a much larger network of relationships that almost inevitably involves formal super controllers, the most powerful type.

So, the moral of the story, just as the Chula Vista example illustrated, is to leverage these networks and find ways to pressure uncooperative place managers to act.[15] But do we always have to be this harsh with place managers? No. And in fact, the ordinance is not where the City of Chula Vista started. They applied pressures in stages proportional to a motel's level of compliance. Thus, there are many options to choose from.

A Hierarchy of Interventions

Although the City of Chula Vista observed a concentration of calls for service at a few motels, the reasons for the calls could vary. Some high call volume motels may have managers who refused to act, whereas other motel managers may simply have been unaware of how to address their crime problems. Thus, Chula Vista rolled out a three-stage process: 1. outreach; 2. code enforcement and public accountability; and 3. permit to operate ordinance.[16]

The first stage, outreach, involved information-sharing activities. Officers shared report cards with each motel manager detailing the number and nature of calls for service generated by their motels. The police also held motel management seminars to educate managers about best practices. Lastly, the police offered individual onsite assistance to motel owners. Officers would conduct free onsite assessments of the motel's specific problems and offer tangible solutions. Most motel managers applied the officer's recommended solutions. But when outreach failed, police intensified their response.

In stage two, code enforcement and public accountability, the police enlisted the help of the Chula Vista's Code Enforcement Office. Code

Enforcement agents visited the motels that continued to generate high volumes of calls. The agents inspected the motels and issued citations for problems that went unaddressed from the report cards issued in the previous stage. Police also distributed a report detailing and ranking each motel based on the number of calls each property generated. Some additional motels complied with requests in this stage. Two motels closed. But a third group continued to generate a high volume of calls. This third group is what prompted the city to advance their response to a third stage.

As described at the beginning of the chapter, stage three involved a permit-to-operate ordinance. Any motel that exceeded the allowable number of calls per service per room was required to take corrective action or face losing their permit to operate. The threat of losing their business permit prompted a few prolific motels into complying. Another handful decided to close. As previously mentioned, these actions led to a 53% decrease in calls for service. In addition, crime at motels declined by 70% and drug arrests at motels declined by 64%.[17]

The three-stage process Chula Vista used illustrates two important ideas. First, there are many options police and city managers can use to pressure place managers to change negligent management practices. Second, the police did not jump to the most coercive tactics to gain compliance. The interventions police can use to elicit compliance from place managers range from cooperative to coercive. Crime researchers, such as Herman Goldstein,[18] Ian Ayres, and John Braithwaite[19], have urged police to consider this range of options carefully for many years.

Goldstein was interested in how police could shift the responsibility for handling a crime problem from the shoulders of the police to others who could handle it better and more sustainably. He noted that police have used a wide variety of methods to get controllers to prevent rather than facilitate crime, ranging from highly cooperative to highly adversarial.[20]

Similar to a police use of force continuum,[21] Goldstein arranged these tactics into a hierarchy with the most cooperative, and most frequently used tactics at the base and the most adversarial and least used tactics at the top. As shown at the bottom of figure 11.2, police can provide information. Often the police need do nothing more than provide the facts and place managers (or other controllers) will improve their actions.

FIGURE 11.2 Goldstein's Hierarchy of Interventions

This is frequent when the owners are not aware of the harm their places are causing. Just above this tactic are simple straightforward requests for assistance. If this does not work, the police can be a bit more confrontational. Note that until this point, the police are working with the place manager and have not sought the assistance of others.

At the fourth tier, the police start seeking other allies. They can find another organization or agency to take over the problem from them. In some cases, the police might be able to shift an apartment complex problem to the public housing agency, like in the Creston apartments example in chapter 3, if the apartment complex houses many renters subsidized by the agency. Rather than continuing to address a bar problem, the police might be able to shift the problem to the state regulatory agency, such as a liquor board. A problem involving mentally ill people might be shifted to a mental health agency. Typically, the police stay involved, but they step back to a secondary role.

If there is one other entity who can handle the problem, the police might help create a new entity that can handle the problem. The police could petition the city council, for example, to create a regulatory capability within the city attorney's office to address metal recycling issues or ongoing nuisances at properties. Sometimes the mere posting of a notice for a potential fine can be enough to elicit action from place managers.[22]

The police could also work with community and religious organizations to develop a non-governmental organization to help unhoused people, thus reducing their victimization and involvement in disorder.

If shifting responsibility to an existing or new organization is not feasible, then some form of public shaming of the controllers who should be responsible is possible. This tier would involve super controllers: probably diffuse super controllers. Withdrawing police services is the next higher option, should shaming not work. Police can refuse to respond to gasoline stations that routinely report gas theft, if these stations have refused to take relevant precautions. Similarly, police can refuse to respond in-person to calls about minor shoplifting if the store has refused to implement measures to address the problem.[23] Alternatively, the police can charge a fee for responding to excessive calls. In some circumstances, the police have advocated to their elected officials that the city or county mandate particular prevention approaches. This clearly is invoking political super controllers. The top tier is to file a civil suit against the property owner. If the court agrees that the property owner has been negligent, then the court an impose a variety of sanctions, including closing the problem place.

This is a rough hierarchy—whether imposing a fee for service is worse than cutting off service is a matter of debate, and probably varies from circumstance to circumstance. It is useful, nevertheless, because it illustrates the wide array of approaches the police can use to shift the responsibility for addressing crime from them to those who were principally involved in creating the crime opportunities. When deciding which policies to implement, however, it's important to carefully consider the crime types occurring and potential harms.[24] Many cities that have passed ordinances to address excessive calls to police, for example, will have exemptions in place for certain types of calls, such as domestic violence, so as not to discourage the reporting of personal violence.[25]

Conclusions

Engaging super controllers can be a powerful tool for crime prevention. There are many examples showing how super controllers can compel previously unwilling controllers to act.[26] But there is another common question that skeptics wonder about place-based crime prevention: will preventing crime at one place simply push crime to other locations?

Won't offenders just go next door? In the next chapter, we explain this phenomenon, often called displacement, and the considerable research that has gone into testing it. We show that crime does not displace quite like you think. In fact, we show that another phenomenon, diffusion of benefits (the opposite of displacement), holds out the promise that prevention spreads, rather than crime.

Key Points

- Police are not the only ones who can solve crime problems
- Super controllers can compel non-compliant controllers to act
- There are a range of interventions super controllers can impose
- Use the more cooperative interventions first, followed by more coercive interventions
- Ask: what person or agency can compel a controller to act?

Notes

1 Eck, J.E. & Madensen, T.D. (2018). Place management, guardianship, and the establishment of order. In D.S. Nagin, F.T. Cullen, & C.L. Jonson (Eds.), *Deterrence, Choice, and Crime: Contemporary Perspectives* (pp. 269–296). Routledge. https://doi.org/10.4324/9781351112710-10; Eck, J.E. & Madensen, T.D. (2018). Place management. In G.J.N. Bruinsma & S.D. Johnson (Eds.), *The Oxford Handbook of Environmental Criminology* (pp. 629–663). Oxford University Press. https://doi.org/10.1093/oxfordhb/9780190279707.013.22

2 Linning, S.J., Carroll, T., Gerard, D.W., & Eck, J.E. (2025, January). Can the police solve all public safety problems? *Public Management, 107*(1), 40–44. https://icma.org/articles/pm-magazine/can-police-solve-all-crime-problems

3 Bichler, G. & Schmerler, K. (2020). Crime and disorder at budget motels in Chula Vista, California. In M.S. Scott & R. Clarke (Eds.), *Problem-Oriented Policing: Successful Case Studies* (pp. 244–256). https://doi.org/10.4324/9780429457357-22

4 Bichler, G., Schmerler, K., & Enriquez, J. (2013). Curbing nuisance motels: An evaluation of police as place regulators. *Policing: An International Journal of Police Strategies & Management, 36*(2), 437–462. https://doi.org/10.1108/13639511311329787; Bichler, G. & Schmerler, K. (2020). Crime and disorder at budget motels in Chula Vista, California. In M.S. Scott & R. Clarke (Eds.), *Problem-Oriented Policing: Successful Case Studies* (pp. 244–256). https://doi.org/10.4324/9780429457357-22

5 Bichler, G., Schmerler, K., & Enriquez, J. (2013). Curbing nuisance motels: An evaluation of police as place regulators. *Policing: An International Journal of Police Strategies & Management, 36*(2), 437–462. https://doi.org/10.1108/13639511311329787; Bichler, G. & Schmerler, K. (2020). Crime and disorder at budget motels in Chula Vista, California. In M.S. Scott & R. Clarke (Eds.), *Problem-Oriented Policing: Successful Case Studies* (pp. 244–256). https://doi.org/10.4324/9780429457357-22

6 Eck, J.E. (2003). Police problems: The complexity of problem theory, research and evaluation. *Crime Prevention Studies, 15*, 79–114; Clarke, R.V. & Eck, J.E. (2003). Become a problem-solving crime analyst in 55 small steps. London, UK: Jill Dando Institute for Crime Science. Retrieved from: https://popcenter.asu.edu/sites/g/files/litvpz3631/files/55stepsuk_0_0.pdf ; Clarke, R.V. & Eck, J.E. (2009). Crime analysis for problem solvers in 60 small steps. Washington, DC: Office of Community Oriented Policing Services. Retrieved from: https://portal.cops.usdoj.gov/resourcecenter/content.ashx/cops-w0047-pub.pdf

7 Sampson R., Eck, J.E., & Dunham, J. (2010). Super controllers and crime prevention: A routine activity explanation of crime prevention success and failure. *Security Journal, 23*(1), 37–51. https://doi.org/10.1057/sj.2009.17

8 Sampson R., Eck, J.E., & Dunham, J. (2010). Super controllers and crime prevention: A routine activity explanation of crime prevention success and failure. *Security Journal, 23*(1), 37-51. https://doi.org/10.1057/sj.2009.17

9 Clarke, R.V. (2020). Assaults with glasses in bars and clubs in Lancashire, England. In M.S. Scott & R.V. Clarke (eds.), *Problem-Oriented Policing: Successful Case Studies* (pp. 128–136). New York, NY: Routledge. https://doi.org/10.4324/9780429457357-13

10 Sampson R., Eck, J.E., & Dunham, J. (2010). Super controllers and crime prevention: A routine activity explanation of crime prevention success and failure. *Security Journal, 23*(1), 37–51. https://doi.org/10.1057/sj.2009.17

11 San Francisco Department of Health (2021). Food safety placarding. Retrieved May 28, 2021 from: https://www.sfdph.org/dph/EH/Food/Placarding.asp

12 Sampson R., Eck, J.E., & Dunham, J. (2010). Super controllers and crime prevention: A routine activity explanation of crime prevention success and failure. *Security Journal, 23*(1), 37–51. https://doi.org/10.1057/sj.2009.17

13 Linning, S.J. & Eck, J.E. (2024). Clarifying control in criminology: A proposal for six interacting controls of crime. *Canadian Journal of Criminology and Criminal Justice, 66*(3–4), 119–141. https://doi.org/10.3138/cjccj-2024-0053

14 Sampson R., Eck, J.E., & Dunham, J. (2010). Super controllers and crime prevention: A routine activity explanation of crime prevention success and failure. *Security Journal, 23*(1), 37–51. https://doi.org/10.1057/sj.2009.17

15 Linning, S.J., Carroll, T., Gerard, D.W., & Eck, J.E. (2025). When high-crime properties handcuff police. *Public Management, 107*(12), 16–21. https://icma.org/articles/pm-magazine/when-high-crime-properties-handcuff-police

16 Bichler, G., Schmerler, K., & Enriquez, J. (2013). Curbing nuisance motels: An evaluation of police as place regulators. *Policing: An International Journal of Police Strategies & Management, 36*(2), 437–462. https://doi.org/10.1108/13639511311329787; Bichler, G. & Schmerler, K. (2020). Crime and disorder at budget motels in Chula Vista, California. In M.S. Scott & R. Clarke (Eds.), *Problem-Oriented Policing: Successful Case Studies* (pp. 244–256). https://doi.org/10.4324/9780429457357-22

17 Bichler, G. & Schmerler, K. (2020). Crime and disorder at budget motels in Chula Vista, California. In M.S. Scott & R. Clarke (Eds.), *Problem-Oriented Policing: Successful Case Studies* (pp. 244–256). https://doi.org/10.4324/9780429457357-22

18 Goldstein, H. (1997). The pattern of emerging tactics for shifting the ownership of prevention strategies in the current wave of chance in policing: Their implications for both environmental criminology and the police. Presentation at the 6th International Seminar on Environmental Criminology and Crime Analysis, Oslo, Norway, June 23–25, 1997. Retrieved from: https://popcenter.asu.edu/sites/default/files/Responses/responsibility/PDFs/Goldstein.pdf

19 Ayres, I. & Braithwaite, J. (1992). *Responsive Regulation: Transcending the De-regulation Debate*. New York: Oxford University Press. https://doi.org/10.1093/oso/9780195070705.001.0001

20 Scott, M. & Goldstein, H. (2005). Shifting and Sharing Responsibility for Public Safety Problems. In *Problem-Oriented Guides for Police* (Issue 3). Office of Community Oriented Policing Services. Retrieved from: https://popcenter.asu.edu/sites/default/files/shifting_sharing_responsibility_for_public_safety_problems.pdf; Goldstein, H. (1997). The pattern of emerging tactics for shifting the ownership of prevention strategies in the current wave of chance in policing: Their implications for both environmental criminology and the police. Presentation at the 6th International Seminar on Environmental Criminology and Crime Analysis, Oslo, Norway, June 23–25, 1997. Retrieved from: https://popcenter.asu.edu/sites/default/files/Responses/responsibility/PDFs/Goldstein.pdf

21 National Institute of Justice (2009). The Use-Of-Force Continuum. Retrieved from: https://nij.ojp.gov/topics/articles/use-force-continuum#0-0

22 Payne, T.C. (2017). Reducing excessive police incidents: Do notices to owners work? *Security Journal, 30*(3), 922–939. https://doi.org/10.1057/sj.2015.2

23 Zidar, M.S., Shafer, J.G., & Eck, J.E. (2018). Reframing an obvious police problem: Discovery, analysis and response to a manufactured problem in a small city. *Policing: A Journal of Policy and Practice, 12*(3), 316–331. https://doi.org/10.1093/police/pax085

24 Desmond, M. & Valdez, N. (2013). Unpolicing the urban poor: Consequences of third-party policing for inner-city women. *American Sociological Review, 78*(1), 117–141. https://doi.org/10.1177/0003122412470829

25 Payne, T.C. (2017). Reducing excessive police incidents: Do notices to owners work? *Security Journal, 30*(3), 922–939. https://doi.org/10.1057/sj.2015.2

26 Shader, C.G., Gill, C., Zheng, X., & Carleton, B. (2024). City government as super-controller: A systematic review of non-police mechanisms that city governments can apply to reduce crime at hot spots. *Aggression and Violent Behavior, 78*, 101957. https://doi.org/10.1016/j.avb.2024.101957

12

Won't Offenders Just Move Around the Corner?

So far, we have shown that: 1) most crime is concentrated at a few places; 2) often these stable high crime places are poorly managed; and 3) when place managers apply situational techniques to high crime places, they can reduce crime. You might agree now that you've seen the evidence. But you may still be wondering: won't offenders just move somewhere else? If we reduce crime at one place, won't offenders just go around the corner to offend? And if this happens, what is the point? Wouldn't the net amount of crime still be the same?

These are logical questions to ask. Researchers call this concern crime displacement. It's based on the idea that offenders are so driven to commit crime, they will find a way to carry it out no matter what. It is a reasonable concern. However, in this chapter, we will show that displacement is not inevitable. Instead, it is an overstated concern.

In this chapter, we explore the displacement hypothesis. We describe the different ways displacement might occur. We then shift to the research that has explored the threat of displacement. Overall, studies suggest that it is not as much of a threat as most people think. In fact, there is good evidence that an opposite effect, the diffusion of benefits, often occurs. So, the second part of this chapter explains how reducing crime at one place can make nearby places safer.

DOI: 10.4324/9781003430155-15

The Displacement Hypothesis

The displacement concern is that tinkering with the environment—social or physical—will not stop a dedicated offender. If a store that an offender steals from improves its security, the offender will go to another store. The newly secured store wins, but at the expense of the other store. From society's point of view, there is no change. The offender produces the same amount of crime. This worry is based on the assumption that most, if not all, offenders are determined.

Many criminologists feel that if offenders have strong propensities to commit crimes, only two things will stop them from committing crimes. First, we can incarcerate them. While incarcerated, they cannot commit crimes among the free public (even if they can commit crimes against other inmates).[1] Second, we can treat their propensities. If offenders' urges to commit crime develop from their upbringing, then social and psychological programs to stop this development might be useful.[2] Alternatively, we could rehabilitate offenders to curb their propensity.[3] Anything less will leave the offender with an unquenchable inclination to get in trouble. If they cannot get into trouble one way, they will find another.

That is what many criminologists believe, and many people in the public share these beliefs. Since preventing crime at places does not alter deep seated propensities, believers in propensities conclude such efforts will not reduce crime. Crime will just shift around and we will be playing a continual game of whack-a-mole. Even though situational crime prevention works at places, according to the displacement hypothesis it only moves crime.

Displacement may not be just geographical. In the 1970s, Thomas Reppetto made the displacement hypothesis explicit and listed the types of displacement.[4] Others have modified Reppetto's list over the years.[5] There are six types of displacement (with alternative names) about which researchers worry (table 12.1). Only the first, geographic or spatial displacement, deals with shifting crime from place to place. For purposes of explanation, we will pretend that there are pure forms of each type, but as you will immediately see, some types must include elements of the other types.

Temporal displacement involves the offender changing the times he will commit crimes. If he steals copper from abandoned homes on Mondays, he could shift to other days of the week if this would allow him

Table 12.1 Types of Displacement

Type	Explanation	Example
Geographic (Spatial)	The offender moves elsewhere	Unable to break into cars in one parking lot, the offender switches to another parking lot.
Temporal	The offender switches times	Unable to deal drugs in the early evening hours, the drug dealer shifts to later at night.
Method	The offender changes procedures	Unable to enter homes through unlocked doors, the burglar uses tools to break windows.
Target (Victim)	The offender selects other targets	Unable to shoplift electronic equipment, the thief switches to shoplifting clothing.
Type	The offender switches crimes	Unable to pickpocket commuters on a subway, the thief starts breaking into their cars.
Perpetrator (Offender)	New offenders replace old offenders	After all sex workers are arrested, their pimp recruits new women.

to circumvent a new prevention effort. Any time switch falls within this category: time of day, day of week, week of month, month of year, and so on. As a practical matter, most temporal displacement is likely to be of the first two types.

Method displacement involves changes in the way offenders commit crimes. This can include changes in their procedures, tools, and other ways of committing crimes. In the late 1980s, for example, when police first started going after street-level crack cocaine dealers, the police found that the arrestees were holding drugs, money, and firearms. Dealers then changed the way they did business. They used lookouts, and others who would hold the drugs, money, and guns. Knowing officers would likely chase those who fled on foot, dealers paid runners (who carried no drugs, guns, or money) to flee when the police arrived so the dealers could escape or have time to hide their illegal wares. Often these runners were juveniles.

If offenders, in response to enforcement or other prevention, change who or what they attack or steal, then this is a form of target (or victim) displacement. For example, if gangs are blocked from raiding drug stores to gain narcotics and other drugs, they could hit doctors' offices. If robberies of shoppers were no longer possible, then perhaps the robbers would switch to robbing college students.

If following some prevention effort, offenders change their crime type—theft from restaurant cash registers to robbing customers coming out of restaurants, for example—then this is called crime type displacement. Any form of crime type displacement will require changes in methods, targets, time, or geography. So, crime type displacement is really a combination of displacement forms. Although it is not a pure type, it may be worth considering. If you are studying displacement, you might want to look for rises in other crimes that correspond to your intervention.

The final type, offender displacement, may not be a form of displacement at all. Rather, think of it as another phenomenon—offender replacement. This is not just splitting hairs. The first five forms of displacement involve individual offenders making decisions—unable to commit the crime of his choice, when, where, and how he wants, the offender finds an alternative set of criminal behaviors. Offender displacement operates very differently. The original offenders are removed, and new offenders come in. None of the original offenders are making decisions about how to change their behavior. The only circumstance where offender displacement is likely to matter is when the criminals removed had been originally recruited by another criminal. A corrupt metal recycler might recruit new copper thieves, for example, if the gang that used to supply him with stolen copper no longer can.

Why Is Displacement Unlikely?

Having reviewed the case for displacement, let's turn to the case against it. Whereas displacement criminologists argue that criminal propensities will always win out, the displacement skeptics argue that displacement may occur, but it also may not. We should not prematurely assume that situational prevention will not work. Displacement skeptics do not claim crime never displaces.

The case against displacement comes from the rational choice perspective. The places that attract offenders are attractive for a reason. Think back to the principles of situational crime prevention (in chapter 10); good crime opportunities provided limited risk, reasonable rewards, low effort, good provocations, and decent excuses.[6] Alternative places, where the offenders could have chosen to commit their crimes, were less attractive. That's why they did not offend there in the first place. We suspect this is true because if the two types of places had been equally attractive, then offenders would probably have committed crimes in both at roughly equal frequency. In short, hotspots are hot for a reason.

When a prevention effort blocks offending at the places offenders like the most, offenders are left with less desirable places. At these places risks will be higher. Or rewards lower. Or more effort is needed. Or there are fewer provocations. Or there are no excuses. You get the idea. Consequently, a reasonably rational offender will not automatically choose to go to these places. These places may not be good enough for crime.

There is another reason offenders may not switch. They might not know of the alternative places. Recall from chapter 9, Patricia and Paul Brantingham's offender search explanation showed that offenders commit crimes in their awareness space.[7] Offenders only know about crime opportunities at the places where they spend their time. If the offenders are taking advantage of a particularly good opportunity, and the only criminal opportunity they are aware of is taken away, then displacement is unlikely.

The third reason to be skeptical of automatic displacement is that even if offenders know of alternative crime sites, they will have to learn how to tackle them. These offenders knew how to be successful at the now protected places, but that does not mean they know the ins and outs of the alternative sites. Offenders might not want to put in the effort to learn how to avoid the risks. But even if they do, learning takes time, so displaced crime is unlikely to be instantaneous.

Another reason is many people commit crimes opportunistically. As we have consistently discussed, many people who commit crime do not have a chronic urge to commit crime. But if a tempting, low-risk crime opportunity presents itself, they will exploit it. If there was no opportunity, they will not seek out an alternative. But what about those few people who commit most of the crime? Wouldn't they be the most driven to commit crime regularly?

A compelling case in the United Kingdom provides an answer. Ronald Clarke and Pat Mayhew directly challenged the idea that offenders are highly driven to commit crimes regardless.[8] They started by asking, "what types of people would we expect to be very determined to act against social norms?" One of the answers was people contemplating suicide. Further, we would expect such people to be among the least rational, as well as the most driven. It seems reasonable that someone who wants to commit suicide will find a way, regardless of efforts to block opportunities; there are many ways to kill oneself, so blocking one or two should merely shift people to other methods.

Many British homes are furnished with gas for heating and cooking. The gas came from processing coal and was very toxic. Being common and lethal made coal gas the primary way people committed suicide in Great Britain. People would turn on the gas for the oven, put their heads inside, and inhale the fumes. The process was lethal but painless. When oil and natural gas fields were discovered off the Scottish coast, natural gas became cheaper than coal gas and eventually replaced coal gas. Natural gas was far less toxic. Did suicides decrease or stay the same? The automatic displacement enthusiast would assert that suicides numbers would stay the same, only the method of suicide would change.

Displacement skeptics would predict a decline in suicide and that is what Clarke and Mayhew found when they investigated the matter. Suicides declined as the use of natural gas increased.[9] There was no compensating switch to jumping off high buildings or cliffs, taking poisons, throwing oneself in front of trains or cars, drowning, shooting oneself, or other methods. Many people considering suicide refrained from committing suicide when they could not find an easy, convenient, painless, clean, and effective method. More recent reviews in suicide research support the finding that "the risk of substitution or displacement towards other means is small".[10] If displacement is not obvious for a behavior where we expect people to be determined, it may not be common when people are less determined.

In short, crime scientists believe offenders make choices about which places are best for crimes. If these are denied, offenders will either stop committing crimes or reduce the number of crimes they commit. The crime scientist does not deny the possibility of displacement. Rather, she does not believe it is automatic. The amount needs to be addressed on a case-by-case basis.[11]

What the Evidence Shows About Displacement

The suicide study explodes the myth of automatic displacement, but it does not directly apply to crime. Fortunately, many researchers have looked for displacement and other researchers have assembled the big lessons from these many studies. Rob Guerette and Kate Bowers completed the most complete review of displacement to date.[12] They found 102 studies of situational crime prevention that looked for displacement. They discovered displacement in 26% of the observations. Further, they found that in 68 of the studies, no displacement was found.

Guerette and Bowers also discovered that "when displacement occurred, it was never complete".[13] This means that the intervention still produced net reductions. To illustrate, consider a place with 20 crimes per year. Let's say that police carry out a place-based intervention that successfully reduces crime at the place, but displacement occurs. The findings suggest that one nearby property might experience two crimes, and another nearby property might experience three crimes. Thus, even though displacement occurred, not all 20 crimes were displaced. Instead, we still have a net reduction of 15 crimes.

Guerette and Bowers' study is the most comprehensive today. However, others that have examined displacement have found similar results. In general, displacement does occur, but less often than anticipated, and when displacement occurs, it's never absolute. No study showed that displacement made crime worse than before. In short, displacement can happen, but we should not expect it to undermine prevention efforts.[14]

However, in an evaluation of 55 studies on displacement, Rene Hesseling found an anomaly that others had missed.[15] He found six studies that reported evidence of displacement's opposite effect. This weird set of findings puzzled researchers. Why would a prevention effort at one site (say an apartment building) have beneficial impacts at sites nearby (e.g., surrounding apartment buildings) not receiving prevention efforts? The answer would come from another study published the same year.

The Diffusion of Crime Control Benefits

It turned out that the six studies puzzling Hesseling were the tip of a research iceberg. No one expected prevention to spread safety beyond its borders, so no one had a name for this phenomenon. Actually, researchers had many names for it but did not share them: for example, a multiplier effect, halo effect, spillover, and bonus. Consequently, the opposite effect of displacement went undetected. That is, until Ronald Clarke and David Weisburd scoured the research and a list of studies with this apparent finding.[16] In these studies, crime did not shift following a prevention effort. Instead, the prevention benefits spread. Often, if practitioners imposed an effective intervention at one place, not only would crime decrease at that place, but it would also decrease at nearby places. It was like a paleontologist searching through museum drawers and discovering a new dinosaur species: the evidence was already there but no one had noted it. So, Clarke and Weisburd gave this unexpected phenomenon a name, the *diffusion of crime control benefits*. But what could cause the diffusion of benefits?

Clarke and Weisburd proposed two reasons for the diffusion of benefits: deterrence and discouragement. Both deal with how offenders misperceive the scope of an intervention. Deterrence occurs with how offenders misperceive the reach of the intervention. For example, police may increase their presence at a single high-crime property. But offenders may question whether police are patrolling adjacent properties too. This causes offenders to pull back on their offending both at and around the high-crime property. Discouragement occurs when offenders perceive the rewards at nearby locations as being less than before the intervention. So while offenders might not feel an increased risk of getting caught for offending there, they pull back their offending because they think the rewards of crime have declined.[17]

Most recently, Shannon and John, along with Kate Bowers, proposed a different cause of diffusion: reversing crime radiation.[18] Crime radiation is a phenomenon whereby a place elevates the risk of crime at nearby places.[19] Recall in chapter 5, we discussed the Barksdale Market where the owner incentivized drug users to shoplift items at nearby stores to exchange for drug money in the shop. This is an example of crime radiating out from a place. The place manager encouraged crime at nearby places. When the store was closed by the police and put to legitimate work, shoplifting at the stores across the street dropped. Taking ownership of the Barksdale meant the drug users no longer had a place where they could get easy cash for drugs in exchange for their stolen goods. The reward for shoplifting was eliminated. Thus, crime not only declined at the Barksdale, but also at nearby properties. So, crime radiation scholars argue that diffusion may occur after an intervention because the place was radiating crime.[20]

Table 12.2 Types of Diffusion of Benefits

Type	Explanation	Example
Geographic (Spatial)	Protection of nearby areas	Protecting a parking lot from thieves keeps thieves from targeting other neighbouring parking lots.
Temporal	Protection of other times	Suppressing drug dealing in the early evening reduces it at other times.
Method	Blocking substitute means	Getting homeowners to lock windows reduces all forms of burglary entry.
Target (Victim)	Protection of other targets	Protecting electronic equipment from shoplifting suppresses theft of other goods.
Type	Reduction in other crimes	Preventing pickpocketing on the subway reduces break-ins to vehicles in the commuter parking lots.
Perpetrator (Offender)	Blocking new offender entry	Having arrested all the sex workers, their pimp can no longer recruit new women.

Diffusion comes in the same types as displacement (table 12.2). It just works in the opposite direction. Geographic or spatial diffusion occurs when crime decreases at both the primary crime site, and at surrounding locations. Again, closing the Barksdale Market is an example of this.

Temporal diffusion occurs when offenders pull back on offending at times other than what the intervention targets. Method diffusion involves offenders giving up a set of criminal behaviors, rather than just the one targeted by the prevention efforts. Target diffusion may also be quite common. Clarke and Weisburd cite a study of a university library installing electronic book trackers that set off exit alarms.[21] These alarm triggers were installed on other materials. Students and faculty who stole books stopped, but they also stopped stealing library materials that did not trigger the alarm because they were not aware of which materials were linked to the alarm. Again, creating uncertainty helped diffuse benefits in other ways. Crime type diffusion will be, like displacement, a mix of other forms of diffusion. Finally, offender diffusion may be thought of as a different sort of phenomena, though for practical purposes we have left it on this list.

What the Evidence Shows About Diffusion

Rob Guerette and Kate Bowers' systematic review of displacement also assessed whether the diffusion of benefits occurred. Of the 102 studies of situational crime prevention interventions, they found that 27% produced a diffusion of benefits. These findings add to the case against displacement. Again, displacement seems to occur in about 26% of the cases. When displacement happens, it is never absolute. In fact, the diffusion of benefits is equally likely to occur.[22]

So, crime does not automatically displace, thus thwarting crime prevention. In fact, it turns out that some situational prevention efforts have benefits larger than expected, the opposite of displacement. Could prevention have other unexpected results? Yes, offenders sometimes curtail their misbehavior before the prevention effort gets underway.

Anticipatory Benefits

Eight years after the discovery of the diffusion of crime prevention benefits, Martha Smith, along with Ronald Clarke and Ken Pease, revealed that a crime reduction can start before the prevention program.[23] They called this phenomenon *anticipatory benefits*. The authors found several examples where crime declines before a strategy formally starts. Why would this happen?

To illustrate, consider the following example from Barclay and colleagues.[24] In the mid-1990s, the police in Vancouver, Canada, were receiving repeated calls for vehicle thefts in parking lots. They realized these calls came primarily from park-and-ride commuter lots at transit stations. These were prime locations for thieves. People would park their cars for the day and take the train into the city for work. Offenders knew the owners of the vehicles in these lots were unlikely to return for many hours; the vehicles were unguarded targets.

In response, the police created a bike patrol program. They would hire a few employees to act as roaming guardians in the lots. Importantly for anticipatory benefits, the police initiated a publicity campaign the month before the bike patrol started, but did not indicate when the program would start. This created an anticipatory benefit; crime in the lots began falling before anyone on bikes started patrolling (light grey area in figure 12.1). Why?

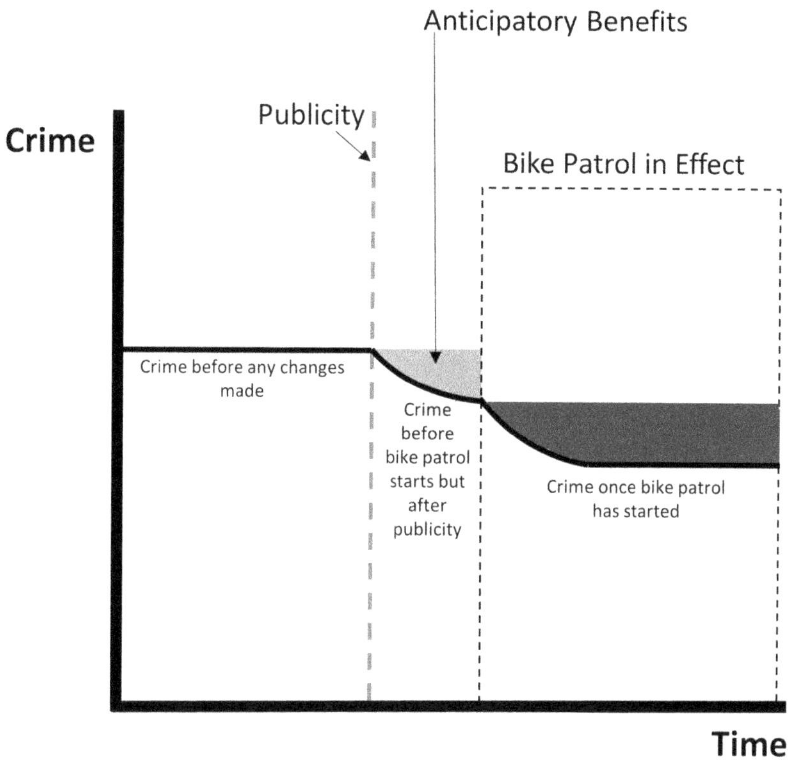

FIGURE 12.1 Anticipatory Benefits

This is the same kind of uncertainty we saw in chapter 2 about residual deterrence following an intervention. But instead of having offenders feel uncertainty after the intervention, it occurred before. They could not tell what the intervention would consist of and when it would begin. Offenders' perceived risk of getting caught increased, so they scaled back their offending before the bike patrols even started. Crime declined further once the bike patrols started (area shaded in dark grey in figure 12.1), a situational crime prevention technique to extend natural surveillance.

Don't Be a Displacement Doomster

We titled this chapter with a question: won't offenders just go somewhere else? Our answer is: probably not. Crime displacement has been on the minds of criminologists for decades. It is a common argument people use to stop the use of place-based crime prevention strategies.

But research continues to suggest that while displacement can happen, it is not common and certainly not absolute. Instead, positive effects—such as diffusion of benefits and anticipatory benefits—are just as likely. When you successfully dismantle crime opportunities at places, you are likely to drive down crime at the chosen place and even some nearby places.

Key Points

- Displacement is not as common as most people assume
- If crime opportunities were as good nearby, offenders would have already been offending there
- Diffusion of benefits is just as likely to occur
- Creating uncertainty among offenders causes them to decrease their offending
- Ask: how can I make an offender second-guess whether to commit a crime at the place in question?

Notes

1 Piquero, A.R. & Blumstein, A. (2007). Does incapacitation reduce crime? *Journal of Quantitative Criminology, 23*, 267–285. https://doi.org/10.1007/s10940-007-9030-6
2 Farrington, D.P., Ttofi, M.M., & Losel, F.A. (2016). Developmental and social prevention. In D. Weisburd, D.P. Farrington, & C. Gill (Eds.), *What Works in Crime Prevention* (pp. 15–75). Springer Publishers. https://doi.org/10.1007/978-1-4939-3477-5_2
3 Lipsey, M.W. & Cullen, F.T. (2007). The effectiveness of correctional rehabilitation: A review of systematic reviews. *Annual Review of Law Social Science, 3*(1), 297–320. https://doi.org/10.1146/annurev.lawsocsci.3.081806.112833
4 Reppetto, T. (1976). Crime prevention and displacement phenomena. *Crime and Delinquency, 22*, 166–177. https://doi.org/10.1177/001112877602200204
5 Barr, R. & Pease, K. (1990). Crime placement, displacement, and deflection. In M. Tonry & N. Morris (Eds.), *Crime and Justice: A Review of Research* (vol. 12, pp. 277–318). Chicago, IL: University of Chicago Press. https://doi.org/10.1086/449167
6 Clarke, R.V. (2011). Situational crime prevention. In R. Wortley, L. Mazerolle, & S. Rombouts (Eds.), *Environmental Criminology and Crime Analysis* (pp. 178–194). New York, NY: Routledge.
7 Brantingham, P.L. & Brantingham, P.J. (1981). Notes on the geometry of crime. In P.J. Brantingham & P.L. Brantingham (Eds), *Environmental Criminology* (pp. 27–54). Prospect Heights, IL: Waveland Press; Brantingham, P.L. & Brantingham, P.J. (1993). Environment, Routine, and Situation: Toward a Pattern Theory of Crime. In M. Clarke & R.V. Felson (Eds.), *Routine Activity and Rational Choice* (pp. 259–294). Transaction. https://doi.org/10.4324/9781315128788-12
8 Clarke, R.V. & Mayhew, P. (1988). The British gas suicide story and is criminological implications. In M. Tonry & N. Morris (Eds.), *Crime and Justice: A Review of Research* (vol. 10). Chicago, IL: University of Chicago Press. https://doi.org/10.1086/449144

9 Clarke, R.V. & Mayhew, P. (1988). The British gas suicide story and is criminological implications. In M. Tonry & N. Morris (Eds.), *Crime and Justice: A Review of Research* (vol. 10). Chicago, IL: University of Chicago Press. https://doi.org/10.1086/449144

10 From page 630 of: Daigle, M.S. (2005). Suicide prevention through means restriction: Assessing the risk of substitution: A critical review and synthesis. *Accident Analysis & Prevention, 37*(4), 625–632. https://doi.org/10.1016/j.aap.2005.03.004

11 Cornish, D.B. & Clarke, R.V. (1987). Understanding crime displacement: An application of rational choice theory. *Criminology, 25*(4), 933–947. https://doi.org/10.1111/j.1745-9125.1987.tb00826.x

12 Guerette, R.T. & Bowers, K.J. (2009). Assessing the extent of crime displacement and diffusion of benefits: A review of situational crime prevention evaluations. *Criminology, 47*(4), 1331–1368. https://doi.org/10.1111/j.1745-9125.2009.00177.x

13 From page 1346 of: Guerette, R.T. & Bowers, K.J. (2009). Assessing the extent of crime displacement and diffusion of benefits: A review of situational crime prevention evaluations. *Criminology, 47*(4), 1331–1368. https://doi.org/10.1111/j.1745-9125.2009.00177.x

14 Barr, R. & Pease, K. (1990). Crime placement, displacement, and deflection. In M. Tonry & N. Morris (eds.), *Crime and Justice: A Review of Research* (vol. 12, pp. 277–318). Chicago, IL: University of Chicago Press. https://doi.org/10.1086/449167; Eck, J.E. (1993). The threat of crime displacement. *Criminal Justice Abstracts, 25*(3), 527–546; Hesseling, R.B.P. (1994). Displacement: A review of the empirical literature. In R.V. Clarke (Ed.), Crime Prevention Studies (vol. 3, pp. 197-230). Monsey, NY: Criminal Justice Press.

15 Hesseling, R.B.P. (1994). Displacement: A review of the empirical literature. In R.V. Clarke (Ed.), *Crime Prevention Studies* (vol. 3, pp. 197–230). Monsey, NY: Criminal Justice Press.

16 Clarke, R.V. & Weisburd, D. (1994). Diffusion of crime control benefits. In R.V. Clarke (Ed.), *Crime Prevention Studies* (vol. 2, pp. 165–183). Monsey, NY: Willow Tree Press. Retrieved from: https://popcenter.asu.edu/sites/g/files/litvpz3631/files/library/CrimePrevention/Volume_02/08clarke.pdf

17 Clarke, R.V. & Weisburd, D. (1994). Diffusion of crime control benefits. In R.V. Clarke (Ed.), *Crime Prevention Studies* (vol. 2, pp. 165–183). Monsey, NY: Willow Tree Press. Retrieved from: https://popcenter.asu.edu/sites/g/files/litvpz3631/files/library/CrimePrevention/Volume_02/08clarke.pdf

18 Eck, J.E., Linning, S.J., & Bowers, K. (2024). Does crime in places stay in places? Evidence for crime radiation from three narrative reviews. *Aggression and Violent Behavior, 78*, 101955. https://doi.org/10.21428/cb6ab371.5adfc466

19 Bowers, K.J. (2014). Risky facilities: Crime radiators or crime absorbers? A comparison of internal and external levels of theft. *Journal of Quantitative Criminology, 30*(3), 389–414. https://doi.org/10.1007/s10940-013-9208-z; Linning, S.J., Bowers, K., & Eck, J.E. (2024). Crime radiation theory: The co-production of crime patterns through opportunity creation and exploitation. *Crime Science, 13*(32), 1–8. https://doi.org/10.1186/s40163-024-00234-6

20 Eck, J.E., Linning, S.J., & Herold, T.D. (2023). *Place Management and Crime: Ownership and Property Rights as a Source of Social Control.* Springer Publishers. https://doi.org/10.1007/978-3-031-27693-4; Eck, J.E., Linning, S.J., & Bowers, K. (2024). Does crime in places stay in places? Evidence for crime radiation from three narrative reviews. *Aggression and Violent Behavior, 78*, 101955. https://doi.org/10.21428/cb6ab371.5adfc466

21 Scherdin, M.J. (1986). The halo effect: Psychological deterrence of electronic security systems. Information Technology and Libraries, September, 232-235. Retrieved from: https://popcenter.asu.edu/sites/g/files/litvpz3631/files/2025-02/161-scherdin-the_halo_effect_psychological_deterrence_of_el.pdf

22 Guerette, R.T. & Bowers, K.J. (2009). Assessing the extent of crime displacement and diffusion of benefits: A review of situational crime prevention evaluations. *Criminology, 47*(4), 1331–1368. https://doi.org/10.1111/j.1745-9125.2009.00177.x; Bowers, K.J., Johnson, S.D., Guerette, R.T., Summers, L., & Poynton, S. (2011). Spatial displacement and diffusion of benefits among geographically focused policing initiatives: a meta-analytical review. *Journal of Experimental Criminology, 7*, 347–374. https://doi.org/10.1007/s11292-011-9134-8

23 Smith, M.J., Clarke, R.V., & Pease, K. (2002). Anticipatory benefits in crime prevention. In N. Tilley (Ed.), *Crime Prevention Studies* (vol. 13; pp. 71–88). Boulder, CO: Lynne Rienner Publishers. Retrieved from: https://popcenter.asu.edu/sites/g/files/litvpz3631/files/library/CrimePrevention/Volume_13/05-Smith.pdf

24 Barclay, P., Buckley, J., Brantingham, P.L., & Whinn-Yates, T. (1997). Preventing auto theft in commuter parking lots: A bike patrol in Vancouver. In R.V. Clarke (Ed.), *Situational Crime Prevention: Successful Case Studies* (2nd ed.). Guilderland, NY: Harrow and Heston.

PART 4
PUTTING THE RULE OF THE FEW INTO PRACTICE

We started off this book showing you the importance of the rule of the few for crime prevention. By now, you should have a sense of what we mean. Though the rule may not always apply, it's common enough that you should always consider it during your problem-solving process. Is the problem concentrated at specific places? Are specific people involved?

Our early chapters highlighted the fallacies that most people have about crime. They suggest the opposite of the rule of the few. Instead of being hyper-focused, they are broad. We assume that crime is widespread, particularly in high crime neighborhoods. Most assume that the more offenders we arrest, the less crime we will have. We also assume that to address crime, we need participation from most residents in a community to address problems. Similarly, we assume that hiring more police or decreasing police response time will reduce crime.

But the world we live in does not align with these fallacies. Many phenomena are concentrated, and crime is no different. Problems repeatedly occur. This makes them patterned. Despite this, many politicians and the public continue to advocate for policies that adhere to the fallacies we have been highlighting. For example, in the wake of crime spikes or terrible events, politicians often pledge to compel the police department to return to community policing practices. Similarly, right-leaning politicians may pledge to hire more police while left-leaning politicians pledge to defund them. But none of these tactics have been shown to reduce

DOI: 10.4324/9781003430155-16

crime. More importantly, they are not specific enough. Community policing is problematic because nobody can define it, let alone implement it operationally. Hiring more police officers only works if a department is immensely short-staffed. This usually isn't the case and if it is true, finding more officers is currently a problem for every agency. Defunding the police could work, but no one has ever outlined anything specific as to what plans would be set in motion to handle the numerous and varied scenarios police are regularly called for. As the rule of the few preaches, we need to be specific. We need to be intentional. It's time for a change.

This final part of the book discusses ways to put the rule of the few into practice to reduce crime. In chapters 13 to 17, we provide specific strategies you can use to address crime. Practices that consider concentration among places, offenders, and targets/victims will likely be the most effective. We draw on real world experiences of police and researchers who have put the rule of the few into practice. As you will see, this requires a particular focus on the few people and places experiencing most of the crime.

13

LESSONS FROM A HOMICIDE SCENE

When Dan worked with the Cincinnati Police Department, he commanded a unit called Vortex. Vortex was designed to reduce gun violence and crime in troubled neighborhoods, through an extremely visible police presence that generated high arrest numbers. At the time, high police visibility and many arrests were believed to reduce crime.

One day, Vortex had 60 officers deployed in a six-block area. You could not look up or down the street without seeing an officer. During this operation, an individual came out of a building onto the street, pulled out a gun and shot two people, killing them both. Officers immediately apprehended the perpetrator. Yet two people were dead despite a large, highly visible police presence.

90 minutes later, while the 60-officer Vortex team was still present, another person came out of a different building, 1.5 blocks away from the initial double homicide, and shot someone, killing him. There were now three outdoor homicides within a 90-minute time frame and with 60 police officers highly visible in the immediate area.

Dan learned a valuable lesson that day. The anticipated deterrent effect, from saturating an area with uniformed police and making many arrests, simply did not work. There had to be a better way to police than the traditional standard model.

DOI: 10.4324/9781003430155-17

Widespread police neighborhood crackdowns and high arrest numbers were both ineffective and hurtful to the community. Using these tactics, police did not drive down gun violence. Instead, the police disrupted the daily activities of the 99% of people in the neighborhood who were uninvolved in the violent incidents and just trying to make their way in life.

Focusing on the many, instead of the very few who were actively engaged in gun violence, generated tremendous animosity towards the police in these already troubled communities. It also did nothing to dismantle the gangs driving the violence or remove the opportunity structure that enabled the violence to routinely occur. Dan wondered, was there a better way to police? He realized that narrowly focusing his efforts would be the most effective. A few other agencies had adopted such a strategy, called focused deterrence, with success.

Focused Deterrence

Around the same time of the Vortex incidents, law enforcement practitioners were developing and applying strategies that accounted for the concentration of crime. Researchers like John had shown the importance of the rule of the few not just at places, but also on the other sides of the crime triangle including offenders and targets. The individuals who committed the three homicides in Cincinnati mentioned earlier were well known to the police; they were repeat violent offenders. Police personnel, like Dan, realized that many of the shootings could be tied to very few people. This prompted police agencies to start developing more focused crime reduction strategies. The new strategies concentrated on the few violent offenders, instead of the usual broad approach that involved the many, including those who were not involved in gun violence.

Focused deterrence was one of the first policing strategies to incorporate the rule of the few. The initial strategy, called Operation Ceasefire, was created in Boston, Massachusetts, during the mid - 1990s.[1] Criminal justice partners and researchers found that less than 1% of Boston's residents between the ages of 14–24 were responsible for more than 60% of the city's homicides.[2] Their discovery that a few prolific offenders drive gun violence holds true in other US cities as well:

- In Cincinnati, 0.5% of the city's population were violent gang members and they were responsible for 75% of the shootings and gun homicides in the city[3]
- In Fort Myers, Florida, 0.3% of the of the city's population were identified as violent gang members and found to be responsible for 67% of the city's homicides and non-fatal shootings between 2012–2017[4]
- In Oakland, California, 0.1% of the city's overall population was found to be at the greatest risk of gun violence[5]
- In New Orleans, Louisiana, less than 1% of the city's overall population were involved in over 50% of the city's homicides[6]

The numbers were clear. Very few people drive violent crime trends across the country. But the difficult question to answer became how can we turn this information into a strategy that effectively reduces gun violence? Boston's Operation Ceasefire had a possible answer: focus your resources on the tiny fraction of people who are committing the violence, usually members of criminal gangs or groups.[7]

In a focused deterrence model, criminal justice partners communicate two messages to gang-involved people. The first message uses a carrot and stick approach. Police offer the few individuals mostly likely to engage in gun violence an option to leave criminal life. Community partners offer targeted services to assist those who wish to find a way out of the criminal lifestyle. The community partners communicate a willingness to welcome the person into their circles and explain what resources are available to help them. The offer of help to leave the criminal lifestyle also provides the police increased community legitimacy. This is especially the case when a police enforcement operation later arrests those individuals who did not take advantage of the opportunity and continued to engage in gun violence.[8]

If the gang-involved individuals choose not to accept this offer and continue to engage in gun violence, the promised swift and certain law enforcement sanctions will follow. This leads to the second message: the consequences of not accepting help to exit the criminal lifestyle. The second focused deterrence message can be delivered in two ways.

The first message option is a deterrence message delivered to a particular individual. It involves direct interactions between specific gun violence-involved persons, law enforcement personnel, and community partners. Together, law enforcement and community partners identify the people most likely to be involved in gun violence, as either a suspect or a potential victim. Next, the partners communicate a clear, direct message to these high-risk individuals: "We know who you are, what you do, and who you associate with. If you do not stop shooting, we will focus all the resources of the criminal justice system on you."

The implicit threat is to use all available resources to arrest and incapacitate the most violent offenders. Ideally, police pursue these violent offenders for their most serious crimes. But if they have insufficient evidence for those offenses, they can pursue other criminal justice levers at their disposal.

Every shift, law enforcement personnel use discretion. If someone on probation is working hard to stay out of trouble and find stable employment but misses his court-ordered curfew once, for example, a police or probation officer can overlook this. But if the individual has been called out in a focused deterrence strategy because law enforcement has seen him engaging in deviant behavior, law enforcement will respond differently to keep their earlier swift and sure punishment promise. So, police can pursue other crimes or probation violations committed by those who chose not to leave the criminal lifestyle.

The second message delivery option makes use of the network structure within violent groups or gangs. It gets the group/gang to control its own members. Police also deliver a deterrence message here. But instead of delivering it to a single person, they deliver it to a criminal group. In some cases, the police warn the entire group that if any individual in their group engages in gun violence, they will take all legal means to sanction everyone in the group. In other cases, the police need only inform specific, usually high-status, individuals within the group of the threat. With either method, certain group members now have a personal stake in controlling the behavior of the other members through peer pressure. The goal is for the groups to police themselves.[9]

Evaluations of focused deterrence suggest the strategy can effectively reduce gun violence.[10] The Boston Operation Ceasefire program reduced youth gang violence by 63%.[11] Other cities adapted the Boston program and had similar successes. For example, the Chicago-focused deterrence program, from 2003–2004, produced a 37% reduction in homicides and 16–34% reductions in shootings depending on the study area.[12] A program in High Point, North Carolina, from 2004 to 2007, saw 26% fewer drug-related crimes and a 57% decline in violent crime.[13] A program in New Orleans, from 2012 to 2014, reduced homicides between 17% and 31%, depending on the neighborhood.[14] To date, researchers have evaluated 24 focused deterrence strategies and found that 19 (79%) of the evaluations produce statistically significant reductions in crime.[15]

The strategy's co-creator, David Kennedy, has attributed much of the strategy's success to making police more purposeful with their time and attention:

> ...focus was on one or a few important things, not on everything; focus on a small number of extreme high-risk groups and networks, not on everyone; and focus on creating real consequences, not on threatening essentially false ones.[16]

Adding a Focused Deterrence Approach to Vortex

Inspired by focused deterrence, Dan re-engineered Vortex to focus on the few people that were driving gun violence in Cincinnati. Vortex transformed from a short-term crime suppression unit, focused on the many, to a data-driven, intelligence-led police unit, that focused their resources on the few; the actual people driving violent crime. Vortex later became the primary enforcement arm of the Cincinnati Initiative to Reduce Violence (CIRV), a focused deterrence-inspired strategy.[17]

Vortex no longer operated under the fallacy that crime is widespread or that a high number of arrests reduce crime (as covered in chapters 2 and 4). Instead of trying to arrest many people, Vortex emphasized arrests of the few prolific violent offenders. The strategy focused on outcomes—in this case reduced gun violence and the harm associated with it—and not merely arrest numbers (i.e., outputs), which only measured police officer activity. As a result, violent offenders came to see Vortex as a powerful deterrent that altered their risk/reward balance.

Given Cincinnati's gang structure at the time, Dan believed that the group message approach would likely work best. In fact, he had Vortex officers penetrate the multiple layers of security at an after-hours nightclub to speak directly with the gang leader who controlled all the criminal activities in a neighborhood long plagued by gun violence. Officers showed him the gang book compiled by investigators, which detailed the structure and roles of the entire gang and clearly identified those individuals who were involved. Police communicated the deterrent message that if the gun violence perpetrated by anyone in the gang did not stop, immediate sanctions to all members of the group were certain to follow.

The following day, the gang leader held a meeting with all his key lieutenants and informed them that "if a body hit the ground" on their territory and he did not personally give the order for it, he would have the shooter killed. After this meeting, one of Cincinnati's most violent neighborhoods did not have a gang member involved shooting or homicide for over 16 months.

This example showed that putting pressure on the few members of a gang with the highest power and status had the most impact. It also showed that the police did not need to directly send the deterrent message to each individual member of the gang. Instead, a pointed individual encounter with one of the gang's top members compelled him to spread the message about the consequences to all if the other members engaged in gun violence.

This example also demonstrates the concept of super controllers (discussed in chapter 11). In this instance, the gang leader served as a personal super controller. He communicated the message to his lieutenants, making them handlers. The lieutenants, as handlers, were then tasked with controlling the behavior of lower-ranking gang members who might have become the shooter in future violent incidents.

We should also note that the violent gang did not get a free pass for their other criminal activities simply because they stopped shooting. Vortex continued to investigate the gang's other illegal activities and was eventually able to dismantle the gang. But to do so, they needed to stop the rampant gun violence first. By stopping the immediate violence, Vortex stabilized the neighborhood in the short term which then allowed for the longer-term investigation of the gang. Their focused deterrence strategy provided Vortex the needed time and space to build criminal cases against multiple gang members and completely dismantle the gang. Doing so stabilized the neighborhood for the long-term, instead of merely disrupting the gang's activities for a brief period.

Overall, the focused Vortex strategy resulted in a sustained violent crime reduction citywide. In fact, the violent crime reduction, and new focus on the few instead of the many, was so successful that it led other troubled neighborhoods to petition the city to have Vortex deployed in their neighborhoods.

Focusing on the Few Who Commit Most of the Property Crime

We have previously established that a small number of prolific offenders commit most of the crime across any area. However, much like violent gun offenders, an even smaller number of nonviolent criminal offenders commit shocking amounts of property crime. Recall from chapter 4 that "the most crime-involved 10% of males account for nearly 66% of all the US crime committed by males" and "the most crime-involved 10% of females account for 59% of all the US crime committed by females".[18] So, even when dealing with property crime, it is in the police's best interest to narrowly focus on the few.

Nonviolent property crimes, such as shoplifting, vehicle theft, and theft of items from automobiles, make up most of the reported crimes in any area. They are committed by a few prolific offenders who concentrate on a few repeat places and victims. A New York Times article highlighted that in 2022, "a third of all shoplifting arrests in New York City last year involved just 327 people, the police said. Collectively, they were arrested and rearrested more than 6,000 times". The same article also showed a narrow concentration of theft offenses by place. The victims are also concentrated: "18 department stores and seven chain pharmacy locations accounted for 20 percent of all New York City theft complaints".[19]

If a community wants to reduce its overall crime, they must reduce their property crime. Most cities have far more property crime than violent crime. So, a reduction in only violence will have less of a significant impact on a city's overall crime rate.

Unlike violent offenders, who usually specialize in one type of crime, such as armed robbery of drug dealers, nonviolent offenders are usually generalists and will vary their crime type based on arbitrary opportunities that present themselves during their daily activities.[20] This is why a narrow focus on the *how* is needed to reduce property crimes. Acting on the how removes the opportunity structure for the prolific property crime offenders to commit future crimes to occur at that location.

Researchers have begun exploring focused deterrence to reduce crimes other than shootings and homicides. For example, a focused deterrence program to reduce intimate partner domestic violence was able to reduce police calls for service and arrest by 20%.[21] However, to date, no one has applied focused deterrence strategies to nonviolent crime. It remains to be seen whether such an approach would work as well as if does with shootings and homicides. But as we have shown throughout this book, focusing on the few is usually the most efficient.

What's The Catch?

Although the evidence for focused deterrence is mostly positive, it has a flaw: sustainability. While focused deterrence consistently reduces crime, it's difficult to maintain these crime reductions. Significant shifts in crime strategy are often seen as one-off special projects, run by specialized police units, and are not used as the overarching crime strategy for an entire police department.

These new strategies require an immense investment of time and resources on the part of the police and other law enforcement agencies. They require police workforce resources that are very costly. Police departments often create task forces or special units to bring more police attention to the few problematic offenders. However, the new special units divert the already limited number of operational patrol officers from existing agency staffing resources, at a time when most police agencies are already below their authorized complement of officers and struggle to attract new recruits.

To the delight of high-ranking police officials and politicians, these narrowly-focused deterrence efforts usually deliver immediate declines in violent crime.[22] Once the immediate threat of violence declines, however, both public and police officials shift their focus to other pressing problems. The police can seldom sustain these special task forces due to both workforce and economic constraints. This makes it challenging to maintain the internal and external support and resources needed to keep focused deterrence strategies operating. With time, the most prolific offenders learn to adapt to this. They learn to retreat and wait for the initiative to subside.

Changes in both police and political leadership also regularly occur. Often the new leaders have their own individual agendas. So, the leaders implement new strategies and initiatives because they are not associated with the previous strategy and will receive no personal credit for its success.

The evidence from Cincinnati, Ohio illustrates this decay in effectiveness. Initially, their focused deterrence strategy, called the Cincinnati Initiative to Reduce Violence (CIRV), saw a 61% reduction in homicides involving high-risk offender groups. However, over time, those reductions declined to 35%.[23] A 35% reduction in homicides is still a win. We simply use the example to show that the strong effects that you might initially observe may not last.

The next logical question then would be: is there a way to sustain these crime reduction effects? Our answer is yes, and it involves merging an offender-focused strategy with a place-based approach to generate sustainable crime reduction. In the next chapter, we cover new innovations in place-based approaches to crime reduction, then in chapter 15 we show you how to merge and offender- and place-based strategy to maximize your crime reductions and keep crime at bay long after your intervention.

Key Points

- A tiny fraction of people commit most of the violent and property offenses
- Offer help to the few who are involved in violent crime and promise sanctions to those who do not accept the help
- Take advantage of the network structure of gangs to spread the focused deterrence message
- Ask: who are the few people committing most of the crime?

Notes

1 Braga, A.A., Weisburd, D.L., & Turchan, B. (2018). Focused deterrence strategies and crime control: An updated systematic review and meta-analysis of the empirical evidence. *Criminology & Public Policy*, 17(1), 205–250. https://doi.org/10.1111/1745-9133.12353; Braga, A.A. & Kennedy, D.M. (2021). *A Framework for Addressing Violence and Serious Crime: Focused Deterrence, Legitimacy, and Prevention*. Cambridge University Press. https://doi.org/10.1017/9781108938143

2 Kennedy, D.M., Piehl, A.M., & Braga, A.A. (1996). Youth violence in Boston: Gun markets, serious youth offenders, and a use-reduction strategy. *Law and Contemporary Problems, 59*(1), 147–196. https://doi.org/10.2307/1192213

3 Engel, R.S., Baker, S.G., Tillyer, M.S., Eck, J., & Dunham, J. (2008). Implementation of the Cincinnati initiative to reduce violence (CIRV): Year 1 report. Cincinnati, OH: University of Cincinnati Policing Institute.

4 Haberman, C.S., Desmond, J.S., Gerard, D.W., & Henderson, S.M. (2018). Fort Myers Gun Violence Reduction Initiative Gang Activity: Year 1 report. Cincinnati, OH: University of Cincinnati Institute of Crime Science.

5 McLively, M. & Nieto, B. (2019). *A Case Study in Hope: Lessons from Oakland's Remarkable Reduction in Gun Violence*. Giffords Law Center.

6 Corsaro, N. & Engel, R.S. (2015). Most challenging of contexts: Assessing the impact of focused deterrence on serious violence in New Orleans. *Criminology & Public Policy, 14*(3), 471–505. https://doi.org/10.1111/1745-9133.12142

7 Braga, A.A., Weisburd, D.L., & Turchan, B. (2018). Focused deterrence strategies and crime control: An updated systematic review and meta-analysis of the empirical evidence. *Criminology & Public Policy, 17*(1), 205–250. https://doi.org/10.1111/1745-9133.12353; Braga, A.A. & Kennedy, D.M. (2021). *A Framework for Addressing Violence and Serious Crime: Focused Deterrence, Legitimacy, and Prevention*. Cambridge University Press. https://doi.org/10.1017/9781108938143

8 Braga, A.A., Weisburd, D.L., & Turchan, B. (2018). Focused deterrence strategies and crime control: An updated systematic review and meta-analysis of the empirical evidence. *Criminology & Public Policy, 17*(1), 205–250. https://doi.org/10.1111/1745-9133.12353; Braga, A.A. & Kennedy, D.M. (2021). *A Framework for Addressing Violence and Serious Crime: Focused Deterrence, Legitimacy, and Prevention*. Cambridge University Press. https://doi.org/10.1017/9781108938143

9 Kennedy, D.M. (2006). Old Wine in New Bottles: Policing and the Lesson of Pulling Levers. In D. Weisburd and A. Braga (Eds.), *Police Innovation: Contrasting Perspectives* (pp. 155–170). Cambridge, UK: Cambridge University Press.

10 Braga, A.A., Weisburd, D.L., & Turchan, B. (2018). Focused deterrence strategies and crime control: An updated systematic review and meta-analysis of the empirical evidence. *Criminology & Public Policy, 17*(1), 205–250. https://doi.org/10.1111/1745-9133.12353; Braga, A.A. & Kennedy, D.M. (2021). *A Framework for Addressing Violence and Serious Crime: Focused Deterrence, Legitimacy, and Prevention*. Cambridge University Press. https://doi.org/10.1017/9781108938143

11 Braga, A.A., Kennedy, D.M., Waring, E.J., & Piehl, A.M. (2001). Problem-oriented policing, deterrence, and youth violence: An evaluation of Boston's Operation Ceasefire. *Journal of Research in Crime and Delinquency, 38*(3), 195–225. https://doi.org/10.1177/0022427801038003001

12 Papachristos, A.V., Meares, T.L., & Fagan, J. (2007). Attention felons: Evaluating project safe neighborhoods in Chicago. *Journal of Empirical Legal Studies, 4*(2), 223–272. https://doi.org/10.1111/j.1740-1461.2007.00096.x

13 Corsaro, N., Hunt, E.D., Hipple, N.K., & McGarrell, E.F. (2012). The impact of drug market pulling levers policing on neighborhood violence: An evaluation of the high point drug market intervention. *Criminology & Public Policy, 11*(2), 167–199. https://doi.org/10.1111/j.1745-9133.2012.00798.x; Kennedy, D.M. & Wong, S.L. (2009). *The High Point Drug Market Intervention Strategy*. Washington, DC: US Department of Justice, Office of Community Oriented Policing Services.

14 Corsaro, N. & Engel, R.S. (2015). Most challenging of contexts: Assessing the impact of focused deterrence on serious violence in New Orleans. *Criminology & Public Policy, 14*(3), 471–505. https://doi.org/10.1111/1745-9133.12142

15 Braga, A.A., Weisburd, D.L., & Turchan, B. (2018). Focused deterrence strategies and crime control: An updated systematic review and meta-analysis of the empirical evidence. *Criminology & Public Policy, 17*(1), 205–250. https://doi.org/10.1111/1745-9133.12353; Braga, A.A. & Kennedy, D.M. (2021). *A Framework for Addressing Violence and Serious Crime: Focused Deterrence, Legitimacy, and Prevention*. Cambridge University Press. https://doi.org/10.1017/9781108938143; Scott, M.S. (2017). *Focused deterrence of high-risk individuals: Strategies for policing*

innovation. Problem-Oriented Guides for Police Response Guide Series, No. 13. U.S. Department of Justice. Retrieved from: https://popcenter.asu.edu/sites/default/files/spi_focused_deterrence_pop_guide_final.pdf

16 From page 211 of: Kennedy, D. (2019). Advocate: Policing and the Lessons of Focused Deterrence. In D. Weisburd & A.A. Braga (Eds.), *Police Innovation: Contrasting Perspectives* (2nd ed; pp. 205–226). Cambridge University Press. https://doi.org/10.1017/9781108278423.010

17 Engel, R.S., Tillyer, M.S., & Corsaro, N. (2013). Reducing gang violence using focused deterrence: Evaluating the Cincinnati Initiative to Reduce Violence (CIRV). *Justice Quarterly, 30*(3), 403–439. https://doi.org/10.1080/07418825.2011.619559

18 From page 9 of: Martinez, N., Lee, Y., Eck, J., & O, S. (2017). Ravenous wolves revisited: A systematic review of offending concentration. *Crime Science, 6*(1). https://doi.org/10.1186/s40163-017–0072-2

19 Meko, H. (2023, April 15). A Tiny Number of Shoplifters Commit Thousands of New York City Thefts. *New York Times*. Retrieved from: https://www.nytimes.com/2023/04/15/nyregion/shoplifting-arrests-nyc.html

20 Decker, S.H. (2005). *Using offender interviews to inform police problem solving*. Problem-Oriented Guides for Police, Problem-Solving Tools Series, No. 3. U.S. Department of Justice. Retrieved from: https://popcenter.asu.edu/sites/default/files/tools/pdfs/InterviewingOffenders.pdf

21 Sechrist, S.M. & Weil, J.D. (2018). Assessing the impact of a focused deterrence strategy to combat intimate partner domestic violence. *Violence Against Women, 24*(3), 243–265. https://doi.org/10.1177/1077801216687877

22 Braga, A.A. (2008). Pulling levers focused deterrence strategies and the prevention of gun homicide. *Journal of Criminal Justice, 36*(4), 332–343. https://doi.org/10.1016/j.jcrimjus.2008.06.009; Braga, A.A. & Weisburd, D.L. (2012). The effects of focused deterrence strategies on crime: A systematic review and meta-analysis of the empirical evidence. *Journal of Research in Crime and Delinquency, 49*(3), 323–358. https://doi.org/10.1177/0022427811419368; Braga, A.A., Weisburd, D.L., & Turchan, B. (2018). Focused deterrence strategies and crime control: An updated systematic review and meta-analysis of the empirical evidence. *Criminology & Public Policy, 17*(1), 205–250. https://doi.org/10.1111/1745-9133.12353

23 Engel, R.S., Baker, S.G., Tillyer, M.S., Eck, J., & Dunham, J. (2008). Implementation of the Cincinnati initiative to reduce violence (CIRV): Year 1 report. Cincinnati, OH: University of Cincinnati Policing Institute; Engel, R.S., Tillyer, M.S., Dunham, J., Hall, D., Ozer, M., Henson, B., & Godsey, T. (2009). Implementation of the Cincinnati initiative to reduce violence (CIRV): Year 2 report. Cincinnati, OH: University of Cincinnati Policing Institute.

14

Crime Radiation and Place Network Investigations

In the Franklin neighborhood of Provo, Utah (USA), residents were calling the police in record numbers for issues such as illicit drug and alcohol use, assaults, overdoses, sexual offenses, thefts, trespassing, and disorder. For years the police had been trying to address the problem. When people called for help, they responded, often resulting in arrests of people involved in the illegal activity. But this response did not prevent future crimes. So, calls from residents kept coming in. Tired of responding endlessly to the calls, police decided to try a problem-oriented approach.[1]

The police started tracking where the calls were coming from. Once again, the rule of the few appeared; many of the calls could be traced back to a single address. Looking back on their data, they realized that a 4-unit dilapidated apartment had been generating an average of 135 calls for service to police per year for over a decade. Police also learned that the property had developed a reputation as a haven for people experiencing homelessness, mental health issues, and drug addiction. The apartment was so-well known, in fact, that people from outside of the city would travel to the apartment looking to offend. The tenants, all behavioral health patients, were repeatedly victimized. Collectively, the tenants called the police 184 times in five years. One tenant was suspected of committing six crimes.

 DOI: 10.4324/9781003430155-18

But the police linked 911 calls at other addresses to the apartment too. Nearby residents were reporting that "crimes being committed at this address were bleeding onto their property diminishing property values and scaring away potential customers at surrounding businesses".[2] In essence, crime was *radiating* from the apartment building to other properties.[3] Opportunities for crime at the apartment, such as undisturbed drug use, was encouraging illegal activity elsewhere, such as burglary and theft to fund the drug abuse.

Despite calls coming from properties all over the Franklin neighborhood, the police department realized they had a place, not neighborhood, problem on their hands. So, they took a place-based approach to tackle the problem. They started by moving the apartment's tenants to hygienic housing. They also called upon regulatory agencies to begin regular inspections of the property. Eventually, the owner sold the property.

The new owners renovated the building and began renting the units. Calls to police about the building stopped and calls to police from properties around the building immediately dropped about 50%; a year later, calls had dropped 92%.[4]

The Provo apartment example teaches us three lessons. First, place-based approaches to crime prevention can be quite effective. Much like the Barksdale Market Dan dealt with in chapter 5, authorities could not get a handle on the crime problems until a responsible manager acquired the ownership of the building. The transfer in ownership produced a sustained crime reduction effect. The new owners stopped the revolving door problem; a place-based approach saved the police from having to keep going back to the apartment to address crime.

Second, when places radiate crime, it means that the criminal activity at the place may not stay at the place. Much so-called neighborhood crime can be traced back to a tiny fraction of places within a neighborhood.

Third, if a place is radiating crime, then suppressing crime at that place can create a diffusion of benefits.[5] Not only did crime at the Provo apartment go down, but crime at nearby properties declined once the new owners addressed the problems at the radiator, namely the apartment. In short, we are better off treating places than treating neighborhoods.[6]

In the last chapter we showed you how focusing on the few prolific offenders generates the greatest crime reduction. But the effect can wear off if you do not maintain the program. To fix this, you need to add a place component to your response. So far, we have dealt with crime places in isolation; they assume crime at a place stays at a place, and this is often true. We covered how to address these types of problems with place management (chapter 7) and situational crime prevention (chapter 10).

However, in some cases, like the Provo apartment example, what happens at a place does not stay at a place. Crime produced at a place creates crime at nearby places. So, places are connected. These connections can occur unintentionally or intentionally. Crime radiation explains much of the unintentional connections among crime-involved places. We just saw an example of this in the Provo example, where activity at the apartment created illegal activity at nearby places.

In addition, offenders may intentionally connect properties; researchers call these place networks. Offenders deliberately acquire certain properties to create place networks. These networks provide the infrastructure needed to carry out their crimes. Without each place in the network, they cannot commit their crimes. So, understanding the different types of places and their function can help you identify and dismantle the network.

We start by discussing radiation and its various types. Then we discuss deliberate place networks offenders use to carry out their crimes. We will show that eliminating crime radiation or place networks creates long-term crime reduction.

Crime Radiation

Kate Bowers first coined the term *crime radiation* when she discovered that high theft locations in a British city were associated with more crime at nearby places.[7] A decade later, Shannon and John partnered with her to develop a full explanation of the phenomenon.[8] So far, we have been able to identify three types of crime radiation: hot dot, veiled dot, and cold dot.

Hot dot radiation occurs when a high-crime place increases crime at its neighboring properties.[9] Hot dots have sustained crime opportunity structures. They anchor offenders' searches for good crime opportunities. Consider a high-crime bar as an example. The bar might be known for its lax serving practices and regularly allowing patrons to become overly intoxicated. Knowing this, it draws in offenders who may want to binge drink, get into fights, take drugs, and so on. But in the process of continually going to and from this bar, offenders notice other crime opportunities at nearby places. Thus, hot dot radiators do not change the crime opportunities of nearby places. Instead, they draw in offenders who then notice existing opportunities nearby and exploit them.

In Kate Bowers' original study of theft radiation, she likely detected hot dot radiation.[10] Retail stores known for lax security procedures (e.g., self-checkouts, no anti-theft devices on high value items, etc.) will attract offenders and they will go back repeatedly to pilfer merchandise. But in the process of going to and from these well-known stores, offenders will notice and exploit other crime opportunities nearby.

Thus, an important feature of hot dot radiators is that there is no deliberate attempt to encourage crime at nearby places; crime nearby is merely an unfortunate byproduct of bad place management decisions at the radiator (e.g., choosing not to use anti-theft devices on high value items).

But when a place manager deliberately encourages crime at nearby places, you have *veiled dot radiation*.[11] Veiled dot radiators will host consensual crimes. A metal recycling facility that buys stolen copper is an example. So is an automotive repair shop that purchases stolen catalytic converters, and a convenience store, like the Barksdale Market from chapter 5, that facilitates drug use, thereby encouraging users to shoplift nearby properties to fund their addiction. The place manager encouraged drug users to shoplift items from the neighboring pharmacy and grocery store to purchase or trade for drugs on his property.

Because the inside crimes are consensual, veiled dot radiators will likely appear as low-crime or crime-free properties in police report data. Those engaged in the consensual crimes are unlikely to report the criminal activity. But police intelligence and surveillance can uncover many nefarious activities at these places. Moreover, the place managers of veiled dots profit from encouraging crime at nearby properties. This further incentivizes people involved with veiled dots to keep illegal activities discrete.

However, it is also possible to have crime-free places that unintentionally create crime nearby. Such places are called *cold dot radiators*. Cold dot radiation occurs when low- or no-crime places increase crime at nearby places.[12] These places usually have strong place management so they do not experience any crime on their property. But the activities at the place can unintentionally cause crime nearby.

Consider a cinema located in the downtown core of a major city as an example. Let's say this cinema is located on a busy street but has no onsite parking. Moviegoers who commute by car will have to find street parking nearby. Having watched moviegoers leave their vehicles and enter the cinema, offenders know the vehicles will be left unguarded for a couple of hours. So, they break into the cars.

Offenders likely stumble upon cold dot radiators. Unlike hot or veiled dot radiators, cold dot radiators do not intentionally attract offenders for criminal purposes. Instead, offenders encounter them while going about their daily activities. Other examples could include gyms, churches, sports arenas, and any places which cause people to leave targets unguarded for a period of time.

Like veiled dot radiators, it may be initially difficult to detect a cold dot radiator with police report data. It may require police intelligence or surveillance to see how a series of vehicle thefts, for example, may be connected to the routines of a cold dot radiator. But sometimes it may be intuitive to devise. If a series of vehicle break-ins occurs during a major sporting event, they may be connected to the nearby sports arena. Similarly, if the thefts are occurring during worshipping hours, offenders may be exploiting the routine activities of a church.

All crime radiation types suggest that what happens at places doesn't always stay at places. Sometimes the goings on of one place will influence crime at other nearby places. While researchers are still examining how prevalent crime radiation is, the discovery of this phenomenon has uncovered several important lessons about prevention. We turn to those next.

Addressing Crime Radiation

If a few places radiate crime, then focusing our prevention efforts on these radiators makes sense. This has three important implications for crime reduction. First, crime radiation suggests that place-based approaches are even more important than historically thought. Consider the original crime concentration findings of Lawrence Sherman and his colleagues from chapter 2. They found that 3.3% of addresses experienced 50.1% of crimes in Minneapolis, MN.[13]

Initially researchers argued that police could cut a city's crime in half by addressing crime at 3.3% of places. But if some of these places are radiating crime, you only need to suppress problems at the radiators. In the Provo apartment example, the change in place management at the radiator suppressed crime at the apartment and at properties around it. Once the problems at the radiator were taken care of, the diffusion of benefits occurred; crime at nearby places declined as well. Crime at the nearby places affected by the radiator would be part of Sherman's 3.3% of places; they experienced repeated crime because of the radiator. But if solving crime at the radiator solves crime at nearby properties, then police would need to address fewer than 3.3% of the problem places. Crime radiation suggests that police should prioritize the crime radiators within the few places experiencing crime.

The second implication is that the police will reduce crime more when they can identify crime radiators. This ability will be particularly important when dealing with veiled and cold dot radiators. Residents may be calling about problems at their properties caused by a radiator. But the residents won't always know that the crime they are experiencing is connected to another property. Thus, the police must identify the link among calls, the crime radiator.

Identifying the radiator can be the difference between creating a diffusion of benefits or displacing crime. In fact, one of the most recent studies of crime radiation uncovered a potential link between mistreated radiation and crime displacement. When examining case studies of police problem-solving, Perla Sulaj identified several examples where there appeared to be a crime radiator.[14] Police were receiving calls about crimes occurring at nearby properties. So, the police worked with place managers to apply situational crime prevention techniques at these residential units. However, they also reported that offenders simply moved elsewhere to commit their crimes. Sulaj proposed that because police were focusing their attention on places experiencing "radiated" crime, it did not address the key place (i.e., the radiator) causing the problems. Had police linked the residential crimes to the radiator and intervened at the radiator, they may have reduced crime and avoided displacement.

The third implication is that crime radiation can usually only be addressed by place managers. In the Provo apartment example, it was not until new owners took over the property and began enacting new place management practices that crime at and around the apartment declined. Police will certainly be involved in the crime reduction process. As seen in the Provo example, they were the ones who identified the radiator.

They were also the ones who called upon the appropriate regulatory agencies to inspect the property. Repeated failures to meet building safety codes prompted the negligent owner to sell the property. This left room for a new place manager to take over and use situational crime prevention to suppress crime opportunities at the place. Most importantly, dismantling crime opportunities at the radiator created a long-term crime reduction effect.

In summary, crime radiation is not always deliberately caused by the property owner of the crime radiator. Sometimes the radiation is an unfortunate by-product of the routine activities of the place. But other researchers have found that some offenders select specific properties to create a place network to facilitate their crimes. We turn to this next.

Crime Place Networks

Around 2015, the Cincinnati Police Department (CPD) tasked Captain Maris Herold with developing a city-wide violence prevention strategy. Captain Herold understood the importance of places and the rule of the few for crime prevention. In fact, only a tiny fraction of places drove most of the violence. Specifically, 23 places (1.2% of the city's land mass) experienced over 42% of the city's shootings. These few places experienced most of the shootings in the city. So, she rolled out hotspot policing patrols where her officers would attend to these specific properties. To the delight of Herold's superiors, these patrols almost always reduced crime immediately. They then turned their attention to other issues. But Captain Herold noticed a troubling pattern; within a few weeks or months of the successful patrols, crime would return to these same places.[15]

Captain Herold expressed her frustration to crime science Professor Tamara Herold (formerly Madensen and creator of the ORCA framework). You may recall Tamara from chapter 2. She was the researcher who found that no matter which police department she worked with, officers told her that their crime hotspots have been hot for as long as they can remember. No amount of police efforts could extinguish crime permanently. Police felt like they were playing a game of whack-a-mole traveling from place to place.

But while Captain Herold was trying to solve her crime-place problem, Professor Herold was studying different kinds of places and place management styles.[16] This included places with crime and places without crime. Tamara was starting to discover the importance of places linked to crime but that were not overtly experiencing violence. This led the Professor and the Captain to realize that there was an infrastructure of places that facilitated violent crime. Some places in the network hosted the violence, while other places supported offenders' activities at the violent hotspots. The connection sparked an idea: police should conduct crime place network investigations (PNI).[17]

To understand their PNI strategy, we must first review the four types of proprietary places that Professor Herold (then Madensen) and John Eck identified, called CS4 (table 14.1).[18] CS4 is an acronym capturing the four types of crime-involved places, all of which use terms that start with C and S: crime sites, comfort spaces, convergence settings, and corrupting spots. The CS4 concepts apply to both physical and online places.[19] We include both types of places in the table below but focus our discussion on physical places.

The first type of proprietary place is the *crime site*. This is the property experiencing multiple crime events. In our case, the place experiences violent events, such as shootings. Crime sites are visible to the police. Crimes occur on these properties and people report the crimes to the police. As such, any analysis of crime is based on these crime site data.

Table 14.1 CS4: Four Types of Proprietary Places

	Description	Physical Place Example	Online Place Example
Crime Sites	Properties where crime occurs	A high-crime convenience store	A website that corrupts computers that access it
Comfort Spaces	Private meeting, supplying, and staging locations	A single-family home that an offender rents to use as a club house for his gang	A website where offenders exchange information
Convergence Settings	Public places where offenders meet	A night club	A private message board where offenders communicate
Corrupting Spots	Places that encourage criminal activity at other locations	A metal recycling business that buys stolen metal	A server that controls illicit activity at other websites

Modified from: Madensen & Eck (2012)

But three other types of places are hidden from these data that facilitate crime at the crime sites.

The second type of place is called a *comfort space*. This is a concept coined by Cincinnati Police Captain Matthew Hammer.[20] During his work for CPD, he noticed that offenders acquired private properties (e.g., renting a house) for various purposes: meeting, supplying, and staging. While they use these places as social hangouts (i.e., meeting locations), they are also used for nefarious purposes such as storing illegal drugs and guns (i.e., supplying locations). They also acquire some private places to station gang members in places that allow them to survey open-air drug markets and alert fellow gang members when police are approaching (i.e., staging locations). Due to the supporting nature that comfort spaces serve, offenders make a concerted effort to conceal any illegal activity going on at these places. Though nearby residents may suspect that the place is used by offenders, they do not explicitly observe crimes. Thus, few crimes are ever reported at comfort spaces. So, if we base crime prevention strategies solely on police report data, comfort spaces are hidden and appear as crime-free places.

The third type of proprietary place is called a *convergence setting*. This concept was coined by Marcus Felson.[21] Contrary to the private nature of comfort spaces, convergence settings are public. Felson identified them as public places that bring people together. For crime, these are the locations where offenders meet. He suggested that such places can be useful to offenders looking to recruit members to gangs. A major transit hub or night club are examples of a convergence setting. All people have access to such a place. Offenders, for example, may spend time at bus stations looking for teenagers who have run away from home to recruit into their criminal enterprise. Some use night clubs, for example, to work out illegal business deals. Often, offenders do not commit crimes at convergence settings. So, they are hidden from police report data as well. They often use these places to meet and plan crimes elsewhere.

The fourth type of proprietary place is called a *corrupting spot*. Madensen and Eck argue that a few properties encourage crime elsewhere.[22] For example, a metal recycling business can serve as a corrupting spot if it encourages people to steal copper piping. Such places often offer cash in exchange for metal and ask few questions or require no documentation from the buyer (e.g., no request for identification or paperwork that creates a paper trail of the sale). Similarly, an automotive recycler can be a corrupting spot if it encourages catalytic converter thefts.[23] Often, consensual exchanges of stolen goods occur at these places. It is not in the best interest of the buyer or seller to report the stolen goods brought to their place. So once again, corrupting spots do not appear in police crime data.

Now let's show how CS4 can be used to address violent crime hotspots. Consider a persistently violent apartment complex used by a gang with an open-air drug market. The apartment complex itself is the crime site. It is a violent crime hotspot. Traditionally, police would send officers to the apartment (i.e., hotspots policing) causing offenders to pull back their offending. Intelligence gathered by police and researchers like Captain Herold, Professor Herold, and Captain Hammer revealed that when police crackdown at such a place, offenders will retreat to comfort spaces or convergence settings. It should not be surprising that once police leave the crime site, offenders emerge from their places of comfort or convergence settings and resume their same criminal activities (recall, the concept of residual deterrence discussed in chapter 2).

Those who developed PNI argue that you also need to identify the hidden places in the network. A nearby public park may serve as a public place where gang members recruit juveniles into their drug dealing enterprise (convergence setting). The gang members may also rent two nearby properties (comfort spaces) to facilitate their drug dealing in the apartment complex.[24] The first comfort space may be a single-family home two blocks away to store the drugs and weapons used at the crime site (supplying location). The second comfort space may be an upper floor unit in the apartment building across the street. Gang members can station someone in the unit to watch for police approaching the crime site and alert their confederates before officers arrive (staging location). Last, a business (corrupting spot) that purchases stolen goods from people seeking to buy drugs at the open-air drug market further encourages crime, including violence, at the apartment complex.[25]

The traditional hotspots policing method focuses only on the known crime site, often through police reports of criminal activity (e.g., drug dealing, shootings, robberies). Without police intelligence the other three types of CS4 places remain hidden and are likely the reason why crime returns to the crime site after a police crackdown ends. The reason is that hotspots policing only disrupts the opportunities for crime temporarily. Adding police increases guardianship. When the place network remains intact, offenders simply curtail their offending and wait for the police to leave.[26]

Place network investigations advocate for a multi-agency approach where police must partner with government agencies, place managers, and community members to identify all places in the network (table 14.2).[27] Then they must develop strategies that target not only the crime site, but also the hidden places in the network. In addition to increasing police presence at the apartment complex, for example, you would also want to investigate who owns the comfort spaces that gang members are using to facilitate their crimes. Most place managers do not want people committing crimes on their properties. In many PNI initiatives, place managers were simply unaware of the criminal activity occurring on their property. Once the police notified the owners, they evicted the gang members for violating the terms of their lease agreement (e.g., that tenants are not permitted to have illegal drugs in their possession on the property).

In other cases, Matthew Hammer explained how police could partner with city bylaw enforcement and building inspectors to remove comfort spaces.[28] For example, some gangs will keep tall grass in the front yards of the houses they rent near hotspots. They leave their firearms in the tall grass so that: the weapons are difficult to see by anyone passing by, they have easy access to their weapons, and they can deny possession of the weapon if police locate them. In Cincinnati, Ohio, for example, allowing grass or weeds to grow more than ten inches (25cm) is a violation of

Table 14.2 Cincinnati Example of Agencies They Partnered with to Change Location Dynamics

Police	Community leaders/council	Buildings and Inspections	Community & Economic Development
Traffic Engineering	Public Works/Services	Law/Prosecutors	Community Police Partnering Center
Keep Cincinnati Beautiful	CIRV Leadership Partners	Health Inspector	Recreation Commission
Hamilton County Probation	Property Owners	Fire Department	Blight Control

Modified from Isaac et al. (2017)

the City's Code of Ordinances.[29] Bylaw officers, acting as super controllers, can use these codes to put pressures on the place managers of these homes to maintain their lawns.[30] At best, doing this can alert an unknowing place manager that their property is being used for illegal purposes, causing them to take action. At a minimum, forcing the owner to assure the grass gets mowed eliminates the easy hiding place that gang members were using. This makes crime more difficult to commit.

If the police can partner with the right place managers, governmental agencies, and local stakeholders to address comfort spaces, convergence settings, and corrupting spots, then gang members no longer have the infrastructure to operate their open-air drug market at the apartment complex. They have no places of comfort to retreat to and wait out the police. They have no nearby place to recruit young gang members and potential drug purchasers do not have an easy place where they can obtain money for drugs. Thus, once a place network investigation is successfully carried out, researchers have found that crime declines at the places and does not return.[31]

The original place network investigation strategy earned the Cincinnati Police Department the 2017 Herman Goldstein Award for Excellence in Problem-Oriented Policing. The 23 micro-locations CPD identified (1.4% of the city's land mass) accounted for over 42% of all shooting incidents in the city.[32] One site experienced a disproportionate number of shooting victims. In the years leading up to the intervention, the site experienced five, eight, and 18 shooting victims in 2013, 2014, and 2015 respectively.

After implementing their place network strategy in June 2016, the Cincinnati Police Department reported a decrease of shooting victims of more than 83%. The days between shootings also increased. Prior to the intervention, there was a shooting on average every 32 days. But after the intervention, there was a shooting only every 130 days.[33]

The Cincinnati Police Department experienced such success at their initial site that they expanded their place network investigations to nine violent micro-locations. Captain Matthew Hammer oversaw five initiatives and evaluated them for his doctoral dissertation. Overall, he found statistically significant changes in shootings at four of the five sites. Further, he found that shootings declined between 12% and 92%, depending on the site being evaluated.[34]

The PNI approach has been expanded to other US cities, such as Denver, Las Vegas, Tucson, and Wichita, for further evaluation.[35] Tamara Herold and John Eck's preliminary analyses of PNI in Las Vegas suggest that place network investigations "[are] responsible for the absence of violence (over 180 days) in a site that has historically been one of the most violent locations in Las Vegas, Nevada".[36]

Places Provide the Infrastructure Offenders Need to Carry Out Their Crimes

Crime radiation and place network investigations teach an important lesson about crime. Offenders need infrastructure to carry out their crimes. Places are a key part of that infrastructure. These places can be physical or online (or both!), but offenders use places nevertheless.

Relying on infrastructure is no different from how non-offenders need places to carry out their everyday activities. Students need schools, campuses, and online learning systems to host their lessons. Employers provide workplaces, both physical and digital, so that employees can interact with their co-workers and clients. Athletes need sports arenas and stadiums to practice and play their games. Musicians need theatres to perform in and studios to record in. Retailers rely on highways for their semi-trucks to transport goods to and from their stores. In online contexts, websites rely on servers to stay operational.

In the previous chapter, we showed you how a focused deterrence approach allowed police to successfully stop violent offending among the most prolific offenders. But the strategy fails to prevent other people from taking the place of the apprehended offenders. To create long-term change, you also need to include places in your crime prevention strategy. Incarcerating the few gang members responsible for most of your city's violence will work for a while. But if the places they were using are still controlled by the gang, new members can take over the gang's operations. Dismantling the place networks of offenders, particularly gangs, eliminates the infrastructure they need to carry out their crimes. Dismantling their place networks keeps crime from coming back. Using the rule of the few to focus on the few offenders and few places responsible for most of the crime show the most promise for crime prevention.

In the next chapter we show you why merging an offender- and place-based approach works best. To do this most effectively, you need to deploy your officers with a purpose; have them focus daily on the few people and places causing most of the problems.

Key Points

- Some crime-involved places can intentionally or unintentionally create crime elsewhere
- When you understand how places radiate crime or create place networks, you can be more effective at reducing crime
- Place-based strategies that remove offenders' infrastructure can generate long-term crime reduction
- Ask: are the places experiencing crime connected to other places?

Notes

1 Provo City Police Department (2021). Crime and Disorder at the "Dog House'. Goldstein Award Submission. Center for Problem-Oriented Policing. Retrieved from: https://popcenter.asu.edu/sites/default/files/provo_city_pd_beebe_properties_2021.pdf
2 From page 3 of: Provo City Police Department (2021). Crime and Disorder at the "Dog House". Goldstein Award Submission. Center for Problem-Oriented Policing. Retrieved from: https://popcenter.asu.edu/sites/default/files/provo_city_pd_beebe_properties_2021.pdf
3 Bowers, K. (2014). Risky Facilities: Crime Radiators or Crime Absorbers? A Comparison of Internal and External Levels of Theft. *Journal of Quantitative Criminology, 30*(3), 389–414. https://doi.org/10.1007/s10940-013-9208-z; Linning, S.J., Bowers, K., & Eck, J.E. (2024). Crime radiation theory: the co-production of crime patterns through opportunity creation and exploitation. *Crime Science, 13*, 32. https://doi.org/10.1186/s40163-024-00234-6
4 From page 3 of: Provo City Police Department (2021). Crime and Disorder at the "Dog House". Goldstein Award Submission. Center for Problem-Oriented Policing. Retrieved from: https://popcenter.asu.edu/sites/default/files/provo_city_pd_beebe_properties_2021.pdf
5 Clarke, R.V. & Weisburd, D. (1994). Diffusion of crime control benefits. In R.V. Clarke (Ed.), *Crime Prevention Studies* (vol. 2). Monsey, NY: Willow Tree Press; Eck, J.E., Linning, S.J., & Bowers, K. (2024). Does crime in places stay in places? Evidence for crime radiation from three narrative reviews. *Aggression and Violent Behavior, 78*, 101955. https://doi.org/10.21428/cb6ab371.5adfc466
6 Linning, S.J., Carroll, T., Gerard, D.W., & Eck, J.E. (2026). Fighting neighborhood crime one address at a time. *Public Management, 108*(1), 46-49. https://icma.org/articles/pm-magazine/fighting-neighborhood-crime-one-address-time
7 Bowers, K. (2014). Risky Facilities: Crime Radiators or Crime Absorbers? A Comparison of Internal and External Levels of Theft. *Journal of Quantitative Criminology, 30*(3), 389–414. https://doi.org/10.1007/s10940-013-9208-z

8 Eck, J.E., Linning, S.J., & Bowers, K. (2024). Does crime in places stay in places? Evidence for crime radiation from three narrative reviews. *Aggression and Violent Behavior, 78*, 101955. https://doi.org/10.21428/cb6ab371.5adfc466; Linning, S.J., Bowers, K., & Eck, J.E. (2024). Crime radiation theory: the co-production of crime patterns through opportunity creation and exploitation. *Crime Science, 13*, 32. https://doi.org/10.1186/s40163-024-00234-6
9 Eck, J.E., Linning, S.J., & Bowers, K. (2024). Does crime in places stay in places? Evidence for crime radiation from three narrative reviews. *Aggression and Violent Behavior, 78*, 101955. https://doi.org/10.21428/cb6ab371.5adfc466; Linning, S.J., Bowers, K., & Eck, J.E. (2024). Crime radiation theory: the co-production of crime patterns through opportunity creation and exploitation. *Crime Science, 13*, 32. https://doi.org/10.1186/s40163-024-00234-6
10 Bowers, K. (2014). Risky Facilities: Crime Radiators or Crime Absorbers? A Comparison of Internal and External Levels of Theft. *Journal of Quantitative Criminology, 30*(3), 389–414. https://doi.org/10.1007/s10940-013-9208-z
11 Eck, J.E., Linning, S.J., & Bowers, K. (2024). Does crime in places stay in places? Evidence for crime radiation from three narrative reviews. *Aggression and Violent Behavior, 78*, 101955. https://doi.org/10.21428/cb6ab371.5adfc466; Linning, S.J., Bowers, K., & Eck, J.E. (2024). Crime radiation theory: the co-production of crime patterns through opportunity creation and exploitation. *Crime Science, 13*, 32. https://doi.org/10.1186/s40163-024-00234-6
12 Eck, J.E., Linning, S.J., & Bowers, K. (2024). Does crime in places stay in places? Evidence for crime radiation from three narrative reviews. *Aggression and Violent Behavior, 78*, 101955. https://doi.org/10.21428/cb6ab371.5adfc466; Linning, S.J., Bowers, K., & Eck, J.E. (2024). Crime radiation theory: the co-production of crime patterns through opportunity creation and exploitation. *Crime Science, 13*, 32. https://doi.org/10.1186/s40163-024-00234-6
13 Sherman, L.W., Gartin, P.R., & Buerger, M.E. (1989). Hot spots of predatory crime: Routine activities and the criminology of place. *Criminology, 27*(1), 27–56. https://doi.org/10.1111/j.1745-9125.1989.tb00862.x
14 Sulaj, P. (2025). *Understanding crime radiation from successful police problem-solving strategies*. Unpublished Honours thesis, School of Criminology, Simon Fraser University.
15 Eck, J.E., Linning, S.J., & Herold, T.D. (2023). *Place Management and Crime: Ownership and Property Rights as a Source of Social Control*. Springer Publishers. https://link.springer.com/book/10.1007/978-3-031-27693-4; Isaac, E., Hammer, M.G., Christenson, B.R., & Madensen, T. (2017, June). *Place-based investigations of violent offender territories* (P.I.V.O.T.). Herman Goldstein Award Submission (Winner), Center for Problem-Oriented Policing. Retrieved from: https://popcenter.asu.edu/sites/default/files/17-15.pdf
16 Madensen, T.D. & Eck, J.E. (2012). Crime places and place management. In F.T. Cullen & P. Wilcox (Eds.), *The Oxford Handbook of Criminological Theory* (pp. 1–18). Oxford University Press. https://doi.org/10.1093/oxfordhb/9780199747238.013.0029
17 Herold, T.D. & Eck, J.E. (2020). Gun violence in Cincinnati, Ohio. In M.S. Scott & R.V. Clarke (Eds.), *Problem-Oriented Policing: Successful Case Studies* (pp. 28–39). New York: Routledge. https://doi.org/10.4324/9780429457357-4: Isaac, E., Hammer, M.G., Christenson, B.R., & Madensen, T. (2017, June). *Place-based investigations of violent offender territories* (P.I.V.O.T.). Herman Goldstein Award Submission (Winner), Center for Problem-Oriented Policing. Retrieved from: https://popcenter.asu.edu/sites/default/files/17-15.pdf

18 Madensen, T.D. & Eck, J.E. (2012). Crime places and place management. In F.T. Cullen & P. Wilcox (Eds.), *The Oxford Handbook of Criminological Theory* (pp. 1–18). Oxford University Press. https://doi.org/10.1093/oxfordhb/9780199747238.013.0029
19 Madensen, T.D. & Eck, J.E. (2012). Crime places and place management. In F. T. Cullen & P. Wilcox (Eds.), *The Oxford Handbook of Criminological Theory* (pp. 1–18). Oxford University Press. https://doi.org/10.1093/oxfordhb/9780199747238.013.0029; Zdjelar, I., Linning, S.J., Hart, M.B., & Davies, G. (2025). Using crime place networks to understand terrorist attacks: The importance of in-person and online crime-involved places. *Journal of Policing, Intelligence and Counter Terrorism, 1–20*. https://doi.org/10.1080/18335330.2025.2532760
20 Hammer, M. (2011). *Crime places of comfort*. Unpublished Master's demonstration project paper, University of Cincinnati, School of Criminal Justice.
21 Felson, M. (2003). The Process of co-offending. In M.J. Smith & D.B. Cornish (Eds.), *Theory for Practice in Situational Crime Prevention* (pp. 149–167). Criminal Justice Press.
22 Madensen, T.D. & Eck, J.E. (2012). Crime places and place management. In F.T. Cullen & P. Wilcox (Eds.), *The Oxford Handbook of Criminological Theory* (pp. 1–18). Oxford University Press. https://doi.org/10.1093/oxfordhb/9780199747238.013.0029
23 Eck, J.E., Linning, S.J., & Herold, T.D. (2023). *Place Management and Crime: Ownership and Property Rights as a Source of Social Control*. Springer Publishers. https://link.springer.com/book/10.1007/978-3-031-27693-4; Herold, T.D. & Eck, J.E. (2020). Gun violence in Cincinnati, Ohio. In M.S. Scott & R.V. Clarke (eds.) *Problem-Oriented Policing: Successful Case Studies* (pp. 28–39). New York: Routledge. https://doi.org/10.4324/9780429457357-4
24 Hammer, M. (2011). *Crime places of comfort*. Unpublished Master's demonstration project paper, University of Cincinnati, School of Criminal Justice.
25 Eck, J.E., Linning, S.J., & Herold, T.D. (2023). *Place Management and Crime: Ownership and Property Rights as a Source of Social Control*. Springer Publishers. https://link.springer.com/book/10.1007/978-3-031-27693-4; Hammer, M. (2011). *Crime places of comfort*. Unpublished Master's demonstration project paper, University of Cincinnati, School of Criminal Justice.
26 Eck, J.E., Linning, S.J., & Herold, T.D. (2023). *Place Management and Crime: Ownership and Property Rights as a Source of Social Control*. Springer Publishers. https://link.springer.com/book/10.1007/978-3-031-27693-4
27 Isaac, E., Hammer, M.G., Christenson, B.R., & Madensen, T. (2017, June). *Place-based investigations of violent offender territories* (P.I.V.O.T.). Herman Goldstein Award Submission (Winner), Center for Problem-Oriented Policing. Retrieved from: https://popcenter.asu.edu/sites/default/files/17-15.pdf
28 Hammer, M. (2020). *Place-based investigations of violent offender territories (PIVOT): An exploration and evaluation of a place network disruption violence reduction strategy in Cincinnati, Ohio*. Unpublished PhD dissertation, University of Cincinnati, School of Criminal Justice.
29 City of Cincinnati (2024). Code of Ordinances, Title VII – General Regulations, Chapter 731 – Weed Control, Sec. 731-3. Retrieved from: https://library.municode.com/oh/cincinnati/codes/code_of_ordinances?nodeId=TITVIIGERE_CH731WECO_S731-3HERE#:~:text=Every%20owner%20or%20person%20in,such%20lot%20or%20lands%20immediately.
30 Sampson R., Eck, J.E., & Dunham, J. (2010). Super controllers and crime prevention: A routine activity explanation of crime prevention success and failure. *Security Journal, 23*(1), 37–51. https://doi.org/10.1057/sj.2009.17

31 Herold, T.D. & Eck, J.E. (2020). Gun violence in Cincinnati, Ohio. In M.S. Scott & R.V. Clarke (Eds.) *Problem-Oriented Policing: Successful Case Studies* (pp. 28–39). New York: Routledge. https://doi.org/10.4324/9780429457357-4; Eck, J.E., Linning, S.J., & Herold, T.D. (2023). *Place Management and Crime: Ownership and Property Rights as a Source of Social Control.* Springer Publishers. https://link.springer.com/book/10.1007/978-3-031-27693-4

32 Isaac, E., Hammer, M.G., Christenson, B.R., & Madensen, T. (2017, June). *Place-based investigations of violent offender territories* (P.I.V.O.T.). Herman Goldstein Award Submission (Winner), Center for Problem-Oriented Policing. Retrieved from: https://popcenter.asu.edu/sites/default/files/17-15.pdf

33 Isaac, E., Hammer, M.G., Christenson, B.R., & Madensen, T. (2017, June). *Place-based investigations of violent offender territories* (P.I.V.O.T.). Herman Goldstein Award Submission (Winner), Center for Problem-Oriented Policing. Retrieved from: https://popcenter.asu.edu/sites/default/files/17-15.pdf

34 Hammer, M. (2020). *Place-based investigations of violent offender territories (PIVOT): An exploration and evaluation of a place network disruption violence reduction strategy in Cincinnati, Ohio.* Unpublished PhD dissertation, University of Cincinnati, School of Criminal Justice.

35 Herold, T.D. & Prosser, J. (2023). Crime place networks in Las Vegas: A new violence reduction strategy. *The Police Chief.* Retrieved from: https://www.policechiefmagazine.org/crime-place-networks-las-vegas/

36 From page 35 of: Herold, T.D. & Eck, J.E. (2020). Gun violence in Cincinnati, Ohio. In M.S. Scott & R.V. Clarke (eds.) *Problem-Oriented Policing: Successful Case Studies* (pp. 28–39). New York: Routledge. https://doi.org/10.4324/9780429457357-4

15

Deployment with a Purpose

As you have recognized by now, this book is written for a variety of audiences. At minimum, city and county administrators, elected officials, and law enforcement practitioners can all find value in our ideas.

This chapter is primarily geared to a practitioner audience looking to improve their daily operations. However, government administrators need to understand how their law enforcement agencies may claim to be data driven but are measuring the wrong things. This leads to fallacy-based operational strategies that produce easily quantifiable results, such as number of arrests, but do not solve problems, especially in the long term.

To improve problem solving and ensure the opportunity structure at a problem location is dismantled and does not reoccur, Dan originally designed, and Shannon built upon, a strategy they called *deployment with a purpose*. The Cincinnati, Ohio and Fort Myers, Florida police departments have successfully implemented deployment with a purpose into their daily patrol operations.

Deployment with a Purpose—A New Strategy

When Dan took over his last command, it was the busiest and most crime-ridden patrol district in Cincinnati. The district had a population of 89,000 people, covered over 20 square miles, and had 144 officers to police it. At the time, Cincinnati's Police Department had five patrol

DOI: 10.4324/9781003430155-19

districts. Dan's new command responded to over 12,000 more citizen calls for police service and experienced over 2500 more serious crimes than any other city patrol district.

By relentlessly analyzing the data, Dan realized that the rule of the few drove the district's crime and calls for police service. Four of the 12 district neighborhoods were responsible for 85% of the district's crime and calls for police service. Within those four neighborhoods, 19 one-block street segments drove the crime numbers across the entire district. Each high activity street segment had a particular place location that served as the primary crime attractor for the area. Crime radiated into the neighborhood from the problem places, compounding the issue. Effective place management was absent at these locations.

The comprehensive place-based analysis clearly showed that the *crime is widespread* fallacy[1] (chapter 2) was not a valid idea. Instead, Dan needed to use a strategy based on the rule of the few, which included place managers and not just residents, to reduce the criminal activity.

District crime analysts examined crime patterns and data about individual offenders. The rule of the few again held true. Analysis showed that this district had roughly 90,000 people, but only 104 (0.1%) people were committing the crime across the entire district area. In many cases, these individuals lived outside of the district but chose to commit their crimes there. In addition, the district was about 20 square miles in size, but most of the crime occurred at only 19 street blocks, often because these blocks contained far greater opportunities for crime than other city locations.

The easy police solution, when confronted with problem people and places, would have been to focus on either shutting down the problem places or simply making arrests and hoping to solve the problem. Having previously taken graduate classes from John and understanding the importance of problem places in addition to problem people, Dan designed the first version of deployment with a purpose. The new strategy intently focused the police resources on the district's few problem people and places.

Every day and every shift, district officers applied the rule of the few. They narrowly focused their deployment with a purpose and enforcement efforts on the 19 problem blocks/places and the 104 prolific offenders. Patrol officers and specialized function officers clearly understood their role in the overall strategy. The patrol officers employed precise strategies to transform the street conditions and remove the chronic offenders generating the daily crime and calls for police service. Neighborhood-based officers worked with place managers and other city departments to change conditions contributing to crime at the problem properties. Detectives built strong criminal cases on the most influential and prolific offenders in the district. Every shift, Dan and his entire supervisory staff reminded all officers of the district's problem places and people, in addition to the precise strategies they needed to perform and why, so they could deploy with a purpose.

Dan shared weekly evaluations of the strategy with everyone, including patrol and specialized officers, place managers/owners of problem properties, and neighborhood residents. He shared the reasons for both success and failure with everyone involved. When a strategy was unsuccessful, Dan quickly collaborated with patrol officers to modify the approach or replace it. When a strategy was successful, officers began implementing it in other problem areas.

The new deployment with a purpose strategy that focused on a few prolific offenders and problem places was extremely successful. District crime fell to 12-year historic lows. Citizen calls for police service dropped by over 6500 calls a year. Interestingly, calls for police service in the other district neighborhoods, which did not contain the 19 problem street segments, increased slightly. This showed the narrow focus on the few problem people and places, instead of the many, generated the positive results and not random chance. Deployment with a purpose worked.

Compstat—A Traditional Strategy

But don't police already deploy with a purpose? For the most part, the answer is no. Police do track their activities, but they tend to focus on number of stops and arrests instead of reductions in crime. In other words, they focus on outputs instead of outcomes. This output-focused approach stems largely from a 30-year-old police strategy called Compstat.

In 1994, the New York City Police Department developed their Computer Statistics program, commonly referred to as Compstat.[2] Compstat was designed to track crime and calls for police service data and to hold police commanders accountable for the strategies they employed to reduce crime and calls in their area of operations.[3] It was innovative and reduced New York City's crime and calls for police service. Compstat was soon adopted by police agencies throughout the United States. Over time, in many agencies, Compstat lost its initial focus and became a program that focused primarily on easily measurable outputs—number of arrests, traffic citations, pedestrian stops, and directed patrols—instead of focusing on outcomes-harm reduction and problem solving.[4]

These problems with Compstat-like approaches persist to this day. Here is a scenario that happens daily in police agencies across the world. Though hypothetical, it is similar to true experiences. A police commander attends their agency's version of Compstat. During the meeting, high-ranking officials point out a problem location to the command officer and he is given a mandate to do something about it prior to the next meeting.

The commander returns to his unit of assignment, grabs a few lieutenants and sergeants, and tells them, "I just got my behind handed to me at Compstat about the Interstate Motel. Tell the cops to go there and by the next meeting, I need some extra patrols and enforcement activity to show we are taking care of the problem." The lieutenants and sergeants go to roll calls and briefings and tell the officers the same things.

Officers increase their visibility at the Interstate Motel and make some low-level arrests, primarily for quality-of-life offenses such as public drinking, minor drug abuse, minor warrants, or loud music. At the next Compstat meeting, the commander reports back on the officers' arrest activity and shows a slight reduction in calls for police service at the location. The problem is then deemed "solved" and everyone moves on to other things.

A few weeks or months later, the same criminal activities and increased calls for police service return at the Interstate Motel. Police respond the same way they did before, with increased patrols and low-level arrests. Once again, this traditional strategy reduces crime and calls for police service, but only temporarily.

Much like what we discussed in chapter 4, this repeated process illustrates that increased patrols and arrests disrupt crime opportunities for only a short term. Without dismantling the crime opportunities at the Interstate Motel, crime and increased calls for police service will keep coming back. This leaves officers feeling like frustrated hamsters who spin endlessly in a wheel.

The traditional police response in the example above suffers from a frequent problem; most agencies measure officers' activity (an output), not achievement (an outcome). Agencies use officer activity as their evaluation criteria for whether the strategy is successful. Doing 30 drive-through hotspot patrols of an area with nothing found or making only a few minor arrests does not solve the problem, especially long-term.

The residents in a neighborhood with a problem property do not care about the number of hotspot patrols police do. Instead, they care that the crime events which originally caused them to call the police are no longer happening. Residents also care that fewer of their friends and neighbors are victims of crime and the neighborhood as a whole is experiencing less harm.

Deployment with a Purpose - Action Steps

Instead of simply trying to make sure the Interstate Motel does not appear as a problem property in their next period's statistics, police should have tried to solve the problem. Removing the opportunity structure at the Interstate Motel and creating a sustained reduction in crime and calls for police service would have been an appropriate outcome. It would also eliminate the need for daily patrols at the motel and free up valuable officer problem-solving time.

When deploying with a purpose, for every shift police commanders direct their patrol officers to problem locations with extremely specific information about:

1. **Where** the patrol officers need to go during their shift,
2. **Why** they are going to that place,
3. **When** they should go to the place,
4. **What** precise activities they need to do while at the place,
5. **How** their actions will solve the problem, and finally to
6. **Share** the success, once you have solved the problem.

The first 3 elements require police supervisors to communicate clear, concise guidance and direction as to the **WHERE** the patrol officers must go, **WHY** they are focusing on that specific location, and **WHEN** they need to respond there. For example:

> We are having a problem with crime and repeat calls for police service at the Interstate Motel between 10pm–4am on Thursday through Sunday. Calls are for general disorder in the parking lot, prostitution out of room 224, drug sales in room 221 across the hall, and gambling in the stairwells. Robberies of patrons are starting to occur. The prostitution, drug sales, gambling and robberies are interconnected and controlled by the OG street gang. Gunfire has occurred after 2am the previous three weekends and is related to the robberies and to illegal gambling disputes.

Note the specifics in the **WHY**. Supervisors clearly explain the dates, times, locations, and problem description to their patrol officers. By being specific with these details, nothing is left to individual officers' interpretation.

In the next component, supervisors must ensure that officers understand exactly **WHAT** specific action(s) they need to take at the problem place. For example:

> Every shift, I need you to go to the Interstate Motel, and perform a very specific task while there. You need to get out of your car and interact with the individuals or groups engaged in the problems we've been seeing, such as clients of sex workers and drug sellers or those gamblers playing in the dice games.

The tasks you will ask of officers will vary depending on the unique activity causing the problem. In some cases, such as disorder in the motel parking lot, the mere presence of visible, uniformed police is enough to end the activity for a time. In other cases, a longer-term investigation involving additional police department and partner resources, such as place managers and community support, may be needed. The longer-term responses are more common when dealing with the violent street gang members who control the drug sales, prostitution, and gambling at the motel and who are responsible for the weekly gunfire.

When you deploy officers with a purpose, the officers are focused on the actual problems and use very specific strategies to achieve an identified outcome. They are not using the standard policing model of a blanket approach focused on outputs. Having patrol officers drive through the lot when time permits or making low level arrests of persons, who may not be involved in the actual problem activities, will have little impact on the underlying problem.

In the next component, supervisors make sure officers again know exactly **WHEN** they need to go to the place, **WHAT** actions they need to perform while there and **HOW** their specific actions at the problem location will contribute to solving the problem. For example:

> The activity is occurring Thursday through Sunday between 10pm–4am. During these hours, I need you to go to the Interstate Motel for 15 minutes every two hours and perform the specific tasks we've given you. If you do this consistently, it will remove the opportunity structure needed for the activities to occur. Once we dismantle the opportunity structure, the crimes and calls for police service will not persist.

An expected pushback from patrol officers is that doing the precise work involved in a narrowly focused crime strategy will take away from their time spent doing "real" police work. This argument is easily overcome with agency data which clearly shows that during these peak times, the officers will be handling calls for police service at the problem location anyways.

What you are asking the officers to do is to perform a very specific problem-solving task while they are at the location. Precise tasks, chosen for the problem locations, may differ by the shift performing them, by hour and by day of the week. The task is designed to dismantle the opportunity structure that allows crime to occur. This contrasts with the traditional approach of officers merely showing up, temporarily disrupting the problem activities and then quickly moving on to another call.

The strategies require constant evaluation as conditions at the locations will evolve. To reduce crime, your strategy must continually evolve, and you need to be transparent with your officers about why they are being asked to respond in this way. This leads to the next Deployment with a Purpose component.

Supervisors must ensure officers thoroughly understand **WHY** they need to respond in a particular way and **WHAT** they can expect if they respond that way. For example:

> This strategy is evidence-based and has been proven to work on drug sales and robberies. Let me show you an example from the Overlook Hotel where it has been tried and succeeded.
>
> If you follow the strategy and complete the precise tasks, you will remove the opportunity structure and crime will not reoccur. We won't have to spend all of our patrol time at the Interstate Motel every week managing problems at their facility. If we do it right, it won't reoccur in a few months. Do it right and we won't have to do it again!

People become police officers because law enforcement is the profession they wanted to be part of. If police officers wanted to be the place managers of poorly-run problem apartment buildings, stores, or motels, they would have chosen to be a poor place manager and not a law enforcement officer. Yet, by only temporarily disrupting problematic activities and not dismantling the opportunity structure around them, problem property manager is the role police too often find themselves in.

Finally, when you remove the opportunity structure and successfully solve the problem, police commanders need to share with the officers involved how important their role in the problem-solving process was. This is best done in front of their peers so that the importance of both problem-solving and deployment with a purpose is reinforced throughout the entire agency. For example:

> Great work dealing with the problems at the Interstate Motel these past few weeks. Thanks to your efforts, you convinced the motel's owner to remove their hourly rate and only allow nightly stays. They're adding LED lighting in the areas you suggested and installing a new camera system, which they will link to our real-time center so we can monitor it.

> Multiple charges have been filed against the OG street gang. They no longer control drug sales, gambling and prostitution in the area. Area gun violence has declined 78% and robberies are down 90%.
>
> Since we deployed with a purpose to solve the problem, the calls for police service to the Interstate Motel have substantially decreased. It's no longer a problem property. We will continue to monitor calls to this location. But given problem-solving efforts at other motels, both the research and our experience tell us you probably will not have to go back there. Great work!

Deployment with a purpose gives patrol officers, who make up the majority of any police department's officers, more ownership of the daily problems they encounter. When patrol officers see their success, it encourages them to generate and share new problem-solving ideas. It creates buy-in from those non-involved officers who see their peers recognized for successful problem-solving. Deployment with a purpose produces better analysis as officers see that the reams of data they generate every shift has an actual problem-solving function. So, the data quality improves.

Deployment with a purpose also capitalizes on the experience and expertise of patrol officers. In every police agency, patrol officers are the primary data collectors. It makes far more sense to include them as a primary part of the data-driven problem-solving strategy as well. If *all* patrol officers know why they are performing a specific strategy, clearly understand their role—especially in something new—and they believe in it, they will figure out how to do what needs to be done to remove the opportunity and prevent a problem from reoccurring.

Providing these last explanations increases officer buy-in. When officers understand their role in the problem-solving strategy and can easily see the benefits to responding in the precise way you explain, they are far more likely to follow the directions. They may even suggest their own ideas for improvement of the chosen problem-solving strategy or propose a new strategy based on their direct knowledge of the people and places involved.

There is a huge difference between understanding the importance of data and in making data a priority throughout all levels of your organization, especially in the problem-solving process. Analysis is not only about statistical data. Successful police problem solving requires agency leaders, officers, and analysts to clearly identify the opportunity that allows or encourages the problem to persist.

Deployment with a purpose is more likely to generate sustained crime reductions because it also adds a missing place-focused component to more traditional offender-focused strategies. When you only focus resources on the few prolific offenders, you can drive down crime quickly. But it's usually difficult to sustain this crime reduction. Of the offenders who remain at large, they retreat and wait out your strategy. They know that politicians and major police officials will eventually have to turn their attention to the next pressing problem.

When you add a place component to your offender focused strategy, it dismantles crime opportunities at the place. When you dismantle crime opportunities at the problem place, offenders cannot simply regroup after and restart their illicit activities there. Getting property owners to change the opportunity structure at their places removes the criminal infrastructure that offenders need to sustain their criminal activities. This means the police no longer need to spend their patrol time managing a poorly run facility and that neighborhood harm from crime radiation around it is reduced.

Deployment with a Purpose and Double Displacement

In chapter 12 you learned about crime displacement and that it is not inevitable.[5] In this chapter, we've explained the ideas of deployment with a purpose and showed how to combine an offender-based strategy with a place-based strategy to achieve maximum impact. What would happen if you combined all three ideas? What do you do in the rare instances when you think crime will displace? Don't just wait for it to happen; have a plan in place to avoid it.

Offenders choose places to commit their crimes based not only on the opportunity structure but also by the presence of important location features. Clear lines of sight to identify threats from police or from other offenders, easy access to escape routes, and proximity to both customers/potential victims and comfort spaces all make a location more attractive to offenders.

With knowledge of how places and offenders interconnect and why certain places are more valued by offenders, Dan developed an additional strategy for District Three's problem places. An idea he called *double displacement.*

When the opportunity structure for crime is removed, a few persistent offenders will try to displace elsewhere to commit their crimes. In the District Three example, it was 104 people out of the 90,000 residents who might displace. Dan and his team analyzed the places near the district's 19 problem blocks/places to identify precise locations where the few persistent offenders might displace. They asked and answered the question: why is the crime here and not over there? Often, crime radiators and crime place networks informed the answer.[6] Once officers answered this question and identified the probable displacement locations, officers deployed with a purpose to them as well.

When police dismantled the opportunity structures at the 19 problem blocks/places, a few offenders moved to the probable displacement locations only to discover the police waiting. So, there was no crime opportunity structure in place. This caused the offenders to retreat to their original comfort space[7] to determine their next move. The police officers referred to these locations as "the Alamo", since this was where the offenders were going to make their final stand.

Planning for double displacement worked; the few persistent offenders were initially displaced to a new location but with no crime opportunity present there they quickly returned to their original area. Once they were back, the District Three team identified the offenders' comfort space and used code enforcement, nuisance abatement, and other specific place-based strategies to eliminate it. The combination permanently dismantled both the area's crime opportunity structure and the location features that made it attractive to offenders.

Planning for double displacement lowered crime when the offenders were originally displaced. Crime was lowered again when the offenders were displaced a second time. Then place-based strategies removed the offenders' comfort spaces. Anticipating double displacement resulted in long-term reductions in area crime.

Purposeful deployment has a lesson which goes far beyond how commanding officers work with their patrol officers. But while officers need to have purpose, we can apply the lesson of purpose to crime control outside of agencies. In the next chapter, we go beyond purposeless community involvement. We show you how to identify the purposeful few who can do beneficial work.

Key Points

- Patrol officers are your best resource for rolling out crime prevention strategies; deploy them quickly and purposefully
- Tell patrol officers exactly what they need to do, where, when, and why
- Update all officers daily about the results of their efforts
- Merging a place- and offender-based strategy is most likely to produce sustained crime reductions
- Ask: have I given precise instruction to officers about where problems are occurring, who to focus on, the actions to take at these places, and why?

Notes

1 Linning, S.J., Carroll, T., Gerard, D., & Eck, J.E. (2024). Is crime widespread? *Public Management, 106*(10), 30–32. https://icma.org/articles/pm-magazine/crime-widespread
2 Willis, J.J., Mastrofski, S.D., & Weisburd, D. (2007). Making sense of COMPSTAT: A theory-based analysis of organizational change in three police departments. *Law & Society Review, 41*(1), 147–188. https://doi.org/10.1111/j.1540-5893.2007.00294.x
3 DeLorenzi, D., Shane, J.M., & Amendola, K.L. (2006, September). The CompStat Process: Managing Performance on the Pathway to Leadership. *The Police Chief.* Retrieved from: https://www.policechiefmagazine.org/the-compstat-process-managing-performance-on-the-pathway-to-leadership/; Shane, J.M. (2004, May). Compstat design. *FBI Law Enforcement Bulletin, 73*, 12–19.
4 Eterno, J.A. & Silverman, E.B. (2012). *The Crime Numbers Game: Management by Manipulation.* Boca Raton, FL: CRC Press.
5 Guerette, R.T. & Bowers, K.J. (2009). Assessing the extent of crime displacement and diffusion of benefits: A review of situational crime prevention evaluations. *Criminology, 47*(4), 1331–1368. https://doi.org/10.1111/j.1745-9125.2009.00177.x
6 Eck, J.E., Linning, S.J., & Herold, T.D. (2023). *Place Management and Crime: Ownership and Property Rights as a Source of Social Control.* Springer Publishers. https://link.springer.com/book/10.1007/978-3-031-27693-4; Herold, T.D. & Eck, J.E. (2020). Gun violence in Cincinnati, Ohio. In M.S. Scott & R.V. Clarke (Eds.), *Problem-Oriented Policing: Successful Case Studies* (pp. 28–39). New York: Routledge. https://doi.org/10.4324/9780429457357-4; Linning, S.J., Bowers, K., & Eck, J.E. (2024). Crime radiation theory: the co-production of crime patterns through opportunity creation and exploitation. *Crime Science, 13*, 32. https://doi.org/10.1186/s40163-024-00234-6; Sulaj, P. (2025). *Understanding crime radiation from successful police problem-solving strategies.* Unpublished Honours thesis, School of Criminology, Simon Fraser University.
7 Hammer, M. (2011). *Crime places of comfort.* Unpublished MSC demonstration project paper, University of Cincinnati, School of Criminal Justice.

16
FINDING PUBLIC CHARACTERS

Throughout this book we have emphasized the importance of place managers and their ability to suppress crime opportunities. They usually comprise a small number of property owners who possess a great deal of power. In part 3, we provided several examples of how action by place managers can reduce crime. As we showed in the previous two chapters, merging a place- and offender-based approach to crime is likely to generate the biggest impact. But these examples also highlighted the importance of having the police partner with communities. In this chapter we expand on this further. We clarify what we mean by community partnership.

As the rule of the few dictates, you will have the most success by being hyper-focused. You should identify the specific community members who can help you solve the specific problem at hand. In a few cases, these people might be residents, but usually they will be place managers.[1] Most place managers will take it upon themselves to address problems.[2] Other times, someone must approach them.[3] In yet another set of instances, it may not be obvious who should tackle the problem. We describe these various scenarios and how to best optimize community co-operations with the police.

The standard community policing approach is to assure police are working with residents to identify and address problems.[4] This is often achieved through community meetings. The police appoint community-liaison

DOI: 10.4324/9781003430155-20

officers to meet with residents on a regular basis to hear and address their concerns. Although we believe such work should continue, this approach excludes key players in communities who could create meaningful change in neighborhoods. By now you will not be surprised to hear that such people are usually place managers. They own or operate property within the neighborhood, but often are not residents. As previously discussed, many property owners own multiple properties.[5] But just because they are not residents of the neighborhood does not mean they lack interest in keeping the area safe. Many place managers are busy people. They are running businesses and may not attend community meetings. But if you engage with these people, many will be willing to talk and cooperate with you to solve problems.

However, there is an important distinction to be made. We are not telling you to switch gears from working with residents to working with place managers. Instead, you need to apply the rule of the few to your problem.

Once you have identified a problem, ask yourself who specifically can help you solve the problem. Often it will be a place manager, but not a large group of them. If three convenience stores in your city experience repeat robbery problems, start working with the place managers of those three convenience stores. You need not require action from the other convenience store owners if they are not experiencing robberies.

Similarly, if the police are receiving repeated calls for service to the same apartment building, you do not need to partner with all apartment owners in the community to solve the problem. You need only approach the owner of the apartment in question. Moreover, the rule of the few predicts that your problem is likely concentrated in only a few of the units in the building. If, for example, a group of offenders is selling drugs out of unit 1B, you should focus your discussion with the place manager about that specific unit. It is likely that all other tenants in the building are abiding the law. It is unlikely they are engaged in crime simply because they live in the same building as a few people who are. You do not need to roll out enhanced enforcement throughout the building. Just focus on the problematic behavior at the precise problematic place. This rule of the few approach applies for any type of place, including motels, gas stations, public parks, vacant buildings, retail stores, libraries, and so on.

The specific community members who can help solve the problem may not be immediately obvious. In the next section we provide guidance on how to start thinking with a focused lens. One of the best people to articulate this was architectural journalist Jane Jacobs, whom we introduced in chapter 7. Her ideas, particularly her concept of *public characters*, help advance where our focus should be.

Identifying Public Characters

The major thrust of Jacobs' work is that cities are deliberately shaped and controlled by place managers (see chapter 7).[6] Most place managers are well-intentioned, hard-working people who strive to create vibrant urban areas. The more place managers you have in an area, the more "eyes on the street" there are to watch over the area.[7] Place managers act to keep streets safe.[8] After all, being on a safe street helps profits because customers want to return. Jacobs notes that:

> ...storekeepers and other small businessmen are typically strong proponents of peace and order themselves; they hate broken windows and holdups; they hate having customers made nervous about safety. They are great street watchers and sidewalk guardians if present in sufficient numbers.[9]

Most place managers have an economic incentive to keep their places safe. This allows customers to enjoy their experiences and makes them want to return. By virtue of owning property and a business, they also have skin in the game. They have invested in the neighborhood and have difficulty picking up their stakes and moving elsewhere.

Jacobs frequently describes how involved many place managers can be in day-to-day city life.[10] They hold high social status in communities because they are often a constant fixture in neighborhoods. Even in the poorest neighborhoods there are often a small number of place managers who have been operating businesses in the area for decades. They know the locals and residents know them. They observe what happens along the streets of their businesses and often intervene if problems arise. Jacobs refers to the most involved ones as *public characters*. They are the glue that keep people in check. Specifically, she states that:

> …the social structure of sidewalk life hangs partly on what can be called self-appointed public characters. A public character is anyone who is in frequent contact with a wide circle of people and who is sufficiently interested to make himself a public character … Most public sidewalk characters are steadily stationed in public places. They are storekeepers or barkeepers or the like. These are the basic public characters. All other public characters of the city sidewalks depend on them—if only indirectly because of the presence of sidewalk routes to such enterprises and their proprietors.[11]

The social role of place managers is integral to Jacobs' arguments regarding safe city streets. As place managers get to know people, it creates a sense of community whereby they connect people. She also argues that they take a sense of ownership of the streets to protect those who use the space.

Property owners will usually be the most likely to help you solve the types of problems we have used as examples in this book. They can replace glassware with polycarbonate glasses in their bars. They can install locked display cases to protect high value electronics. They can change the payment systems on gas pumps. They can lock the wheels on the dumpsters next to their churches.

But also remember that some place managers have been delegated their authority from property owners. They could be managers or employees hired by the owner to run the business. The people are often part of a stable prosocial network who consistently have eyes on the street. Offenders will come and go from neighborhoods. Many police officers come and go too; they are frequently transferred to other areas. But many of these public characters are permanent fixtures in neighborhoods, in some cases for years. They guard the area, keep watch, and intervene if problems ensue. As Jacobs notes:

> …a network of doormen and superintendents, of delivery boys and nursemaids, a form of hired neighborhood, keeps residential Park Avenue supplied with eyes … [and] if rents were to slip below the point where they could support a plentiful hired neighborhood of doormen and elevator men, it would undoubtedly become a woefully dangerous street.[12]

These public characters are even less likely to be thought of in problem-solving efforts. They can include doormen, valet drivers, mailmen, bouncers, restaurant hosts, food truck vendors, and so on. They should not be overlooked. These individuals are a stable presence in communities but are seldom residents. They are frequently stationed in public areas, but the least likely to be present at community meetings. Nevertheless, they can be an invaluable source of information and assistance in your problem-solving efforts.

But there are circumstances in which no public characters are obvious. Either no one volunteers their efforts to step into this role, or it is not clear who should take it on. This is where the police can play a crucial role.

The Police as Public Characters

We continue to emphasize the point that the police alone often cannot solve problems.[13] The police can be gatekeepers or consultants, but in most cases, they cannot implement change. The police cannot install locked display cases in retail stores experiencing shoplifting, only the place managers can. The police are unable to change the payment systems at gasoline pumps, only the place managers can. The police cannot replace all glassware with polycarbonate glasses, only the place managers can. You get the idea. Now, the police can identify the problems: frequent shoplifting at the same store; gasoline theft at gas stations; assaults at downtown bars. The police can also attempt to compel place managers to act. But it is ultimately the place manager who needs to solve the problem.

In many situations a public character can step up to address a problem. But in some situations, the public character is not obvious. If drug problems begin in a vacant building whose owner is not apparent, who can address this? If problems recur at a large chain store and the store's manager claims she cannot act because corporate policy forbids it, are our hands tied? Can nothing be done? Similarly, if some residents try to take action as public characters to have speed bumps installed on a school street but are not successful, are they just out of luck?

In such cases, the police could step in as public characters. Although the police may not be able to solve problems outright, they do have a unique power that even place managers do not: authority. If you have ever called or gone to a government office, you have probably had to wait.

Even once you got your turn, you may not have gotten what you wanted. In many cases the agency likely failed to provide what was needed.

Or in an even more frustrating scenario, you may be told that the issue you have brought to them falls under the jurisdiction of another agency. This is a common problem for the average resident. The bureaucracy of agencies can make it difficult to determine who can solve the problem. John Mudd provides an excellent example of this:

> A civic leader in southern Queens phones the local police precinct asking that barricades be placed around a gaping hole in a nearby vacant lot where children play. She is told it is a Highways Department problem. The community relations officer there says the danger is the Board of Education's responsibility, since a school used to occupy the site. The Board of Education reports that a new school has been built several blocks away and the land has reverted to the Department of Real Estate. Real Estate checks and finds that the demolition contractor for the old school was responsible for closing a sewer drain at the bottom of the hole, the contract for the job ran out six months ago, and the department does not have the equipment to deal with it.[14]

Worse yet, as problems evolve, the relevant agency can change. This is what Mudd refers to as "the rat problem":

> If a rat is found in an apartment, it is a housing inspection responsibility; if it runs into a restaurant, the health department has jurisdiction; if it goes outside and dies in an alley, public works takes over.[15]

Police officers are not always faced with the same problem. They certainly can be diverted from one agency to the next. But, unlike residents, the police have a level of authority in society that gets them to the front of the line. They are not told to take a number. At the very least, police often possess institutional knowledge of how to circumvent the bureaucracy, through a loose and often closely guarded network of dependable insiders who can and will get things done. This is particularly the case the higher the rank of an officer. When a police captain, for example, arrives at a government office looking for assistance, they are far more likely to receive first rate service.

In this regard, police officers can use their authority to co-ordinate or even compel problem-solving efforts that require cooperation from many agencies.[16] Dan used his status as a police captain often to do just this. The Barksdale Market example from chapter 5 is a prime example of this. Recall that in addition to its various crime problems, Dan discovered that the Barksdale property had unpaid tax liens, building code violations, and fell short of several health violations. But different government agencies were responsible to address each of these problems. Many of the problems had yet to be addressed and none of the agencies communicated with each other. So, Dan took it upon himself to co-ordinate action with the local police, redevelopment foundation, city, building inspector, health inspector, and prosecutor to address the problem. After a raid, the city seized the property for outstanding liens and code violations. The property was then sold to the non-profit redevelopment foundation to be remodeled into a new business.

Instead of disrupting the opportunity structure, which only temporarily reduces the problem, Dan's strategy completely dismantled the crime opportunities. Taking ownership of the property away from the owner eliminated the infrastructure that offenders needed to carry out money laundering, drug dealing, and shoplifting. Had Dan not taken on the role of a public character to coordinate this strategy, it would be far less likely that crime would have been eliminated at the Barksdale. Residents would not have had access to the resources needed to shutter the business. They also would not have been able to co-ordinate the multi-agency response needed to address the problem.

Closing the Barksdale was not the first crime reduction proposal suggested. Many had been suggested and some tried prior; none were successful. Ideas for crime reduction are never scarce. But most of them will fail. So, the challenge to anyone trying to reduce crime is to separate the many ideas bound to fail from the few ideas that are likely to succeed. This won't be easy because even failure-bound ideas carry a whiff of plausibility and useful ideas are not immediately apparent. But in the next chapter we offer you a tool to do this difficult sorting.

Key Points

- Public characters are people stationed in public places and in frequent contact with people who use a street or property
- Public characters are often stationed in public places for long periods (think: doormen, valet drivers, mailmen, bouncers, food truck vendors, restaurant hosts)
- When no public character is apparent, police can serve as public characters
- Ask: who can address your problem?

Notes

1 Eck, J.E., Linning, S.J., & Herold, T.D. (2023). *Place Management and Crime: Ownership and Property Rights as a Source of Social Control.* Springer Publishers. https://doi.org/10.1007/978-3-031-27693-4

2 Eck, J.E. & Madensen, T.D. (2018). Place management, guardianship, and the establishment of order. In D.S. Nagin, F.T. Cullen, & C.L. Jonson (Eds.), *Deterrence, Choice, and Crime: Contemporary Perspectives* (pp. 269–296). Routledge. https://doi.org/10.4324/9781351112710-10

3 Sampson, R., Eck, J.E., & Dunham, J. (2010). Super controllers and crime prevention: A routine activity explanation of crime prevention success and failure. *Security Journal, 23*(1), 37–51. https://doi.org/10.1057/sj.2009.17

4 Skogan, W. (2019). Community policing. In D. Weisburd & A. Braga (eds.), *Police Innovation: Contrasting Perspectives* (2nd edition; pp. 27–44). Cambridge University Press. https://doi.org/10.1017/9781108278423.002

5 Linning, S.J. & Eck, J.E. (2021). *Whose 'Eyes on the Street' Control Crime? Expanding Place Management into Neighborhoods.* Cambridge University Press. https://doi.org/10.1017/9781108954143

6 Jacobs, J. (1956, June). The missing link in city redevelopment. *Architectural Forum: The Magazine of Building, 104*(6), 132–133; Jacobs, J. (1958). Downtown is for people. In W.H. Whyte Jr. (Ed.), *The Exploding Metropolis* (pp. 140–168). New York: Doubleday; Jacobs, J. (1961). *The Death and Life of Great American Cities.* New York: Vintage; Jacobs, J. (1969). *The Economy of Cities.* New York: Vintage; Jacobs, J. (1981). Can big plans solve the problem of renewal? In S. Zipp & N. Storring (Eds.), *Vital Little Plans: The Short Works of Jane Jacobs* (pp. 177–188). New York: Random House; Jacobs, J. (1985). *Cities and the Wealth of Nations: Principles of Economic Life.* New York: Vintage; Jacobs, J. (2000). *The Nature of Economies.* New York: Vintage.

7 From page 35 of: Jacobs, J. (1961). *The Death and Life of Great American Cities.* New York: Vintage.

8 Jacobs, J. (1961). *The Death and Life of Great American Cities.* New York: Vintage; Linning, S.J. & Eck, J.E. (2021). *Whose 'Eyes on the Street' Control Crime? Expanding Place Management into Neighborhoods.* Cambridge University Press. https://doi.org/10.1017/9781108954143

9 From page 37 of: Jacobs, J. (1961). *The Death and Life of Great American Cities.* New York: Vintage.

10 Jacobs, J. (1961). *The Death and Life of Great American Cities.* New York: Vintage.

11 From page 68 of: Jacobs, J. (1961). *The Death and Life of Great American Cities.* New York: Vintage.

12 From page 40 of: Jacobs, J. (1961). *The Death and Life of Great American Cities.* New York: Vintage.
13 Linning, S.J., Carroll, T., Gerard, D.W., & Eck, J.E. (2025, January). Can the police solve all public safety problems? *Public Management, 107*(1), 40–44. https://icma.org/articles/pm-magazine/can-police-solve-all-crime-problems
14 From page xiii of: Mudd, J. (1984). *Neighborhood Services: Making Big Cities Work.* New Haven, CT: Yale University Press.
15 From page 8 of: Mudd, J. (1984). *Neighborhood Services: Making Big Cities Work.* New Haven, CT: Yale University Press.
16 Sampson R., Eck, J.E., & Dunham, J. (2010). Super controllers and crime prevention: A routine activity explanation of crime prevention success and failure. *Security Journal, 23*(1), 37–51. https://doi.org/10.1057/sj.2009.17; Scott, M. & Goldstein, H. (2005). Shifting and Sharing Responsibility for Public Safety Problems. In *Problem-Oriented Guides for Police* (Issue 3). Office of Community Oriented Policing Services. Retrieved from: https://popcenter.asu.edu/sites/default/files/shifting_sharing_responsibility_for_public_safety_problems.pdf

17
SCRAP What Does Not Work

When people talk about cutting crime, they usually think of several ideas. They think that we need to solve big and complex social problems, such as people's morals, poverty, homelessness, mental health, or drugs. Or, they think that crime can happen at any place at any time. From social media, internet reports, and the news, people worry that they are at risk all the time and anywhere. Or, they think residents' lack of willingness to get involved created the crime problem, so getting residents to act is the key to driving down crime. Or, they think that the police should step up their arrests; it's lax enforcement that has given the bad guys the feeling that they can get away with crime. Or, coupled with demanding more arrests, people believe that police are the proprietors of crime control; the police chief is the anti-crime czar and few other public or private agencies matter.

There is a kernel of truth to these notions to make these beliefs plausible. Big social problems do have something to do with crime; a country with little poverty, much equality, and stern morals probably will have less crime than an impoverished, unequal, and immoral society. There is no place or time that is absolutely crime-risk free. Even low crime neighborhoods have the occasional murder, rape, or robbery. Residents have some role in crime prevention. Importantly, they can put political pressure on elected officials to do something about crime, and knowing that,

DOI: 10.4324/9781003430155-21

most elected officials are hypersensitive about being tarred with the "soft on crime" brush. Arrests can help blunt crime. There are prolific offenders who can cause a great deal of harm if left roaming the streets. Police are the lead local agency to deal with crime emergencies. There is no one else to call when crime threatens people.

But many people take the kernels of insight and inflate them, like popcorn, into bloated hot air-filled nutritionless fallacies. They are fallacies because they fail to obey the rule of the few. As we have shown with research and examples, we do not have to cause major social change to reduce crime. Crime is highly concentrated. Most residents, particularly in areas with high crime levels, have little power to control crime. Fixing the small problems that make crime easy and profitable works. Non-police public and private agencies have important roles in suppressing crime. Broad-brush approaches assume that to reduce crime we need to do a lot to the many, when the truth is we need to do something with a few.

These fallacies violate the rule of the few. In chapter 1 we urged you to shift from thinking like the many to rule of the few thinking. We displayed a table showing the difference between how many people think about crime and rule of the few thinking. Here it is again, except we have put the rule of the few thinking first (table 17.1). We wrote this book because we believe that few people—aside from those promoting political positions or seeking academic status—are interested in accomplishing

Table 17.1 Use the Rule of the Few to Cut Crime

	Think Rule of the Few	Ignore Thoughts of the Many
Key Question	How?	Why?
Cause of Crime	Opportunity	Propensity
Explain	Crime Events	Offenders
Understand	Immediate Situation	Distant Possible Causes
Focus	Solving Problems (Ends)	Improving Processes (Means)
Undertake	Treatment of Causes	Treatment of Symptoms
Problem Solvers	Place Managers	Police & Residents
Default Intervention	Dismantle Opportunities	Addressing propensities

little. We believe you want to succeed in protecting property and lives, and if we are right, then the second column is for you.

Ask *how* offenders commit crime rather than asking *why*? Focus on crime opportunities rather than offenders' propensities towards criminality. Address the immediate situations that prompt offending instead of distant possible causes, such as upbringing or economic recessions. Focus on solving discrete problems, using outcomes as your guide, rather than improving processes, such as having police get to the scene of the crime faster or arresting more people. Be sure to treat the causes of crime instead of the symptoms. Place managers will usually be your best problem-solvers, rather than residents or police. Finally, work to dismantle crime opportunities as opposed to addressing criminal propensities.

Aiden Sidebottom's experience studying bag thefts in bars (chapter 1) is a great illustration of rule of the few thinking. He did not focus on why thieves coveted bags. He also realized that only a few bars had bag theft problems. So, he asked: why here but not there? The answer was that those few bars had two entrances/exits which provided an easier opportunity for thieves to steal bags. A simple opportunity-dismantling solution is to get the place managers of the bars to block off one of the doors. This increases the effort and risk involved in stealing bags.

Knowing how to craft solutions obeying the rule of the few is a big step towards reducing crime. But you will likely be bombarded with crime reduction proposals from others. This is particularly true of police chiefs and city managers. A few of these proposals might be productive. But many may not work.

This was something that happened to Fort Myers, Florida, Police Chief Derrick Diggs. Chief Diggs was being bombarded with many ideas about how to address the city's crime. Externally, city officials, elected officials, the public, and the media were suggesting an abundance of crime reduction ideas. Internally, his own commanders were suggesting their own ideas. Chief Diggs was struggling to sort the few ideas that were likely to succeed from the many ideas that were likely to become costly and embarrassing failures. He consulted Dan about the conundrum. Dan suggested that he use a tool Shannon developed to accomplish this: the SCRAP test. Chief Diggs applied the test internally and externally with great success. The SCRAP test helped the police design strategies that reduced crime while simultaneously making fewer arrests.[1] Later, we wrote a series of articles outlining how city managers could use the SCRAP test.[2]

The SCRAP Test

Crime reduction ideas applying these fallacies can come from anyone: local politicians, colleagues, residents, community activists, police, academics, business leaders, state and national legislators, the media, and others. Sometimes their ideas even sound plausible. Therefore, when looking to reduce crime, you will have two needs: 1. a way to identify proposals that are based on crime fallacies; and 2. a way to adjust proposals so that you can turn fallacy-like ideas into actionable and effective solutions. The SCRAP test addresses both needs. SCRAP is an acronym made from the first letters of the five fallacies. Here is how it works.

First, take any crime reduction proposal and ask yourself if the proposal applies any of the fallacies in the left column of table 17.2. The more fallacies the proposal applies, the more likely it will fail to reduce crime. Second, if the proposal applies most of the fallacies, you should SCRAP the proposal. Third, if the proposal only applies a fallacy or two, you should consult the right column. The right column shows you how to adjust the proposal so that the strategies is more likely to succeed.

You can also use the SCRAP test to design a crime reduction strategy from scratch. First, use the right column to guide strategy design. Then, use the left column to check your strategy for fallacies.

The second column highlights key rule of the few-inspired questions that will lead you in the right direction. First, ask yourself whether you

Table 17.2 The SCRAP Test

If your strategy assumes...	Instead, ask yourself...
Solutions to crime are complicated.	What is the problem?
Crime is widespread.	Does the rule of the few apply?
Residents matter most.	Who is the place manager?
Arrests reduce crime.	What is the desired outcome?
Police can solve all crime problems.	How can I dismantle crime opportunities?
...Scrap it!	...Try this!

can break the problem down into smaller, solvable components. As discussed in chapters 6 and 8, you are unlikely to solve major societal issues particularly swiftly and certainly not during an 8-, 10- or 12-hour shift. Just as important, responding to only immediate troublesome events will not lead to long-term crime reductions. Instead, you need to find the "goldilocks" problem that will generate the most gains if solved. The CHEERS criteria will help you zero in on solvable problems.[3]

Second, ask whether you've applied the rule of the few to your problem. If you analyze all the cases, does a hockey stick graph appear? If so, this means crime is concentrated at a few places, and caused by only a few people, or things.[4] Then ask yourself why here but not there? Why do a tiny number of places, people, or items on the blade of the stick have so many problems, while all the others on the handle do not? What accounts for this? Often you can find answers by asking *how* instead of *why* the crimes are being committed. It is critical to understand both the *why* and *how* when crime occurs. Acting on the *why* is what ultimately makes a police agency data driven. Acting on the *how* removes the opportunity structure for future crimes to occur at that location.

Third, ask whether you have identified the relevant place manager.[5] There are two types of place managers who can be the most helpful. The first type are the ones who can actually do something about the problem. These are the people on the blade of the hockey stick who own or operate the properties experiencing the problem.[6] Remember to be specific here. As chapter 16 discussed, if you have a problem at an apartment building in the city, you do not need to contact all landlords. You need only work with the landlord of the building in question. The second type you can consult with are the managers of places that do not have a problem. These are the ones on the handle of the hockey stick. Continuing with our apartment example, landlords with buildings that do not have the problem in question may have some good ideas on how to address the problem. Perhaps they dealt with the same problem five years prior and figured out a way to address it. This makes them experts on that problem. They are a great resource. As described in chapter 7, many of these place managers work together to spread safety at and around their properties. They have a vested economic interest in making sure their place users feel safe and want to return to their properties.[7]

Fourth, instead of thinking we can arrest ourselves out of a problem, the SCRAP test prompts you to ask: what is the desired outcome? Using metrics like number of stops or arrests made, number of community meetings held, or number of streetlights installed is no guarantee that you are reducing crime (see chapter 4). They are simply a reflection that somebody acted. Whether those actions solved the problem cannot be determined by tracking outputs. You need to have a clear outcome (i.e., goal) in mind: reduce the number of burglaries, reduce the number of car crashes, reduce the number of people getting killed in car crashes. Hiring more police officers to go out and arrest wrongdoers is unlikely to produce these outcomes. Police often can only react to crime and even if they apprehend a prolific offender, crime will continue if the opportunity structure remains in place. Other offenders will eventually find and exploit these opportunities too. In general, what police officers do matters more than how many officers you have.[8]

Fifth, instead of assuming the police should deal with the problem, ask: how can we dismantle the opportunity? This book has been filled with examples where the most effective solutions to crime problems were not carried out by the police. Often, the police do not have the legal authority to address the crime opportunities. The police cannot go onto private property and block doors in bars. The police cannot change the payment systems on gasoline pumps. They cannot develop and roll out kill switch technologies to lock our smartphones. They cannot install locked glass display cases in retail stores or replace pint glasses with shatterproof ones (chapter 5). Only place managers can do these things (chapter 7).

The police and government can encourage or assist place managers to make these changes (chapter 10). The police can offer advisory services and make recommendations about better security measures to place managers, for example. Similarly, governments can offer grants or tax breaks to cover the costs of replacing pint glasses with polycarbonate ones. In more extreme cases, governments can compel place managers to act (chapter 11). This can occur through regulation or legislation.[9] Mandating a shift to pay-before-you-pump systems at all gas stations is an example. But at the end of the day, all these efforts are to get place managers to make different and more effective decisions. So, if you are faced with a problem, start by asking who *owns* the problem? That place manager is the person who can use situational crime prevention to dismantle the crime opportunity.

Applying the SCRAP Test

You've seen the SCRAP test in action throughout this book. Many of the problem solvers behind the examples intuitively rejected the SCRAP fallacies and designed effective programs to prevent crime. Take Dan's fatal car crash prevention example (highlighted in chapters 1 and 8).[10] Dan did not try to fix major societal issues—such as alcoholism or drug addiction, risk-taking behavior, or social media addiction—that could contribute to car crashes. While intoxicated drivers, speeders, and distracted drivers certainly contribute to some car crashes, Dan's analysis of the crashes found that the worst crashes were due to rain on curved roads where drivers lost control of their vehicles.

Dan also did not assume that these fatal crashes occurred all over the city. So, he did not roll out widespread police patrols attempting to thwart dangerous driving. Instead, he had his team analyze where the crashes occurred. They found that the fatal crashes were concentrated at only seven locations in the city.[11]

When thinking about a response, Dan did not immediately default to involving residents or police, and especially not a strategy where they would try to arrest their way out of the problem. He knew that if fatal crashes occurred mostly at seven locations during bad weather, he should investigate whether he could improve the road conditions at those seven locations. So, he became a public character and began consulting with the City of Cincinnati Traffic Engineering Department and a paving contractor. They determined that loss of traction, particularly on curved roads in rain, was usually to blame. Finding a way to increase the coefficient of friction of the road could address the problem. The traffic department, and their contractors, used special equipment to create rougher pavement on the short stretches of road that experienced the accidents. The road roughening ended the vehicle-related fatalities at these fatality hot spots.

Dan was able to save lives by avoiding the common fallacies. He did not mobilize residents; residents have no authority over government-owned roads. Nevertheless, he did consider that residents living near these roads would object to a noisy solution, so he had the traffic department experiment with alternative grinds to find the one that could stop deaths but allow locals to sleep. Dan also did not make this problem a police problem. In fact, he shifted the problem to the city agency that was responsible for roads. The police department did not carry out the road grinding. Instead, the place manager, the Traffic Engineering Department, did. The solution Dan promoted also avoided having to arrest speeding drivers.

Dan's problem-solving strategy passed the SCRAP test. He identified the problem: poor road conditions causing car crashes. He identified the few places experiencing the problem: seven locations (street blocks or intersections). He identified the relevant place manager: the Cincinnati Traffic Engineering Department. He identified his desired outcome: to reduce fatalities caused by car crashes. He dismantled the opportunity: increasing the coefficient of friction of wet roads.

When Aiden Sidebottom and Samantha Muncaster encountered the lead thefts from churches, they too came up with a SCRAP-approved solution. Locking the wheels on dumpsters to prevent thieves from getting access to church roofs has nothing to do with major social issues, like poverty or substance abuse, that might increase thieves' propensities to steal. They also identified the tiny fraction of churches that needed to lock their dumpsters' wheels (17 out of 100). The solution did not involve residents. Instead, it involved working with the churches' place managers to do something simple: lock the dumpster wheels. The police did not lock the dumpster wheels.[12]

In the glassing example, British police did not try to address major societal issues like alcoholism or hooliganism among the British population. They also did not roll out a blanket patrol to reduce intoxication and fighting or get a group of residents together to discuss the issues. Instead, they identified pubs with many glassings and worked with the place managers through a grant program to replace their pint glasses with shatterproof polycarbonate glasses. Residents could not implement this strategy; they have no control over pubs that they do not own. The strategy only worked once police got the right place managers onboard.[13]

In the Kia Boyz car theft example, police did not try to address major societal issues like poverty or social media influence. They also did not adopt widespread, blanket patrols in attempts to apprehend thieves. They also did not try to get residents involved in the problem. Instead, the police deduced vehicles manufactured by Kia and Hyundai between 2015 and 2019 as the targets of thieves. They also deduced that thieves CRAVED these vehicles because they had no engine immobilisers and thus were easy to steal.[14] So, the police prompted the Attorney Generals in the United States to pressure the product manufacturer to address the problem. New models of Kias and Hyundais contain engine immobilisers making the opportunity to steal more difficult, and the manufacturers have also installed software updates in the older cars to make their thefts more difficult. None of this response involved residents or police.[15] It also did not require that we solve major social issues or arrest our way out of the problem. Instead, they used the rule of the few; they got the two vehicle manufacturers who produced vehicles that were easier to steal to use situational crime prevention in their vehicles.

In the Provo apartment example, the police did not try to address major societal issues like drug addiction or poverty. They also did not apply a blanket city-wide approach to address drug-related offences, burglaries, thefts, and the like. Instead, the police identified a dilapidated four-unit apartment as the source of the crime. While residents did provide police with information about the problem, the residents did not implement the solution. Instead, the police relocated the tenants to hygienic housing and called upon regulatory agencies to conduct inspections of the apartment that was radiating crime.[16] Due to regulatory pressures, the owner sold the apartment. The new owner made necessary repairs prior to renting to new tenants. By obeying the rule of the few the crime problems in and around the Provo apartment nearly disappeared.

Get to Work

At some point, all political and police leaders will be confronted with a crime problem they are expected to solve. It may seem overwhelming in scope, especially if there are resource limitations that impact solving it. Using a combined offender- and place-based strategy, you will be able to narrow your focus to the very few people and places who drive crime.

Then, deploy with a purpose every day to eliminate the crime opportunity. We provide a quick reference guide to problem-solving tools in the appendix.

Once you develop your problem-solving strategy, implement it with a great sense of urgency. City and county managers and police leaders often over analyze a strategy, trying to think through any possible contingencies, prior to implementation. The critical window to make a positive difference with a sound strategy, slams shut as the street conditions change prior to roll out and the chosen strategy is no longer as effective.

Conduct ongoing evaluations of your chosen strategy. It does no good to evaluate your strategy 6–12 months after implementation and realize it has been ineffective. Regular evaluations allow for timely strategy modifications when needed and increase the likelihood of success.

Finally, talk about your new problem-solving and deployment with a purpose strategy internally and externally. Explain to your officers, government administrators, neighborhood place managers, and the community what you are doing, why you are doing it, their expected role, and what they can expect. Clear expectations and established outcomes reduce surprises later and increase buy-in as those involved feel part of the solution.

Obeying the rule of the few will be your best bet to cut crime. Use the hockey stick as your prime tool to solve problems. But like any tool, you need to use it properly. Will you use your hockey stick to slash an opponent to block a play in the short term and risk ending up in the penalty box or strategically use it in a powerplay to score a game winning goal? It's up to you!

Key Points

- When trying to reduce crime, always start with the rule of the few
- Apply the SCRAP test to your or anyone else's crime reduction proposal
- SCRAP crime prevention suggestions that rely on many common fallacies
- Revise proposals that have potential but apply a few crime fallacies
- Consider proposals that pass the SCRAP test
- Ask: does the proposed strategy pass the SCRAP test?

Notes

1 Linning, S.J., Carroll, T., Gerard, D.W., & Eck, J.E. (2025). How can you SCRAP crime proposals that are likely to fail? *Public Management, 107*(2), 36–40. https://icma.org/articles/pm-magazine/how-can-you-scrap-crime-proposals-are-likely-fail; Smith, B. (2021, April 12). Fort Myers Police Department says statistics becoming key in the war on crime. Fort Myers News-Press. Retrieved from: https://www.news-press.com/story/news/local/2021/04/12/fort-myers-police-say-studying-trends-helped-cut-violent-crime-50/7190188002/

2 Linning, S.J., Carroll, T., Gerard, D.W., & Eck, J.E. (2024). Do solutions to crime need to be complicated? *Public Management, 106*(8), 36–39. https://icma.org/articles/pm-magazine/do-solutions-crime-need-be-complicated; Linning, S.J., Carroll, T., Gerard, D.W., & Eck, J.E. (2024). Is crime widespread? *Public Management, 106*(10), 30–32. https://icma.org/articles/pm-magazine/crime-widespread; Linning, S.J., Carroll, T., Gerard, D.W., & Eck, J.E. (2024). Do residents matter the most in reducing crime? *Public Management, 106*(11), 30–34. https://icma.org/articles/pm-magazine/do-residents-matter-most-reducing-crime; Linning, S.J., Carroll, T., Gerard, D.W., & Eck, J.E. (2024). Do more arrests reduce crime? *Public Management, 106*(12), 38–41. https://icma.org/articles/pm-magazine/do-more-arrests-reduce-crime; Linning, S.J., Carroll, T., Gerard, D.W., & Eck, J.E. (2025). Can the police solve all public safety problems? *Public Management, 107*(1), 40–44. https://icma.org/articles/pm-magazine/can-police-solve-all-crime-problems; Linning, S.J., Carroll, T., Gerard, D.W., & Eck, J.E. (2025). How can you SCRAP crime proposals that are likely to fail? *Public Management, 107*(2), 36–40. https://icma.org/articles/pm-magazine/how-can-you-scrap-crime-proposals-are-likely-fail

3 Clarke, R.V. & Eck, J.E. (2003). Become a problem-solving crime analyst in 55 steps. Jill Dando Institute of Crime Science, University College London. Retrieved from: https://popcenter.asu.edu/sites/g/files/litvpz3631/files/library/reading/PDFs/55stepsUK.pdf

4 Eck, J. E., Lee, Y., Oh, S., & Martinez, N. (2017). Compared to what? Estimating the relative concentration of crime at places using systematic and other reviews. *Crime Science, 6*(1), 1–17. https://doi.org/10.1186/s40163-017-0070-4

5 Eck, J.E., Linning, S.J., & Herold, T.D. (2023). *Place Management and Crime: Ownership and Property Rights as a Source of Social Control.* Springer Publishers. https://doi.org/10.1007/978-3-031-27693-4

6 Eck, J.E., Linning, S.J., & Herold, T.D. (2023). *Place Management and Crime: Ownership and Property Rights as a Source of Social Control.* Springer Publishers. https://doi.org/10.1007/978-3-031-27693-4

7 Linning, S.J. & Eck, J.E. (2021). *Whose 'Eyes on the Street' Control Crime? Expanding Place Management into Neighborhoods.* Cambridge, UK: Cambridge University Press. https://doi.org/10.1017/9781108954143

8 Lee, Y., Eck, J.E., & Corsaro, N. (2017). Conclusions from the history of research into the effects of police force size on crime—1968 through 2013: A historical systematic review. *Journal of Experimental Criminology, 12*(3), 431–451. https://doi.org/10.1007/s11292-016-9269-8

9 Eck, J.E. (2018). Regulation for high-crime places: Theory, evidence, and principles. *The Annals of the American Academy of Political and Social Science, 679*(1), 106–120. https://doi.org/10.1177/0002716218778764

10 Corsaro, N., Gerard, D.W., Engel, R.S. & Eck, J.E. (2012). Not by accident: An analytical approach to traffic crash harm reduction. *Journal of Criminal Justice, 40*, 502–514. https://doi.org/10.1016/j.jcrimjus.2012.08.003

11 Corsaro, N., Gerard, D.W., Engel, R.S. & Eck, J.E. (2012). Not by accident: An analytical approach to traffic crash harm reduction. *Journal of Criminal Justice, 40*, 502–514. https://doi.org/10.1016/j.jcrimjus.2012.08.003

12 Muncaster, S.J. (2012). *The theft-price relationship: Observations on the theft of lead.* Unpublished Master's thesis, Department of Security and Crime Science, University College London, United Kingdom.

13 Clarke, R.V. (2020). Assaults with glasses in bars and clubs in Lancashire, England. In M.S. Scott & R.V. Clarke (Eds.), *Problem-Oriented Policing: Successful Case Studies* (pp. 128–136). New York, NY: Routledge. https://doi.org/10.4324/9780429457357-13

14 Clarke, R.V. (1999). *Hot products: Understanding, anticipating and reducing demand for stolen goods.* Police Research Series Paper 112. London, UK: Policing and Reducing Crime Unit. Retrieved from: https://popcenter.asu.edu/sites/g/files/litvpz3631/files/hot_products_understanding_anticipating_and_reducing_demand_for_stolen_goods_clarke_1999.pdf ; Valdes-Dapena, P. (2023, January 28). Some auto insurers are refusing to cover certain Hyundai and Kia models. *CNN Business.* Retrieved from: https://www.cnn.com/2023/01/27/business/progressive-state-farm-hyundai-kia/index.html

15 Samra, M. (2023, March 21). Raoul urges Kia, Hyundai to take 'comprehensive action' over Chicago-area car thefts. *Chicago Sun Times.* Retrieved from: https://chicago.suntimes.com/news/2023/3/21/23651031/illinois-attorney-general-kwame-raoul-kia-hyundai-chicago-car-theft-crime

16 Provo City Police Department (2021). 'Crime and Disorder at the "Dog House"'. Goldstein Award Submission. Center for Problem-Oriented Policing. Retrieved from: https://popcenter.asu.edu/sites/default/files/provo_city_pd_beebe_properties_2021.pdf

APPENDIX

Ten Problem-Solving Tools

We know some of you may be frustrated with us. We have yet to provide a magic formula to solve your crime problems. Though many policing strategies provide a formula, we have shown that they have limited effectiveness. Hotspot policing, for example, gives fairly simple directions: identify the few places that experience most of the crime and send police to patrol those places more often. But there are several problems with this: what should the police do when they get there? How long should they spend there? Can they take the same action at each hotspot? If the address the officer is dispatched to contains a large geographic area, how should she handle her time there? Do police need to continue the hotspot patrols forever to keep the crime from reoccurring?

Throughout this book we have advocated for you to engage in problem-solving. We want you to consider and address the cause of the problem as opposed to treating its symptoms. We want you to dismantle the crime opportunities as opposed to temporarily disrupting them, so that six months or a year later you don't have to do it again. The issue with our approach is that there is an array of problems in the world and as situational crime prevention shows, each problem requires an individual response tailored to that specific problem. So, it is impossible for us to identify all possible problems and then spell out all the possible solutions.

Instead, we have been working to make you a problem-solver. We gave you a new way to see the world, and more specifically crime (e.g., the rule of the few). We have given you tools to address these problems (situational crime prevention) and shown who is best equipped to implement them (place managers).

When you engage in problem-solving, there are several questions you should ask yourself: is this even a problem for me to address? If so, how? Is there a systematic problem-solving framework I can follow? Is it a police problem or a place management problem?

Fortunately, many have developed tools to answer these questions. Here, we discuss the ones that are most widely used. This is a quick reference guide to the tools. There are many, but we provide ten of the most prominent ideas that have either been used or more recently proposed to solve problems, especially those involving crime. Some you have seen in this book already. Others are additional resources you can seek out to help in your problem-solving process. Table A.1 summarizes the questions you will likely ask and corresponding tools that can help you address them.

Table A.1 Questions to Start the Problem-Solving Process

	Question	Where to start
1	Do I have a problem?	The CHEERS Criteria
2	How do I solve a problem?	The SARA Model
3	Who are the key players in the problem?	The Crime Triangle
4	Why here, but not there?	The Hockey Stick (j-)Curve
5	How do I fix the problem?	Situational Preventions
6	When should I expect effects?	The Time-Course Framework
7	Did I apply the right dosage?	Weak Intervention Backfire
8	How do I keep track of the process?	Checklists
9	How do I implement a narrowed response?	Deployment with a Purpose
10	Why should we celebrate successes?	Goldstein & Tilley Awards

The CHEERS Criteria

As discussed in chapter 8, when we refer to problems, we mean a collection of unwanted or harmful events that need solving. Problems are patterned; they are not random. So, they must recur and will do so in a predictable manner. If there is no pattern, there is nothing to be solved or prevented. You cannot intervene in a random event. The patterns themselves reveal the true causes of problems.

If you are dealing with crime, you can consult the CHEERS criteria, developed by Ronald Clarke and John Eck to define police problems (table A.2).[1] This is the tool used in the scanning phase of the SARA model. Sometimes people raise concerns to the police, but the issues they raise may not be within the scope of policing. This tool helps determine what is considered a police problem. There are six criteria: community, harm, expectation, event, repeat, and similar. All must be met to be considered a police problem.

First, the trouble being described must occur in the community. It cannot be a concern solely of police administration, such as officers not wearing their hats. Second, there must be something harmful involved: death, injury, taking or destroying something that belongs to someone else; or even fear of using public space. It cannot be just a state of being, such as homelessness, or something that makes people uncomfortable, such as teenagers standing on a street corner. Third, there must be some expectation among some members of the public that the police should be involved substantially. It cannot be something far removed from policing, such as addressing bad sewer smells, or removing flood waters from basements.

Fourth, all problems involve events, such as break-ins, threats, or transactions. It cannot be general states such as poverty or racism, or other general conditions like declining morals. Fifth, the events need to repeat or have a high likelihood of repeating. This is because solving problems is supposed to prevent bad things, and if it is unlikely to repeat, there is no need to prevent it (unlike a meteor strike). Finally, these events that repeat must have something in common, a basis of similarity that indicates a common set of causes. They cannot be an arbitrary set of unconnected unfortunate events.

Table A.2 The CHEERS Criteria: Defining Police Problems

Criteria	Must	Cannot	Good Example	Bad Example
Community	The difficulty must affect the public	It cannot just be a concern to the police	Break-ins to cars parked along a street block	Police cars scraping each other in the police station parking lot
Harm	There must be a tangible harm	Cannot just be a dislike	Death; injury; theft; psychological trauma	Discomfort with teenagers on sidewalk
Expectation	Some in the public must see this as something for the local government to handle	Cannot be something completely outside local government mandate	Traffic crashes; burglaries; and fights	A pandemic
Event	Discrete incidents make up the problem	Cannot be a general state	A prostitution transaction; a terrorist bombing	Homelessness (is a state, not an event)
Repeat	Events must recur, or are likely to	Cannot be a singular event with little chance of recurring	A building with frequent burglaries; reports of aggressive panhandling at an ATM	A train derailment with injuries; a bridge collapse
Similarity	Events must share important characteristics	Cannot be an arbitrary collection of unlinked events	Crimes occurring at the same address; shootings between two rival gangs; wallet thefts from elderly men	A car crash, burglary, report of a loud teen party, and theft all in the same week on the same block

Modified from Clarke & Eck (2005)

Anything that does not meet all six CHEERS criteria is not a police problem, in the technical sense. If you are dealing with a non-crime problem, you will need to modify these criteria. For example, expectation will not be relevant if the police are not involved in solving your problem. But if your problem meets all six CHEERS criteria, you have a police problem. You can then start the problem-solving process by applying the SARA model.

The SARA Model

In the 1970s and 1980s, John worked for the Police Executive Research Forum, a non-profit agency that partnered with US police departments to improve policing approaches. In the late 1980s, John and his team worked with the Newport News (Virginia) Police Department to create a problem-solving framework: the SARA model (figure A.1).[2] Though originally developed for police to advance problem-oriented policing, the model can be used to address any type of problem. In fact, Shannon and John once attended a community meeting in Cincinnati, Ohio where an attendee brought up the SARA model to address a littering problem not realizing that one of its original creators was in the room!

SARA is an acronym for the four problem-solving steps: scanning, analysis, response, and assessment. The first step—scanning—is to detect,

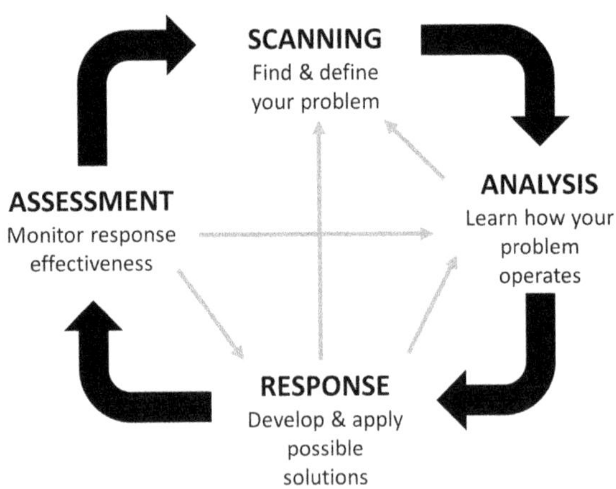

FIGURE A.1 The SARA Model

Adapted from Spelman & Eck (1987)

identify, and define a problem. You must verify whether you have a problem on your hands. This is where you can use the CHEERS criteria. If you are dealing with a different kind of issue, you could apply the inverted triangle we provided in chapter 8 (to evaluate whether you are dealing with a problem, immediate troublesome event, or major societal issue).

For the rest of our explanation of the SARA model we will assume you are dealing with a crime problem and the police are involved. In this case, if your problem meets the CHEERS criteria, you can move to the second step: analysis. This is where you can put the crime triangle to use (discussed in chapter 2 and Tool 3 below). Here you identify the key players in the inner triangle and corresponding controllers, or super controllers (recall chapter 11). Ask yourself who is involved, and how. Be sure to also ask where the problem is occurring and why. The objective is to understand both how and why the problem occurs so that you can identify possible solutions. Acting on the *why* is what makes an agency data driven. Acting on the *how* removes the opportunity structure for future crimes to occur at a location.

The third step, response, is developing those solutions. This is where you can apply the techniques of situational crime prevention (recall chapter 10). Here you need to ask what should be done about the problem and who the best person is to address it (recall chapter 7 and 16). Be sure to search widely for possible solutions. Solutions will often go beyond things the police can do themselves. Remember, you can reach out to other government agencies, businesses, and the community to create tailor-made interventions that have a high likelihood of success. Furthermore, these solutions should be the things that involve the least coercion possible.

Finally, at the assessment stage, you determine if the response you applied in the previous step actually worked. If your goal was to reduce the problem, then you need to make sure you achieved this outcome. Remember from chapter 4, do not mistake outputs (e.g., arrests) with outcomes (e.g., a reduction in the number of impaired drivers). This final stage requires two types of evaluations: process and impact. Process evaluations answer two questions: did the response occur as planned? Did all the response components work? The impact evaluation asks additional questions: Did the problem decline? If so, why did it decline? Did the response cause the decline?[3]

It is important to note that problem-solving processes need not follow a linear path; it is an iterative process. Ronald Clarke and John Eck describe this in their helpful (free) guide for crime analysts; *Crime Analysis for Problem Solvers in 60 Small Steps*.[4] As the SARA diagram suggests, you may need to move back and forth between the SARA steps. It is possible that an attempt made in the response stage does not work. You may realize this in the assessment stage, but you do not need to return to the scanning stage and start all over again. Perhaps the analysis stage revealed several potential solutions. The one you happened to try did not work, but there are others at your disposal. It is also possible that you may want to return to the analysis stage in case you missed an important detail that could shed more light on the true cause of your problem.

For a more recent version of the problem-solving process, see Jerry Ratcliffe's book *Reducing Crime: A Companion for Police Readers*.[5] Within it, he suggests splitting the response strategy into two phases: nominating a strategy and deploying a strategy. These change leads to a different problem-solving acronym: PANDA. PANDA tells problem solvers to: **P**roblem scan, **A**nalyze the problem, **N**ominate a strategy, **D**eploy the strategy, and **A**ssess outcomes.[6]

The Crime Triangle

We first introduced the crime triangle to you in chapter 2. We return to it here with hopes that you now understand how it fits in with the problem-solving process. John developed the crime triangle to establish who the key players are in a crime problem.[7] After reading routine activities theory (discussed in chapter 9), John realized that the elements of crime had parallels to the fire triangle. Just as fire cannot occur without heat, fuel, or oxygen, crime cannot occur unless an offender converges with a target at a place that lacks capable guardianship. These make up the inner triangle (figure A.2). Often, police, government officials, and the community overcomplicate crime prevention. If any one of these three elements are absent, crime cannot occur. So, you do not need to remove all three elements to prevent crime.

The outer triangle denotes the potential controllers who could intervene in the crime process. Handlers have emotional attachments to offenders and can often compel them to refrain from offending.[8] The offender

FIGURE A.2 The Crime Triangle

genuinely cares what the handler thinks about them. Offenders may refrain from acting on crime opportunities so they do not disappoint the handler who cares about them. Guardians, such as security guards, can protect targets.[9] Managers are the owners and operators of the place.[10] If a single effective controller is present and operating, then even if the three necessary conditions (depicted in the inner triangle) come together, crime is unlikely. A single crime might occur if by some odd chance the inner elements converge when all of the controllers are momentarily inattentive. However, to have a recurring problem (i.e., a hotspot), both the convergence and inattentiveness must routinely occur.

You should use the crime triangle when in the analysis phase of the SARA process. The crime triangle helps you ask important questions, such as: where the problem is occurring (place)? Who may be causing the problem (offender and sometimes manager)? Who is impacted by the problem (target)? Who might be able to intervene (manager, guardian, or handler)? Again, Jerry Ratcliffe (2019) has offered a revised problem-solving model for this phase summarized by the acronym VOLTAGE. This model reminds problem-solvers in the analysis phase to analyze **V**ictims, **O**ffenders, **L**ocations, **T**imes, **A**ttractors, **G**roups, and **E**nhancers.[11] Another helpful question to ask rests with our next tool, the Hockey Stick (j-)Curve.

The Hockey Stick (j-)Curve

In chapter 1, when faced with theft problems in bars and churches, British researcher Aiden Sidebottom asked an important question: why here, but not there? He had analyzed bag thefts in 26 locations of the same chain of bars in London.[12] The data produced a hockey stick curve (Figure A.3): most places had no crime (the handle), but a few experienced a lot (the blade). For years, the police had been responding to calls for service at places in the blade of the hockey stick (Bars T, P, R, & M). No matter what they tried, crime persisted.

But something changed when Sidebottom showed the hockey stick graph to police. The questions officers started asking changed: why here, but not there? It was only then that police realized the locations in the blade had two entrances/exits.[13] Those on the handle did not. Similarly, the metal thefts from roofs of churches occurred at churches with mobile dumpsters. Churches whose dumpsters could not be moved to access the roof did not experience theft problems.

Sometimes comparing places with problems to places that serve a similar function but don't experience the problems is very helpful. It causes you to think about the physical characteristics of the place, how the place is managed relative to others, and how people use the place. The Hockey

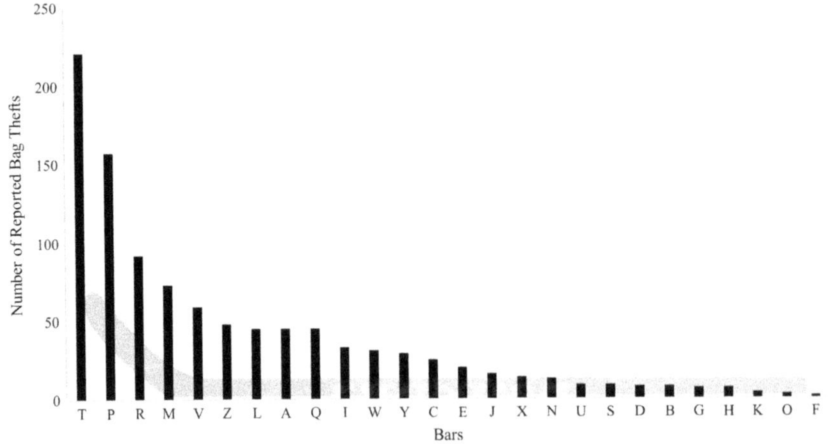

FIGURE A.3 Bag Thefts Across 26 Bars of the Same Chain in Central London, 2005–2006

Adapted from Sidebottom & Bowers (2010)

Stick (j-)Curve is a useful tool in the analysis phase of the SARA model to help you establish how the problem operates.

But once you figure out how the problem is occurring and the key players involved, what do you do about it? This is where situational preventions enter the picture.

Situational Preventions

Once you know how the problem operates and who is involved in the problem, you need to do something about it. This is where the response phase of the SARA model comes in. This is the phase in which situational crime prevention is the most relevant to apply.

Because we covered situational crime prevention extensively in chapter 10, we will not rehash it here. You should mainly focus on dismantling crime opportunities. In trying to dismantle a crime opportunity, recall Ronald Clarke's offender choice criteria.[14] Put yourself in the shoes of an offender and ask: would I need to invest a lot of effort into committing this crime? Am I likely to get caught? Are there few rewards for carrying out this crime? Are there few provocations for acting badly? Do few excuses exist to justify my criminal actions? If the answers to these questions are mostly "yes", then crime is unlikely. But if the place signals "no" to some of these questions, then crime will be a tempting and a likely choice by many people who use the place.

In such cases, you need to see which of the 25 techniques of situational crime prevention you can apply that change peoples' answers to those 5 questions (table A.3). Remember to consider the COSTS criteria (**C**rime-specific, **O**ffender's perspective, **S**ituation modification, **T**ime, and **S**pace) when designing your strategy to make it as direct as possible (see chapter 10).[15] Situational crime prevention forms the basis of your *response* in the SARA model. But as you implement this response, be sure to anticipate and consider the timing of effects and the potential backfires you may observe.

The Time-Course Framework

When designing your prevention strategy, you also need to consider timing. Crime can change at different times surrounding an intervention: before you implement your strategy, during your strategy, or after your strategy.

Table A.3 The 25 Techniques of Situational Crime Prevention with Examples

Increase Effort	Increase Risk	Reduce Rewards	Reduce Provocations	Reduce Excuses
1. Target Harden • Steering column locks & engine immobilizers • Multi-factor authentication	**6. Extend guardianship** • Go out in groups at night • "Cocoon" neighborhood watch	**11. Conceal targets** • Secure lockers for package deliveries • Place surplus stock out of customers' sight	**16. Reduce frustration** • Efficient queues • Air conditioning in transit	**21. Set rules** • Rental agreements • Hotel rules/registration
2. Control access • Key fobs for door entry • Gated entries	**7. Assist natural surveillance** • Improve street lighting • Support whistleblowers	**12. Remove targets** • Cashless payment on transit • Do not stock high-theft items	**17. Avoid disputes** • Separate enclosures for rival sports fans • Fixed cab ares	**22. Post instructions** • "No Parking" signs • "Private Property" signs
3. Screen exits • Ticket needed for exit • Electronic merchandise tags	**8. Reduce anonymity** • Taxi Driver IDs • Greeters at stores and banks	**13. Identify property** • Vehicle licensing and parts marking • Anti-theft devices on clothing	**18. Reduce emotional arousal** • Create a friendly, calm environment • Ban offensive symbols	**23. Alert conscience** • Roadside speed display boards • "Shoplifting is stealing" signs
4. Deflect offenders • Street closures • Separate bathrooms for women	**9. Use place managers** • Two clerks in convenience stores • Train bar staff on safe serving practices	**14. Disrupt markets** • Monitor pawn shops • Regulate metal recyclers	**19. Neutralize peer pressure** • Allow only one teenaged shopper into store at a time • "It's OK to say No" campaigns	**24. Assist compliance** • Easy checkout • Frequent clearing of litter bins
5. Control tools/weapons • Swap pint glasses with shatterproof glasses in bars • Baggage screening	**10. Strengthen formal surveillance** • Red light cameras • Security guards	**15. Deny benefits** • Ink merchandise tags • Smartphone kill switches	**20. Discourage imitation** • Rapid repair of vandalism • Limit crime details to media	**25. Control drugs and alcohol** • Assign alcohol-permitted area • Allow consumption of alcohol only bought on premises

Table modified from: https://popcenter.asu.edu/sites/g/files/litvpz3631/files/twenty_five_techniques_of_situational_prevention.pdf

We've already covered some of these effects. For example, in chapter 11 we showed how crime can decline *before* an intervention starts if publicity is used. This is what Martha Smith and her colleagues call *anticipatory benefits*.[16] Per Lawrence Sherman's concept of *residual deterrence*, crime can also remain low for a period *after* an intervention has ended.[17]

These different effects were discovered in isolation. More recently, Shannon and John, along with Kate Bowers, developed a *time-course framework* that links them together.[18] It creates a useful tool to plan and administer your intervention. We point out that the changes before, during, or after the intervention can produce benefit (crime declining) or backfire (crime increasing). As figure A.4 shows, several researchers have published works detailing interventions that reduce crime (benefit). Fewer have documented examples of backfire. We discuss the backfire example in the next tool. In this time-course tool, we focus on the timing of effects.

With these three time periods in mind, you can begin thinking about the rollout of your intervention. Your intervention will produce benefit or backfire depending on which mechanisms you trigger and how you trigger them.[19] A mechanism is the logical and plausible explanation for why a change you make should impact your outcome of interest.[20] Some strategies will trigger multiple mechanisms and at different times.

Let's use a police crackdown as an example (figure A.5). Recall from chapter 11 that police crackdowns are temporary noticeable increases in police presence at known crime hotspots. If you do not engage in any

	BEFORE	DURING	AFTER
BENEFIT	Anticipatory Benefits (Smith et al., 2002)	Initial Deterrence (Ross, 1981)	Residual Deterrence (Sherman, 1990)
BACKFIRE	Anticipatory Backfire (n/a)	Initial Backfire (Linning & Eck, 2018)	Residual Backfire (n/a)

FIGURE A.4 Intervention Effects Consolidated into the Time-Course Framework

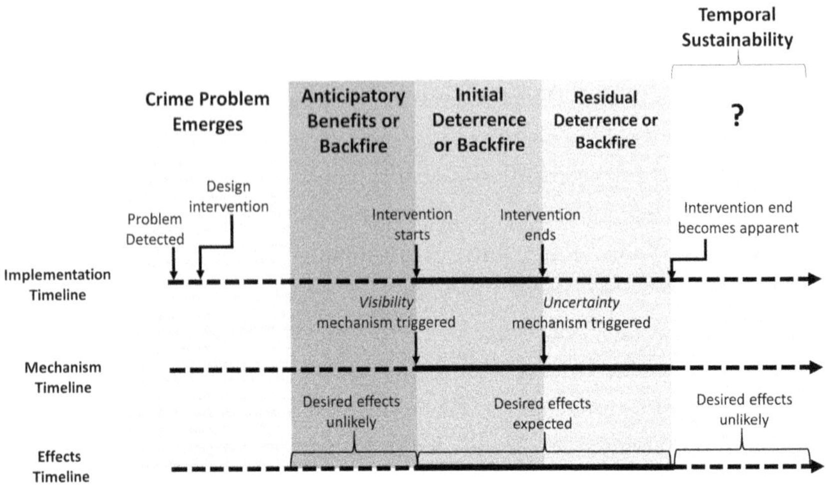

FIGURE A.5 Time-Course Example: Police Crackdown

kind of pre-intervention publicity, it is unlikely that you will observe any changes in crime before the crackdown begins (no anticipatory effects). Once officers begin patrolling the hotspot, crime should begin declining (initial deterrence). However, the theory behind hotspots policing suggests that the mere presence of officers is not enough. They need to be seen. Offenders need to perceive an increased risk of getting caught. This will only happen if you trigger the visibility mechanism. If you send several plain clothes officers to the hotspot, you are unlikely to get the desired crime reduction benefits because offenders would not know their risk of getting caught is higher.

Properly triggering the visibility mechanism during the crackdown also allows you to trigger the mechanism that creates residual deterrence: the uncertainty mechanism. Recall from our discussion of residual deterrence that there is a temporary sustained reduction in crime after a crackdown ends (chapter 2). Once police patrols of the hotspot stop, potential offenders are not sure whether the police will return. So, offenders wait things out. If after a while, officers do not return, the uncertainty mechanism wears off and offending usually starts up again. We call the connection between two mechanisms a "mechanism cascade",[21] meaning the uncertainty mechanisms cannot be triggered unless the visibility mechanism is triggered first.

In this example, we see effects during and after the intervention, but not before. Had we added some form of pre-intervention publicity, we could observe effects before the intervention. The point here is to get you thinking about which mechanisms you are trying to trigger and when you will trigger them. Some advance planning is always wise. Not only will it help you roll out your intervention, but it will also help you decide how to evaluate it. For example, if you believe your intervention will cause some kind of anticipatory effect, you need to decide whether to collect your pre-intervention crimes before or after the publicity mechanism is triggered.

In addition, you want to consider whether the changes you make will trigger mechanisms in ways that reduce crime, as opposed to increase it. Backfire is to be avoided, but we have a limited knowledge of why backfire occurs. We have one explanation: the dosage or intensity you are using in your strategy. This is where the seventh tool is most helpful.

Weak Intervention Backfire

Strategies fail when either no change is observed, or it worsens the problem you are trying to solve. Understanding why interventions fail can be as informative as understanding why interventions work. There are two reasons why interventions can fail. First, the intervention is simply ineffective. It does not trigger the correct mechanism, for example. No matter how we you roll out the intervention, it simply will not work. The second reason for failure is because the intervention was not implemented correctly. If the second reason applies, it means you could have an effective strategy, but it simply was not carried out the right way or the intensity you applied was too weak.

Shannon and John developed the concept of weak intervention backfire to account for the second reason.[22] We hypothesized that researchers have written off several crime prevention and policing strategies as ineffective, when the strategies were simply implemented at the wrong dosage or intensity. Weak intervention backfire was inspired by Shannon's introduction to a concept in biology called hormesis. Hormesis is a biphasic (meaning two phases) "dose-response phenomenon characterized by low-dose stimulation and high-dose inhibition".[23] The idea is that when organisms are exposed to low doses of something harmful, they can develop a resistance to them. At higher doses, the harmful agent may kill the organism. But at low doses, the organism can develop an immunity or tolerance and become stronger.

The flu shot is a good example of this. Each year, medical professionals try to predict which strains of the flu will be most prevalent and include these into the flu shot. You are then injected with a weakened or inactivated dose of those virus strains. Usually, you do not get sick from them, though you may feel a little unwell for a day or so. Instead, your body develops an immunity to those strains of the virus. If you are exposed to the virus in higher doses later, your body is better equipped to fight it off.

Shannon realized that, with a few modifications, many crime prevention and policing strategies work the same way. A prime example is the amount of time police should spend at hotspots. Chris Koper published the most famous study on this topic.[24] He broke police patrol data into five groups to characterize police stops that lasted up to 20 minutes: 1–5, 6–10, 11–15, and 16–20 minutes. Koper found 11–15 minutes was the optimal amount of time for police to spend at hotspots. The 6–10- and 16–20-minute time intervals also generated favourable results, though not significant ones. The one exception was the shortest time interval, 1–5 minutes. Koper's results suggested that if the police spent only 1–5 minutes at hotspots, crime would increase. This would be a backfire effect. Why would this be?

Shannon argued that the concept of hormesis provides a plausible answer. Put yourself in the shoes of a potential offender. Let's say you are at a hotspot about to commit a crime because you know the place has many crime opportunities. But a police officer rolls up and parks beside it. After 90 seconds, the officer drives away. What do you think is the likelihood that another officer will come back to this place any time soon? Probably very low. The officer leaving the scene eliminates the uncertainty mechanism we talked about in the previous tool. Now, you likely perceive your risk of getting caught in the next 5 minutes as quite low. So, you offend. Conversely, if the officer had spent 11–15 minutes at the hotspot, your decision would likely change. After ten minutes you may begin to wonder why the officer has been there for so long. Is she staking out a place across the street? Will she stay here all day? Many would choose to abandon offending at the place.

Shannon encountered another example when attending one of Dan's seminars on gang violence. Dan explained that while working as a police captain he spearheaded a violence reduction strategy by using social network analysis. This is a technique where researchers identify all members of a gang and the number of connections between members. Gangs are structured in a hierarchy. The leaders at the top of the hierarchy tend to be older and have the most connections to other members in the group. Whereas those who are on the street carrying out many of the illegal activities tend to be younger and less connected.

Dan had his team analyze the connections of a Cincinnati, Ohio gang. Knowing the importance of the rule of the few, he knew he needed to focus his police resources on the individuals with the most power; those who were most connected. If the most connected members were incarcerated, the gang would lose its organizational structure and be unable to function.

He asked his analysts to rank members from the most connected to the least connected. Then he had the analysts run simulations of what the gang network would look like if the police could apprehend the 20 most connected individuals in the gang. Results suggested that several strong connections sub-groups at large would remain. So, Dan asked the analysts to re-run the analyses and increase the dosage; simulate removing the 25 most connected individuals in the gang. Results suggested that the higher dosage would dismantle the gang entirely. Too few members and connections between them would remain. So, Dan designed his focused deterrence strategy on the 25 most connected members, instead of the 20 most connected.

Shannon asked Dan what he thought would have happened if he had focused on the top 20 instead of the top 25. His response was that the violence likely would have increased. Why would that be? When a network is disrupted but not dismantled, it leaves many young gang members at large. With high-ranking members incarcerated, the younger ones see promotional opportunities among remaining gang members. The most common way to gain power within the gang is to prove they are the toughest one in the group. The way to achieve this is to engage in violence to prove oneself.[25]

The police time at hotspots and gang network examples reveal an important idea behind weak intervention backfire: dosage matters. In both examples, the intervention is the same. The difference is the dosage or intensity that the intervention is applied. In the case of the police hotspots example, it was 11–15 minutes of presence instead of 1–5 minutes. In the gang network example, it was to remove the top 25 connected members instead of the top 20 connected members.

So, when you are planning out your intervention, do not forget to consider the dosage you are applying. This could dictate whether you create benefit or backfire in the various stages of your intervention.

Use Checklists

It may seem ridiculous to suggest this, but checklists are one of the most effective tools you can use. If you do not believe us, do not worry, you are not alone. Harvard-based professor, surgeon, and writer Atul Gawande recounts many professionals having the same feeling towards such a suggestion. In his 2010 book, *The Checklist Manifesto*, Gawande provides a compelling case for why checklists should be more widely adopted to reduce avoidable failures and near misses.[26] He provides examples from medicine, aviation, engineering, and construction, to name a few. All personnel within these fields are highly trained individuals working in an increasingly complex world. As knowledge and expertise becomes more specialized, sometimes we lose sight of the most basic components of the task at hand.

To illustrate, put yourself in the shoes of a surgeon. Let's say you have years of schooling and practical training. Your technique is impeccable and you have an impressive track record for completing surgeries with few complications. You arrive at work on a Wednesday morning and ready yourself for the first surgery of the day. You make the incision and begin assessing the problem you need to solve, only to find that it is not there. Why? Because you are operating on the wrong patient. With the flurry of things that need to be done before surgery, did someone stop to check that the correct patient was on the table? You, the surgeon, may be focused on making sure all of your personal protective equipment, clothing, and instruments are sterile and safe for use. The anesthesiologist may be trying to calm the patient to get her to sleep. The nurses may be making sure all of the surgical machines are functioning properly, and so on.

Double checking the identity of the patient seems simple, but if no one is delegated that job, it can be easy to overlook.

Or consider another, albeit related, scenario that Gawande provides. The most common complication of surgery in children is infection. Aside from using proper antiseptic practices during the procedure, administering antibiotics prior to incision can often prevent this problem. However, the timing of when the antibiotic is given is crucial. If done more than 60 minutes before, the antibiotic wears off. If the antibiotic is administered after the incision is made, it does not adequately get spread through the blood stream to the tissues being operated on. Though giving antibiotics before surgery seems like a simple step to carry out, it is often missed. In fact, in 2005, staff at Columbus Children's Hospital found that more than one-third of its appendectomy patients failed to receive the necessary antibiotic at the correct time.[27]

Checklists can reduce many of these oversights. As Gawande explains, hospitals use checklists to reduce complications from surgeries. Airline companies use checklists for routine activities: such as before starting the engine, before pulling away from the gate, before taxing on the runway, and so on. But they also have checklists on hand in case non-routine problems arise: smoke in the cockpit, warning lights turning on, a dead radio, a co-pilot becoming disabled, and so on. The pre-flight checklists reduce avoidable problems, such as making sure the plane has been filled with enough gasoline, crews have loaded all luggage into the plane and securely shut the hatch, all flight attendants are onboard, and so on. Most pilots never need to use the non-routine checklists, but they are there in case of emergency. Development and engineering companies use checklists while designing and constructing buildings. The structural integrity of even the most well-designed building can become compromised if you do not take the soil composition you are building on into consideration. Different types of soils will settle in different ways. Failing to account for this one detail can have catastrophic consequences.[28]

So how can you use checklists? You probably already do. You use them to remember what to buy at the grocery store or how to make your favourite chocolate cake (yes, recipes are checklists too!). There is no reason you cannot apply them to your problem-solving process. Aiden Sidebottom, along with Nick Tilley and John Eck have made a case for using checklists

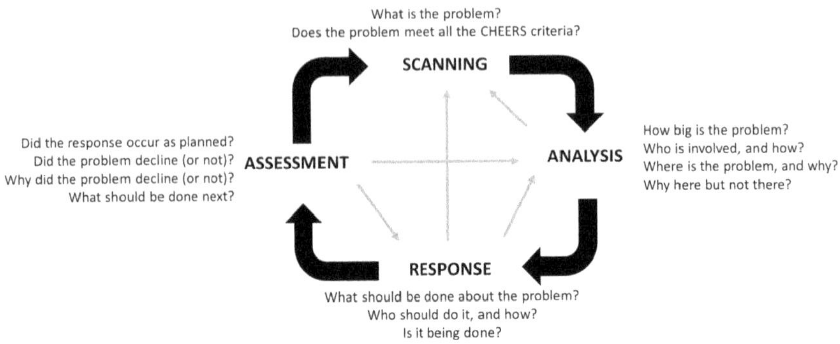

FIGURE A.6 Example Checklist to Use with the SARA Model

Adapted from Eck & Spelman (1987) and Eck (2013)

in problem-solving, particularly by police.[29] These can be applied in different phases. For instance, they can be helpful in identifying the causes of problems. But they can be just as helpful when implementing your proposed solution. Did you carry out all the steps of your strategy? Was your timing right? Did you target the correct places?

We provide an example of this in figure A.6. Using the SARA model we described before, we have added some examples of questions to be answered to help carry out the process. To assure you complete your assessment and action about a problem, you need to assure it meets the criteria of a problem in the first place. You also want to ensure you have learned as much about that problem as you can. This might include who is involved in the problem, where it is happening and why. Missing a component of this checklist could cause you to select a less effective response. Though you may learn this by the assessment stage, it would be better for you to identify the blind spot before getting that far in the process.

Deployment with a Purpose

A detailed checklist-style strategy should be used in each individual phase of the SARA model. That is, you should expand upon the items or questions you ask in each of the phases. In the response phase of the model, too often the police answer is extra patrols in the problem areas.

The problem with extra patrols is the police must keep doing them to be effective. Police are merely reacting to crime. They are not proactively addressing the factors that caused it. Your communities don't care about how many extra patrols the police have done. They do care about whether there are fewer of their family, friends and neighbors being victimized.

Once the extra police patrols stop, crime will eventually return at either the same or a higher level than it was originally. The increased patrols did nothing to remove the opportunity structure that allowed crime to regularly occur there. They merely momentarily disrupted the activity. Offenders know this and react accordingly. They simply move their criminal activities out of view of the police until the extra patrols end. Then it's business as usual again.

Instead of just adding extra patrols, you need to do an in-depth analysis of the data and identify the key causes of the crime. Unfortunately, in far too many police agencies, a simple year-to-date comparison or density map passes for crime analysis. A year-to-date comparison or density map shows you that crime is occurring at a particular location but tells you nothing about why or how. This lack of understanding about the primary cause of crime leads to an ineffective short-term strategy like extra patrols to reduce it.

If agencies conduct a detailed data analysis, they will understand precisely what their crime problem is, where it is occurring, who is driving it, why it's being committed at certain locations and how offenders are taking advantage of the opportunity to regularly commit crimes at a particular location. Once you understand the who, what, when, where, why and how of your crime problem you'll be in a far better position to solve the problem instead of just temporarily disrupting it.

After you've completed a detailed analysis and have a thorough understanding of the crime problem, you can implement an actionable strategy and deploy with a purpose to remove the opportunity structure allowing the crime to occur. As we detailed in chapter 15, deployment with a purpose means a police department's patrol officers are sent to a problem place with clear, concise guidance and direction as to the specific tasks they need to perform while there, know when they need to perform the tasks, and clearly understand both why they need to perform these specific tasks and the expected result if they do so.

Deployment with a purpose means instead of random patrol, every day and every shift an agency sends its patrol resources to those few identified problem places, focuses on the few problem people committing most of the crime, and takes very specific actions to dismantle the opportunities that allow crime to occur there. Deployment with a purpose greatly increases the odds of a long-term crime reduction, instead of a temporary one, and you won't have to rely on extra patrols forever to sustain it.

Goldstein and Tilley Awards

Finally, you should acknowledge all of your successes and those of your peers. This has many positive effects linked to some of the other concepts mentioned in this list. First, it encourages innovative problem-solving. Any organization, whether it is police or a community group or a company, will be made up of a diverse set of people with different experiences. All organizations have natural problem-solvers who are successfully overcoming problems under the same resources constraints as everyone else. It's in your best interest to identify these people and praise their innovation. This encourages them to solve additional problems and publicizes innovative solutions so that others can take advantage of their ingenuity too.

You can acknowledge victories internally by publicly, in front of their peers, acknowledging the good work your people have done. At a local level, you may even want to publicize the wins to the community. This can be done through local newspapers or radio television news broadcasts and via social media platforms.

There are other national and international outlets that help acknowledge this good work and provide like-minded people in other organizations with additional ideas on how to solve the problems they are facing. For example, in 1993 the Police Executive Research Forum created The Herman Goldstein Award to recognize innovations in problem-oriented policing. The submissions from winners and finalists are publicly available so that practitioners can learn from past successes in other departments. All submissions are organized using the SARA model. The Center for Problem-Oriented Policing took over the award in 2007 but keeps all submissions since 1993 available for public view.[30] Similarly, the United Kingdom Home Office Policing and Reducing Crime Unit established the Nick Tilley Award in 1999. The award was designed to encourage and celebrate successful problem-oriented projects that resolved issues faced by the police, partners, or the community. You can find summaries of the submissions and award winners for free online as well.[31] These two awards alone provide hundreds of examples of police problem-solving that you can look to for ideas on how to address the problems you are facing.

Conclusions

These ten problem-solving tools are some of the most commonly used in policing and crime prevention. Many police agencies have applied them with great success. Remember to keep the rule of the few in mind as you apply these tools to your crime problems.

Notes

1 Clarke, R.V. & Eck, J.E. (2003). *Become a Problem-Solving Crime Analyst in 55 Small Steps*. London, UK: Jill Dando Institute of Crime Science. Retrieved from: https://popcenter.asu.edu/sites/g/files/litvpz3631/files/55stepsuk_0_0.pdf ; Clarke, R.V. & Eck, J.E. (2005). *Crime Analysis for Problem Solvers in 60 Small Steps*. US Department of Justice. Retrieved from: https://portal.cops.usdoj.gov/resourcecenter/RIC/Publications/cops-w0047-pub.pdf

2 Eck, J.E. & Spelman, W. (1987). *Problem-Solving: Problem-Oriented Policing in Newport News*. Washington, DC: Police Executive Research Forum.

3 Eck, J.E. (2003). Police problems: The complexity of problem theory, research and evaluation. *Crime Prevention Studies, 15*, 79–114.

4 Clarke, R.V. & Eck, J.E. (2005). *Crime Analysis for Problem Solvers in 60 Small Steps*. US Department of Justice. Retrieved from: https://portal.cops.usdoj.gov/resourcecenter/RIC/Publications/cops-w0047-pub.pdf

5 Ratcliffe, R. (2019). *Reducing Crime: A Companion for Police Leaders*. Routledge Publishers.

6 Ratcliffe, R. (2019). *Reducing Crime: A Companion for Police Leaders*. Routledge Publishers.

7 Eck, J.E. (2003). Police problems: The complexity of problem theory, research and evaluation. *Crime Prevention Studies, 15*, 79–114; Clarke, R.V. & Eck, J.E. (2003). *Become a Problem-Solving Crime Analyst in 55 Small Steps*. London, UK: Jill Dando Institute of Crime Science. Retrieved from: https://popcenter.asu.edu/sites/g/files/litvpz3631/files/55stepsuk_0_0.pdf

8 Felson, M. (1986). Routine activities, social controls, rational decisions, and criminal outcomes. In D. Cornish & R.V. Clarke (eds.), *The Reasoning Criminal: Rational Choice Perspectives on Offending* (pp. 119–128). New York, NY: Springer-Verlag.

9 Hollis, M., Felson, M., & Welsh, B. (2013). The capable guardian in routine activities theory: A theoretical and conceptual reappraisal. *Crime Prevention and Community Safety, 15*, 65–79. https://doi.org/10.1057/cpcs.2012.14

10 Eck, J.E., Linning, S.J., & Herold, T.D. (2023). *Place Management and Crime: Ownership and Property Rights as a Source of Social Control*. Springer. https://doi.org/10.1007/978-3-031-27693-4

11 Ratcliffe, R. (2019). *Reducing Crime: A Companion for Police Leaders*. Routledge Publishers.

12 Sidebottom, A. & Bowers, K. (2010). Bag theft in bars: An analysis of relative risk, perceived risk and modus operandi. *Security Journal, 23*(3), 206–224.

13 Note that Sidebottom discovered this finding after publishing his 2010 paper with Kate Bowers.

14 Clarke, R.V. (1980). Situational crime prevention: Theory and practice. *British Journal of Criminology, 20*, 136–147. https://doi.org/10.1093/oxfordjournals.bjc.a047153; Clarke, R.V. (2011). Situational crime prevention. In R. Wortley, L. Mazerolle, & S. Rombouts (Eds.), *Environmental Criminology and Crime Analysis* (pp. 178–194). New York, NY: Routledge.
15 Shen, J-L. & Linning, S.J. (2025). Direct and indirect situational crime prevention: Using the COSTS criteria to improve interventions. *Security Journal, 38*, 60. https://doi.org/10.1057/s41284-025-00507-y
16 Smith, M.J., Clarke, R.V., & Pease, K. (2002). Anticipatory benefits in crime prevention. In N. Tilley (Ed.), *Crime Prevention Studies* (vol. 13; pp. 71–88). Boulder, CO: Lynne Rienner Publishers.
17 Sherman, L.W. (1990). Police crackdowns: Initial and residual deterrence. *Crime and Justice, 12*, 1–48. https://doi.org/10.1086/449163
18 Linning, S.J., Bowers, K., & Eck, J.E. (2019). Understanding the time-course of an intervention's mechanisms: A framework for improving experiments and evaluations. *Journal of Experimental Criminology, 15*(4), 593–610. https://doi.org/10.1007/s11292-019-09367-0
19 See also: Eck, J.E., Ceccato, V., & Guerette, R.T. (2024). A general problem-solving matrix (GPSM): Combining crime prevention and public health tools. *Security Journal, 37*(3), 468–488. https://doi.org/10.1057/s41284-024-00438-0
20 Johnson, S. D., Tilley, N., & Bowers, K. J. (2015). Introducing EMMIE: An evidence rating scale to encourage mixed-method crime prevention synthesis reviews. *Journal of Experimental Criminology, 11*(3), 459–473. https://doi.org/10.1007/s11292-015-9238-7
21 From page 597 of: Linning, S.J., Bowers, K., & Eck, J.E. (2019). Understanding the time-course of an intervention's mechanisms: A framework for improving experiments and evaluations. *Journal of Experimental Criminology, 15*(4), 593–610. https://doi.org/10.1007/s11292-019-09367-0
22 Linning, S.J., & Eck, J.E. (2018). Weak intervention backfire and criminal hormesis: Why some otherwise effective crime prevention interventions can fail at low doses. *The British Journal of Criminology, 58*(2), 309–331. https://doi.org/10.1093/bjc/azx019
23 From page 184 of: Calabrese, E.J. (2002). Hormesis: Changing view of the dose-response, a personal account of the history and current status. *Mutation Research, 511*, 181–189. https://doi.org/10.1016/s1383-5742(02)00013-3
24 Koper, C.S. (1995). Just enough police presence: Reducing crime and disorderly behavior by optimizing patrol time in crime hot spots. *Justice Quarterly, 12*(4), 649–672. https://doi.org/10.1080/07418829500096231
25 Linning, S.J., & Eck, J.E. (2018). Weak intervention backfire and criminal hormesis: Why some otherwise effective crime prevention interventions can fail at low doses. *The British Journal of Criminology, 58*(2), 309–331. https://doi.org/10.1093/bjc/azx019
26 Gawande, A. (2010). *The Checklist Manifesto: How to Get Things Right*. Metropolitan Books.
27 Gawande, A. (2010). *The Checklist Manifesto: How to Get Things Right*. Metropolitan Books.
28 Gawande, A. (2010). *The Checklist Manifesto: How to Get Things Right*. Metropolitan Books.
29 Sidebottom, A., Tilley, N., & Eck, J.E. (2012). Towards checklists to reduce common sources of problem-solving failure. *Policing: A Journal of Policy and Practice, 6*(2), 194–209. https://doi.org/10.1093/police/par054
30 See: https://popcenter.asu.edu/content/about-goldstein-pop-awards
31 See: https://popcenter.asu.edu/content/tilley-award-submissions

Index: Terms

Index: People

Index: Cities/Countries

For Product Safety Concerns and Information please contact our EU
representative GPSR@taylorandfrancis.com
Taylor & Francis Verlag GmbH, Kaufingerstraße 24, 80331 München, Germany

www.ingramcontent.com/pod-product-compliance
Ingram Content Group UK Ltd.
Pitfield, Milton Keynes, MK11 3LW, UK
UKHW022348190926
475702UK00015B/2163

* 9 7 8 1 0 3 2 5 5 0 5 2 7 *